MONTANA: Two Lane Highway In A Four Lane World

MONTANA:
Two Lane Highway in a Four Lane World

Edited by: Frank Chesarek and Jim Brabeck

Text By Jim Brabeck
Graphics & Illustrations by Frank Chesarek
Research Articles Prepared by Mary L. Lenihan

This book was researched, edited, and assembled in collaboration with students of Lolo Middle School and is a product of the Montana History Project, a continuing project of Lolo Middle School.

Project Director	Frank Chesarek
Project Coordinator	Rachel Veilleux
Project Consultant	Jim Brabeck
Project Consultant	Mary Lenihan
Project Sponsor	John K. Smith, Supt.

Mountain Press Publishing Co.
Missoula, Montana
1978

Library of Congress Cataloging in Publication Data
Main entry under title:

Montana: two lane highway in a four lane world.

   Bibliography: p.
   SUMMARY: Discusses the Treasure State from its geologic beginnings through its fears and dreams for the future.
   1. Montana — Juvenile literature. [1. Montana]
I. Chesarek, Frank. II. Brabeck, Jim.
FT31.3M66   978.6   77-18868
ISBN 0-87842-101-7

ACKNOWLEDGEMENTS:

K. Ross Toole...the difference between an idea and *reality*. Dr. Toole not only loaned his name and his time, but also arranged for a grant from the Hammond Fund, University of Montana, Department of History.

John K. Smith...provided faith, encouragement, and a place for it to happen.

Violet Cowan...not only tolerated and solved the financial maze dropped upon her, but most of all, she gave of herself.

Hazel Cowan...everything from soup to nuts!

Bonnie Franks
Gabrielle Prandoni
Billie Schwartz
B.J. Douglas...made field research possible.

Jeri McIntyre...like Hazel, she not only let us invade her office, but supplied some amazing legwork.

Johnathun Pearson...a patient supporter, helped minimize the effects of doing two jobs at once.

Mike O'Donnell...lender of considerable time and talent.

Ed Eschler...interested, enthusiastic, and always helpful.

Lolo School Board of Trustees...allowed, encouraged, and enabled this project to happen...
    Howard Lemm (past member)
    Billie Schwartz (past member)
    Earl Springer (past member)
    Pat Rowley
    David Glidewell
    Chuck Kaparich
    Simon Gerhart
    Wayne Robinson

"Writing the History of Montana" is a project of the Montana Bicentennial Administration. The Administration, under the direction of Hal Stearns and Paul McCann recognized the value and the need of a text as a lasting observance of the Bicentennial year. The administration's enthusiasm and farsighted concern for education has made this book possible.

Students of Lolo School's class of "76" were responsible for the research phase of this project and the preliminary editing of that research. In alphebetical order, they are:

Jack Aubert
Lori Belcher
Charlene Brown
James Carter
Robbie Chalmers
Jackie Cooper
Mark Courter
Edward Driscoll
Tina DuMontier
Deane Foley
Susan Fuchs
Ron Goldman
David Hall
Lowell Hall

Lori Hintz
John Johnson
Allen Jones
Lisa Kozak
Marci Kratovil
Karla Lane
Ron Larson
Marvin Larum
Joe Lee
Howard Lemm
Montie Lockwood
Robbie Managhan
Tom Oie
Theresa Reinhard

Ronda Rothley
Melody Sauter
Sherri Stubb
David Swartz
Julie Taylor
Donna Templin
John Toomey
Dean Vann
Chris Walling
Kelly Wicklander
Robin Wise
JoAnn Yaeger
Greg Young

Publication of this book was partially funded by an E.S.E.A. Title III Grant made available through the Office of the Superintendent of Public Instruction, Georgia R. Rice, Superintendent.

Students of Lolo Middle School's class of "78" were responsible for the production, publication, marketing, and sales phase of this project. In alphabetical order, they are:

Albert Aisenbrey	Wayne Ellegard	Christi Manning	Julie Rowley
Lynda Allen	Tim England	Mike Massey	Carol Sackett
Rachel Aplin	Pam Fuchs	Scott Massey	Kim Sauter
Wade Ayala	Lisa Gerhart	Shannon Moore	Mike Seifert
Blaine Baker	Peggy Graham	Jan Olson	Lori Sellers
Debbie Birdsong	James Green	Leif Onsum	Melinda Sellers
Tracy Brendal	Jana Greenfield	Linda Orbe	Tony Skaja
Bob Buckmaster	Kevin Groff	Stacy Parker	Diana Spencer
Kim Chapieski	Eldon Hall	Doug Phillips	Susan Spencer
Luke Cowan	Alan Johnson	Wayne Povsha	Darlene Sturm
Emery Curran	Clyde Jordon	Stanley Prazma	Kelly Williams
Greg Daniels	Robbi Lane	Ricky Reinhard	Kathy Wofford
Chris Eden	Rene Lee	Liz Robinson	Murray Young

In this phase a student company was formed:

BOARD OF DIRECTORS
Kelly Williams
Doug Phillips
Liz Robinson
Tony Skaja
Kevin Groff

CORRESPONDING SECRETARY
Lisa Gerhart

ACCOUNTANT
Pam Fuchs

PRESIDENT
Chris Eden

VICE PRESIDENT (PRODUCTIONS)
Pam Fuchs

VICE PRESIDENT (SALES)
Kim Sauter

PREPARATION

Chris Eden	Liz Robinson
Peggy Graham	Kim Chapieski
Murray Young	Lisa Gerhart
Christi Manning	Mike Massey
Jana Greenfield	
Pam Fuchs	
Kim Sauter	

ASSEMBLY
Bob Buckmaster
Chris Eden
Tracy Brendal
Christi Manning
Peggy Graham
Murray Young
Pam Fuchs

DISTRIBUTION

Ricky Reinhard	Liz Robinson	Luke Cowan
Kevin Groff	Lynda Allen	Wade Ayala
Kim Chapieski	Diana Spencer	
Greg Daniels	Christi Manning	
Murray Young	Peggy Graham	
Chris Eden	Pam Fuchs	
Eldon Hall	Lisa Gerhart	

PERSONAL NOTES

to Lisa Gerhart for handling over 2000 pieces of correspondence and always knowing where everything and everybody was or wasn't.

to Chris Eden for a lot of work and subtle pressure and not so subtle questions.

to Pam Fuchs for labor at every level, the "Broadway idea," and a lot of work to come.

to Christi Manning for correcting the corrected corrections and a knowing smile.

to Peggy Graham for always finding a way to be there for anything and anybody.

to Murry Young for quiet, constructive criticism all summer long.

to Theresa Reinhard for editing and arranging Book I.

to Rosie Brabeck for being a patient partner and leaving the light on.

to Katy Jeanne Brabeck for learning to walk without me.

to Rachel Veilleux for sorting things out and lending order we needed badly.

to Sharon Meinders for finding a place closer to the end of the world than a homestead in eastern Montana.

to John Hoar for a mellow environment, good dinner conversation, and the 11:00 PM review.

to Don Sheppard for inspiring the "Copper King Ball game."

to Rachel Viellieux for "the flower that was the plains culture was only briefly magnificent."

to Harry Ray for giving "credits" where credit was due.

to Dick Adler for helping untangle who did what, where and how.

to Whitewater School for buying 15 copies before anyone else believed there'd be a book.

to Scott Chesarek for missing a lot of time and stories. Now we have a new book to read together — it's for planners and dreamers.

to Dawn Chesarek for waiting, and working, and raising, and fixing, and washing, and mowing, and making, and bringing, and getting, and taking...and waiting.

to all preceeding Montanans without whom we would have had little to say.

PREFACE

by K. Ross Toole

History means a lot of different things to a lot of different people. In fact, if you were to ask for a definition from professional historians across America, you'd get as many different definitions as there are professional historians.

But there are some ingredients to the recipe for history which everybody *ought* to agree to. First, history is the story of *people,* great and small, who did things, or failed to do things, in the past. Second, what they did or did not do matters to us today because in some part we are the product of their actions. Third, it is bunk to say that history is dull. True, it can be made to *seem* dull by dull teachers, and dull books, but history itself just cannot be dull. Why? Well, it consists of what people did — so it involves love, hate, treason, spies, mysteries, courage, cowardice, murder, robbery, heroes, thieves, wars, battles, creepy people, wonderful people, saints, sinners, and people almost exactly like you. Is all that *dull*? No! I repeat dull teachers and dull books can make it *seem* dull but it just isn't so.

As you go through this particular book, there are a few things you might keep in mind. Let me start with a question. Can only professors and teachers write history? No. This book could never have been written without the eighth grade at Lolo School, Lolo, Montana. They did not write it all, but they were the ones who said what should go into it and what should not. There was a huge pile of material — enough to write many books. You may believe it or not, but they went through all that material and separated out what they wanted in *this* book — and how they wanted it arranged.

Could your eighth grade write a book about your town or your county or your valley? You bet you could — and a good one. Sure, it is a lot of work; it is also a lot of fun.

I'm a professional historian and I have written a number of books on Montana. I happen to think that this is the best book *ever* written for younger Montanans. Funny, isn't it — because if the eighth grade had not tied into the project, it just would not be as good a book.

So as historians, don't sell yourselves short. And you might try asking your teacher if *you* couldn't do this kind of thing for your town, county, or valley. I don't care where you live, from Ekalaka to Eureka, you are *surrounded* by history and mystery and true stories. Sure, you will have to dig for them, chase them. They tend to hide in old papers and letters in old barns and attics and also in the memory of old minds. But you can dig them out and put them down on paper — and that's history.

Well, have fun with this book. And then go ahead and do your own. If you do, I'll bet you that you will never think history is dull again.

FOREWORD

Montana's history is a fast moving drama of explorers, thieves, millionaires, murderers, heroes, statesmen and ne'er-do-wells. Pieces of her past have provided the material for novels, motion pictures, TV series, magazine articles and just about any story telling media you could think of. All the elements of a good story are there; love, hate, conspiracy, tragedy, comedy, intrigue. There is a tale to touch any emotion. Suppose then, a student arrives on the scene, ready to hear, eager to look, primed for action... Our student buries himself in the first available book only to discover he is hopelessly lost on a zig-zag circling trail of regional and chronological half-stories.

Montana's past could be considered as a collection of histories of from two to seven state-like regions, depending on whose opinion you value. It could be separated into from two to ten chronological time periods, depending on your purposes. It's not too difficult then to sympathize with our student circling in an endless holding pattern.

Our student could seek a course of study based on the regional approach and come away convinced that each region has a sort of jerky but sensible story to tell, unrelated to the other regions. He or she may well decide that history's spotlight fell on each region only to fade and move to focus on another region. Such is not the case.

Should the student follow the chronological approach instead, he or she might realize that Montana's history is a rather staggering list of unrelated events where the scenes change so rapidly they begin to blur. This is also not the case.

If you accept this dilemma, and I think most do, let me suggest another problem. Montana history does not command a large enough financial audience to interest any large textbook publishers.

Consider then, the author of a Montana text. To have fought their way through the student dilemma and survived, we can safely assume they are somewhere between college graduate and college professor. Inspired to produce an accurate text, they surround themselves in research, books and memorabilia to get it all together.

They are now faced with the task of retelling a story, accurately and methodically. Two critical problems, however, have arisen in their preparation. They have become too steeped in the story to go back and relate it to a beginner without having to patch and splice the regional and chronological relationships it took them so long to master. They have also crossed over into a new level of language that may well cloud the very concepts they are trying to pin down for the beginner.

Our poor student is still in a holding pattern. To push him or her at this point (and push we must — we only have a semester) would be fatal. One more student of history fades away — but don't worry, someone or something later on may resurrect that student's enthusiasm. It happens, sometimes. Is it not a shame, though, that such a wonderful story is adequately shared by so few?

It was our intention from the beginning of this project to provide a start, an invitation, if you will, to the beginners. A walk-through tour that lets them look and touch the story at will. Let's get them in the door and tempt them a little. They will satisfy their curiosity — provided we can arouse it.

This, then is a book never intended to be a wholistic study of our State. Instead, it is a loose, general account with as many encounters and enticements as we could weave within it. It is a book about real people and their stories are presented to play upon your emotions.

During your walk-through, if you catch yourself nodding in agreement feeling sad, upset, or even violently opposed to what you think we're trying to infer — great! It was only a start, remember? A push — a pull — a gentle nudge, maybe. Where it takes you is your decision; how far — how fast — you decide.

Our format and graphics were designed to simplify the zig-zag trail that has been hidden to so many. In any of the seven books herein you can follow the mining story through that time period in Chapter TWO and then return to find out whats happening above ground in Chapters THREE and FOUR. You can look in on the "big shots" and the "heavies" in Chapter FIVE and return to find out what "plain old folks" are doing in Chapter SIX. When you're ready for the overall effect of the period, Chapter SEVEN will help you see where the dust settled. It's a time to stop, take a breath, reflect on where we've been; consider where we're going.

We've waged war on the language barrier throughout this book. There is not one word from page 1 on that wasn't read and considered by at least one seventh grader. We are awfully proud of *our* seventh graders but they share a language with junior high students everywhere. Students know what interests students and they know what bores them; they're not too shy about making it known. You'll recognize the language; it's not too formal. Oh yes, we get a little "folksy," and there will be a few outdated words and jokes here and there, but our meaning should be clear. We change our vantage point now and then and you may sometimes wonder how a side article got where it is. Students' interests vary; we've reprinted selections from over a hundred different sources. There should be something for everybody.

We would not attempt to portray this book as the perfect Montana History text. Lolo is a distant vantage point for much of what has and is happening in Montana. Perhaps where you sit is a better point of reference. Maybe you know someone or something we didn't consider. You may find some mistakes or disagree with our interpretations. Come on along! With your research, thoughts, comments, criticisms, and contributions the first revision of this text can be a further step in the right direction.

—FHC

THE TEXT...

Although the major thrust of my undergraduate work was in Political Science-history, I've always viewed myself as an interested bystander, not a political scientist or a historian. Aided by hindsight, that one quality possessed by Monday morning quarterbacks and 6 P.M. stockbrokers, I proceeded to write the text for this book. I wrote the way I teach, that is wanting to inform and hoping to hold interest. Wake Up!

To accomplish this, I chose to use an informal, humorous or just plain human point of view. Being human, there are undoubtedly areas of disputed information. Don't let the casual approach throw you. It is as accurate as it is casual. To say that bias was eliminated would be naive, to say an honest attempt was made to minimize it would be true.

One has to remember that one of the main goals of this book is to arouse the reader, a student of history, to look further into matters concerning the State's past, present and future *on his or her own*. It is my premise that the reader will be more apt to do this in either support or in an attempt to disprove a particular viewpoint. When was the last time someone chose to dispute a name, date or place? (that which historians call identity). This identity, although important, has taken a secondary role to what our kids felt is the true substance of history, cause and effect. The *importance* of the event overshadows its identity. For this reason then, little time was spent on the actual Lewis and Clark Expedition. Instead I dealt with the kids questions of "Why did they go?" and "so what?" Besides, there are numerous books and articles, not to mention Lewis and Clark journals, that cover the trip. If the reader finds that aspect of history particularly interesting and takes off in that direction, one of our goals is accomplished.

You see, this approach was designed to strike sensitive chords. I aimed at the heart not the head. Make 'em laugh. Make 'em cry. Make 'em empathetic, not apathetic.

The style was not meant to sweeten bitter medicine. It was meant to show that history is not merely dust and dead heroes. History is the story of real people, the great and the ordinary. People who made both good and bad decisions based on good and bad information. People who made mistakes. Mistakes from which we can learn.

It is my belief that if, indeed, we haven't learned from history, it is due to the way it is written. Great men making great decisions, losing only to still greater men. Readers of history are placed in awe of such men and their accomplishments, and rightly so in many cases. The harm comes when the reader feels he or she couldn't possibly have measured up to the challenges of yesteryear, thus a lesser person. Probably, our ancestors even in the iciest of graves would not trade places to face the challenge of today's future generations. For this reason, I sought not to diefy anyone. Instead, each has been portrayed as a flesh and blood person, capable of moments of both greatness and weakness. All were people. I hope I did them justice.

—JB

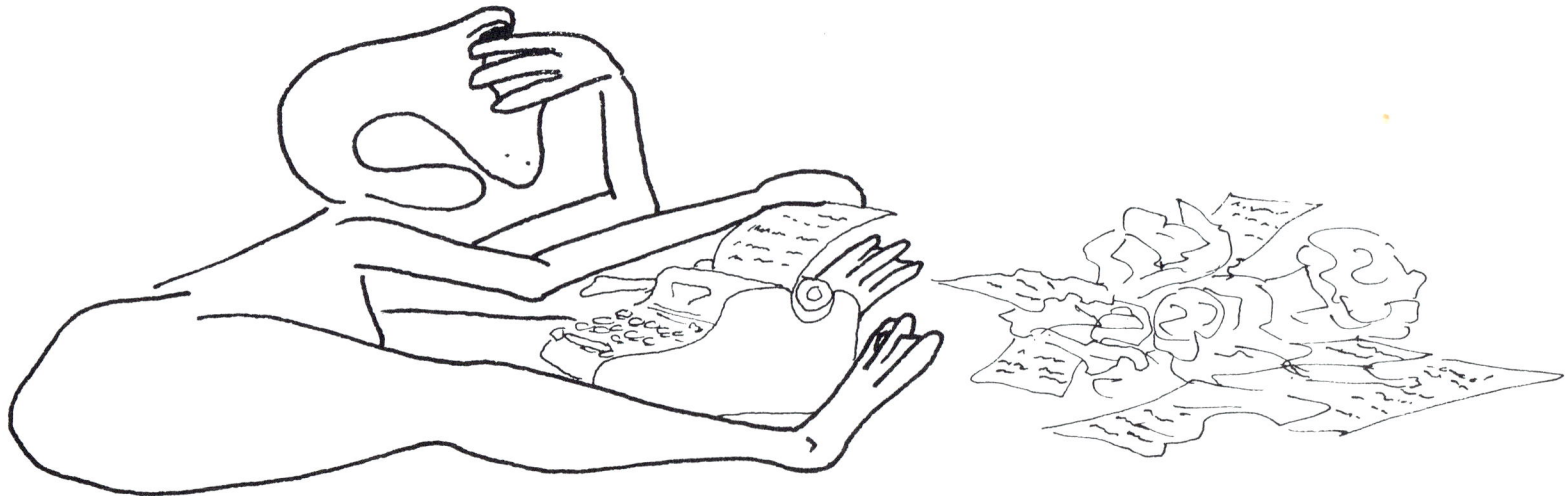

THE GRAPHICS...

It was our intention from the beginning to make the graphics an intergral part of the text, rather than extra. The purpose, then was to both stimulate a mental image that would help clarify the text and at the same time remove some of the burden of names, dates, and places from it. The answer seemed simple, a color-coded time line that weaves throughout the pages with appropriate illustrations silhouetted within the time line. While the concept seemed simple enough, doing it was next to impossible. We had a format designed to remove the pressure of regional and chronological events and a time line designed to remove the burden of names, dates, and places, but they continually created problems for each other. Chapters that followed an aspect of a time period allowed us to follow a theme through the time period, then return to pursue a new theme in another chapter. They also ruled out a chronological time line.

The colors of the time line are true to a chronological period, the illustrations are not. They follow the theme of the chapter.

The illustrations were a comfortable compromise for me. Silhouettes that are to be overprinted do not allow too much detail, which in general, meant less time to complete. On the other hand I am still not real comfortable with what I consider "Drawing in reverse." Everything not in the drawing is done in ink. Illustrations writing the time line also limits the size of the drawings. This is why I chose to draw from and around the time line on chapter title pages. It was a nice break from "small, inside-out" work.

Bonnie Franks and her eighth-graders came up with the idea of a cartoon commentator to serve as a sort of guide. After ruling out numerous characters for one reason or another, they settled for a frog. We have tried for two years to name him (her?) and never came up with a good enough name. I sort of got to liking the thing after a few attempts. The frog proved to be a pretty flexible little character and provides for occasional breaks and emphasis in the graphics. It turned out to be a rather cheeky guide and from time to time I let it voice some of the bias of the class and the feelings of the historical underdogs.

I feel that I made an honest effort to represent events in an historically accurate way. I checked photos and articles for almost every drawing to be sure that things I pictured were in fact in use at that time. There were, of course, no good photographs of dinosaurs and such, and surprisingly enough, I found little description of several recent scenes. In these cases, I made the drawings conform to my mental images of the "way things were." These drawings, if nothing else, are guaranteed to please at least one person.

While admittedly I don't draw pictures for a living (and there are some who've thanked me for that), I have added some subtleties and personal reflections within the graphics. I hope some student or teacher somewhere takes exception with me at least once in a while. That would mean they took the time to look carefully.

My greatest frustration was the fact that the graphics involve overprinting or a "double run" process. Like you, I have to wait until this book comes back from the printer to see just how it really looks.

—FHC

THE RESEARCH ARTICLES...

When Frank Chesarek and I first discussed my job as researcher for this project, my initial response was that I would not be able to find enough suitable material. Locating historical documentation takes much time; generally, hours spent searching for possible items result in perhaps one or two (and often, none) which are appropriate. This project was different, however. It seemed that no matter what sources I turned to, dozens of interesting items caught my attention. My most difficult task, then, was to narrow the selection to those most suitable.

This "difficulty" should be encouraging to students and teachers of Montana history. To find the material used here, I spent hours sifting through books, newspapers, and documents, and found hundreds of items dealing with all facets of Montana history. However, finding the sources was easy; once found, most of these sources immediately proved worthwhile. A visit to any public library, even in the smallest towns, should result in similar luck. The trick will be to convince students that reading "old" newspapers, pamphlets, and other documents, is worthwhile. Once they begin reading, I would be willing to bet that it will be difficult to stop them.

Montana is a "young" state. Many older Montanans originally came here in covered wagons. Many remember the earlier years of statehood, and many are more than willing to talk about their experiences. Newspapers, especially from the years when each town, no matter how small, had its own, contain first-person accounts of mining, cattle ranching, farming, and even the Indian wars. A few of these accounts have been included here. They were chosen because of the stories they tell and because of the way they are told. A newspaper article about Custer written in 1920 tells us as much about 1920 attitudes toward the Indians wars as it tells us about 1876.

Young students should be encouraged to seek out the older residents of their towns, to ask them about early events, such as the "great shutdown," the homesteading boom, or just plain "what it was like back then." They should read some of the older newspapers available. Most of all, they should be allowed to decide on their own which topic interests them, and then be encouraged to follow up this interest. Active participation in historical research, even if it is just for fun, is hsistory, in the best sesnse of the word.

It is impossible for me to single out any specific source or excerpt as my favorite. Each item is significant and equally interesting. Those I most enjoyed reading were some of the Indian legends, what amazed me is how similar these "fabled" explanations of natural phenomena are to scientific truth. I also personally enjoyed the newspaper account of William Andrews Clark's anonymous visit with a group of miners. At the time he was traveling on his private railroad to make a multi-million dollar deal; this story shows he was, at heart, a man who delighted in simplicity.

While completing this project, we became aware of its informal tone. The prose we have used is less than formal; the students preferred this, and we felt this style makes the text more readable. History basically is "story telling," and an informal style seemed appropriate.

I sincerely hope that this project will inspire hundreds of young Montana historians. We have barely scratched the surface of Montana history. Like the "richest hill on earth," there is a wealth of information just waiting to be discovered. Unlike that hill, however, these riches are never exhausted. And the "discoverer" will be enriched by them for a lifetime.

—MLL

CONTENTS:

PHOTOGRAPHS

LEGENDS and LIZARDS... (up to 10,000 BC)

Howdy!

The kids at Lolo Middle School thought you might like a guide to take you down the trails and get you through the tales of Montana's sometimes jubilant, sometimes lamentable, but always flamboyant past.

I've seen to it that some of them are positioned at detours, side trips, etc., to enable you to make your journey as fruitful and worthwhile as time will allow.

In this first book, you will become aware of some of the changes that have taken place in and under Montana. These changes, which span the last three billion years, have been gradual but each has contributed, in some way, to the Montana we know today.

As you are reading this book, imagine how the area in which you live may have looked 300 years ago. Remember now, no white man had ever seen Montana, let alone lived here. There were no houses, shopping centers, farms, or roads; no telephone lines, county lines, or Forest Service trails. Only 300 years ago!

Now, try to imagine how this same area looked 3,000,000,000 years ago!

Maybe turning the page will aid you in visualizing 3 billion years ago...

3

3,000,000,000

100,000,000

1,200,000,000

400,000,000

4

Scientists have been able to piece together Montana's land history by studying the rocks and land formations. They feel confident they can establish a sequence of events that has made this area what it is.

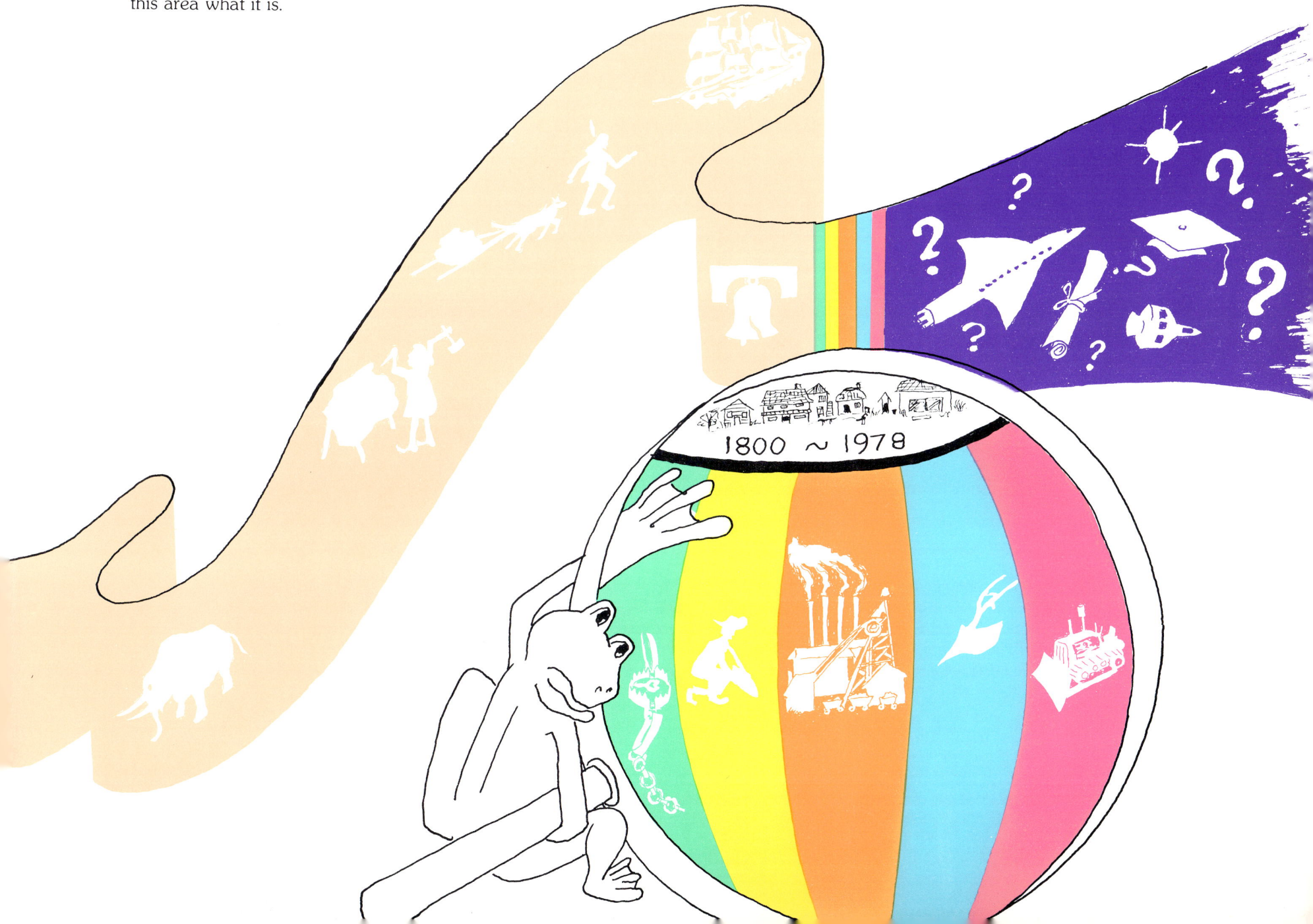

1800 ~ 1978

In the shaddowy beginnings, several billion years ago, a great lifeless ocean washed tons of sediment from the barren lands it surrounded.

There are many Indian legends which explain the formation of interesting geological features on Montana's landscape. For example, Maiden Rock, a formation located in central Montana, was supposed to have been formed during a time of war between the plains Indians. A warrior left his tribe to join a war party, and his lover sat on a cliff awaiting his return. He never did, and out of grief, she turned to stone.

How truthful are Indian legends? Strangely enough, many came close to explaining Montana's geologic past. Scientists now believe that the earth in its earliest times was a great sea, which gradually dried out. Here is the Crow (a tribe which now lives in eastern Montana) version of the earth's beginning.

"Long ago there was no land, only water. The only creatures were the Old Man (the Sun) and the ducks. One day the Old Man told the ducks to dive down into the sea to bring up some earth, so that there might be some land. Three of the ducks dived far down, but found no bottom. Finally, the fourth duck brought some mud back to the surface in his webbed feet. The Old Man held the mud in his hand, and started on his trip, from east to west. He said, 'I'll make it large so that we shall have plenty of room.' As he traveled along his westward journey, he spread the mud and made the land."

Condensed from Robert Lowie, *Myths and Traditions of the Crow Indians*, (New York, 1918).

The layers of rock that formed the ocean floor were slowly buried deeper and deeper to where they were ultimately cooked, squeezed, twisted, and warped until they changed both physically and chemically. They became the "basement" rocks of the continents.

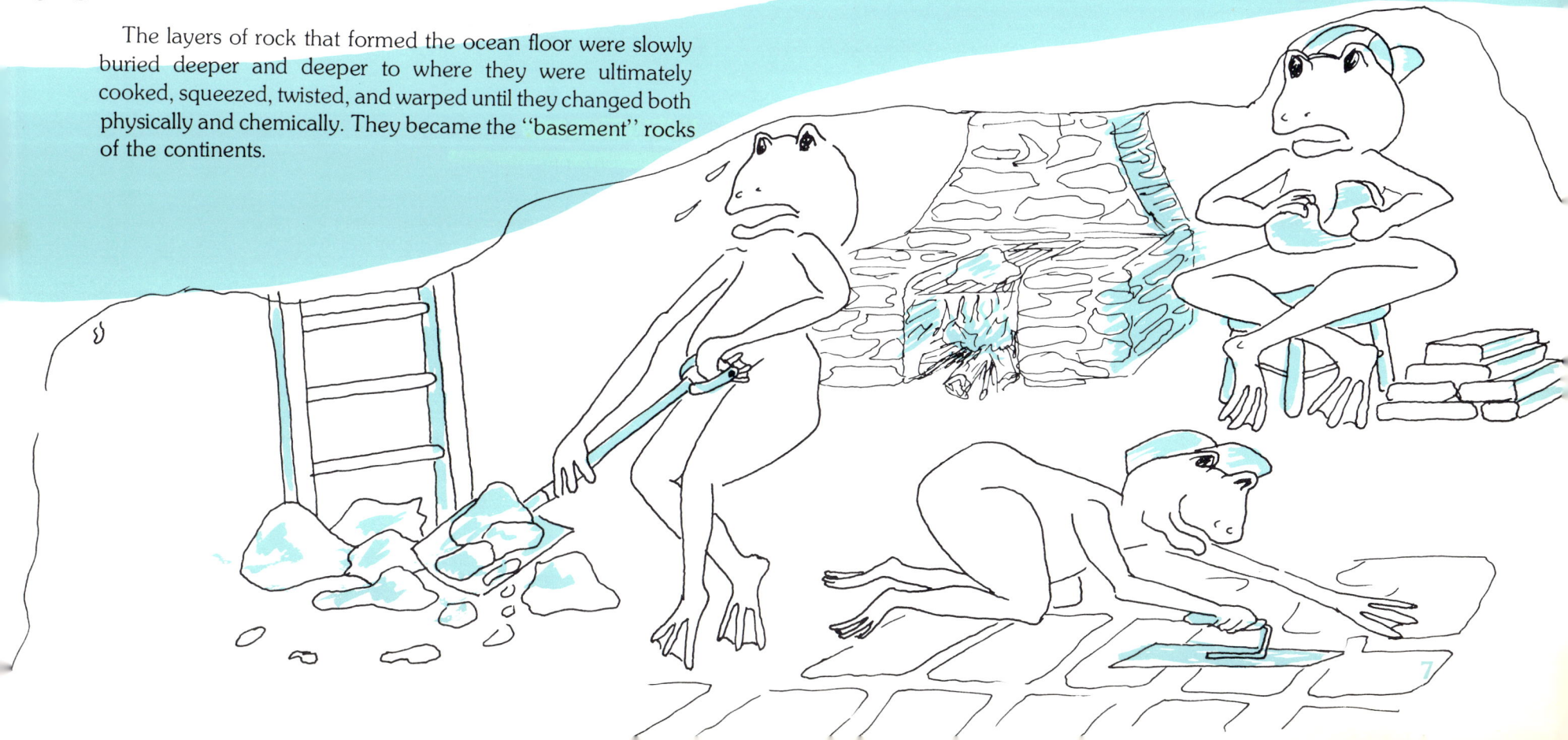

Three billion years ago Montana was on its way up in the world. Lifeless peaks thrust their way upward into empty skies. The mountain ranges were formed...temporarily. For at the same time, wind, water and other erosive forces were carving the landscape until Montana was once again smooth. Thousands of feet of rock were worn away. To get some idea of the forces involved, think of how long it would take to level the Rocky Mountains with dynamite and dump trucks. This leveling exposed the basement rocks, the metamorphic gneiss which melted and squeezed upward through the cracks in the rocks where it cooked and hardened into igneous granite. These metamorphic rocks contain some of Montana's riches in the form of talc, mica, chromium, iron, and other less common minerals.

As this leveling process occurred, Montana again sank beneath the waters of a muddy sea. Sandstone and mudstone once again covered the basement rocks in layers thousands of feet thick. These colorful mudstones have been used in modern times for building materials complete with strangely preserved mudcracks, ripple marks, and raindrop prints. These rocks are known as "Belt" sediments because they have been exposed in the Belt Mountains of central Montana. They are, however, found in other areas of the Northern Rocky Mountains. These rocks contain evidence of primitive fossil seaweed which were likely the first types of plants to appear on earth. Their process of photosynthesis introduced oxygen into the atmosphere setting the stage for the appearance of the first animals.

"Because most valuable metals such as gold and silver formed through volcanic activity, they are found in regions where volcanic deposits have been pushed to the upper layers of the earth's crust. Butte is such an area; the rock formations nearby are igneous rock, or volcanic in origin. Early miners probably did not realize this, but by trial and error they discovered the richest hill on earth."

Mineral Statistics — Montana — 1926
1/2 of the entire national output of precious stones is produced in Montana.
1/3 of the copper mined in the U.S. and
1/6 of all the copper in the world has been produced in Butte.

from *Facts About Montana*, 1926.

Perhaps the first plants to establish roots on dry land were those sea plants left high and dry as the shallow seas withdrew. The vertibrate animals who by now inhabited the shallow seas, probably followed these plants to the land in the form of amphibians. Plantlife thrived and became increasingly diverse. The dominent forms of plantlife were the gymnosperms: cycads, gingkos, ferns, and conifers (the forerunners of our evergreen forests).

The time from 600 million years ago to 100 million years ago was marked by periodic flooding by shallow seas, the shorelines of which are now referred to as the Rimrocks near Billings and Hardin. The waters teemed with plant and animal life. The skeletons of these animals formed a layer of limestone at the bottom of these seas. (Remember, as each flood receded, it left behind a layer of sediment.) The basement rocks now formed the bottom floor of a skyscraper of rock layers. The most recent of these floods ("recent" being 100 million years ago or more) contributed mudstones, shale, sandstone as well as economically important phosphate, gypsum, and bentonite to the accumulating layers of sediment.

Many varieties of animals developed due to the wide range of climate and land formations. The amphibians gave way to reptiles; dinosaurs ruled the land. Fossilized remains of such giants as Triceratops and Tyrannasaurus have been found near Glendive and Fort Peck. The first mammals and toothed birds were also present. As you may have already guessed, a more tropical climate was necessary to sustain or maintain this abundance of life. Consequently, the animals died off. As they died, their remains sank into the brakish swamps which also engulfed the lush vegetation. These accumulations were buried under sediment where the combination of heat, pressure, and time transformed them into Montana's "black gold," the petroleum and low sulphur coal which underlie large areas of the eastern two-thirds of the state.

Ah ... Now I can breathe!

9

These changes in Montana coincided with changes occurring at that time throughout the world. Some geologists theorize that 200 million years ago the continents were but a single, huge land mass. In response to changes deep within the earth, the continents and the "plates" of earth's crust beneath them began to very gradually "float" apart. As the continents ran into one another, the plates tipped, folded, and crumbled. For example, the result of the collision of India into Asia is said to be the Himalaya Mountains. (Scientists have referred to the recent series of earthquakes, January through August, 1976, as a part of this on-going process). Also, the plate under the Pacific Ocean was overrun by the plate comprised of North and South America. The subsequent rise in the edge of this plate formed the great chain of western mountains.

As in the previous mountain building era, characteristic metamorphic rocks were formed by extensive movements of molten rock below the surface. As the soft covering soils were worn away, the central Montana mountains were formed. Meanwhile parts of those things living on land also changed. The angiosperms or flowering plants became the dominant plant life. As gymnosperms diminished in numbers, so did the dinosaurs; their eventual disappearance may be interrelated to these changes. At any rate, by 60 million years ago, the great "Thunder Lizards" were gone.

"Montana has more square miles of known coal fields than any other state. M.R. Campbell, of the U.S. Geological Survey, estimates that there are more than 38,000 square miles of workable coal fields in the state, and a thousand square miles more that may probably be worked. This authority estimates the total original tonnage of coal in Montana as more than 380 billions of tons. At the present rate of production the supply would last something like 95 centuries, or nearly ten thousand years! It thus looks as though Montana has a fuel supply for the indefinite future.

Daniel Willard, *Montana: The Geological Story*, Lancaster, Pa., 1935).

The Northern Rocky Mountain area became a desert. The streams which washed sediments out of the newly formed mountains received so little rain, they dried up before they reached the sea, leaving thousands of feet of sand, mud, and gravel in the lower valleys. At the same time, the inland swamps in the eastern part of the state, remnants of the great seas, began to recede. These swamps were the beginning of additional coal deposits such as the famous Fort Union deposit.

Washington, Oregon and Idaho were covered by surface floods of molten rock which hardened to form basalt plateaus.

The mineralization which accompanied this mountain building activity contributed to Montana's wealth of precious metals, for it was during this time that gold, silver, copper, lead, and zinc were emplaced. These metals are found in association with the great granite intrusion in western Montana known as the Boulder Batholith. These changes, don't forget, took place over a geologic time span of millions of years. Nevertheless, the frequent earthquakes in Montana may indicate that this mountain building is not yet complete.

Of the world's coal supply, Montana has 80×, or 409,000,000,000 tons, a total of 635,000 tons for each inhabitant.

Facts About Montana, 1926

Whew!...○○○ glad we've seen the last of him!

○○○○○

11

Geologic Antiquity
Explained by Geologist

Tropical Plant Life Onetime Flourished Here in Broadwater county.

Search for Potential Oil-Bearing Acreage has Resulted in Learning Much of Prehistoric Central Montana Times.

Search Also found Uranium Possibilities Near Radersburg

Exclusive: The Townsend Star
 By Ray E. Colton, Geologist and
 Science Writer.

As far as the eye can see there is tropical grandeur, a vast lake whose waters are occasionally rippled by the giant Mosazaur "sea lizard" as he darts after a luckless fish. How big is the fish? Close to 500 pounds, but the Masazaur the most deadly of the sea lizards of his time is about forty-five (45) feet in length. He catches the fish, the rendering of flesh is heard. The fight is over. Nearby along the shoreline of the lake a terrible roar is heard among the jungle growths and giant ferns. A prehistoric boa constrictor length about 80 feet and as big around as a barrel glides up a palm tree. Soon the reason for the roar is manifest. A giant reptile of the class of Tyranosaurus Rex "king of the tyrant lizards" has been caught up with a luckless Brontosaur "thunder lizard" who was quietly munching some choice leaves off a tree, and having no protecting armor, and being slow in movement, has very little chance of escape unless he can reach the nearby water where he would be safe, as the flesh eaters could not swim. He fails. Tyranosaurus Rex springs for the kill. Grabbing the long necked dinosaur in the middle of the throat he almost severs the neck from the body. The fight is soon over and the meal is being eaten by the giant carnivor. Overhead the shrill scream of the Ptderactyl "winged reptile" is heard as he hovers around waiting for scraps of the kill. Tyranosaurus Rex pays him no mind but keep right on eating the ninety ton plant-eater which he has selected for dinner.

This scene was enacted here in this area of present day central Montana and Broadwater county about eighty (80) million years ago according to records given in fosil remains.

"Fish fossils believed to be over 300 million years old and of a type never before found in North America, have been discovered in Montana....To date, 12 different kinds of fish, all extinct, have been found."

from the Great Falls *Tribune*, July 22, 1969.

Wouldn't it be nice if one or all of you planned a self-discovery trip in your area using Roadside Geology of the Norther Rockies *by David Alt and Donald Hyndman? If you can't make the trip — get out the trusty map and do it in the classroom. The book is clearly written and full of pictures. (It would be a little more fun to take the trip. Hope you make it!)*

"A few million years ago eastern Montana was the home of various kinds of ancestral horses that walked on three toes, of varieties of camels and rhinoceroses that must have looked even funnier than the ones living in Africa today, and of an absolutely extraordinary kind of gopher that actually had horns in its head — no doubt the ancestral inspiration for our modern "jackalope." Saber-toothed tigers lurked in what little shrubbery there was, waiting to catch a meal."

Dave Alt and Jon Talbot, "The Prairie Surface," *Montana, Magazine of the Northern Rockies,* Fall, 1975 (Vol. 5, p. 4).

Probably 10-20 feet of peat was required to produce a single foot of bituminous *or semi-bituminous coal.*

A bed of coal 20-30 feet thick would require an accumulation of vegetable matter 400 feet in depth.

In bituminous coal it has been estimated that plant stems and fragments of plants would be reduced in size to form coal 1/17 it original size.

Geologists have estimated that in 1,000 years enough vegetation might accumulate to form less than 1-1/2 inch of coal.

A bed of coal 20 feet thick would require roughly 20,000 years to develop.

Daniel Willard, *Montana: The Geological Story,* (Lancaster, Pa., 1935).

"Erosion laid down a strata at the rate of one foot in 5,000 years; deposition, one foot in 2,500 years; and coal at the rate of one foot in 10,000 years. 100 years were required for production of 100 tons of coal on a single acre."

Dr. J.C. Siegfreidt of Bear Creek, as related in a story in the Phillipsburg newspaper, no date (probably the 1930's).

This was the Age of Mammals. Fossilized remains indicate that camels, 4-tusk elephants, rhinoceros, and primitive 3-toed horses roamed the land. These animals moved extensively, eventually crossing the land bridge from Alaska to Siberia. The paddlefish which still can be snagged in the Missouri River had its origin in this ancient time.

About three million years ago, for reasons not fully understood, Montana ceased to be a desert; ice began to build up in the northern hemisphere faster than it melted. Although the climate was not much colder, it was much wetter. Snow gradually accumulated to form huge glaciers, 1,000 to 2,000 feet thick. These glaciers advanced across the face of the land. Then...as mysteriously as they came, they disappeared. These continental glaciers were accompanied by more localized valley glaciers. This has happened at least four times...so far! Each time, the land was significantly altered; the waters of the Missouri, Musselshell, and Yellowstone Rivers were no longer able to find their way north to Hudson's Bay forcing new eastward courses to be carved. Even these new river routes changed, as evidenced by the Shonkin Sag, an empty river valley north of the Highwood Mountains in north central Montana. Enormous lakes were formed by the blockage of rivers near Great Falls and Missoula. Other blockages formed smaller lakes near Cut Bank, Musselshell, Jordan, Circle, and Glendive. Old shorelines now far above the valley floor, giant ripple marks, the outwash plains formed when the dams broke, all bear mute testimony to their existence. The land under the ice was scoured and leveled by its action. As glaciers melted, the deposits of Canadian soil and rock trapped inside were left in ridges hundreds of feet thick forming low hills. High mountain valleys once filled with ice now assume characteristic U-shapes and often contain lakes.

GLACIAL LAKE MISSOULA

During the last ice age, more than 10,000 years ago, an enormous glacier pushed slowly southward down the broad Purcell Valley of British Columbia into the panhandle of northern Idaho where it finally reached the Clark Fork River. When the glacier advanced across the Clark Fork, it dammed the River, impounding Glacier Lake Missoula. Pend Oreille Lake now fills a basin created by that same glacier where it once formed an ice dam.

After the glacier had blocked the river, water began backing up behind it forming a lake that grew larger with every year that passed. The highest shoreline left by Glacial Lake Missoula was just over 4,150 feet above sea level, so at one time the lake flooded the entire Clark Fork drainage of Montana to that elevation. At that time of maximum filling, water must have flooded the Bitterroot Valley as far south as Darby, the Clark Fork Valley as far east as Drummond, all of the Jocko, Camas Prairie and Little Bitterroot valleys, and the Mission Valley as far north as Polson where lake waters lapped against the ice front of another huge glacier. A total of about 2,900 square miles of Western Montana were flooded by the waters of a lake that contained, at maximum filling, a little more than 500 cubic miles of water.

Ice is lighter than water so an ice dam will normally float if the water behind it gets deep enough. That must have been what happened to Glacial Lake Missoula.

The fiercest torrents raging today seem like the merest trickles when compared to what must have happened when the lake emptied. Our best estimates suggest flow velocities through the narrower parts of the Clark Fork and Flathead valleys must have been something like 45 to 60 miles per hour. Considering that the valley walls are scoured to a height of almost 1,000 feet and that the valleys are about a mile wide, the flow rate then works out to approximately 8 or 10 cubic miles of water per hour — 200 times the flow rate of the Mississippi River at maximum flood.

Montana: Magazine of the Northern Rockies, Spring 1976, (Vol. 6, p.2).

"The Missouri River once continued northward to Havre, flowed east in the channel that is now used by the Milk River at Poplar, meandered off in a northeasterly direction to empty into Hudson Bay....Giant springs near Great Falls, one of the natural wonders of the west, is probably nothing but Missouri River water following an underground channel formed during the time of the glaciers. The Musselshell River once flowed north through the lower half of Phillips County to join the Missouri near Bowdoin.

Article in the Great Falls *Tribune*, March 11, 1934.

After the glaciers subsided they left in Montana the headwaters of "the two great rivers of America, the Columbia and the Missouri....The annual flow of water out of the state is sufficient to cover all the New England states (Maine, Vermont, New Hampshire, Massachusetts, Connecticut, and Rhode Island), plus New York, New Jersey, and Maryland, with water to a depth of six inches."

From *Facts About Montana*, published by the state in 1926.

"Bones and teeth of animals found in the gravels beneath the high plains surface in Montana turn out to be remains of animals known to have lived during the latest Meocine and Pliocene time — between 15 and 3 million years ago. Evidently that was the time interval in which the high plains formed. Montana must have had an extremely dry climate during those years and eastern Montana must have looked about the way central Australia does today, except that we had camels instead of kangaroos.

David Alt and Jon Talbot, "The Prairie Surface," *Montana, Magazine of the Northern Rockies*, Fall, 1975, (Vol. 5, p.4).

"All Montana rivers east of the Rocky Mountains, including the Missouri and the Yellowstone, flowed north into Hudson Bay....Both flowed, separately, eastward to the Dakotas before flowing north....Both, as well as smaller rivers, were blocked from their northward course when mountains of rock and dirt picked up by the glacial ice flow moved across Canada. This changed their course to the south into the Gulf of Mexico....This last giant ice flow is estimated to have measured between one and two miles in depth, and also gouged out the Great Lakes....The ice flow was beneficial because it deposited a large variety of rocks and an odd mixture of soil all across Montana."

Paul Buck, then head of the science department at Great Falls High School, in an article in the Great Falls *Tribune*, September 24, 1959.

Volcanic activity continued throughout this period, especially in the areas of Yellowstone Park and the Snake River. Some of the sediments which built up in the valleys during the time of scarce water were removed. Most of the mountain valleys have lost a thousand feet of sediment so far, and still have two or three thousand feet to go.

To the south, in the areas which escaped valley glaciation, the land shows the work of the Yellowstone River as it cuts its way through each successive elevation of land. This type of erosion is in sharp contrast with the action of the ice which left broad valleys with terraces, benches, and badlands.

Although man appeared elsewhere earlier, he probably did not appear in Montana until 10,000 years ago. Perhaps he followed the herds of bison, woolly mammoth, elk, antelope, caribou, and moose across the land bridge between Asia and North America. This was the same route used by the camel and horse (eohippus), only the direction was the opposite.

16

TIPIS and TRAVOIS... (10,000 BC — 1800 AD)

Chapter One

CROSSING

Where did the Indian come from? How did he get here? When did he arrive? These are questions that have bothered Westerners (Europeans primarily) since they first landed on this continent. It is generally believed the first Americans arrived via a land bridge which extended between northeastern Siberia and southwestern Alaska. Other "authorities" have attributed the initial settlement to the Egyptians, Chinese, Phoenicians, or Greeks. Other notions attribute settlement to the Lost Tribes of Israel, a Welsh prince named Madog, or the inhabitants of the Lost Continent of Atlantis. Verrrry Interesting!!!

INDIANS

An alternative to the land-bridge theory:

"Other peoples probably came from the westward, too, drifting along the northeast set of the Japan current as the water took and held their fishing rafts. The seacoast where they landed was bare and desolate, the mountains rose to the skies behind them, but here again was food and a place to live. They had been coastal people in the islands they had called their home, and they remained coastal people on the new mainland where they landed."

Mariott and Rachlin, *American Epic: The Story of the American Indian,* New York: Putnam, 1969.

As to the exact date of arrival, it was Tuesday, the twelfth of February, Fifteen Thousand One Hundred and Thirty-Seven B.C., at high noon MST (mountain standard time). Actually, this date may be off by thirty or forty thousand years, but....we keep trying. (Actually, as new information is found, the date is changed. A discovery in California during the summer of 1976 places the date of the Indian arrival at least 40,000 years ago.)

The migration may have been all at one time, two separate times, or a gradual trickle of small bands merely in search of game.

the LAND

It is generally agreed, however, the migration of Asians, from the area of Mongolia, to North America took place during an ice age. No, not because it was easier to skate across!! However, ice played an important role. You see, the great amount of water in the glaciers that covered the land was from the ocean causing it to drop nearly 300 feet. As this happened, the land bridge, nearly 1,000 miles wide, was exposed, providing "an adequate path." Because this bridge was so wide, it is felt that as the Indians (Asians) moved eastward and southward in search of game, they never realized they were crossing into previously uninhabited land. Therefore it may not have been a migration (having a place as a goal or destination) but rather a flow or gradual movement.

Many animals expanded their ranges by crossing the land bridge into North America, thus introducing NEW species to this continent. Hot on their trails were the first men and women to arrive in North America, also a NEW species. Of course it depends on which side of the bridge you're on as to how you'll interpret this. For instance, a Mongolian history book may view this as "some hunters, the LAST people to settle down, followed some super-plentiful game (e.g. elk, bison, moose, and caribou) across the land bridge for thousands of miles, to the LAST place we'd go for a caribou burger."

As far as we know, there is no evidence that shows these people ever returned to Mongolia, the earlier route of the eohippus (early horse) and camel, after having come to North America. This just might prove that some people would walk thousands of miles for a caribou burger, but wouldn't walk a mile for a camel. My how times have changed.

EOHIPPUS about the size of a fox. Forerunner of modern horse. Lived in N. America and Europe 50,000,000 years ago.

19

As to which Ice Age was used, two stand out, one some 75,000 years ago, the reason being some experts feel it would have taken some 25,000 years for this migration to reach South America's Cape Horn. The second was during the Wisconsin glaciation period some 12,000 to 15,000 years ago. The route taken in either case is said to have been the valleys along the eastern foothills of the cordillera to the extreme south and finally Cape Horn. Some people feel there is evidence of this travois-worn Old North Trail parallel to the continental divide near Heart Butte just south of Browning, Montana.

Montana's written history suffers not only because of its relatively few well-developed archaeological sites, but also because of the unwillingness on the part of some "trained" historians to recognize oral history. A few of the sites preserved in Montana are: the MacHaffies Site in Jefferson County, which establishes man's presence there to be at least 10,000 years ago, the Madison Buffalo Jump State Monument near Logan, and Pictograph Cave State Monument near Billings.

This may be hard to believe, but prior to the arrival of the white man, Indians did not have horses. Dog-pulled travois carried the Indians' belongings while they legged it along side. It was due more to the Indians ingenuity than the white man's generosity that the Indian got the horse. In fact, the white man tried pretty hard to keep the horse from the Indian. But, by the early 1700's, the Plains Indians were becoming equestrian nomads.

The Indians now found in eastern Montana did not arrive there until after Sixteen Hundred A.D. They lived in the northeastern regions of the U.S. It was the advance of the white settlers that forced them from their ancestral home, to the alien conditions and environment of the Northern Great Plains. Their ability to adapt to this new and hostile environment, and as quickly as they did, is a sad tribute to these peoples' ingenuity.

Re pre-horse Mountain Indians:

They lived in pit houses, hunted rabbits, ate seeds, grasses, camas roots, water lillies. They made blankets of rabbit skin, made baskets, followed a complex kinship system, sometimes could find no food other than grasshoppers and caterpillars.

From Mariott and Rachlin, *American Epic.*

"Buffalo jumps are not just a rich repository of arrowheads, and other artifacts of prehistoric Indian culture. The centuries' accumulation of buffalo bones is also a valuable source of fertilizer. Tons of it have been hauled from the base of the pishkuns around Montana, and, in the process, priceless archeological relics have been destroyed."

Ray Ozman, article in Great Falls *Tribune*, 2-25-68.

Chapter Two

BENEATH the LAND

Gold, silver and other valuable mineral deposits are resting peacefully beneath the surface of the land. Man did not yet have the technology or the desire to master all the demensions of his planet...

Chapter Three

GROWING ON

The characteristics of the vegetation found in Montana, east of the divide reflect the personality of the land itself. Grasses are suited to withstand drought, poor soil, intense cold and wind, and frost. Only hardy cottonwoods and their relatives of the river bottoms can survive the rigors of the environment. This semi-arid region receives between 10 and 20 inches of precipitation annually, the bulk of which falls during the early months of summer. However, some of this precipitation comes in the form of damaging hail. A singular intimacy exists between the land and the wind. The land is level and treeless, allowing for free movement of wind currents; the wind imposes with its eternal presence. If its mood is good, the eastern slopes of the Rockies may enjoy a chinook; if bad, the plains suffers a blizzard.

The grass itself is primarily in the gama, bluestem and buffalo grass varieties. Plants typical of desert-like areas such as sagebrush, yucca, and cactus are found. These plants form sod, a heavy, erosion-resistant carpet with shallow roots. In places where moisture is insufficient to support continuous growth, bunch grass grows in tufts. In spite of the landscape's *seemingly* bleak appearance, it was able to support enormous herds of buffalo, deer, antelope and elk. The history of the Northern Great Plains is indeed a history of grass.

the LAND

In the Rocky Mountains, the uneven distribution of timber is a result of determining factors of altitude and precipitation. West of the divide grows fir, spruce, cedar, pine, larch, hemlock, and juniper. The lodgepole pine also grows in the mountains east of the divide along with some deciduous trees.

WHEW! SURE GLAD THERE WEREN'T OOOOO ANY FROG EATERS!

"In the 7th century the Snakes probably held the lands west of the Rockies...there was little big game...the very names they gave their groups indicate their absorption in the quest for food. They were the Root Eaters, Rabbit Eaters, Squirrel Eaters, Salmon Eaters, Seed Eaters, Pine Nut Eaters, had one poor group known as the Earth Eaters. The Mountain Sheep Eaters in the north were the only group named for a game animal..."
(This was before the height of the buffalo culture).

George Hyde, *Indians of the High Plains*, (Norman: U. of Oklahoma Press, 1959).

Chapter Four

LIVING OFF the LAND

The Montana Plains Indians are relatively new to the area. In fact, none of them were here prior to 1600. Here's what happened:

As Europeans began to settle the Atlantic Coast in greater numbers, they forced tribes such as the Iroquois from their ancestral homelands. These Indians in turn, encroached upon the lands of other tribes forcing them further west (an early form of the Domino Theory?). Adding to the Indians problems was the concommitant settlement of the Pacific Coast. The free-roaming tribes were caught between two white waves; it wouldn't be long before they'd go under.

All of the tribes of eastern Montana were originally dwellers of America's northeastern woodlands. Many had lived in fixed homes and engaged in farming and hunting of only small game. Because of the already mentioned pressures, they began their long westward trek to a new, more hostile environment. Stops along the way provided new associations with tribes living in various areas. Many new practices and procedures for survival were assimilated. Adaption through adoption.

If you go back the 300 years as you tried in Book I, you would probably be surprised at the wildlife you'd find in Montana, especially east of the divide. The Plains were alive with enormous herds of buffalo, so many as to be innumerable. It is believed that at one time buffalo roamed almost the entire length and breadth of the continent. The same was true of the wapiti (American elk). You see, the elk is most at home on the plains, not the mountain forests. Haven't you ever wondered why an animal with such large, seemingly awkward antlers would live in the forest and not the plains?

The grizzly too, inhabited the plains. Lewis and Clark mentioned in their notes that contact with the grizzly, a new species to white men, was made much more frequently in eastern and central Montana than in the mountains of Western Montana.

Beaver and other fur-bearing animals were also in great abundance on the Plains, as well as higher ground. If by now the picture in your mind resembles a zoo without cages, you're starting to get the idea.

Bison

"The bison (American Buffalo) came to the North American continent from Asia, crossing over the land bridge that once connected the two continents. It is believed these ancestors of our buffalo arrived during the warm periods between the great glaciers that periodically covered a large part of North America. They ranged as far south as Mexico and as far East as New York. Buffalo were found in the greatest numbers in the plains from the Rockies to the Mississippi. At their peak it is thought that they may have numbered 60 to 70 million. Probably no other continent — not even Africa — has ever produced a wild game animal in such great numbers... We know now that the great north-south migrations once ascribed to the buffalo never occurred. The treks were probably not more than 300 or 400 miles long... By 1870-71, not more than 5½ million remained...by 1900, less than 300."

U.S. Dept. of Interior, Conservation Note No. 12, Fish and Wildlife Service, 1972.

Bears

"For centuries, before the first white man set foot in North America, the grizzly was the most dominant species on the continent. It ruled a vast domain from the Pacific Ocean to the Mississippi River, and its numbers were estimated at well over a million, probably closer to four million if you add the territories of western Canada and Alaska. Left undisturbed by the Indians and early white settlers who shared its land, the giant bear was free to roam where it pleased. The few braves that were able to kill a grizzly kept its claws as a symbol of their great hunting skill, and often ate the bear's heart in hopes of gaining the grizzly's great courage and strength. All of this was changed with the introduction of the repeating rifle... In 1970, the Interior Department Bureau of Sport Fisheries Wildlife estimated that a mere 800 grizzly bears were left in the U.S. — a reduction of over 99%. Of the 800 grizzlies which remain in the western U.S., most are found in a narrow corridor stretching from Glacier National Park south to the Yellowstone and Grand Teton National Parks."

Steven Seater, "Vanishing Point: The Grizzly Bear," *Environmental Quarterly*, July, 1973.

This would be a good time to read *Night of the Grizzlies* by Jack Olson.

Antelope

"The pronghorn, often called the antelope, is believed to be the only hoofed mammal native to the North American continent. Others — the bison, the deer, the moose, the elk, the caribou, and mountain sheep, and the mountain goat — have been here a long time, but scientists believe that their ancestors moved into North America from Asia over natural causeways since submerged. The pronghorn is no relative of any of these others, nor can his relationship to any animal native to any other continent be established....As late as the summer of 1858, at least 40 million pronghorns inhabited an area extending irregularly from the southern part of Alberta to central Mexico. They ranged in herds in the open grasslands and foothills, stopping short of the mountains...On at least 100,000 of the 147,000 square miles which were to become Montana, some 4 million of them lived...(to visualize, 4,000,000 could form a line six abreast and stretch from Havre to West Yellowstone.) By 1908, only 100,000 remained." (these are now protected by hunting regulations).

Lewis T. Poole, article in the Montana *Standard*, 8-31-58.

Cheyenne Tells How Magpie Saved the Indians

WHY the Indian considers the crow, magpie, hawk and coyote as his best friends among animal acquaintances and why the magpie has been especially honored by plains tribes in symbolical drawings and ornamentation is explained by an old Cheyenne legend, which is said to be found also among legends of many other tribes.

Although the art of story telling as a means of educating the young in the language and customs of their people has declined in importance, there are still a few of the older members of the Cheyenne tribe who remember and repeat stories learned in tepees of elders.

O-ne-hiah, one of the oldest women on the Tongue river reservation, who spends part of each year in the camp near Lame Deer, tells the story of the magpie as follows:

Animals Ate Men

"A long time ago the animals were accustomed to eat the Indians. That is, instead of Indians setting out to hunt buffalo, antelope, deer and elk, the elk or buffalo or deer or antelope would go out in bands and hunt men. This was hard for Indians, as they lived in constant fear of being eaten.

"At last the Indians had a great council with the animals to see if some arrangement could not be made which would give the Indians more power.

"Now, there was among the buffalo at that time a swift runner. She could out-run any buffalo, antelope or other creature on the prairies. The buffalo were confident that she could outrun anything, so they made a proposition to the Indians that all the birds and animals on the prairies have a great race and if the men could beat the animals, they could eat them, and if the animals could beat the men, they should continue as before.

"There were some animals and birds who agreed to be on the Indians' side in the great race — the hawk, crow, magpie, coyote and several others. They would race in the great contest and if any of them won, the men should have the victory, but if they lost, they would share the fate of the Indians.

Around Black Hills

"A race course was laid out completely around the Black Hills. The runners were to start at a certain point on the prairies, near the base of the hills, were to encircle the hills and return to the starting place.

"The morning of the race the prairies were covered with animals and Indians. Great bands of buffalo reached as far as the eye could see. Antelope, birds of all kinds and sizes, bears, deer, wolves, coyotes and all creatures on the plains and Indians of every tribe camped along creek bottoms.

"The fastest runners of every species lined up for the start. When the signal was given, the buffalo leaped ahead and plunged on and on at terrific speed. The hawk started like an arrow and was soon far ahead of everything else. Other animals were scattered across the plains as far as one could see.

"The buffalo went on and on, never slacking her pace until every blood vessel in her great body burst from the effort and she sank down to the earth and her blood flowed in great streams into the dry ground.

"The hawk, straining every muscle to keep far in the lead, was suddenly seen to fall like a stone to the earth. He, too, had overworked and his blood flowed from his broken heart into the ground.

"The other animals, so great was their eagerness to win, one by one dropped to the earth, with bleeding bodies. Their blood flowed softly into the ground, into the very rocks beneath the ground, and there it even colored the rocks, so that to this day there are places on the plains near the Black hills where blood-red rocks may be found.

Magpie Wins Race

"Now the magpie ws not a very swift flier, and when the race started she was soon left far behind. She could see beneath her the great mass of animals, moving like the wind across barren plains. She fluttered on, however, on and on, never stopping, never looking back. She saw the animals and birds before her drop one by one to the ground. She still kept on.

"At last the magpie reached the place where the race had started. No one else was left in the race. All had dropped out or had been killed by the strain. She had won over the fastest of every race on the prairie.

"That is why the Indians have hunted the buffalo, elk, deer and antelope. They have remembered their friends and no good Indian kills the crow, magpie, hawk or coyote."

Daniels County Leader
April 12, 1928

This would be a good time to read *Indian Legends From The Northern Rockies* by Ella Clark.

The Plains Indian, relatively small in number, barely diminished any of the animal population. They didn't care to eat the fur-bearing animals as long as buffalo, deer, antelope or elk were available. The grizzly was an impressive opponent, to say the least, for an Indian armed with only a bow and arrows. However, bear claws worn as ornaments, show that a few brave individuals responded to the challenge. Even the appearance of the horse and gun, in the hands of the Indian, did little to diminish the species. They merely made the Indian a more efficient hunter.

BUFFALO NOT STUPID; JUST HAD POOR SIGHT

Buffalo Jumps

An archeological expedition in Yellowstone National Park found "compounds, also called traps or corrals, where bison or other animals were driven into a corral or snowbank to be slaughtered or butchered. Jumps, where animals were driven over cliffs to their destruction, are lacking in the park proper, but they are common along the Yellowstone, Gallatin and Madison Rivers, just north of the park."

Dr. Carling Malouf, UM anthropology prof., in article in *Missoulian*, 7-11-59.

"In the old days, a white buffalo robe would grace the tepee of an Indian medicine man, or (the white buffalo) would be sacrificed to the Great Spirit at elaborate ceremonies in which it was burned, and the skull of the animal used in making 'big medicine' in connection with various Indian ceremonies." (the Indians believed white bison belonged to the Sun god.)

Peyton Moncure, article in Spokane *Spokesman-Review*, 3-13-49

Unlike the white men who were to come later, the Indian used almost every part of the buffalo.

The tastiest morsel was the tongue and the tender meat in the hump. Those of the tribe who were meat jerkers would cut a hind quarter into one big sheet of meat which they would leave to dry in the sun. This dried, or jerked, meat would then be cut in strips and pounded into a flakey mass by the squaws who would then intersperce layers of meat with melted buffalo fat to produce pemmican.

This delicacy was packed in bags of buffalo skin and kept sometimes for years. Some of this cache, when located, was to provide a staple food for the fur traders who came later.

As useful as the flesh of the buffalo were the droppings — especially in the Great Plains region where wood was scarce. It became standard fuel for campfires because it produces a hot fire with more glow than flame which was ideal for cooking.

In the event of a sudden blizzard, the Indian would crawl into a freshly killed and still warm buffalo carcass to keep from freezing.

With the coming of the white man things changed. The buffalo hides brought a higher price than the meat and attracted thousands of white hunters to the ranges.

Montana Standard, August 13, 1967.

Rocky Cliffs Meant Death for Countless Buffalo

By GROVER C. JARRETT

Buffalo furnished the early Indian with many of his most urgent needs.

Before the Indian could get all these things from a buffalo, he had to kill it. And, on foot this was no mean task. Though the horse was said to have originated on this continent, he disappeared and didn't return until Cortez landed with his troops in Old Mexico. Until this time the Indian was on foot.

The piskun, according to stories coming down from the early days, furnished the Indian with an answer to his problem. After maneuvering a herd into the vicinity of a cliff, the tribe would chase the buffalo over the precipice. Those not killed as a result of the fall were finished off with bows and arrows.

It is doubtful that these places were used much after the Indians became owners of horses. With a good mount and a bow and arrow with a steel point, it was easy for the Indian to get his meat.

Getting the buffalo herd over the cliff was no easy job though. This was the job of the medicine man who owned a "buffalo stone." A rock about the size of a man's fist, the "buffalo stone" was said to possess the magical power of luring the big animal toward it.

The medicine man, with his stone held tightly in his hand, worked his way along the brink of the cliff and, since he was covered with a buffalo skin, the animals soon became curious and moved closer for a look at the "thing." In the meantime the rest of the tribe was sneaking up behind the herd to keep it from turning back.

Pretty soon the herd, becoming more curious about the funny creature up front, was running toward the cliff. The medicine man, stripping off his buffalo skin robe, made a mad dash for safety and the animals went over the cliff.

Fortunes Made in Sale of Hides and Bones. Indian was Loser in the Bison's Passing.

The Surround

The true sportsman-like attack was by direct onslaught with all hunters mounted on fleet and trained buffalo ponies. This Indian method was known as "the surround." It was managed by the same preliminaries that were observed in all the great buffalo hunts by Indians. The attack was made in careful order under strict discipline, directly upon the herd until the latter had fully scented the danger, when the hunters broke into a wild gallop, each free to go where he chose, chasing and slaying amid the thunder of hoofs, the bellowing of the beasts and the clouds of dust raised in the mad rush of so many animals. So completely panic-stricken would these mighty herds become and so little sensible of where to flee, that most of them fell victims to their pursuers, and the ground would soon be strewn with mighty carcasses.

The Sane Hunters

There were, it is true, many men such as the Earl of Dunraven, Dr. Allen and others, who came west and hunted western game as did the Indian, for meat or trophies, but the final extinction of the bison and other wild game on the prairies was accomplished by the most cowardly and inhuman methods.

The commercial slaughter of the bison and the sale of buffalo hides reached vast proportions in the seventies. In St. Louis, one firm received 250,000 robes in 1871. There were many trading posts dealing in these and smaller peltries. In Cheyenne, in 1872 there was at the Union Pacific tracks a shed that measured 175 feet long, 60 feet wide, and 30 feet high, and this was literally so packed with buffalo hides that the walls bulged. Fort Benton, Montana, sent 80,000 buffalo hides to the St. Louis market in 1876. It is estimated that from 1872 to 1874 there were 1,780,461 buffalo killed and wasted, the meat being left to rot on the plains, the hides only being utilized. During this same time, also, 3,158,780 were killed by white hunters and the hides transported over the Santa Fe Trail. Add to these figures the 540,000 killed by the Indians during those years and you have a grand total of 3,698,780. By 1879 the great southern herd had been exterminated.

The Mineral Independent
March 3, 1977

BUFFALOS ROAM AGAIN IN MONTANA

Mineral Independent 2-1-40

CROW TRIBAL HERD HAS GROWN TO 600 HEAD, REPORTS SUPERINTENDENT

Old Watch-Fire Prophecy of Medicine Men Has Been Fulfilled; Once More These Indians in Southern Montana Have Favorite Meat and Hides Available.

By WALTER E. TAYLOR

A recent report of Robert Yellowtail, superintendent of the Crow Indian reservation, reveals that the Crow buffalo herd now numbers more than 600 head. The buffalo are roaming once again over the grassy hills in the land of the Crow and an old watch-fire prophecy of Crow medicine men has been fulfilled. Once more the Crow have buffalo meat and hides available for times of need. Once again the women sew dancing garments with buffalo sinew.

In pre-Columbian times the Crow country, a vast territory lying between the Yellowstone river and the Big Horn mountains of Wyoming, was one of the finest buffalo hunting regions in the northwest. From remotest times it had been the private preserve of the Crow and they defended it against all comers. They were among the most peaceful of western Indian peoples but when their hunting country was threatened they could fight fiercely. The bunch grass grew knee deep on the rolling hills and the buffalo that grazed there were fat, famed among distant tribes for the fine quality of the robes they provided.

Then, in latter years of the 19th century the robe hunters, white men looking for quick riches, came to the land of the Crow. Within two decades the buffalo were almost exterminated. Carload after carload of stiff buffalo robes went east on the newly constructed railroads and countless thousands of buffalo carcasses lay rotting on the prairies. The Crow people could not, would not believe that in so short a period of time all of the buffalo, their chief source of food, clothing, and shelter, had been killed off. No, it could not be said the chiefs and the medicine men. The chiefs were of the opinion that the buffalo had migrated to the far north, but the medicine men had a different theory. The buffalo, said they, had not been all killed off, for Old Man Coyote had seen to that. He had caused a great hole to open in the earth and into the hole he had driven the buffalo. Some day, according to the medicine men's prophecy, the buffalo would return to the land of the Crow. And they did.

The present immense Crow reservation, one of the largest in the United States, includes a large portion of the original Crow hunting ground. Of course the buffalo have not come back in the great numbers the Crow once knew, but there are enough to make up one of the largest herds remaining within United States borders. The buffalo herd is part of the Indian rehabilitation program of Robert Yellowtail, first full-blood Indian reservation superintendent appointed west of the Mississippi.

In 1935 Yellowtail conceived the plan of stocking the reserve with wild game. Although some of his critics said so, Yellowtail had no idea of sending his people "back to the blanket" or providing them with the thrills of the old-time hunt. His objective was to have a ready supply of food for the Crow in times of economic stress.

From Yellowstone park the Crow got 200 head of buffalo. The animals were shipped to the reservation by truck and loosed in a vast pasture of more than thirty thousand acres, a pasture surrounded on three sides by canyons of the Big Horn river and two tributary streams. These deep river courses on the north, east, and west sides of the grazing area have steep sides that prevent the animals from wandering away. All that is needed to prevent their escape to the south is a 700-yard fence. This comparatively short piece of fencing keeps the buffalo in the great pasture. The fence is eight feet high and is built of heavy timbers. Buffalo walk nonchalantly through ordinary cattle fencing.

Since it was started the Crow herd has shown a steady increase. Come what may, the Crow people will have meat when they need it, and officials of the United States Indian bureau are watching Mr. Yellowtail's experiment with interest. It may be tried on other reservations.

To date there has been no need for the Crow to turn to their buffalo herd for meat and only about 70 animals have been slaughtered for tribal ceremonials and festive barbeques. Robes, bones, sinews have been used to revive tribal arts in the making of ceremonial costumes.

Far from any village or town, the Crow buffalo range gives the animals living conditions identical with those of olden times, and in their new home the buffalo have become as wild as their ancestors. The sight of man, afoot or on horseback, sends them thundering over the hills in wild flight. And migratory instincts have not dimmed in the thundering herd. After the melting of the snows each springtime the buffalo travel to the highest point on their range to summer. They travel in groups made up of a bull, several cows, and the calves. The old law of survival of the fittest is still in force and when a young bull attacks an oldster in an attempt to steal his family, the ensuing fight is fierce and may be hours long. If the challenger is successful and the patriarch is driven off, the latter retires from the heard to live out his life as a hermit.

Re: buffalo jump site between Ulm and Vaughn in Cascade County — "Dr. Dee Taylor, UM anthropologist, said 'All indications are this could be one of the deepest, and therefore oldest buffalo kills known.' Taylor said it is thought the site contains bones of prehistoric 'bison antiquis,' — a larger type of buffalo existing prior to 15,000 years ago. He said the bones could probably present unknown facts related to the 'few roving bands of humans' who killed buffalo by driving them over steep cliffs."
Article in Great Falls Tribune, 1-9-58.

29

Many of the animals are regarded as typifying some form of wisdom or craft.

Among the animals especially respected and supposed to have great power, are the buffalo, the bear, the raven, the wolf, the beaver, and the kit-fox. Geese too, are credited with great wisdom and with foreknowledge of the weather. As is quite natural among a people like the Blackfeet, the buffalo stood very high among the animals which they reverenced. It symbolized food and shelter. Not a few considered it a medicine animal, and had it for their dream, or secret helper. It was the most powerful of all the animal helpers.

A reverence for the bear appears to be common to all North American tribes, and is based not upon anything that the animal's body yields, but perhaps on the fact that it is the largest carnivorous mammal of the continent, the most difficult to kill and extremely keen in all its senses. The Blackfeet believe it to be part brute and part human, portions of its body, particularly the ribs and feet, being like those of a man. The raven is cunning. The wolf has great endurance and much craft. He can steal close to one without being seen.

There were various powers and signs connected with these animals so held in high esteem by the Blackfeet, to which the people gave strict heed. Thus the raven has the power of giving people far sight. Often, in going to war, a man would get a raven's skin and stuff the head and neck, and tie it to the hair of the head behind. If a man wearing such a skin got near the enemy without knowing it, the skin would give him warning by tapping him on the back of the head with its bill.

The wolves are the people's great friends. If, as they are travelling along, they pass close to some wolves, these will bark at the people, talking to them. Some man will call to them, "No, I will not give you my body to eat, but I will give you the body of some one else, if you will go along with us." If a man goes away from the camp at night and meets a coyote, and it barks at him, he goes back to the camp, and says to the people: "Look out now; be smart. A coyote barked at me to-night." Then the people look out, and are careful, for it is a sure sign that something bad is going to happen.

If a person is hungry and sings a wolf song, he is likely to find food. Men going on a hunting trip sing these songs, which bring them good luck.

Blackfoot Lodge Tales: The Story of a Prairie People, George B. Grinnell, Lincoln, University of Nebraska Press, 1962.

The buffalo and the beaver were hunted and trapped into near extinction for sport and money. The grizzly, elk, big horn sheep, deer and other animals were forced to retreat to the mountains, for in the presence of the white man they could no longer roam freely. They had to move and adapt, much the same way as another, far more precious creature, the American Indian.

It was the arrival and settling of the white man that changed everything. Put simply, the white man did two things to the animals of the area:
1. massacred them into near extinction.
2. forced them into the wilderness areas of the mountains.

Chapter Five

Which tribe entered Montana first? It is hard to say. The Blackfeet, the Crow, the Atsina, the Sioux, the Cheyenne, and the Assiboine all eventually established nomadic residency here. The Chippewa or Ojibway and the Cree arrived in the mid-1800's, the last to settle.

At first there was room for all who came, but as numbers increased, competition for choice hunting grounds grew fierce. (Not different from today's hunting problem, huh?) Consequently, tribes adopted warlike postures toward some tribes and allied themselves, for strength, with others.

INTER-TRIBAL INDIAN WARS

"Although regarded as migratory and wandering, these tribes moved back and forth in a comparatively restricted area which was a homeland, sacred as the land of their fathers. Their resentment was great because they considered as their property the bison which roamed their land. This strong personal attachment to the land and the compelling economic dependence on the buffalo were the basic causes for intertribal warfare....War was waged for horses to maintain mastery over the bison range, to augment one's personal wealth, and to have the means to establish a family. (One's wealth was measured by how many horses he owned.) The compelling urge to revenge the injury or death of kinsmen and friends resulted in a vicious circle of death and reprisal."

Arthur K. Buntin, *Battleground: A Narrative and Evaluation of Intertribal Warfare on the Buffalo Plains of Eastern Montana and in Adjacent Areas Prior to 1880,* unpublished MA thesis, U. of M.

A majority of the Indians believed that they had the right to roam at will on any land inhabited by the buffalo, for Wakunda, the Creator, had made the prairie and the buffalo for the sole use of all Indians. In case of scarcity of game in its customary hunting place, a tribe extended its hunting operations into another part of the plains, which the Creator intended for Indian support. They sought not land but the means of subsistence which every Indian believed himself entitled to, even though it was necessary to destroy his enemies or to risk his own life to obtain it."

Paraphrased from Edward T. Denig, "Indian Tribes of the Upper Missouri," *40th Annual Report of the Bureau of American Ethnology,* Washington, D.C., 1930.

The first modern horses were brought to this continent by the Spanish settlers of the southwest. The Spanish tried to prevent the Indians from acquiring these animals realizing it would be detrimental to their plans for domination. In spite of rigorous Spanish efforts, the Indian did acquire horses and within a short period of time, adopted a culture centered around its use. At first, the tribe that possessed horses, reigned supreme. Horses offered mobility, speed to aid the hunt, strength to move belongings (instead of dogs). Such an asset was not to be kept by few, however, and over the years all tribes were able to travel with greater ease across the open expanses of Montana. With the horse, the Indians changed from semi-sedentary people who relied on farming for at least part of their food, to complete nomads following the game across the prairies. These tribes showed an amazing adaptibility to changes forced upon them (moving) and adoptibility to changes sought by them (the horse).

Effect of finding horses on Indian culture:

With horses, Indians could hunt buffalo, so dwellings were now tipis made of leather. These shelters could be considerably larger than pit houses, so tribes moved in larger groups.
Pottery-making and basket-making was forgotten, as buffalo hides were used to make lighter, easier-to-carry containers for storage and transporting.
Textile skills were abandoned as tribes relied on buffalo, antelope, and deer hides (which they could now obtain in larger quantity) for their clothing and blankets.
The peak of Indian buffalo-based culture was at about 1800. It only lasted about 100 years altogether.

From Mariott and Rachlin, *American Epic*.

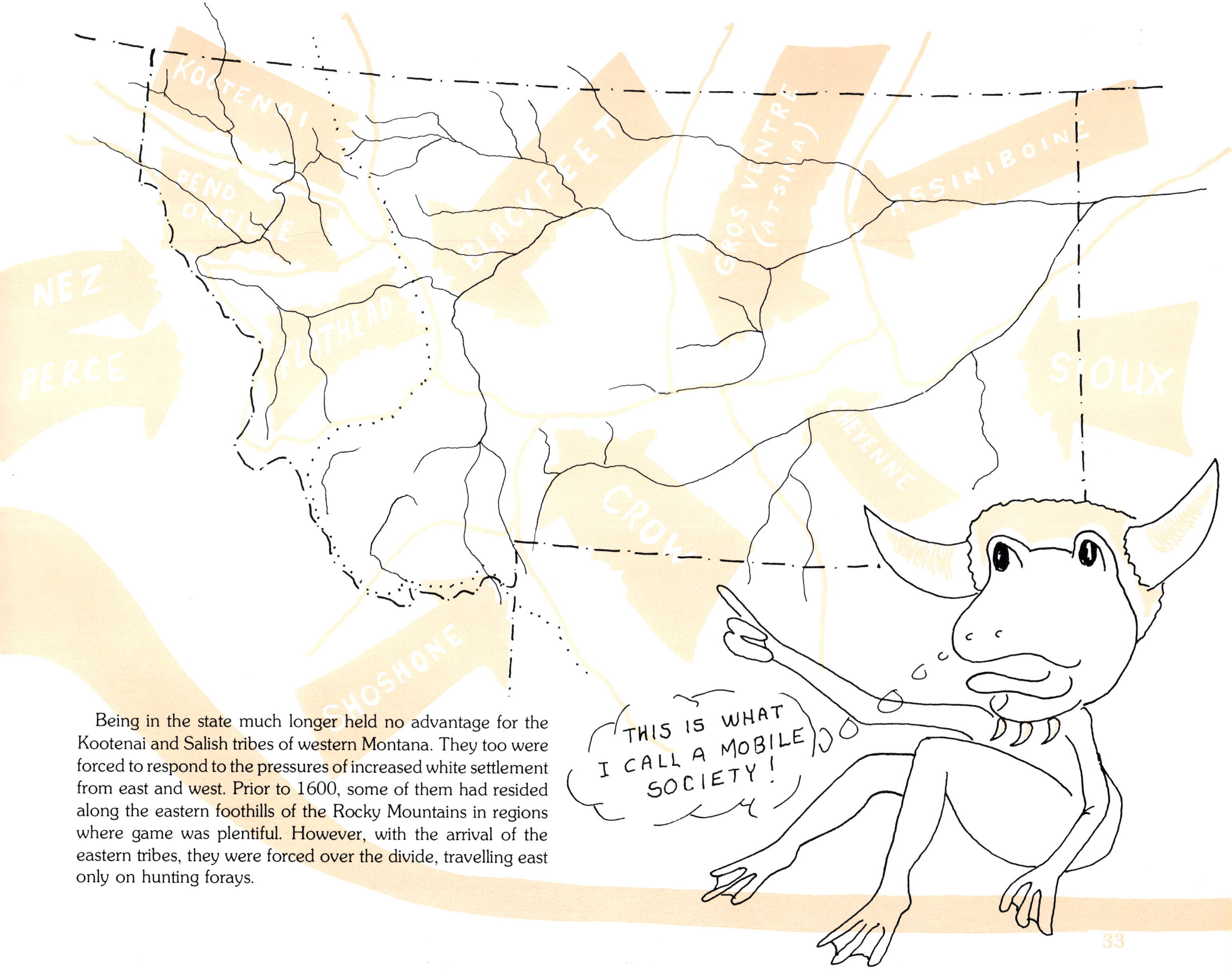
KOOTENAI
PEND OREILLE
NEZ PERCE
FLATHEAD
BLACKFEET
GROS VENTRE (ATSINA)
ASSINIBOINE
SIOUX
CHEYENNE
CROW
SHOSHONE
THIS IS WHAT I CALL A MOBILE SOCIETY!

Being in the state much longer held no advantage for the Kootenai and Salish tribes of western Montana. They too were forced to respond to the pressures of increased white settlement from east and west. Prior to 1600, some of them had resided along the eastern foothills of the Rocky Mountains in regions where game was plentiful. However, with the arrival of the eastern tribes, they were forced over the divide, travelling east only on hunting forays.

HOW THE FLATHEAD GOT HORSES

The story of the diffusion of the horse has been told me many times. The following version is quoted because it is almost a literal translation of the story told by an old warrior with an authentic "coup." Since it agrees with the versions of other competent informants, it is changed as little as possible.

A long, long time ago the Salish had no idea of a horse (estimated between 1600 and 1750). This was before Lewis and Clark came here. Then it happened that two lodges of Salish were camped way to the south. Since they were usually at peace with the Shoshonean Snake, the Flathead felt safe. Upon that occasion a party of Shoshoni surprised these lodges and wiped them out, then returned to their own camp. Very soon after this the main band of the Salish came upon the remains of their massacred kin and swore vengeance. A small party undertook this and stole to the south, scouting the trail of the murderers.

Apparently the Shoshoni had not expected a return visit, for the camp was very poorly guarded and very few men were present. Seeing how easy revenge would be, one of the warriors said, "Now let us rush this small camp and wipe out two Shoshoni lodges for what they did to our people." But the man who carried the pipe saw something which amazed him. There was a herd of hobbled animals, the like of which they had never seen before. What was perhaps the strangest of all was that these animals seemed content where they were, in associating with people, and were not trying to run away. They would even let people come up to them without trying to run away and save themselves. In view of these strange sights the chief refused to rush the Shoshoni camp, and said to his war-brothers, "No, boys, let us wait here and see what this means."

So the Salish waited and spied on the Shoshoni camp with its strange animals for three days. The Shoshoni warriors came and went without discovering them. Our people noticed that the men liked these animals and were good to them. But what surprised them most was that the Snake warriors got on top of them and rode on their backs. So at the end of the third day the leader of the Salish party said, "Tomorrow will be the fourth day we have watched. When the Shoshoni warriors go away tomorrow let us rush that camp and drive away all those animals and take them home, for we see that the Snake prize them." And they did that; they drove all of them away. There were only a few Snake men around and the Salish shot them with arrows.

They drove the horses northward and soon found the main band of Salish. These friends were very much surprised at all their war party told them and admired the horses very much. All of this band then broke camp and started northward to the Salish country in the Bitter Root Valley. But there was one thing they did not know, because they had no experience with horses. The Snakes did not keep all their horses in one herd. The great herd was over in the hills, and that is what the Shoshoni men were doing, grazing their main herd out of sight of camp.

When the Shoshoni warriors came back and found their horses stolen, they formed a large war party and pursued the Salish. It did not take them long to catch up, for they knew how to ride horses and the Salish did not. Our people had to walk on foot and drive the horses. Since this was in the open country south of Dillon the scouts saw the Snake party coming a long way off and gave warning. The Salish prepared to receive the attack of the Shoshoni, which scared them. The Shoshoni are not as good fighters as the Salish. That is one of the reasons we make fun of them and make snake signs when we speak of them. They had more warriors than we did, no women along, and they were on horses, but they did not attack.

This would be a good time to read *Coyote Tales of the Montana Salish* by Harriet Miller and Elizabeth Harrison.

The Snake rode up on their horses and made peace signs, showing they wanted to parley. They came up and got off their horses, and they begged and begged and begged. They begged the Salish to give them back their horses. But the Salish chief said, "No, we will keep them. You wiped out two of our lodges and we will keep these horses instead of wiping out two of your lodges, as we could have done." And that is what they did, and even though they begged and begged, the Shoshoni had to go back to their camp without their horses.

For quite a while the Salish were afraid of horses. As they were driving them back to the Bitter Root they formed a large circle around them, and were a little afraid when the horses came too close. One of the young men who had been on the revenge party was brave, however, and he caught one of the horses. Everyone stood around to see what would happen, but the young man rode the horse as long as it walked. Then he thought he would make it trot, as he had seen the Shoshoni warriors do. But when the horse trotted this young man got dizzy, even when it was only trotting, and fell off. Some people say he fainted.

The Salish learned to ride horses and to prize them, as everyone knows. We are fine horsemen even today. These warriors who captured the horses notched their "coup" sticks and were always given great honor. This is the truth.

All Flathead informants say that the horse diffused to all the northern and western tribes from them, as well as a few of the nearer people of the Plains. The story is very vivid as to how the Kalispel were entranced when one of their village came upon a horse track one day. They called a council and debated about the animal which had made the track. Some wise men thought it might be a horse, since the story of such animals had already reached them. About that time some people looked down the Clark's Fork River, and there came a Flathead who had been visiting his Upper Pend d'Oreille friends, sitting nonchalantly on the loping horse and smoking his pipe. When he swam the horse across the river they all came and gathered around him to observe the strange beast.

H.H. Turney-High, *MAAA*, "Flathead Indians."

Indian women were responsible for most of the "household chores," with some variation from tribe. Men were the warriors and hunters. Women gathered roots and berries, prepared the meats and hides brought by their husbands, and did beadwork and quillwork which decorated their apparel and household items. The life of an Indian woman was demanding, but by her standards, rewarding.

Guns were an important addition to the Indian's arsenal. They were first introduced to Montana by Cree traders dealing with the French and British. The hunting success of the Indian increased immeasureably with the acquisition of the gun. So too was their ability to establish a territory. Those tribes acquiring horses and guns became the rulers of the land.

BLACKFOOT BEHAVIOR IN WAR — EXPECTATIONS, PUNISHMENT

In their hostile encounters, the Blackfeet have much that is common to many Plains tribes, and also some customs that are peculiar to themselves. Like most Indians, they are subject to sudden, apparently causeless, panics, while at other times they display a courage that is heroic. They are firm believers in luck, and will follow a leader who is fortunate in his expeditions to almost any danger. On the other hand, if the leader of a war party loses his young men, or any of them, the people in the camp think that he is unlucky, and does not know how to lead a war party. Young men will not follow him as a leader, and he is obliged to go as a servant or scout under another leader. He is likely never again to lead a war party, having learned to distrust his luck.

If a war party meets the enemy, and kills several of them, losing in the battle one of its own number, it is likely, as the phrase is, to "cover" the slain Blackfoot with all the dead enemies save one, and to have a scalp dance over that remaining one. If a party had killed six of the enemy and lost a man, it might "cover" the slain Blackfoot with five of the enemy. In other words, the five dead enemies would pay for the one which the war party had lost. So far, matters would be even, and they would feel at liberty to rejoice over the victory gained over the one that is left.

The Blackfeet sometimes cut to pieces an enemy killed in a battle. If a Blackfoot had a relation killed by a member of another tribe, and afterward killed one of this tribe, he was likely to cut him all to pieces "to get even," that is, to gratify his spite — to obtain revenge. Sometimes, after they had killed an enemy, they dragged his body into camp, so as to give the children an opportunity to count "coup" on it. Often they cut the feet and hands of the dead, and took them away and danced over them for a long time. Sometimes they cut off an arm or a leg, and often the head, and danced and rejoiced over this trophy.

Women and children of hostile tribes were often captured, and adopted into the Blackfoot tribes with all the rights and privileges of indigenous members. Men were rarely captured. When they were taken, they were sometimes killed in cold blood, especially if they had made a desperate resistance before being captured. At other times, the captive would be kept for a long time, and then the chief would take him off away from the camp, and give him provisions, clothing, arms, and a horse, and let him go. The captive man always had a hard time at first. When he was brought into the camp, the women and children threw dirt on him and counted "coups" on him, pounding him with sticks and clubs. He was rarely tied, but was always watched. Often the man who had taken him prisoner had great trouble to keep his tribesmen from killing him.

Blackfoot Lodge Tales: The Story of a Prairie People, George B. Grinnel, Lincoln, U. of Nebraska, 1962.

Chapter Six

Prior to the acquisition of the horse, plains life was very difficult. This was especially true for people accustomed to farming and hunting mostly small game. Since the sole source of transportation was the dog, lodgings were by necessity small. As if it wasn't enough to drive the Indians westward from their land, the whites introduced (sometimes purposely) new diseases which caused large numbers of Indians to die, due to the lack of natural immunity.

As these Indians moved westward, they acquired some of the cultural traits of the tribes living in the Dakotas and the Missouri River Valley. Pottery making, certain religious ceremonies, social structures, farming techniques, use of canoes and bull boats and earthen lodges were just some of the things learned along the way.

The single feature that made the plains inhabitable in those early years was the American Buffalo (bison or just plain "buffalo"). The buffalo provided the Indian with life's necessities: food, shelter, and clothing. Uses were found for nearly every part of the animal.

While the Indians were still on foot, buffalo hunting was a communal effort. The most common method was the buffalo jump or pishkun. By this method, the animals were stampeded over a cliff. If the fall did not kill them, the spears and arrows of the persons waiting below did. As soon as the animals were skinned, women and children began to preserve the meat through drying or other methods.

INDIAN CUSTOMS (though these are Blackfoot, they are fairly representative.)

"Whenever a Blackfoot counts a coup, he is entitled to a new name. A Blackfoot will never tell his name if he can avoid it. He believes that if he should speak his name, he would be unfortunate in all his undertaking.

It was considered a grave breach of propriety for a man to meet his mother-in-law, and if he spoke to her, she demanded a very heavy payment, which he was obligated to make. The mother-in-law was equally anxious to avoid meeting or speaking to the son-in-law.

Three modes of burial were practiced by the Blackfeet. They buried their dead on platforms in trees, on platforms in lodges, and on the ground in tipis. If a man died in a dwelling, it was never used again. The people would be afraid of the man's ghost. If the deceased was a man, his weapons and often his medicine were buried with him. With women a few cooking utensils and implements for tanning robes were placed on the scaffolds....If a man had a horse, he might order it to be killed at his grave. In ancient times, it is said, dogs were killed at the grave. Women mourn for deceased relations by cutting their hair. For the loss of a husband or son (but not a daughter) they not only cut their hair but often take off one or more joints of their fingers.

The children, at least the boys, played about and did as they pleased. Not so with the girls. Their duties began at a very early age. They carried wood and water for their mothers, sewed moccasins, and as soon as they were strong enough, were taught to tan robes and fires, make lodges and travois, and do all other woman's (menial) work. The boys played at mimic warfare, hunted around in the brush with their bows and arrows, made mud images of animals, and in the summer spent about half their time in the water. In winter they spun tops on the ice, slid down hills on sleds of buffalo ribs, and hunted rabbits."

George B. Grinnel, *Blackfoot Lodge Tales: The Story of a Prairie People*, Lincoln, U. of Nebraska Press, 1962.

This would be a nice time to watch *Vision Quest* from MSU Film and Television Center.

If no cliff was available, the animals were driven into a "surround" where the confusion caused by great numbers of animals milling around enabled the Indians to make their kill. Sometimes too, individuals would try sneaking up on a herd to kill an animal. Try that on for size!!

The Indians of this era roamed only periodically, and then only for short distances in search of game, for they did not have the means to roam extensively.

The true Plains Culture did not develop fully until the middle of the eighteenth century, when the Indian acquired the horse. This is the culture most often depicted on T.V. and in movies; the stereotyped Indian wearing a war bonnet, sitting on a painted pony. This culture developed only on the Great Plains and only after the introduction of the horse and gun, by the white man.

This increased mobility brought about some changes that are not as obvious as 'just' being able to hunt greater areas. Prosperity increased; time spent gathering food was greatly reduced. With increased leisure time, tribes had a chance to develop their art forms as well as rituals and ceremonies. Contacts with other tribes increased. This resulted in the spreading of cultural traits and various adaptions to the new way of life. In other words, tribes had SOME similarities and used SIMILAR methods for doing CERTAIN tasks. (Americans and Italians both use cars, fire extinguishers, some are Catholics, etc.)

This increased contact also increased the amount of predatory warfare. However, the Indian fought for honor, not decimation. They thought it foolish to kill a person who exhibited bravery. Bravery was shown by being able to "count coup" upon an enemy (get close enough to actually strike an opponent with a "coup" stick). Horse-stealing became a favorite pastime, particularly because the horse became THE standard of wealth.

PHILOSOPHY OF "COUP" AND WAR

An expression often used in these pages, and which is so familiar to one who has lived much with Indians as to need no explanation, is the phrase to count "coup." Like many of the terms common in the Northwest, this one comes down to us from the old French trappers and traders, and a "coup" is, of course, a blow. As commonly used, the expression is almost a direct translation of the Indian phrase to strike the enemy, which is in ordinary use among all tribes. This striking is the literal inflicting a blow on an individual, and does not mean merely the attack on a body of enemies.

The most creditable act that an Indian can perform is to show that he is brave, to prove, by some daring deed, his physical courage, his lack of fear. In practice, this courage is shown by approaching near enough to an enemy to strike or touch him with something that is held in the hand — to come up within arm's length of him. To kill an enemy is praiseworthy, and the act of scalping him may be so under certain circumstances, but neither of these approaches in bravery the hitting or touching him with something held in the hand. This is counting "coup".

The man who does this shows himself without fear and is respected accordingly. With certain tribes, as the Pawnees, Cheyennes, and others, it was not very uncommon for a warrior to dash up to an enemy and strike hom before making any attempt to injure him, the effort to kill being secondary to the "coup."

Blackfoot Lodge Tales: The Story of a Prairie People, George B. Grinnell, Lincoln, U. of Nebraska, 1962.

BLACKFOOT INTER-TRIBAL JUSTICE AND PUNISHMENT

The following were the crimes which the Blackfeet considered sufficiently serious to merit punishment, and the penalties which attached to them.

Murder: A life for a life, or a heavy payment by the murderer or his relatives at the option of the murdered man's relatives. This payment was often so heavy as absolutely to strip the murderer of all property.

Theft: Simply the restoration of the property.

Adultery: For the first offense the husband generally cut off the offending wife's nose or ears; for the second offense she was killed by the All Comrades. Often the woman, if her husband complained of her, would be killed by her brothers or first cousins, and this was more usual than death at the hands of the All Comrades. However, the husband could have her put to death for the first offense, if he chose.

Treachery (that is, when a member of the tribe went over to the enemy or gave them any aid whatever): Death at sight.

Cowardice: A man who would not fight was obliged to wear woman's dress, and was not allowed to marry.

If a man left camp to hunt buffalo by himself, thereby driving away the game, the All Comrades were sent after him, and not only brought him back by main force, but often whipped him, tore his lodge to shreds, broke his travois, and often took away his store of dried meat, pemmican, and other food.

Blackfoot Lodge Tales: The Story of a Prairie People, George B. Grinnell, Lincoln, U. of Nebraska, 1962.

DIET OF FLATHEADS

The Salish considered everything connected with digging and caring for the pit woman's work. In fact, the presence of men was tabued while the women were baking in the pit lest bad luck and famine overtake all.

Camas was always cooked before being eaten or stored. Its taste in the raw is quite unpleasant. Occasionally it was cooked by itself, in which case it was dried and stored without pulverizing. In this state it was sometimes squeezed into little cakes which were subsequently dried and stored. Yet camas cooked plain was not the rule. Its chief blend was with the black lichen mentioned before, which baked with camas produces a black, gelatinous mass. This was later dried and pulverized. The lichen baked by itself was considered more of a tonic for the sick than a food.

While the hot pit was primarily for camas, flesh foods were also prepared in it. Dried meat was made more palatable by this slow steaming, while fresh meat was very superior when baked in this manner. A large haunch of fresh meat will cook thoroughly in a little over an hour. It was the favorite method of cooking fresh bear meat because it tended to overcome the bear's strong flavor. Small rodents were seldom cooked in any other way. These were not sknned, but carefully scraped, drawn, filled with tallow, and cast into the pit in large numbers.

The Salish women also cooked by boiling, broiling, and roasting. Boiling was accomplished by digging a hole in the ground about one foot deep and of about the same diameter. This was then lined with a permanent bag of bison skin which had been carefully fitted and sewn to size. This was sunk convenient to the fire. In this the stones were placed to get as hot as possible, then dropped into the nearby water-filled receptacle. When the food had been boiled the bag was immediately removed, washed; then hung up to dry. The Kalispel sometimes say that the Flathead at one time long ago lined the boiling hole with baskets of the flexible Nez Perce type. The principals insist they did not; that they did not know how to make these basketry wallets at any time. As will be seen they traded with the Nez Perce for these wallets: this they insist is a very old condition of trade and material culture; all of which may or may not be true.

Very delicious soups and stews were made in this way. Basic soup was made of shank bones, the grease of which was skimmed away and used for mixing with pemmican. A thick broth of boiled pemmican was a hardy food. The most highly prized soup delicacy was one of simmered blood mixed with camas-lichen powder. Fruits dried of fresh were not boiled with meat, but after fresh meat had been boiled Flathead like to dip dried berry cakes into the broth. The broth from fresh meat was also a favorite medium in which to boil camas, bitter root, and other dried roots and berries. Fish was often boiled, especially the smaller species. Boiling was also the normal way of preparing salmon pemmican and mussels.

Turtles might be roasted in the manner described in the next paragraph or, if large enough, in a special manner. This was to bury the reptiles in a shallow hole, cover with earth, and keep a fire going over the spot until the flesh was considered done.

Roasting was a simple process. Numerous stakes of about two and one half feet in length were driven into the ground near the camp fire. Onto their pointed ends fresh meat or large fish were cast.

As for meal times, the Flathead had two. Any other eating during the day was mere incidental snacking. Breakfast was served when the men of the lodge came from watering and feeding the primary chargers, ordinarily just before dawn. Supper was served just before sundown when the day's work was over. There was no difference in the menus of the two meals. Several dishes of the foods mentioned above were set out each meal.

The family assembled and ate together; inside in severe weather, before the lodge when it was fine. No tabu kept husband and wife, parents and children apart. Husband and wife indeed ate from the same bowl or bark basket. Large, long bowls were used as serving dishes and were placed in the three principal living portions of the lodge. From these inhabitants and guests served themselves, urged to more helpings by the cook when the food permitted.

Fingers were used for the solid materials while horn spoons scooped up the soups. After eating, Flathead cleaned their hands by running them through their hair unless they had eaten fish.

The Salish possessed excellent wooden dishes and spoons. The typical dish was carved from a knot of pine but preferably cedar, was of elliptical shape, about sixteen inches long and nine inches broad, and was undecorated. They knew of rather elaborately decorated bowls and frequently obtained them by inter-tribal trade from the west. A few of these native bowls may yet be seen, but the decorated ones have long since disappeared. Spoons with which to eat soups of soft cooked vegetables were made of mountain goat or sheep horn, or sometimes of basketry.

H.H. Turney-High, *MAAA*, "Flathead Indians."

Nearly all the Plains cultural traits were present prior to the arrival of the horse. The horse merely permitted them to become intensified or more elaborate. The major source of food was still the buffalo. Due to their constant movement, the Indians were unable to farm, the exception being some ceremonial tobacco grown by the Cree. The transportable hide tepee increased in size as did the travois. Although most tribes had acquired basketry, weaving and pottery skills in their prior habitat, they were no longer practical. Easily transported items and leather items replaced them. Because of this, tribes developed elaborate techniques for the tanning and the use of rawhide. Quillwork was eventually replaced by beadwork; geometric artwork adorned functional items. Most transportation was on land. In fact, when Fort Benton, one of the early trading posts, was established on the south side of the Missouri River, the Blackfeet would not trade there until it was moved to the north side of the river.

The tribes were organized into bands for most of the year, coming together in larger tribal groups for ceremonial occasions such as the Sun Dance. Each tribe had men's societies (today's Elk, Moose, Eagle organizations?). Sweat lodges were used for ceremonial purification.

Although the gun was an important addition to the Indian's lifestyle, it is important to remember that they were very effective hunters with a bow and arrows. An experienced warrior could shoot from a horse so rapidly as to keep at least one arrow in the air at all times with a force sufficient to drive the shaft of the arrow through the body of a buffalo.

Although the nature of the land resulted in a superficial similarity among the Plains Indians, it is important to remember that the tribes preserved their identities very distinctly. Although they all had hide moccasins, their methods of sewing them were unique to each tribe. Thus, the tribal identity could be determined by a footprint. Each tribe has its own social organization, means of determining relationships, (e.g. whether through the mother's clan or the father's or some other combination), religion, and mythology.

Their nomadic ways brought them into continual contact with members of other tribes who, like themselves, retained the languages they had developed from their origins in the eastern woodlands. It was because of this that the tribes devised a universal sign language. This language was sophisticated enough for even the conveyance of abstract ideas. Sign language attained its highest form of development among the Plains Indians.

This would be a nice time to watch *People of the Buffalo* from Encyclopedia Britannica Films.

While the Kootenai and the Salish Indians of Western Montana shared some common characteristics with the Plains Indians, they were also representative of the Plateau peoples. The arrival of the great numbers of Indians to eastern Montana, particularly the Blackfeet, prevented them from traveling and living, at will, on the eastern slopes of the divide. Thus the development of a culture dependent upon the buffalo never occurred. These tribes hunted not only buffalo, but also smaller game such as deer. Unlike eastern tribes, they developed several fishing techniques reminiscint of their origins in the Columbia Basin. They had efficient modes of water transportation. They harvested such plants as bitterroots, camas, and berries. They had some basketry and pottery, but little developed art. Although they used the tepee, they also used the long house. They had no Sun Dance, but did have a Mid-Winter Festival or Winter Spirit Dance. Thus, although these Indians were unique within their own tribal groups, they also exhibited characteristics common to other Montana Indians. They were less warlike than their eastern neighbors and more receptive to the coming of the whites.

TRIVIA FACTS ON INDIANS

a. Before whites arrived, it is estimated that there were 600,000 Indians in North America. By 1850, there were 250,000.

b. Dog breeding was the task of women, and it was women who managed the drag dogs outside of the village.

c. The Nez Perce developed the only true American-bred horse, the Appoloosa.

d. Indians first called horses "elk dogs" and used them for food.

e. Flatheads, Pen d'Oreille and Kalispells all sought guardian spirits in the mountains.

f. The Crows were one of the earliest tribes to move from the East.

g. The Blackfoot considered everyone to be either a warrior or a woman, if a man was not a good warrior, he had to dress in women's clothes and do women's work.

FLATHEAD CALENDAR OF MONTHS

The year was divided into twelve lunar months. The phases of the moon were carefully observed. The first month or moon corresponds roughly to January. Hence:

1. First month: The Wandering
2. Second month: Three Bands Spread All Over
3. Third month: The Goose Flight
4. Fourth month: The Lovemaking
5. Fifth month: Bitter Root Month
6. Sixth month: Camas Month
7. Seventh month: Service Berry Month
8. Eigth month: Onion Month
9. Ninth month: The Harvest of Ripe Things.
10. Tenth month: Half-autumn, or Half-summer
11. Eleventh month: Autumn
12. Twelfth month: Continuous Snow

H.H. Turney – High, *MAAA*, "Flathead Indians".

Chapter Seven

The Plains Indians had a land ethic very different from that of the white men who were to follow them into this area. To the Indian, the land and its wealth were objects of worship, treasured gifts from supernatural spirits. Their idea of conservation was total utilization of the land about them with the least amount of disturbance to its natural state. A dead buffalo presented a variety of useful objects in addition to hide and meat. The horn, hooves, bones, and the entrails became useful additions to their household. Although a buffalo jump seems like wanton slaughter, even this sudden windfall was preserved for later use. And always, man and other animals had equal rights to the land; in fact the world to them was inhabited by thousands of spiritual entities endowned with supernatural powers with whom they must coexist.

WEATHER LORE OF FLATHEADS

The Flathead can generally give reasons for most changes in weather. Below are listed beliefs regarding weather control.

Every time one whips a snake it will thunder.

If one catches a skunk and throws it in the water, it will rain.

If one finds a night hawk nest and disturbs the eggs or kills the young it will soon thunder and rain.

It will rain if one bothers robins.

If it rains steadily for several days and one wishes it to cease, he must look under stones for an ant nest. Destroy this nest. In order to allow the insects to rebuild their homes, the Ant Persons will have to make it stop raining.

If one sees a robin in water, be sure of a storm.

If one sees a certain little bird (gomene, English uncertain) diving, an early and cold winter may be expected.

If one should loose the forces making for rain and storm unintentionally he may prevent the consequences by taking a swim as soon as possible.

Thunder always was a portent and some shamans acquired their medicine from the Thunder Bird, and could therefore stop storms. Anything red attracted lightning, and as thunder was thought to be the cause of lightning, everything of that color was concealed at the first rumble. The first thunder of the spring was considered especially portentous and was the recipient of prayers for well-being. The leaves of a fir called pam were gathered, dried, and pounded. When it thundered threateningly people took a little pam powder and scattered it on the fire. The smoke ascended to the clouds and made the weather moderate. Men would offer smoke to Thunder during a storm and beseech it to depart, while women would often throw their hide fleshers outdoors for the same purpose.

Should one come unexpectedly upon a nest of eggs, even ant eggs, it is a sign of approaching rains. Hence the expression, "Eggs found by chance bring rain." Should the eggs be deliberately sought they are of no value as portents.

H.H. Turney — High, MAAA, "Flathead Indians."

CREATION OF THE RED AND THE WHITE RACES

This creation myth can not be a very old tribal tradition, for the Flatheads who saw the Lewis and Clark party in 1805 were puzzled by the strange appearance of them. These Indians did say, however, that they could go in six days to where the white traders came and that they had seen bearded men who came from a river a six days' march north of them. Stories about the creation of the races, sometimes including the black race, are found among tribes as far apart as the Assiniboines of Alberta and the Chickasaws of our southeastern states. According to Salish myths, Old Man Coyote was the figure of good, and Mountain Sheep was the symbol of evil.

Long, long ago when the world was young, Old Man in the Sky drained off the earth which he had made. When he had it crowded down into the big salt holes, the land became dry. About that time, Old Man Coyote became lonely and so went up into the Sky Land to talk to Old Man. Old Man questioned him.

"Why are you unhappy and crying? Have I not made much land for you to run about on? Are not Beaver, Otter, Bear, and Buffalo on the land to keep you company? Why do you not like the Mountain Sheep? Did I not place him up in the hills, so that you need not fight? Why do you come up here so often, just to talk?"

Old Coyote sat down and cried many more tears. Old Man became very cross and began to scold. "Foolish old Coyote, you must not drop as much water upon the land. Have I not worked many days to dry it? Soon you will have it all covered with water again. What is the trouble with you? What more do you want to make you happy?"

"I am very lonely because I have no one to talk to," Coyote answered. "Beaver, Otter, Bear, and Buffalo are busy with their families. They do not have time to visit with me. I want a people of my own, so that I may watch over them."

Old Man replied: "If you will stop this shedding of water, and stop annoying me with your visits, I will make you a people. Take this rawhide bag, this parfleche, and carry it to the mountain where there is red earth. Fill it full and bring it back to me. Hurry!"

Old Coyote took the bag and traveled many days and nights. Finally he came to a mountain where there was much red soil. Though weary after his long journey, he managed to fill the parfleche. Then he was sleepy.

"I will lie down to sleep for a while. When I awaken I will run swiftly back to Old Man in the Sky."

Coyote slept so soundly that he did not hear Mountain Sheep come along and look at the red soil in the bag.

"Foolish Coyote has come a long distance to get such a load of red soil," Mountain Sheep said to himself. "I wonder what he wants if for. I will have fun with him."

He dumped the red soil out upon the mountain. Then he filled the lower half of the bag with white earth and put some red soil on the upper half. Laughing to himself, Mountain Sheep ran away to his hiding place.

When Old Coyote awakened, he tied the top of the parfleche and hurried with it to Old Man in the Sky. The sun was going to sleep when he arrived. It was so dark that they could scarcely see the soil in the bag. Old Man in the Sky took the dirt and said, "I will make the soil into the forms of two men and two women."

He did not see that half the soil was red and half white.

"Take them to the dry land below," he said to Coyote when he had finished shaping them. "They are your people, and you can talk with them. So do not come up here to trouble me."

Old Coyote put the new people in the parfleche and carried them to dry land. In the morning when he took them out to put breath into them, he was surprised to find one pair red and the other pair white. Instantly he knew the trick that had been played upon him.

"I see that Mountain Sheep came while I slept," Coyote said. "What shall I do now? I know that I can not keep these two colors together."

So he carried the white ones to the land by the big salt hole. The red ones he kept in his own land, so that he could visit with them.

That is how Indians and white men came upon the earth. And that is why Coyote was a friend of the Indians.

Ideas of group cooperation, a supernatural world, and tribal warfare for honor were difficult for early Europeans to comprehend. Their misunderstandings persist today in the "Noble Savage" myth. Few of the white settlers were able to duplicate the Indian's skill in living in an inhospitable environment without the aid of more modern conveniences such as the gun. Probably none of them were able to change the face of the land as little as did the Indians. Their motivations were very different: the Europeans sought to exploit the land for a personal gain of monetary wealth in "civilized" terms. The Indian exploited the land in such a manner that it would continue to maintain their life style endlessly. In this clash of two cultures, the Indians were bound to lose because their desires were not prompted elsewhere. They sought only maintenance of a status quo. There was no way possible for these two ethics to exist within the same area. The flower that was the Plains culture was only briefly magnificent.

PROPHECY OF THE COMING OF THE WHITE MEN

"Throughout the northern region west of the Rocky Mountains one hears in almost every tribe a tradition that before the appearance of the first white man, a dreamer, or in some instances (and nearer the truth) a wandering Indian of another tribe prophesied the coming of a new race with wonderful implements."

This Nez Perce prophecy was related by Lucy Armstrong Isaac.

An old man in Lapwai — I forget his name — used to see the future in his dreams. He would see white-faced animals a little bigger than deer coming over the hill. They would come down Thunder Hill, between Lapwai and the Clearwater River. Behind the white-faced deer was a white-faced man.

"Another kind of human being is going to be here soon," the old man would tell his people. Other men laughed at him.

"We are going to have some writing given us," he told them. "We must have our ears open so that we can understand it. A white-faced man will explain it. We will have seven sleeps, and the seventh day will be a holy day.

"The earth will be plowed up. There will be many ways of going fast to other places. People will go fast on the land and fast in the air, like big birds."

People laughed at the old man's dreams, laughed at what he said would happen. But everything he prophesied came true.

This is a true story, not a myth or legend.

48

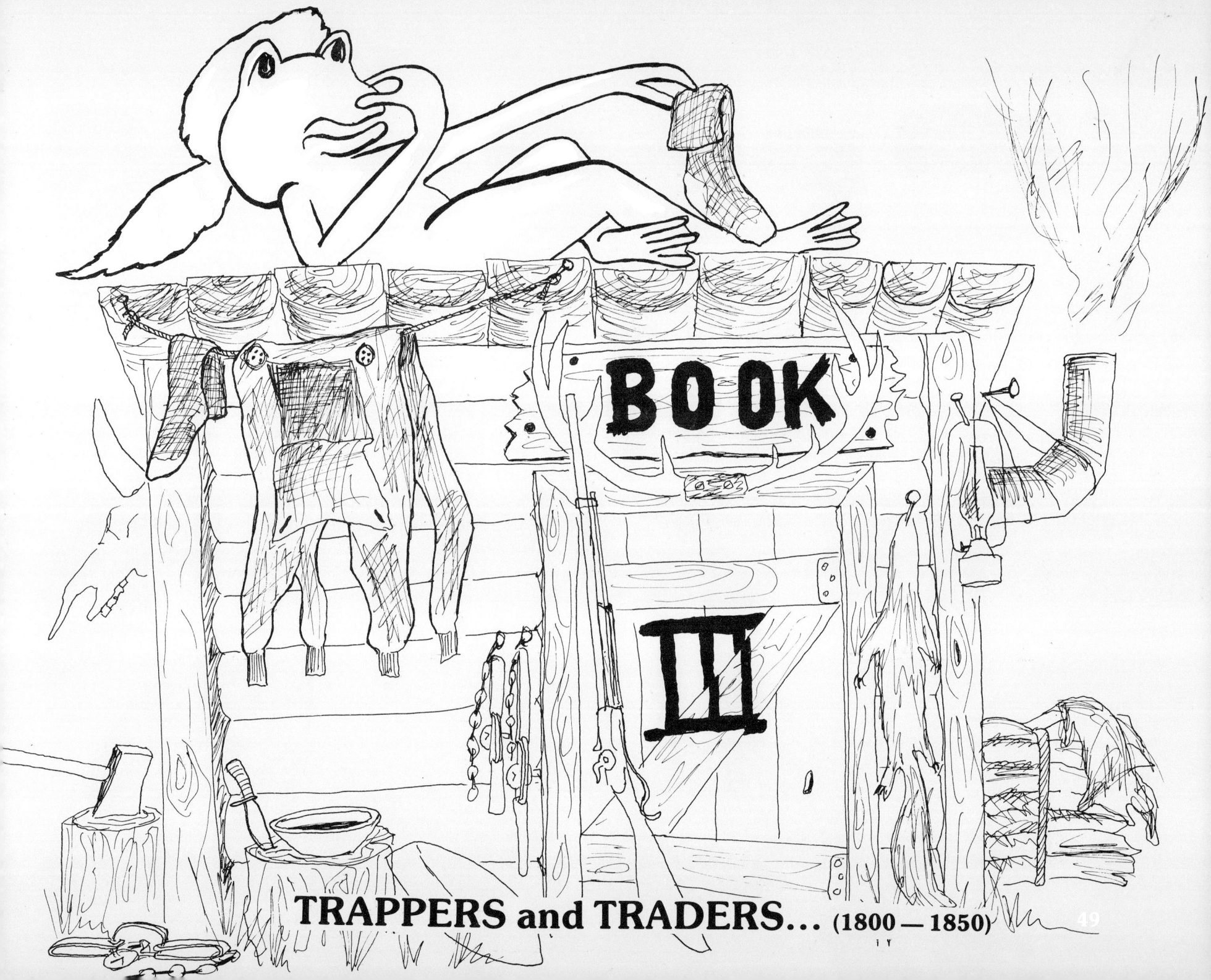

TRAPPERS and TRADERS... (1800 — 1850)

Chapter One

CROSSING the LAND

At various times and places the Indian made many prophecies concerning the coming of the white man. For the most part, they were based on simple observation. They dealt mainly with the white man's implements or "things" (e.g. guns, holy book, booze.)

The Indian coundn't possibly have known or been expected to know the total impact the white man was to have on their lands. At least not from the initial, seemingly innocent "backpacking" trips of the first explorers. What the heck? What harm can a few wealthy tourists cause on a walk through? What lasting changes could they possibly bring?

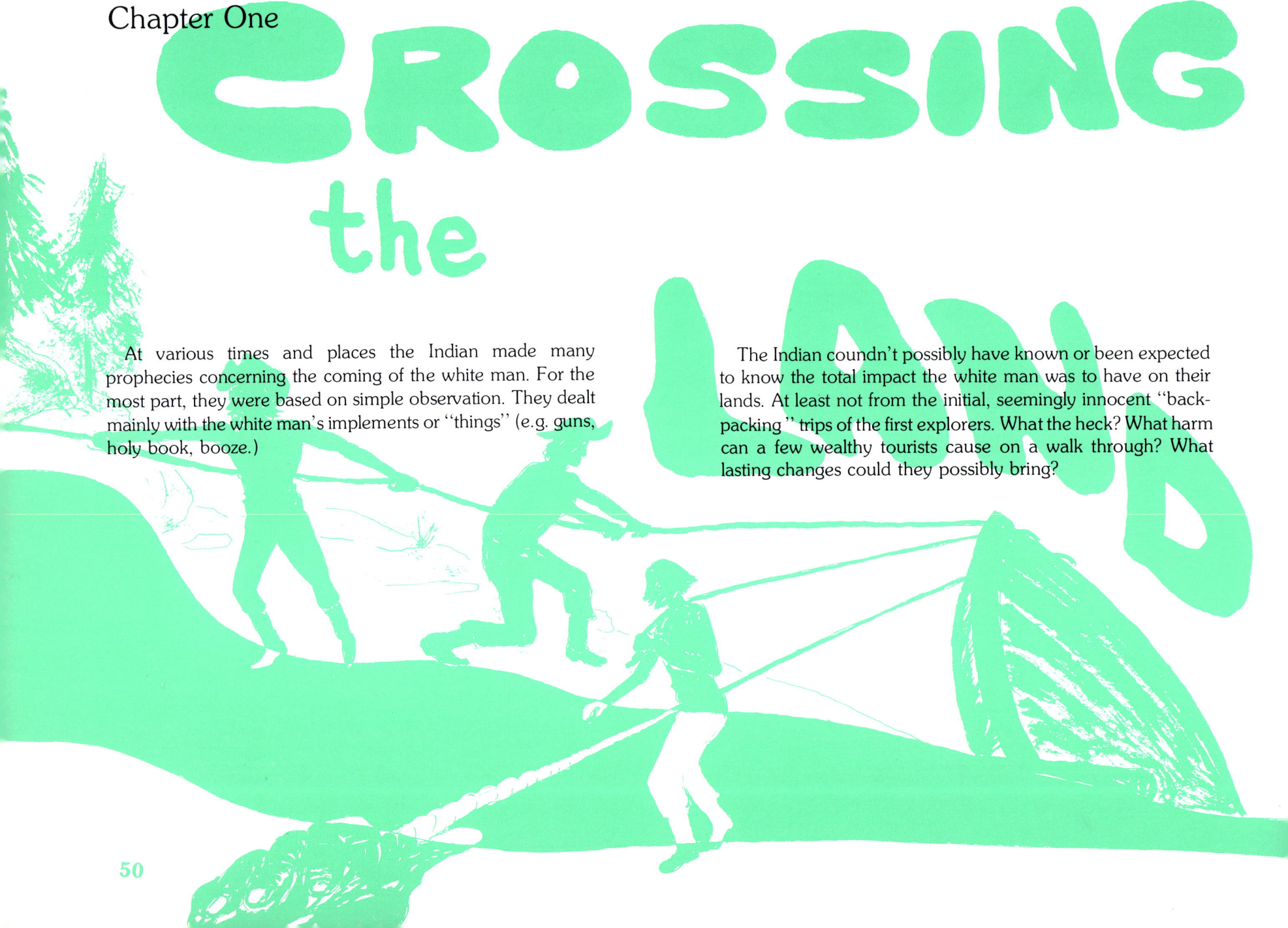

The year is 1742, the place is a Mandan Indian village in present-day North Dakota. There are white men in the village. Louis-Joseph and Francois Verendrye are the leaders of the white party. The objective of the Verendrye brothers is to find the much sought after "Northwest Passage," that elusive waterway through North America which would permit Europe an easy access to Asia. (Were the Verendrye brothers tourists, or were they on a business trip?)

The Verendryes travelled westward, encountering numerous tribes. In January of 1743, while travelling with a war party of the "Bow People," possibly Crows, they came to what they called the "Shining Mountains." It was here the "Bow People" turned back. Discretion being the greater part of valor, the Verendryes followed suit and turned eastward.

The "Shining Mountains" of the Verendryes, depending on which historian you read, were either the Black Hills of the Dakotas or the Big Horn Mountains of Montana and Wyoming. If indeed they were the latter, the Verendryes were probably the first whites in present day Montana.

The next major group of white tourists to roam to and through the "Shining Mountains" to the Pacific Ocean was the Lewis and Clark expedition of 1804-06. Besides their own journals, there are numerous books and articles giving accounts of their amazing feat. This book chooses to deal primarily with why they went, and the repercussions of the journey.

The latter half of the 18th century witnessed intense rivalry among the major European powers of Britain, France, and Spain for control of vast territories in the Americas. The newly formed United States was well aware of these political rivalries. To say the United States was concerned is a gross understatement. You see, the western boundary of the U.S. was the Mississippi River. Across the river was the Louisiana Territory, whose ownership flip-flopped from France, to Spain (1762-1802), back to France. As is the case with the homeowner, the U.S. was interested in its neighbors. Would the holder of the Louisiana Territory cut off U.S. privileges at the all-important port of New Orleans, forcing overland transportation to the western states? Good grief! Think of the money, time, and hardship that would have cost the people of the frontier.

"On August 12, 1806, Lewis and his men met two fur trappers moving upriver, John Dickson and Forrest Hancock. The two Illinois trappers were the first white men encountered in 16 months. And they were the first representatives of a massive wave of American furmen which would follow the expedition into the Rockies."

A Visual History of Montana; Helena: OSPI, 1976

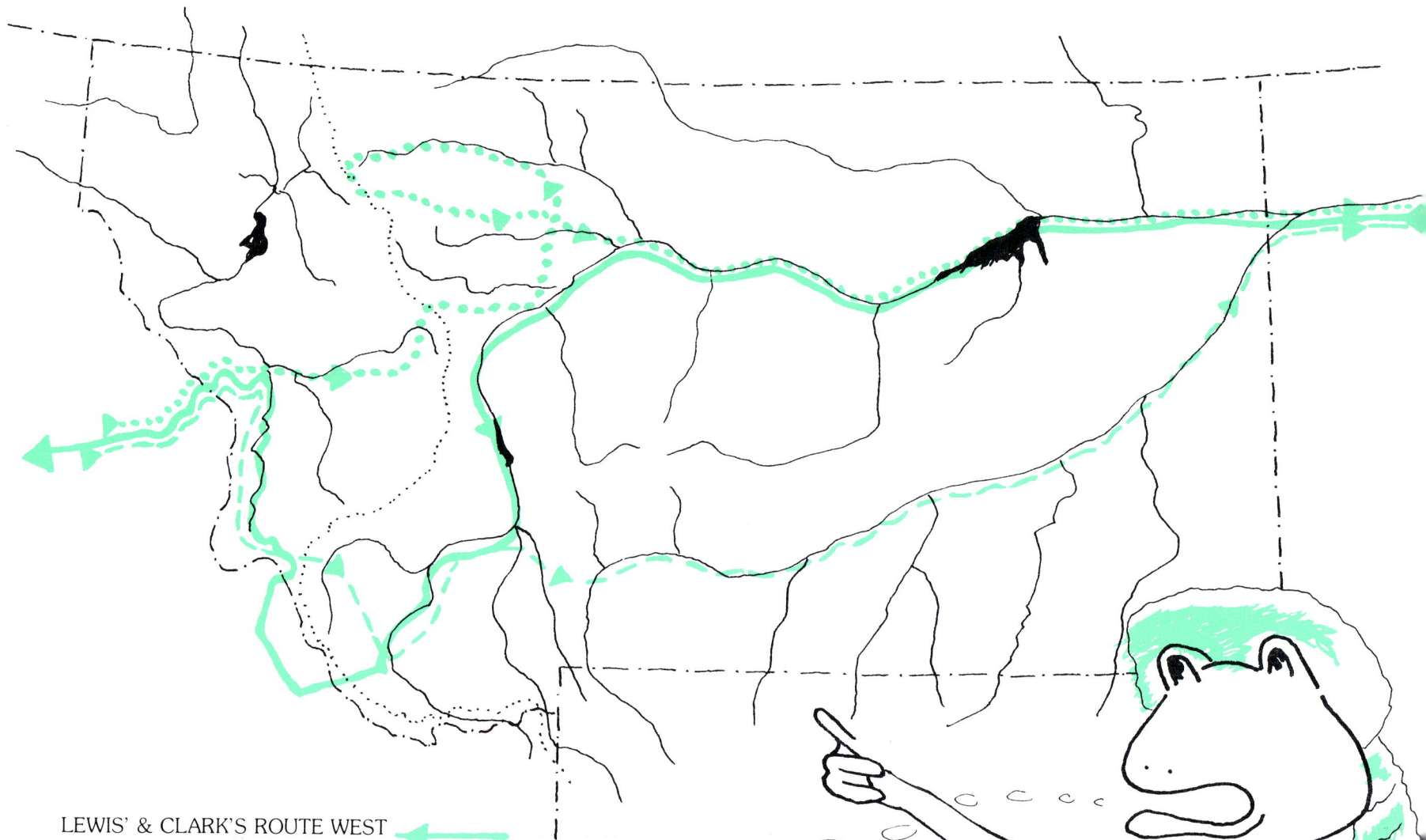

LEWIS' & CLARK'S ROUTE WEST

LEWIS'S ROUTE EAST

CLARK'S ROUTE EAST

THIS TURNED OUT TO BE QUITE A CAMPING TRIP!...

Information used to develop this map courtesy of *Montana Outdoors*. This article appears in the Jul/Aug issue with maps prepared by the Cartography Bureau, DNR & C.

LEWIS AND CLARK EXPEDITION
• IN MONTANA •

THE CORPS OF
DISCOVERY

In its scope and achievement, the Lewis and Clark Expedition of 1804-06 stands as a giant among the major explorations of the North American continent — and the world. The expedition carried the destiny as well as the flag of a young and vibrant nation westward across thousands of miles of uncharted wilderness — up the wide Missouri, over the Rocky Mountains and on to the Pacific Ocean.

During their long journey through Montana, the explorers encountered alien tribes and menacing animals. On foot, astride fleet Indian ponies and by boat, they pushed over formidable mountain ranges, floated surging rivers, portaged over sagebrush plains laced with pads of prickly pear-cactus.

And what was accomplished? Most obvious, of course, was that the expedition served as a catalyst in sparkling the imagination of a growing nation that would develop into one of the greatest nations in the world. Assigning high priority to the quest for knowledge, Meriwether Lewis and William Clark meticulously recorded observations about the characteristics, inhabitants and resources of the land through which they passed.

The expedition traveled in Montana about six months of the total time consumed and about one-half of the total distance explored. During the westward journey through Montana in 1805, the explorers followed the Missouri River to the Three Forks of the Missouri, and then up the Jefferson and Beaverhead rivers to the present site of Clark Canyon Reservoir. At this point, the expedition headed west and traveled overland, crossing the Continental Divide over Lemhi Pass into Idaho. After proceeding northward through Idaho, the travelers re-entered Montana and exited the state via the Lolo Trail over the Bitterroot Mountains.

On the return trip through Montana, Lewis and Clark separated at Travelers' Rest, just south of present-day Missoula. Lewis, accompanied by nine of his men and five Nez Perce guides set off in a northeasterly direction, crossing the Continental Divide over Lewis and Clark Pass and returned to the plains country to check the source of the Marias River and other tributaries of the Missouri. During the return leg of the trip, Lewis and three of his men clashed with eight Piegan Blackfeet Indians resulting in the death of two Indians.

Clark, with the largest setment of the party, headed southward to recover the canoes that were cached near the forks of the Beaverhead River. At the Three Forks of the Missouri, part of the crew pushed down the Missouri to rendezvous with the Gass detachment of the Lewis party at the Great Falls of the Missouri. Clark and the rest of the group, including Sacagawea, headed east, crossed Bozeman Pass and dropped down to the upper Yellowstone at a point nine miles from the pass near present Livingston. Water travel was resumed east of what is now Columbus. Just east of present-day Billings, the expedition stopped on the south side of the Yellowstone near a remarkable sandstone formation. Clark named it Pompy's Tower (now Pompeys Pillar) after Sacagawea's infant son whom he had nicknamed "Pomp." Near a spot on the path leading to the top of the formation, Clark inscribed his name and the date.

The separated portions of the expedition finally united on Aug. 12, 1806, in North Dakota, some 30 miles upstream from the entrance of the Little Missouri River.

This would be a good time to read *Let's Go With Lewis & Clark* by Kirk Polking.

In 1802 the French regained the Louisiana Territory from Spain. President Thomas Jefferson's concern was now indeed well-founded, for gaining a following in France was none other than Napoleon Bonaparte, the "Little Corporal," the man who was to conquer the bulk of the European continent.

In Napoleon's game plan of conquest was an empire in the Western Hemisphere. It was to be based both in Louisiana and on the Caribbean island of Santo Domingo. However, the black slaves and mulattoes of the island had a plan of their own...independence. (No doubt they were spurred on by both the American and French revolutions). Black generals Francois Dominique Toussaint L'Overture and Jean Jacques Dessalines finally defeated the French and drove them out in 1803. Dessalines later became the first president of the first independent country in Latin America, the Republic of Haiti.

With this crushing defeat, Napoleon's dream of a western empire abruptly ended. On April 11, 1803, French Foreign Minister Talleyrand suprised Robert Livingston, the U.S. Foreign Minister, by bringing up the idea of selling the Louisiana Territory. Obviously Livingston was overwhelmed by the idea, for he had been sent to France by President Jefferson for the express purpose of reaching some kind of settlement concerning the problems facing the western frontier. If necessary, we were willing to ally ourselves with Britain against France.

Anyway, on April 30, 1803, France received $15,000,000, and the U.S. took over the Louisiana Territory. What the boundaries were, no one really knew for sure. The treaty specified that the western boundary was the land drained by the Mississippi and Missouri rivers. Northern and southern boundaries, with Canada and Mexico, were not as yet fixed.

What, then, did the United States buy? Enter, stage left: Lewis and Clark. They were to be the fellows who were going to check out the merchandise and take an accurate inventory of all existing varieties of plant and animals (human included) they might come upon. Another aim of their journey was to establish an American precedent of having reached the Pacific via a northwestern route. This was purely political, a move which would show the British and Canadians that we had serious intentions in the area. Also, if along the way they "just happened" to find a "Northwest Passage" (a then-dying dream), it would be nice.

A letter by John Ordway, a sargeant on the expedition, to his parents: "We expect to be gone 18 months or two years; we are to receive a great reward for this expedition: $15 per month and at least 400 acres of first-rate land..."

A Visual History of Montana; Helena: OSPI, 1976

Sacajawea was able to convince skeptical Indians of the expedition's friendliness since "a woman never would accompany a native war party."

A Visual History of Montana; Helena: OSPI, 1976

To make a long, grueling, yet rewarding, story short, they made it to the Pacific Ocean, to the mouth of the Columbia River, on November 7, 1805, after having left St. Louis in mid-May, 1804. The return trip saw the expedition split at "Traveller's Rest" at present-day Lolo on July 1, 1806, until their reunion at the confluence of the Missouri and Yellowstone rivers on August 12, 1806. They arrived back at St. Louis on September 23.

Charbonneau's (Sacajawea's husband) special treat for the men — a combination of meat cuts, flour, salt and pepper, stuffed in a section of buffalo intestine, which was boiled and then fried in bear grease.

A Visual History of Montana; Helena: OSPI, 1976

After reaching what they called the Gates of the Mountains, Lewis and Clark expected to find Shoshoni tribesmen, who, it was hoped, with the influence of Shoshoni Sacajawea, would offer assistance and provide horses. While they knew they were close on the trail of the tribe, they did not catch up with them for some time — the Shoshoni had mistaken them for a Blackfeet band moving into the mountains to attack.

A Visual History of Montana; Helena: OSPI, 1976

The simple summation of their journey's accomplishments is not to minimize its importance, it is rather an attempt to focus on the lasting effects it had on the United States, and, more specifically...Montana.

First of all, the collection of scientific data in the form of plant and animal life encountered was of obvious value. Secondly came the detailed and accurate maps. Thirdly, good relations were established with the Indians along the way, the exception being the Blackfeet. This was due to an unfortunate incident which left two Indians dead. Fourthly, it showed the British and Canadian interests that, yes, the United States was genuinely interested in laying claim to the Pacific Northwest. This was an early stage of the 19th century's "Manifest Destiny" cry, which was to make possible the words "from sea to shining sea." And lastly, it put to rest the search for the "Northwest Passage," (until 1958, that is, when the USS *Nautilus* became the first ship to pass *beneath* the North Pole.)

Separately, these accomplishments were extraordinary, to say the least. In combining the first four, however, for the purpose of re-examination, we now begin to see an unmistakable significance.

One more time — with feeling! Not only did Lewis and Clark tell people that beaver, otter and other fur-bearing mammals abounded in numbers "richer than any country on earth" (#1), but also they provided accurate maps (#2), which would enable people to seek the aid of friendly Indians and avoid the hostiles (#3). Lastly, and possibly most subtly, their successors were granted the implied, if not expressed, blessings of the United States government in their quest for wealth.

What one culture may have seen as a group of tourists jotting down notes regarding natural beauty, might possibly have been one heck of a long and dangerous business trip to the other.

What the heck, what harm can a few wealthy tourists cause? What possible changes could they bring?

On the return trip, in the vicinity of Bozeman, Clark was "constantly amazed at the immense numbers of beaver and buffalo: this valley could be a fur trader's paradise!"

A Visual History of Montana; Helena: OSPI, 1976

56

Chapter Two

BENEATH the LAND

Gold, silver, and many other valuable minerals are still resting peacefully beneath the land, but their time is running out.

57

Chapter Three

GROWING

"The land is level, fertile, open and beautiful beyond description...." The words were those of Meriwether Lewis. The scene described was that of eastern Montana in the spring of 1805. A short time thereafter, at some distance past the confluence of the Missouri and Musselshell rivers, Lewis again remarked, "We have now got into a country which presents little to our vision but scenes of barrenness and desolation...the upland is almost entirely without timber and consists of large prairies or plains the boundaries of which the eye cannot reach. The grass is generally short in these Immense Natural Pastures."

It was nearly fifteen years later, however, that Major S.H. Long made his description of "the West," which, of course, encompasses Montana. Long's mission in the West was to build a fort on the Yellowstone River to serve as a base for the enforcement of the newly-formed boundary with Canada, the 49th parallel. Instead, he followed the Platte River to its headwaters. Any way, talk about generalizations, listen to this: Long described "the West" (the area west of the Mississippi from Canada to Mexico) as a place where no man could live, and the land was unsuitable for agriculture...in other words, a desert. Good Grief! One statement to cover *that* much territory? Looking at *some* of the vast stretches of semi-arid, treeless prairie, his notion *is* somewhat understandable. Long's description was accepted as gospel for nearly fifty years, hence the title "Great American Desert" became synonymous with "the West."

The word "desert" kept many people away, much to the delight of the fur trappers, who knew fortunes were to be made in the form of beaver and other fur-bearing mammels which filled the streams of the region.

Montana's agricultural roots (no pun intended) have a somewhat magical, mystical, or maybe spiritual aura about them. On one side, the white man's, there was no such mystery; on the other, however, the Indian's, there was almost total amazement. Once again we have a story of cultural difference. Here's how it goes....

Many of the Canadian fur trappers that entered western Montana in the early 19th century were French Roman Catholics. (Fur trappers? What's that have to do with agriculture? Don't worry, we'll get there.) These trappers brought with them a sizeable number of Iroquois, celebrated Indian trappers of the northeast woodlands. The Iroquois were to teach local Indians the "tricks of the trade," so to speak. Along with information concerning trapping, they also passed on some information about men in "Black Robes." These men possessed the "Book of Heaven" which was rumored to contain the secret to "life after death." (Quite a feat to say the least, one which mankind in general has sought after since the invention of death.) Seriously, it is little wonder that the Flatheads and Nez Perce would actively seek out these "Black Robes." (The Indian interpretation, to search for *physical* life after death, differed from the white man's view of a *spiritual* life after death.)

Four times, in 1831, 1835, 1837, and 1839, they set out across enemy nations to St. Louis, in hopes of bringing a priest and his book back to their people. The fourth trip paid off. It was then that Bishop Rosati of St. Louis promised to send a priest. The man for the job was Pierre-Jean DeSmet, a Belgian-born Jesuit. DeSmet ventured westward with an American Fur Company caravan to the site of the 1840 "rendezvous" (their last). There he was greeted by a great number of Flathead and Nez Perce. From there they travelled to the area of the Three Forks of the Missouri. DeSmet was greatly impressed by their willingness to respond to "the Book." In late summer, 1840, he left to raise money for a mission among the Indians of the mountains. He promised he'd return.

The spring of 1841 saw DeSmet's promise kept. With him came two other priests, Gregory Mengarini and Nicholas Pooint. This time they settled in the Bitterroot Valley. It was in this "last valley," as Lewis and Clark so appropriately called it, that St. Mary's Mission, in presentday Stevensville, was begun in the fall of 1841. (Get ready, we are getting close to the part about agriculture. Remember, this is a story about agriculture!).

As the mission was being constructed, Father DeSmet made his way to Fort Colville on the Columbia, the nearest source of supplies. It was here he purchased seed wheat, oats, and potatoes. With the planting of these seeds, at the mission, agriculture had its beginnings in Montana.

Blackfoot Trail Route To The Bison

Silver State Post, 4/11/45

No more beautiful scenery can be found in Montana than along the Blackfoot trail's western slope. Myriads of streams, beautiful lakes, fertile valleys and mountain grandeur meet the eye from the time the trail enters the dark portal of Hell Gate canyon east of Missoula till it debouches on the gray and arid plains of the eastern Rocky Mountain slopes. In early times it was a hunter's paradise. It remains so to this day.

Along its picturesque way passed the Selishes, the Nez Perces, the Kalispells, the Pen d'Rilles, constantly on the alert for the war parties of the fierce Blackfeet and Crows that lurked along its course, waiting to attack from ambush.

It was because of the deadly menace of these fierce tribes that the western canyon gate of the trail was named "Missoula," the Selish word "Port of Fear," for the "Gates of Hell." The enemy would steal westward to make war or to steal the ponies of the Selish (Flatheads), often lying in wait there to attack, or to race forth with their blood curdling war cries.

From the Jesuit missionary Father De Smet we know the story of one of the annual Buffalo hunts of the tribes of the Western slope. The Selishes among whom he labored, persuaded him to accompany them, and all went well until they came into the Musselshell area, and a band of Blackfeet

braves engaged the party in battle. So fierce and cruel were both sides that the Blackrobe could never again be persuaded to hunt with them. Defeating the hostile Redmen, they wended their way westward over the Blackfoot trail, laden with the spoils of the chase.

There was constantly something happening along the Blackfoot trail. Here were fought Indian battles. Along this trail traveled Lewis and Clark. Over this route passed Governor Stevens and Captain C.P. Higgins after concluding the treaty with Chief Victor at Council Grove near Missoula. When the lure of gold brought thousands to the Territory it was broadened by the bull train and the stage coach. Over it passed the cattle and sheepmen who settled the North End.

Automobiles now roll over the expanses trod by Indian feet. Airplanes pass overhead where once the smoke of Indian signal fires was the only man-made thing to rise into the blue. No longer does the Selish or the Blackfoot tread its path. The Buffalo has long since vanished from the plains it leads to.

But it is still a beautiful trail, and rich in historical lore, from the time it enters the dark portal of Hell Gate canyon until it reaches the crest of the Continental divide to commence its descent of the Eastern Slope.

The Indians were very curious about the process of plowing, sowing, and harvesting. They would sit for hours on the fence watching, waiting for the seeds to come to life, as they had been told they would. This was truly a miracle, but one understood by one culture and not the other. When the first shoot appeared they were delighted, and waited impatiently for the ripening and harvesting of the crops.

It is important to remember that the Indians were hunters, nomads who followed game. As they travelled, they would gather plants such as the bitterroot and camas, but never before did they deliberately cultivate. Farming required them to be stationary, that is, to remain settled for a considerable length of time.

Life at the mission was considerably different from the traditional lifestyle of the Indian. The days were planned for work, study, and worship: "Rising at daybreak, prayers; mass; breakfast, and instruction for about an hour; work until midday. In the afternoon: catechism from two to half past three; work until sunset; prayers; instruction; canticles (Bible hymns), and rest." Compare that schedule with the one the Indians may have had prior to the coming of the "Black Robes." Hmmmmm!

This would be a good time to read *Montana Genesis* by the Stevensville Historical Society.

All went well, for a few years. It was after the summer hunt of 1846 that the attitude of the Flathead changed. They didn't seem to care any longer for the "Black Robe's sacred medicine." They were outwardly antagonistic toward the priests.

Some people feel the Flatheads merely had enough of the farming business and the changes of lifestyle that went with it. Another theory was that DeSmet himself made the Flatheads hostile through his efforts to take the "sacred medicine" to the Blackfeet, the mortal enemies of the Flathead. You see, the Flathead figured the "sacred medicine" had kept the enemy off their backs. To them this was fact, because they hadn't had any difficulties with the Blackfeet since the arrival of the "Black Robes" some five years before. So you see, they weren't overly excited about sharing their good fortune (the sacred medicine) with an enemy.

Whatever the cause, the relationship between the Flatheads and the priests deteriorated until finally the mission closed its doors in 1850.

Chapter Four

LIVING OFF the LAND

As stated in Book II, Montana, at the time of Lewis and Clark, was a kind of zoo without cages. Wildlife abounded in both the mountains and on the plains. By comparison there were relatively few domesticated animals. Both the Indian and the white man possessed horses and dogs. The Jesuits and John Owen had a few head of cattle in the Bitterroot.

During this particular period (1800-1850) one animal drew more attention than any other. This animal was to be trapped relentlessly to near extinction. It was to be the source of great wealth for some, and adventure for others. The animal, of course, was the beaver. This li'l dude would probably rather have seen the elk, grizzly, or buffalo pursued as eagerly, instead of himself, but...their time would come. Can't you see a beaver family inside its lodge saying, "Why us?" If they only knew what you are going to know, that is, the cause for which they were dying, they might have died laughing (or crying, depending on how they felt about European fashion.) European fashion?? What's that have to do with anything? Everything!!

Today we think of the Bitterroots as abounding in game. In the time of the expedition, the only animals found were pheasant, grouse, squirrel and coyote. Most large game still inhabited the plains area of the state.

A Visual History of Montana; Helena: OSPI, 1976

"The rise in the demand for furs in Europe was originally, to some extent, caused by a shortage of leather. Not everyone, however, was permitted furs; during the time of England's King Henry VIII his royal edict limited the wearing of furs to the nobility. His daughter, Queen Elizabeth I, aware of the increasing demand for furs, authorized the Muscovite Fur Company, one of history's first such enterprises. Subsequent history saw the development of the beaver hat as the single greatest outlet for furs of any kind."

Ralph Henry, *Our Land Montana*

This would be a good time to read *Mountain Men* by George Ruston.

Remember, nylon, dacron, and all of the other synthetics of today were not around. For warmth the choice was wool or fur. If one were poor the choice was wool or wool. Wool was warm but bulky and drab, unless dyed with indigo or cochineal (a reddish dye made from squashing the cocheneal insect-yuck!). But furs were something else. Furs were warm. Furs were elegant. Furs came in an assortment of colors and textures. Furs for coats. Furs for hats. Furs for trim. Furs "fur" ever'thin'! As more furs were brought to market, prices came down. Lower prices enabled the middle class to buy furs. Demand increased. So did supply...for a while.

*The following, regarding Lewis and Clark, are taken from Sargeant Patrick Gass's journal. Of all the various journals kept during the expedition, this is probably the most simply written, and therefore is most appropriate for junior-high level students. (*Journal of the Lewis and Clark Expedition, *Patrick Gass, Ross and Haines, Minneapolis, 1958).*

After reaching territory in what is now the state of Montana on the 27th of April, 1805, the expedition saw the following wildlife, within a space of a few days:
big-horn sheep
elk
buffalo and deer
"very large brown bear (Grizzly?) which measured 3'5" around the head, 3' 11" around the neck, 5' 10½" around the breast, 8' 7½" in length, 23" around the middle of the fore legs, and talons of 4¾"."
beaver
"another brown bear about the size of the one lately killed"
"Some of the men discovered a large brown bear, and six of them went out to kill it. They fired at it, but having only wounded it, it made battle and was near seizing some of them, but they all fortunately escaped, and at length succeeded in dispatching it. These bears are very bold and ferocious; and very large and powerful. The natives say they have killed a number of their brave men."

Journal of the Lewis and Clark Expedition, Patrick Gass, Ross and Haines, Minneapolis, 1958

"One day Lewis was charged by a Grizzly bear. He jumped into the river, and the bear left. Just as Lewis waded out of the water a herd of buffalo came near and the bulls charged him. They halted short, however, and Lewis was saved. He made his bed that night along a tree, and the next morning discovered a giant rattlesnake coiled near him."

Ralph Henry, *Treasure State: The Story of Montana for Junior Montanans;* Helena, State Publishing Company, 1962

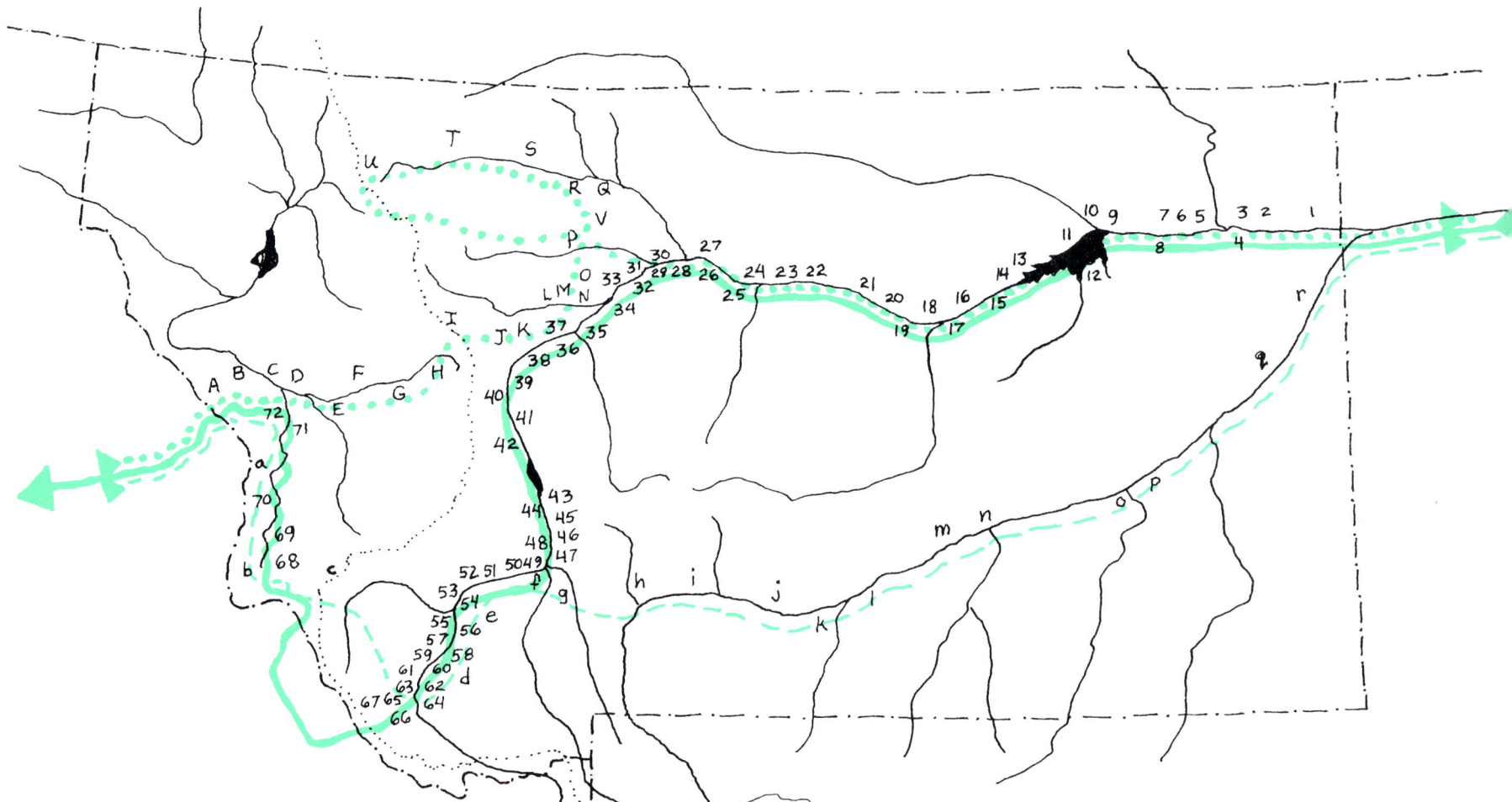

WE MAY HAVE DISCOVERED THE FIRST OPEN-AIR, SELF-SERVE SUPER MARKET!..

Information used to develop this map courtesy of *Montana Outdoors*, this article appears in the Jul/Aug issue with maps prepared by the Cartography Bureau, DNR & C.

WILDLIFE SIGHTINGS
• MAMMALS •

1 mule deer, elk, antelope, buffalo, grizzly, beaver (4/28)
2 deer, elk, antelope, buffalo, grizzly, wolves (4/29)
3 elk, antelope (4/30)
4 elk, antelope, buffalo, beaver (5/1)
5 deer, elk, buffalo, beaver (5/2)
6 white-tailed deer, elk, antelope, buffalo, beaver, porcupine (5/3)
7 buffalo (5/4)
8 antelope, grizzly, wolf, coyote (5/5)
9 moose (5/10)
10 white-tailed and mule deer, elk, ante-lope, buffalo, wolves, beaver (5/8)
11 elk, buffalo (5/9)
12 grizzly (511)
13 grizzly (5/14)
14 deer, buffalo, beaver (5/15)
15 deer, antelope, buffalo, grizzly, mountain lion (5/16)
16 buffalo (5/17)
17 deer, elk, grizzly, beaver (5/19)
18 deer, elk, buffalo (5/21)
19 deer, black bear (5/22)
20 deer, elk, antelope, buffalo, grizzly, Richardson ground squirrel (?) (5/23)
21 beaver, Richardson ground squirrel (?) (5/24)
22 buffalo, bighorn sheep, striped skunk (5/25)
23 elk, whitetail jackrabbit (5/26)
24 bighorn sheep (5/28)
25 buffalo, bighorn sheep, wolves, beaver (5/29)
26 buffalo (5/30)
27 mule deer, elk, buffalo, bighorn sheep, red fox (5/31)
28 mule deer, buffalo, bighorn sheep (6/1)

29 mule deer, elk, buffalo, grizzly (6/2)
deer, elk, antelope, buffalo, wolves (6/3)
elk, buffalo, grizzly, wolves, red fox, longtail weasel (6/4)
mule deer, elk, antelope, buffalo, wolves, red fox, blacktail prairie dog, Richardson ground squirrel (?) (6/5)
mule deer, antelope, buffalo, grizzly, wolves (6/6)
30 elk (6/11)
31 mule deer, antelope, buffalo, grizzly, wolves, beaver, Richardson ground squirrel (?) (6/12)
32 buffalo (6/13)
33 buffalo, grizzly, wolverine (?) (6/14)
34 deer, elk, antelope, buffalo, grizzly, wolves, beaver (6/16-6/28)
35 deer, elk, antelope, buffalo, grizzly, kit fox, beaver, river otter, bushytail woodrat, thirteen-lined ground squirrel (6/22-7/12)
36 buffalo (7/13)
37 deer, elk, buffalo, river otter (7/15)
38 elk, buffalo (7/16)
39 bighorn sheep (7/17)
40 deer, elk, bighorn sheep (7/18)
41 elk, antelope, bighorn sheep, beaver, river otter (7/20)
42 deer, elk, antelope, otter (7/22)
43 deer, elk, antelope, beaver, river otter (7/23)
44 deer, antelope, grizzly, beaver, river otter (7/24)
45 deer, elk, antelope, grizzly, beaver, river otter (7/25)
46 deer, grizzly, beaver, river otter (7/26)
47 deer, elk (7/28)
48 deer, antelope, bighorn sheep, beaver, river otter, muskrat (7/27)
49 white-tailed deer (7/29)
50 deer, antelope, grizzly, beaver (7/30)

51 grizzly (7/31)
52 deer, elk, antelope, bighorn sheep, grizzly (8/1)
53 deer, elk, antelope, beaver, Columbian ground squirrel (8/2)
54 deer, antelope, mountain lion, beaver, river otter (8/3)
55 deer, elk (8/6)
56 deer, antelope, beaver, river otter (8/4)
57 deer (8/10)
58 deer, antelope (8/5)
59 deer, beaver, river otter, muskrat (8/8)
60 deer, antelope, beaver, river otter (8/11)
61 antelope (8/9)
62 deer, wolverine (?) (8/12)
63 deer, antelope, beaver, river otter (8/13)
64 deer, antelope (8/14)
65 deer (8/15)
66 deer, antelope (8/16)
67 deer, antelope, beaver (8/17-8/23)
68 deer, bighorn sheep (9/4)
69 badger (9/5)
70 deer (9/7)
71 (9/8)
72 deer (9/9)
deer, beaver (9/10)

LEWIS' EASTWARD ROUTE — 1806

A mule deer (6/27)
B deer 6/29)
C deer, elk, bighorn sheep, red squirrel (6/30)
D deer (7/2)
E Columbian ground squirrel (?) red squirrel (7/4)
F antelope (7/5)
G deer, antelope, Columbian ground squirrel (7/6)
H moose, beaver (7/7)

I deer, antelope, buffalo, wolves, blacktail prairie dog (7/8)
J deer, antelope, buffalo, wolves (7/9)
K elk, buffalo, grizzly (7/10)
L elk, buffalo (7/11)
M buffalo (7/13)
N grizzly (7/15)
O antelope, grizzly (7/16)
P buffalo (7/17)
Q antelope, buffalo, wolves, whitetail jackrabbit (7/18)
R antelope, buffalo, wolves (7/19)
S elk, antelope, buffalo, wolves (7/20)
T Columbian ground squirrel (?) 7/23
U deer, antelope, wolves, kit fox (7/26)
V buffalo (7/27)

CLARK'S EASTWARD ROUTE — 1806

a deer, bear, Columbian ground squirrel (7/3)
b deer, bighorn sheep (7/4)
c snowshoe hare (?) (7/6)
d deer, antelope, bighorn sheep, beaver, river otter (4/13)
e deer, beaver (7/11)
f deer, elk, wolves, beaver, river otter (7/13)
g deer, elk, antelope, beaver (/13)
h deer, antelope, black bear (?) (715)
i elk, antelope, bear (7/16)
j deer, elk, buffalo (7%17)
k deer, elk, antelope, buffalo, grizzly,
l deer, elk, buffalo, coyote, beaver (7/24)
m elk, buffalo, bighorn sheep, wolves (7/25)
n deer, elk, antelope, buffalo, bighorn sheep, beaver (7/27)
o beaver (7/29)
p grizzly (7/30)
q buffalo, grizzly, wolves (7/31)
r buffalo (8/1)

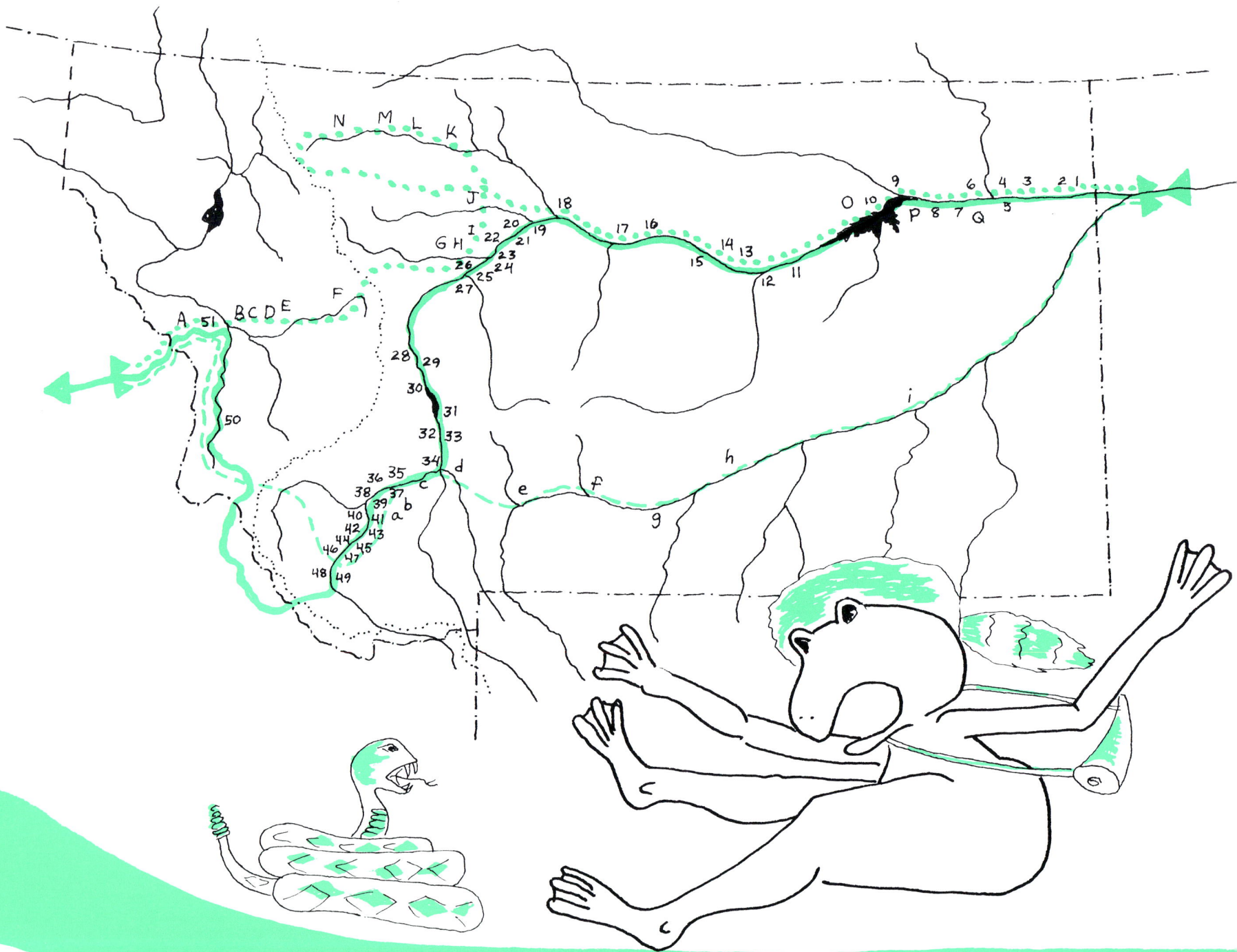

Information used to develop this map courtesy of *Montana Outdoors*. This article appears in the Jul/Aug issue with maps prepared by the Cartography Bureau, DNR & C.

WILLDLIFE SIGHTINGS
• BIRDS • REPTILES • FISH •

LEWIS' AND CLARK'S WESTWARD ROUTE — 1805

1 trumpeter swan, black-billed magpie (4/27)
2 Canada goose (4/28)
3 common crow (4/30)
4 Canada goose (4/30)
5 American avocet (5/1)
6 Canada goose, whistling or trumpeter swan, brant (?) (5/3)
7 Canada goose, snow goose, brant (?) (5/5)
8 bald eagle, belted kingfisher (5/7)
10 willet 5/9)
11 poor-will (?), prairie rattlesnake (5/17)
12 great horned owl (5/20
13 sharp-tailed grouse (5/21)
14 sharp-tailed grouse, channel catfish (5/22)
15 Canada goose (5/23)
16 softshell turtle (5/26)
17 hairy woodpecker or downy woodpecker (5/28)
18 cliff swallow (5/31)
19 long-billed curlew, McCown's longspur (?) (6/4)
    turkey vulture, sage grouse (5/5)
    mourning dove, house wren, American goldfinch, robin, Brewer's blackbird (?), common grackle (?) (6/8)
    mountain bluebird, loggerhead shrike, eastern kingbird (6/10)

20 goldeye, Flathead chub (?) (6/11)
20 cliff swallow, goldeye (6/12)
21 Canada goose, cutthroat trout, goldeye, Flathead chub (?) (6/13)
22 Canada goose (6/14)
23 Canada goose, common crow, Brewer's blackbird (?), prairie rattlesnake, cutthroat trout, channel catfish (6/15)
24 wood duck, common merganser, chestnut-collared longspur or McCown's longspur, Brewer's blackbird (?), horned lark, western meadowlark (6/19-6/23)
25 painted turtle (?), cutthroat trout, channel catfish, goldeye (6/25)
26 common nighthawk (630)
    Canada goose (7/2)
    Flathead chub (?) (7/10)
27 golden eagle, passenger pigeon, belted kingfisher, long-billed curlew, mourning dove, brown-headed cowbird (7/11-7/13)
28 Lewis' woodpecker, common merganser (7/20)
29 Canada goose, cutthroat trout (7/21)
30 Canada goose, sandhill crane, mountain plover or upland plover (7/22)
31 Canada goose, sandhill crane, hognose snake (7/23)
32 Canada goose, sandhill crane, long-billed curlew, common merganser; common, western or plains garter snake (?) (7/24)
33 Canada goose (7/25)
34 sandhill crane, mallard, wood duck, cliff swallow, belted kingfisher (7/27-7/29)
35 blue grouse, pinion jay (8/1)
36 Canada goose, mallard, Lewis' wood

pecker, common merganser, prairie rattlesnake (8/2)
37 Canada goose, long-billed curlew, cutthroat trout, mountain whitefish (8/3)
38 Canada goose, sandhill crane (8/4)
39 Canada goose (8/5)
40 Canada goose, sandhill crane (8/8)
41 Canada goose (8/9)
42 bald eagle, osprey, prairie rattle snake (8/10)
43 Canada goose (8/11)
44 sage grouse (8/12)
45 prairie rattlesnake (8/15)
46 cutthroat trout (8/16)
47 cutthroat trout (8/18)
48 longnose sucker (8/19)
49 Arctic grayling (8/22)
50 sandhill crane (9/7)
51 sharp-tailed grouse, red-headed woodpecker, pileated woodpecker (9/9)

LEWIS' EASTWARD ROUTE — 1806

A spruce grouse (?) (6/26)
B spruce grouse (?) (6/29)
C pileated woodpecker (7/1)
D sandhill crane, sharp-tailed grouse, common raven, long-billed curlew, robin, mountain plover or upland plover, Lewis' woodpecker, western meadowlark, horned lark, mourning dove, eastern kingbird, brown-headed cowbird, common flicker (7/2)

E white pelican, passenger pigeon (7/5)
F whistling or trumpeter swan, common raven, long-billed curlew, robin, mourning dove, eastern kingbird (7/6)
G passenger pigeon, mourning dove, brown-headed cowbird (7/11)
H passenger pigeon (7/12)
I red-headed woodpecker, black-billed cuckoo (?) (7/16)
J American avocet (7/17)
K Canada goose (7/19)
L Canada goose (7/20)
M passenger pigeon, common raven, common crow, mourning dove (7/19)
N passenger pigeon (7/25)
O bald eagle, golden eagle, black-billed magpie, red-headed woodpecker (8/3)
P common nighthawk (8/4)
Q Canada geese, white pelican (8/5)

CLARK'S EASTWARD ROUTE — 1806

a Canada geese (7/10)
b Canada goose, sandhill crane (7/11)
c Canada goose (7/13)
d Canada goose (7/16)
e mountain sucker (7/16)
f white pelican, American avocet (7/17)
g passenger pigeon (721)
h Canada goose, passenger pigeon, common crow, mourning dove, cliff swallow (7/23)
i softshell turtle, channel catfish (7/29)

SOME MONTANA FUR FORTS

Name	Date Established	Location	Built By
THE MISSOURI FUR COMPANY			
Fort Remon or Raymond	1808	On Yellowstone at mouth of the Bighorn River	Manuel Lisa, named for Lisa's son
Fort Lisa, Fort Manuel Lisa, or Bighorn Post	1809	On Yellowstone at mouth of the Bighorn River	Lisa and the Missouri Fur Company
Three Forks Post	1810	Three Forks of the Missouri	Andrew Henry and Pierre Menard
Fort Benton	1821	On Yellowstone at mouth of the Bighorn River	Joshua Pilcher
THE CANADIAN FUR COMPANIES			
Kootenai Post	1808	Kootenai River, opposite Libby	Finan McDonald for North West Fur Company
Saleesh House	1809	Clark Fork, near Thompson Falls	David Thompson for North West Fur Company
2nd Kootenai Post	1811	Kootenai River, opposite Jennings	Finan McDonald and Nicholas Monteur
2nd Saleesh House — Flathead Post	1824	Clark Fork, near Eddy	James McMillan and Ross Cox for Hudson's Bay Company
Fort Connah	1846	Near St. Ignatius	Neil McArthur and Angus McDonald for Hudson's Bay Company. Named for River Connen in Scotland
THE ROCKY MOUNTAIN FUR COMPANY			
Big Horn Post	1824	On Yellowstone at mouth of the Bighorn River	Andrew Henry
Fort William	1833	On Missouri, just below mouth of Yellowstone	William Sublette, Robert Campbell Named for Sublette
THE AMERICAN FUR COMPANY			
Fort Union	182-20	On Missouri River, just above mouth of Yellowstone	Kenneth McKenzie
Fort Piegan	1831	On Missouri River, at mouth of Marias	James Kipp
Fort McKenzie	1832	On Missouri River, six miles above mouth of Marias	David D. Mitchell, Francis A. Chardon, Alexander Culbertson. Named for Kenneth McKenzie
Fort Cass	1832	On Yellowstone, three miles below mouth of Bighorn on south bank	Samuel Tullock. Named for Lewis Cass of Michigan
Fort Jackson	1833	On Missouri, at mouth of Poplar River	F.A. Chardon. Named for President Jackson
Fort Van Buren	1835	On Yellowstone River, at mouth of Rosebud	Samuel Tullock. Named for President Van Buren
Fort Alexander	1842	On Yellowstone River, near mouth of Armell's Creek	Charles Larpenteur. Named for Alexander Culbertson
Fort Chardon	1844	On south bank of Missouri, at mouth of Judith	Francis Chardon and Alexander Harvey. Named for Chardon.
Fort Lewis, also called Fort Cotton, Fort Honore or Henry and Cotton Bottoms	1845	On south bank of Missouri, 18 miles above Fort Benton	Alexander Culbertson. Fort Lewis for Meriwether Lewis. Fort Honore for Honore Picotte
Fort Benton	1847	Missouri River, on site of present town	Alexander Culbertson. Named for Senator Thomas H. Benton
1st Fort Sarpy	1850	North bank of Yellowstone, below mouth of Rosebud	Alexander Culbertson. Named for John B. Sarpy
2nd Fort Sarpy	1857	On Yellowstone, 25 miles below mouth of Bighorn	Robert Meldrum

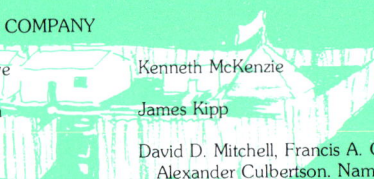

Fort Mortimer	1842	On Missouri, just below mouth of Yellowstone on old Fort William site	Fox, Livingstone & Company
Fort Cotton	1842	On Missouri River, 18 miles above Fort Benton — later Fort Lewis	Fox, Livingstone & Co. Named for a partner
Fort Campbell	1846	Adjacent to Fort Benton	Harvey, Primeau and Company. Named for Robert Campbell
Fort Stewart	1855	On Missouri, near present Blair, Montana	Frost, Todd & Co.
Fort Kipp	1860	On Missouri, above mouth of Big Muddy	Named for James Kipp
Fort Dauphin	1860	On the Missouri, at mouth of the Milk	Louis Dauphin
Fort Poplar	1861	On the Missouri, near the Poplar River	Charles Larpenteur
Fort Andrews	1862	On the Missouri, 15 miles above mouth of the Musselshell	George Steel. Named for Andrew Dawson
Fort LaBarge	1862	Adjacent to Fort Benton	LaBarge, Harkness & Company. Named for brothers, John and Joseph
Fort Galpin	1862	North side of Missouri, 12 miles above mouth of Milk River	LaBarge, Harkness & Company

From "The Fur Trade in Montana," Paul C. Paul C. Phillips, *A History of Montana*, M.G. Burlingame and K. Ross Toole, eds. N.Y.: Lewis Publishing Co. 1957.

It is impossible to put an exact number on the number of beaver, otter, and other fur-bearing animals "trapped out" in Montana and other areas of the west. It will have to be enough to say that trapping went on and on for more than fifty years with a heyday of some twenty to twenty-five years (1820-1845). Thousands of men, both red and white, were employed in the business of trapping so as to enable wealthy Europeans and eastern Americans the joy of sauntering about in fashionably warm apparel.

What may or may not be significant is the apparent change of attitude on the part of the Indian in respect to the hunting of wildlife.

"Trappers were of many nationalities, some literate, others unable to either read or write. To most of them, and to the Indians, money values were puzzling. Monetary systems based on dollars and cents, English pound sterling, French francs, and Spanish pesos meant little to most of them in determining fur prices or trade values. Gradually there developed the recognition that the beaver pelt had an understandable value for exchange and barter. A gun priced at 20 beaver pelts meant a definite price; the same gun priced at $50.00 meant confusion. This recognizable currency, which could not be counterfeited, was acceptable to the trappers and Indians, who bartered their credit for many items of merchandise, priced in the same terms. Trade goods might be priced at five beaver for an axe, ¼ beaver for a string of beads. ⅛ beaver was the smallest denomination. Beaver became the monetary system of the Montana frontier. The impact of beaver pelt currency appeared in the Flathead-Salish language when the word 'ska-le-oo,' originally meaning beaver, became the term for money."

Albert J. Partoll, pamphlet *When Beaver Pelts Were Legal Tender in Montana*, Western Montana National Bank, Missoula, 1964.

"Hudson Bay blankets, sometimes seen in Montana, carried a bar or two or three along the edge; in the fur-trading days the bars signified the number of beaver skins necessary for purchase."

Ralph Henry, *Our Land Montana*

deer, elk, or moose. Not only that, but the hides of other animals were better suited for moccasins, clothing, and teepees. Even more important was the fact that among many of the Indians the beaver, as well as the bear, was thought to possess some supernatural character. Not only did they dislike killing them, they hated killing them.

For these reasons, the population of these fur-bearing animals was in the millions. The domestic use by a relatively small group of inhabitants ensured their existence forever...or until fashions changed. The slaughter of the beaver is second only to the still later slaughter of the buffalo. (My, how styles change!)

Prior to the coming of the whites, Indians killed fur-bearing animals for their domestic use only. They seldom killed for sport. Actually beaver, muskrat, and others were relatively safe, for their meat was not considered to be as appetizing as buffalo,

This would be a good time to read *The Big Sky* by A.B. Guthrie.

Chapter Five

"The object of your mission is to explore the Missouri River...and the waters offering the best communication with the Pacific Ocean...for the purpose of commerce." These were the instructions of President Thomas Jefferson to Meriwether Lewis at the onset of the famous expedition.

As Montanans, and those people who wish they were Montanans (all non-Montanans) travel across the state, the names Lewis and Clark turn up constantly. Deservedly so, in the long-held tradition of naming things after the first person to do something notable. They were the first Americans to stump, map, and describe the Missouri and Columbia rivers to the Pacific Ocean.

But in the view of the people living in these areas, these guys (Lewis and Clark) were just "passing through." They didn't know what it was like to experience a winter in the northern Rocky Mountains or the northern great plains. Their description of the areas over which they travelled were accurate but, like any other "one shot deal," did not provide patterns, such as weather, animal migrations, etc. In all fairness, it wasn't meant to, obviously. This other information had to be added later from word of mouth descriptions related by those who lived there either permanently, such as the Indian, or temporarily, such as the white fur trapper or "mountain man."

Actually, not all white fur trappers could be categorized as "mountain men." You see, fur trapping was conducted by primarily two methods. The British and Canadian way was the "brigade" method. This procedure usually employed thirty to forty trappers, but on rare occasions as many as two or three hundred. It was a "safety in numbers" strategy. Not a bad idea when one considers the fact that some of the "neighborhood people," notably the Blackfeet, weren't all that excited about seeing their furry friends biting the dust. If the Blackfeet would have known that the beaver, an animal of spiritual significance, was being made into hats, goodness knows what they would have done. As it was, they successfully kept the white fur trappers out of their territory for thirty years. In fact, trappers, both white and red, looked over their shoulders for Blackfeet even outside the "normal" Blackfeet territory.

The second trapping method was the free trapper system. The free trapper was the "mountain man." By this method individuals would live and trap all year in the wilderness, coming out in the early summer to meet at a pre-determined location for the purpose of selling their pelts. This was known as the "rendezvous." The first of these was held in 1824, the biggest in 1832, and the last in 1840. In actuality they were week-long drunks at which the trapper was ripped off by being paid low prices for pelts and charged high prices for supplies to get him through another year.

Originally the brigade method was employed by both British and Canadian groups and the American groups. Changes in circumstances required changes in methods. The Blackfeet definitely provided different circumstances. They were constantly killing trappers who ventured near their territory. It was in part due to this that the brigade method was scrapped by the Canadian fur companies. Enter — the free trapper system.

The friction between the Blackfeet and the white is often attributed to a skirmish between the Meriwether Lewis party, exploring the Marias River, and a band of Blackfeet. The story has it that Lewis had been warned about the Blackfeet by the Nez Perce and the Flathead Indians. The Blackfeet tribe was a nation feared by other red men, and soon, white men. Well — Lewis decided to share a camp with Blackfeet. During the night there was a scuffle over some rifles. When the dust settled two Blackfeet lay dead. The remainder of the Blackfeet vanished. The whites figured that if they didn't do likewise they might not get a second chance. Lewis and company made it to the Missouri, some 100-120 miles, by daybreak. Undoubtedly, the fastest segment of the expedition! Whew!!

Others attribute the Blackfeet animosity toward the white to John Colter, a veteran of the Lewis and Clark expedition. At the time of this incident, however, Colter was employed by Manuel Lisa of the Missouri Fur Company. It took place in the spring of 1808 just after Colter's amazing winter trek through what is now known as Yellowstone Park, but was then known as "Colter's Hell." (Nobody believed his stories of the "boiling water."

Some time later, John Colter led a party from Maneul's Fort on the Yellowstone to the Three Forks of the Missouri, and in so doing retraced the route by which he had escaped. Thomas James was a member of that party, and the firsthand information he received from Colter about that event must have made a profound impression upon him, judging from the vivid and colorful description in his narrative. The version given by James does not have the literary merit of other accounts, but is an enthusiastic memorial to a personal friend. The following description by James is more realistic and logical than the other account, except for the hardly plausible statement about Colter's having hidden in a beaver lodge.

"He [Colter] had gone with a companion named Potts to the Jefferson river, which is the most western of the tree Forks, and runs near the base of the mountains. They were both proceeding up the river in search of beaver, each in his own canoe, when a war party of about eight hundred Black-Feet Indians suddenly appeared on the east bank of the river. The Chiefs ordered them to come ashore, and apprehending robbery only, and knowing the utter hopelessness of flight, and having dropped his traps over the side of the canoe from the Indians, into the water, which was here quite shallow, he hastened to obey their mandate. On reaching the shore, he was seized, disarmed and stripped entirely naked. Potts was still in his canoe in the middle of the stream, where he remained stationary, watching the result. Colter requested him to come ashore, which he refused to do, saying he might as well lose his life at once, as be stripped and robbed in the manner Colter had been. An Indian immediately fired and shot him about the hip; he dropped down in the canoe, but instantly rose with his rifle in his hands. 'Are you hurt,' said Colter. 'Yes,' said he,' to much hurt to escape; if you can get away do so. I will kill at least one of them.' He leveled his rifle and shot an Indian dead. In an instant, at least a hundred bullets pierced his body and as many savages rushed into the stream and pulled the canoe, containing his riddled corpse, ashore. They dragged the body up onto the bank, and with their hatchets and knives cut and hacked it all to pieces, and limb from limb. The entrails, heart, lungs etc., they threw into Colter's face. The relations of the killed Indian were furious with rage and struggled, with tomahawk in hand, to reach Colter, while others held them back. He was every moment expecting the death blow or the fatal shot that should lay him beside his companion. A council was hastily held over him and his fate quickly determined upon. He expected to die by tomahawk, slow, lingering and horrible. But they had magnanimously determined to give him a chance, though a slight one, for his life. After the council, a Chief pointed to the prairie and motioned him away with his hand, saying in the Crow language, 'go — go away.' He supposed they intended to shoot him as soon as he was out of the crowd and presented a fair mark to their guns. He started in a walk, and an old Indian with impatient signs and exclamations, told him to go faster, and he still kept a walk, the same Indian manifested his wishes by still more violent gestures and adjurations. When he had gone a distance of eighty or a hundred yards from the army of his enemies, he saw the younger Indians throwing off their blankets, leggings, and other incumbrances, as if for a race. Now he knew their object. He was to run a race, of which the prize was to be his own life and scalp. Off he started with the speed of the wind. The war-whoop and yell immediately arose behind him; and looking back, he saw a large company of young warriors, with spears, in rapid pursuit. He ran with all the strength that nature, excited to the uttermost, could give; fear and hope lent a supernatural vigor to his limbs and the rapidity of his flight astonished himself. The Madison Fork lay directly before him, five miles from his starting place. He had run half the distance when his strength began to fail and the blood to gush from his nostrils. At every leap the red stream spurted before him, and his limbs were growing rapidly weaker and weaker. He stopped and looked back; he had far outstripped all his pursuers and could get off if strength would only hold out. One solitary Indian far ahead of the others was rapidly approaching, with a spear in his right hand, and a blanket streaming behind from his left hand and shoulder. Despairing of escape, Colter awaited his pursuer and called to him in the Crow language, to save his life. The savage did not seem to hear him, but letting go his blanket, and seizing his spear with both hands, he rushed at Colter, naked and defenseless as he stood before him and made a desperate lunge to transfix him. Colter seized the spear, near the head, with his right hand, and exerting his whole strength, aided by the weight of the falling Indian, who had lost his balance in the fury of the onset, he broke off the iron head or blade which remained in his hand, while the savage fell to the ground and lay prostrate and disarmed before him. Now was his turn to beg for his life, which he did in the Crow language, and held up his hands imploringly, but Colter was not in a mood to remember the golden rule, and pinned his adversary through the body to the earth by one stab with the spear head. He quickly drew the weapon from the body of the now dying Indian, and seizing his blanket as lawful spoil, he again set out with renewed strength, feeling, he said to me, as if he had not run a mile. A shout and yell arose from the pursuing army in his rear as from a legion of devils, and he saw the prairie behind him covered with Indians in full and rapid chase. Before him, if anywhere, was life and safety; behind him certain death; and

NOT HOSTILE... JUST CIVIC-MINDED... CLEANING UP THE NEIGHBORHOOD, SO TO SPEAK...

running as never man before sped the foot, except, perhaps, at the Olympic Games, he reached his goal, the Madison river and the end of his five mile heat. Dashing through the willows on the bank he plunged into the stream and saw close beside him a beaver house, standing like a coal-pile about ten feet above the surface of the water, which was here of about the same depth. This presented to him a refuge from his ferocious enemies of which he immediately availed himself. Diving under the water he arose into the beaver house, where he found a dry and comfortable resting place on the upper floor or story of this singular structure. The

Indians soon came up, and in their search for him they stood upon the roof of his house of refuge, which he expected every moment to hear them breaking open. He also feared that they would set it on fire. After a diligent search on that side of the river, they crossed over, and in about two hours returned again to his temporary habitation in which he was enjoying bodily rest, though with much anxious foreboding. The beaver houses are divided into two stories and will generally accommodate several men in a dry and comfortable lodging. In this asylum Colter kept fast till night. The cries of his terrible enemies had gradually died away, and all was still around him, when he ventured out of his

hiding place, by the same opening under the water by which he entered and which admits the beavers to their building. He swam the river and hastened towards the mountain gap or ravine, about thirty miles above on the river, through which our company passed in the snow with so much difficulty. Fearing that the Indians might have guarded this pass, which was the only outlet from the valley, and to avoid the danger of a surprise, Colter ascended the almost perpendicular mountain before him, the tops and sides of which a great way down, were covered with perpetual snow. He clambered up this fearful ascent about four miles below the gap, holding on by the rocks, shrubs and branches of trees, and by

morning had reached the top. He lay there concealed all that day, and at night proceeded on in the descent of the mountain, which he accomplished by dawn. He now hastened on in the open plain towards Manuel's Fort on the Big Horn, about three hundred miles ahead in the northeast. He travelled day and night, stopping only for necessary repose, and eating roots and the bark of trees, for eleven days. He reached the Fort, nearly exhausted by hunger, fatigue and excitement. His only clothing was the Indian's blanket, whom he had killed in the race, and his only weapon, the same Indian's spear which he brought to the Fort as a trophy. His beard was long, his face and whole body were thin and emaciated by hunger, and his limbs and feet swollen and sore. The company at the Fort did not recognize him in this dismal plight until he made himself known. Colter now with me passed over the scene of his capture and

wonderful escape, and described his emotions during the whole adventure with great minuteness. Not the least of his exploits was the scaling of the mountain, which seemed to me impassible even by the mountain goat. As I looked at its rugged and perpendicular sides I wondered how he ever reached the top — a feat probably never performed before by mortal man. The whole affair is a fine example of the quick and ready thoughtfulness and presence of mind in a desperate situation, and the power of endurance, which characterize the western pioneer."

"The Crows tried to starve out the white traders at Ft. McKenzie at the confluence of the Marias and Missouri rivers. Days went by and the people in the fort began to suffer greatly. They ate all their food and then they ate all the dogs in the fort. Then they began to eat strips of boiled buffalo hide. Finally they told their leader, Alexander Culbertson, that they could stand it no longer and would surrender. But Culbertson had another idea. He knew the Indians were not acquainted with the cannon held at the fort. They had never heard anything like cannon fire. He called out to the Crow chief that if his men did not leave by noon of a certain day the fort would hurl thunderbolts among them. The chief laughed. Right at noon of the day mentioned one of the cannons was aimed directly at the center of the Indian encampment. A shot went bounding among the Indians, greatly frightening them. The medicine man did not know what to do, and the chief really believed it was a thunderbolt. He ordered his men to leave at once, and in a few hours all the Indians had gone."

Ralph Henry, *Treasure State*

Anyway, it seems that Colter was among the Crow Indians for the purpose of establishing trade. While he camped with them, they were attacked by the Blackfeet, an event that occurred with a degree of regularity. Colter was a pretty good shot, and he made his presence known. In this particular case the Blackfeet should have stayed home; they lost. Having lost, and having seen a white man fighting along side their hated enemy might have been too much for one day. They already hated the Crow; the only logical thing to do was hate the white man, too. Think about how different things might have been if Colter had been with the Blackfeet, instead!

Whichever, if either, explanation is true, doesn't really matter. We know the Blackfeet were, indeed, the rulers of the land, along with, but not along side, the "Mountain men." Both boldly moved about their business for a great number of years. The Blackfeet maintained their territorial integrity, while the mountain men, with the aid of friendly Indians, extracted the much sought after fur for "the Company." The depletion of the beaver, and the age of the silk hat, finished the age of the "mountain men."

74 The sad truth is that the Blackfeet were "done in" by a combination of diseases introduced by the whites. The first was alcohol, supplied in quantities adequate to continue the trade they finally established in 1831 at Fort Piegan. The second was the smallpox epidemic of 1837. The epidemic followed the route of the whiteman. It made its way up the Missouri with the fur traders. Its impact varied from tribe to tribe. The Mandans for instance were all of a sudden referred to the past tense. It staggers the mind to think a disease could totally eliminate a tribe. The Assiniboine didn't fare much better. The Crow maybe because of their relative closeness to the whiteman, fared better. They heeded warning and made themselves scarce for awhile.

Such was not the case of the Blackfeet. They too were warned about the disease, but whether they didn't trust the whitemans words or they were just curious isn't clear. They went to the trading posts as usual, then returned home. Some time passed and no Blackfeet traders. The whites went to see what happened to their customers. Alexander Culbertson from Fort McKenzie, came across a good sized camp in which death lost but two rounds. Bodies and carcasses littered the camp. A major village, now had only two living residents. The Blackfeet nation was halved. These people, reknowned for their superior military genius, were killed by a foe that even their best tacticions could not outwit — smallpox.

Chapter Six

Jeremiah Johnson, Kit Carson, Jedediah Smith, Hugh Glass, John Colter. Five names, five men larger than life. It is almost impossible to find where myth ends and the man begins. Their exploits have captured the imaginations of millions everywhere. The romanticized versions of their lifestyles have appeared in dime novels, magazine articles, books, and more recently, television. Many successful T.V. series have portrayed the rugged individual pitted against the wiles of nature in its primitive state. Another popular theme is that of man versus beast. How about the one that shows the blending of cultures in the old "blood brothers" bit?

But we still ask...what were they *really* like? What did they eat? Did they wash behind their ears? What did they do? I mean there was no electricity for T.V., radio, power tools, no running water for plumbing. Wait a minute! These guys were in a super minority at the time. What about the Indians of this area and era? How did they live? You know, a kind of a day in the life of a mountain man and an Indian.

First of all, why would a person live alone in the wilderness, or at best with two companions, for years at a time? (Not including the time spent with others at the rendezvous.) The answers were as varied as the individuals. In general, it's safe to say that adventure and money were the biggest reasons.

The "mountain men" were some of the first to adopt the natural look. Their dress set them apart from all others, not only by the way they looked, but also by the way they smelled. Their greasy buckskins, and coonskin caps were covered with liberal coats of bear grease for waterproofing. Combine this with the fact that many bothered to bathe only once a year, (at the rendezvous) and you have the reason for their "natural" odor. They were a breed apart. As for shelter, the "Big Sky" provided enough overhead for many. Some constructed crude log structures. Still others followed the theory "if it's good enough for the natives, it's good enough for me," and used hides for shelter.

"Meat's meat!" This was a common saying among the mountain men, whose diet was almost exclusively meat. Whether they couldn't afford to be fussy, or they just happened to like everything hasn't been established. All that is known is that the mountain men ate anything that moved, from buffalo to rattlesnake, every fowl that flew, every reptile and insect that crept. According to an informal survey taken to determine the meat most preferred, the dog came out #2, beating out buffalo, beef, venison, mountain mutton, turkey, grouse, wild fowl, rabbit, hare, beaver, etc. The only animal to place higher was the panther (cougar.) These meats were regularly eaten, having been prepared by various methods, ranging from raw to burned.

"The Mountain Man seemed a forlorn and pathetic primitive out of the past. 'They are stared at as though they were bears,' wrote Rudolph F. Kurz, a Swiss artist who traveled the Upper Missouri."

Goetzmann, "The Mountain Man as Jacksonian Man"

Historian William Goetzmann studied 446 Mountain Men who were engaged in trapping between 1805 and 1845. He found 182 had been killed during their trapping days, and only five remained trappers after that date. Of the rest, 36 became farmers or ranchers, 17 became traders, 4 became Indian agents. But a few entered the civilized world in a big way, becoming bankers, newspaper editors, lawyers, real estate agents. One became a superintendent of schools, one the governor of New Mexico. And three trappers went on to found the city of Denver.

William Goetzmann, "The Mountain Man as Jacksonian Man," *American Quarterly*, Volume XV, #3, Fall, 1963.

This would be a good time to read The Indian Culture Series, a great selection of short paperbacks printed by Montana Indian Publications, Billings.

By comparison, the Indian lived a far more "civilized" existence. In part this must be attributed to the traditional breakdown of work that occurred in the extended family. The mountain men lived much as single men (visions of dirty dorm rooms and bachelor "pads") do today.

The Indian was a nomad. The possible exception to this were the Flathead and Nez Perce, who, for a short time, farmed. In varying degrees they all aided the white man. Even the Crow and Blackfeet did their part. The Crow encouraged the whites to take healthy walks by constantly stealing their horses, starting with Lewis and Clark's. The Blackfeet continually helped lessen competition by use of their own *elimination* methods, until 1831.

If indeed time helps place things in their proper perspective, then we must say that of the two, the regions and the Indian, the region fared better (if you could call it that.) The region lost an infinite number of fur-bearing animals, whose value as a part of the ecosystem was immeasurable, and whose monetary value was appreciated and experienced by a mere handful of distant individuals. The Indian, on the other hand, was the real loser in this episode. Not only did they fall victim to liquor and smallpox, but even more devastating was the fact that those who survived were kept dependent on the white man for firearms, liquor, and supplies. The red man lost what the white man had acquired only fifty years earlier — independence.

Days of the Fur Traders in the Northwest

The Old-Time Fur Trader Was a More Picturesque Character than any Other in the West; His Daily Life was Replete with Dangers and Thrills; Hostile Indians Were Ever Present Peril

(By Mrs. M.E. Plassmann)

When our next president of the United States, elects to take his summer outing in Yellowstone or Glacier park, it is to be hoped a committee of our promiment citizens will wait upon him, and invest him, not with the toga of the statesman, but the fringed and beaded buckskin shirt girded with a scarlet sash, a fisher cap, leggings and moccasins, likewise beaded, and a gay kerchief to tie about his neck. For weapons, there would be a hunting knife and revolver — if a gun, then a cartridge belt might take the place of the scarf.

He could fish, if he chose, but with no fancy tackle or flies. What he uses in this line, would necessarily be the work of his own hands. He should sleep in a tent, a tepee, or on the ground, with the starry heavens as a canopy. His meals should be cooked at a campfire, and of an evening, beside this same campfire he will hear tales of the old, old days, like some that follow.

A Virginia boy ran away from home and by wagon, horseback, or on foot, ultimately found his way to St. Louis, where he heard wonderful stories of the Far West, of encounters with wild animals and almost as wild men; of fortunes to be gained by trapping beaver, and the freedom to be had out there, from all the restraining influences of civilization. It was an alluring picture this, when viewed from the standpoint of an adventure-loving youth of nineteen.

William Sublette, of the Rocky Mountain Fur company was then in St. Louis, buying supplies and drumming up recruits. To him went the boy, and asked to join his company.

"You will be killed before you are halfway there," was Subiette's reply to the callow youth before him. "Then I can die." retorted the boy.

This answer made Sublette form a favorable opinion of the applicant, and he was engaged as a hired trapper, who received the needful supplies from the company, was subject to its orders, and all the fur he brought in belonged to the company and not to himself. At the end of the year, the hired trapper received a salary of four or five hundred dollars. The free trapper on the contrary, was subject to no one. He came and went as he chose; but when he sold his furs, he discovered, that according to financial methods later common, the price he received was dictated by the fur company that controlled the market.

While serving his apprenticeship, it was better in every way for the boy to be a hired trapper. He was forced to submit to discipline, and taught the things it was imperative he should learn in order successfully to contend with the wilderness. This included more than becoming a horseman, swinging a lasso, or branding cattle. He learned to ride? Yes. He also learned to walk long distances and for days at a time, over snow, and when blizzards raged; to have no warm bunkhouse awaiting him nightly, to sleep out of doors, no matter what the weather; to expect no coddling when the victim of an accident, or an Indian markmanship; to have a straight diet of meat, or go without eating, just as it happened — in other words to adapt himself to his environment as the Indians did. This was part of the schooling of a mountain man.

Once, when in the mountains, the boy and a companion strayed away from the main company on a hunting expedition. They were fortunate in killing a buffalo cow. It was quickly skinned, a fire built that would not make their presence known to roving bands of Blackfeet, and the choicest pieces cooked for their immediate consumption. It was late in the afternoon. When their meal ended and the hunters were too far from the man camp to reach it that night.

Weary, but no longer hungry, the two made the best of the situation, by seeking the shelter afforded by a grove of aspen, and wrapping their blankets about them, laid down to sleep.

They were awakened early in the morning by the sound of sniffing, and the weight of some large animal walking over them. At once the boy, being from the south, "reckoned" it was a grizzly, and a good-sized one, judging from its weight, that was making the disturbance. The bear was in search of some pieces of buffalo meat the hunters had providently hidden under their heads and their blankets the night before.

Not understanding what had awakened him, the other man half rose to see what was tramping over him, when the boy whispered, "Lie down! It's a bear." The man disappeared under his blanket just in time; for the bear, hearing the voice, rushed back to investigate. He found the meat under the boy's head, and retired to devour it, when something was said that brought his bearship in a rush to the spot.

A full-grown grizzly is no light weight, and it took a good deal of will power to keep from crying out when the animal used the recumbent hunters as a rug, but they managed to endure in silence, until the boy, peeping from under cover sighted the bear busily engaged in stowing away the buffalo meat, when cautiously aiming the gun lying by his side, he killed the creature, and saved the remainder of the buffalo, which was taken back to the main camp, after the two had breakfasted. Note.

(This should have been the manner of the killing; in truth the bear became frightened, ran down the mountain, when the boy followed and killed him.)

The disposition of meat was made in this manner. A man, standing with his back toward it, called a number, designating one of the messes into which the company was divided, and the meat went to it, or the name of the bourgeois — the leader — was called, and he became the recipient.

Not always were the boy's experiences of an amusing nature, like the foregoing. Sublette had chosen to trap on middle ground, almost unknown to white men. He had gone to the headwaters of the Snake river where there was an abundance of beaver, but also it was a favorite hunting ground of the Blackfeet, the most feared of all the northern Indian tribes.

These tolerated no invasion of their territory by either white man or Indian.

The company, led by Sublette were traveling in a north-easterly direction, and were on the Gallatin, when the Blackfeet attacked them, killing two men, and putting the rest to flight. The boy escaped, but only to find himself alone, surrounded by Indians, and with no knowledge of the country.

It was November, and very cold in the mountains already white with snow. Concealing the mule he had ridden in the timber, the boy climbed to the top of the highest peak in the vicinity, and looked about him. His company was not in sight, but a wonderful landscape view unrolled itself in every direction. Below him was the Yellowstone flowing eastward. To the north he caught glimpses of the Missouri on its way to join the Mississippi; back of him was the Sanke river hastening to the Columbia and south, mountain after mountain towered, their peaks snow white against the faultless blue of the sky.

He pondered long what he should do, but not unboylike, he had wept bitterly. Deciding to go southeast into the Crow Country. "a land of plenty — as the mountain man regards plenty — and there he could at least live, provided the Crows permitted him to do so."

Retrieving his mule he set out. He dared not build a fire on account of the Indians, and to spend the night without one meant freezing to death. The morning found him some thirty miles from his starting point. He had crossed the Yellowstone, and was again among the mountains, where he was forced to leave the mule and go on foot, taking only one blanket, and his gun, and he had eaten nothing for two days.

About twenty miles south he came upon a band of mountain sheep, one of which he killed and ate; then he slept. On awakening a bitter wind was blowing, and again he set out taking with him as much of the meat as he could carry. Not a sound broke the silence. No bird could live in that frozen waste, and whatever other animals the mountains harbored made no sound. It was a solitude Zimmerman might have envied.

On the fifth day of his journey, the boy ate the last of his mutton, and then climbed an eminence east of his camp. When he was startled to see a vast field covered at intervals by cone-shaped elevations, from which issued steam, and columns of boiling water. It was a strange sight, reminding the boy of Pittsburg as he had last seen it. Complimentary or not to that city; the boy said it looked like the hell described by the preachers, and it might be that for all he knew.

One thing was certain. He was cold and below was warmth. So down he climbed, to find the earth, when he reached the plain, giving back a hollow sound as he went forward. While thawing out he reflected "If it war hell, it war a more agreeable climate than he had been in for some time."

Once more comfortable in body, but hungry and lonesome, the boy was suddenly startled by hearing two shots fired, followed by blood-curdling Indian war whoops. Grasping his gun in preparation for defense, a voice spoke in good English. "Well, I swan! If it isn't the boy." The latter had passed his initiation , and was now recognized as a member of the honorable fraternity of Mountain men.

These two stories from "The River of the West," are enough for one evening; the campfire is burning low, and dawn comes early in summer, yet as a kind of verbal nightcap to induce pleasant dreams, is added this of a hunting expedition undertaken by the boy and Milton Sublette. When they were entirely unprepared, a large grizzly charged out of a thicket, and took after Sublette, who promptly sought the tallest tree. The boy, seeing his companion was likely to be overtaken, fired, and killed the bear. Approaching the tree, he found Sublette sitting on the ground, arms and legs encircling the trunk.

"What are you doing there?" inquired the boy.

"What! Where! Oh I thought I was twenty feet up the tree." Only he said it with expletives it is unbecoming one of the Victorian age literally to quote.

Philipsburg Mail 9-2-27

It must be noted that it wasn't the individual trapper who was responsible for the deterioration of the Indian, but rather "the Company," the masterminds who sat back and reaped the profits. The mountain men and trappers actually worked *with* the Indians. They knew, understood, and respected them for what they were. Intermarriage was common-place. It was these first few whites, the ones who took the time to see what the Indian had to offer, that sadly became the exception to the rule. This brand of cultural exchange was not to be seen again for many years to come.

Chapter Seven

In an attempt to categorize the men who headed the major fur-trading companies, many adjectives come to mind: wealthy, brutal, energetic, ruthless, aggressive, well-bred, unscrupulous, shrewd, and parasitic. To say that all of these words apply in all cases would not only be unfair, but would also be untrue. However, to say that most applied to most would be fairly accurate.

In defense of these men it has been said that it was just the nature of their business that made them so; the killing and skinning of animals for something as frivolous as *fashion* requires people with hearts of stone. (Remember, there is a difference between fashion and necessary clothing.)

In protest of what they did, it can be stated objectively that the fur trading era was, generally speaking, the beginning of a series of low points for present-day Montana. Relations between the red and white men were, to say the least, somewhat strained. Meanwhile, valuable natural resources were being rapidly depleted for the advancement of a select few (and *they* lived thousands of miles away.) Who were these "few?"

Manuel Lisa and his backers, under that name of the Missouri Fur Company, were the first Americans to attempt to make millions in the northern Rockies and great plains. The year was 1807. The Company did well until fire, the Blackfeet and Gros Ventre, the War of 1812, and pressure from Canada's Hudson Bay and Northwest companies put them out of business.

In 1819 Lisa started the company again. At his death, in 1820, Joshua Pilcher took over. Again things went well, for a while. In 1823, as could have been expected, the Blackfeet again did them in, causing considerable loss of humans and pelts. The Company staggered to halt in 1830.

The Rocky Mountain Fur Company, led by General William H. Ashley, a Missouri businessman and politician, and Andrew Henry, one of Lisa's old partners, lasted some twelve years, from 1822 to 1834. It was then absorbed by the American Fur Company. It was Ashley and Henry who introduced the "free trapper" system.

Another company was the Columbia Fur Company. This company came into being when Canada's Northwest Company merged with the Hudson Bay Company. Angry and disenchanted Scotsmen of the Northwest Company moved south and formed the Columbia. It was this group which provided stiff competition with the American Fur Company on the upper Missouri. Competition was something the American did not tolerate. In 1827 the Columbia became the "upper Missouri" outfit of the American Fur Company. This "outfit" was led by Ken McKenzie, whose base of operation was Fort Union, located at the confluence of the Missouri and Yellowstone rivers.

Manuel Lisa of the Missouri Fur Company in 1810 sent Andrew Henry and Pierre Menard to the Three Forks with the objective of building a post at the point where the rivers come together. This was in hostile Blackfeet Country. The fort was actually built. The Blackfeet began a series of attacks, and twenty men were killed, among them George Drouillard, a veteran of the Lewis and Clark expedition. The siege lasted for months. The post was abandoned.

Ralph Henry, *Our Land Montana*

Fort Union, built at the confluence of the Yellowstone and Missouri Rivers, was built by Kenneth McKenzie's American Fur Company in the late 1820's. Trade there flourished until the early 1840's. Two Company men, Alexander Harvey and F.A. Chardon, were placed in charge during the last year. Both hated the Blackfeet bitterly. A war party of Blackfeet killed a pig belonging to the fort. The Indians moved on; some men from the fort pursued them, and fell into an ambush. One member of the fort party was killed. Back at the fort, revenge was plotted. They placed the fort's cannon, charged with 150 one-half ounce lead bullets, to cover the area in front of the main gate. They did not differentiate between hostile and friendly Blackfeet; the next Indian party to appear was a peaceful group intent on trade. The cannon was discharged. 21 Indians were killed outright; many were wounded.; nine later died. That night the whites held a drunken scalp dance in front of the fort. They mutilated the dead Blackfeet, whooped, danced around a fire in the manner of the Blackfeet scalp celebration. They realized that in all probability the fort would be under unceasing attack. They moved equipment downstream to the mouth of the Judith River. The Blackfeet burned Fort Union, which thereafter became known as Fort Brule, or Burnt Fort.''

Ralph Henry, *Our Land Montana*

Fur Trade Was Lush Business for Those in Upper Brackets But Skimpy for Free Trappers

Kenneth McKenzie, the king of the Missouri, who ruled in regal splendor at Fort Union, was one of the most colorful men of the fur trade. With as much display of the purple as was compatable with the wilderness, MacKenzie ruled the realm of the Missouri under the overlordship of this all-powerful American Fur Co., founded by John Jacob Astor. From the time of its establishment in 1832, this trading station remained the port of Montana until the rise of Fort Benton caused it to decline and ultimately to be dismantled.

McKenzie, year after year, defied all rivalry. Company after company was formed to capture a rich share of the trade with the Indians, only to succumb to McKenzie's diplomacy and superior energy. Without a charter, with no governmental grant to shut the door to competition, the American Fur Co. yet maintained its supremacy in the vast region of the Missouri as effectively as the Hudson's Bay Co., with the strong arm of the British empire at its back, domineered in western Canada and the Columbia river valley.

Business Was Good

To give you an idea of how fat the business was, it may be stated that the value of the St. Louis fur trade, most of which passed through Fort Union after that post was established, was valued at $200,000 to $300,000 annually from 1807 to 1847.

Yet the Indian and free trapper saw little of this golden flow. McKenzie, like all the others, operated on the theory that these individuals were born to be gyped. When the government slammed the door on liquor traffic with the Indians, it was too tough a pill for McKenzie to swallow. He established a still at Fort Union and there manufactured liquor to be used in the fur traffic.

And here, McKenzie, at times openly defiant of the orders of the United States government, was king. It was a veritable court that he maintained in the wilderness. At one time he ordered a complete suit of armor from England. He even had medals struck to award to his loyal followers.

"From the style in which he dressed I really thought he was a king," wrote Larpenteur in his "Forty Years a Trader On the Upper Missouri," in telling of his first meeting with McKenzie.

Yes, there were signs of wealth all about. The fur trade was a nice business, but not so good for the Indians and free trappers.

The golden harvest was comfined, for the most part, to the boys in the upper brackets. John Jacob Astor did very well for himself, and so did William H. Ashley, the Sublettes, Maj. Andrew Henry, Kenneth McKenzie and other kingpins in the business.

For the most part, however, actual producers, the Indians and the free trappers who hied forth and bagged the beaver and brought in the buffalo hides, had little to show for it but a few grand sprees a year and the accompanying hangover.

The fur trade was glorious for the boys at the top because their cash outlay for the rich pelts was mere peanuts compared to the fabulous profits they received in the eastern markets.

What the Indians and free trappers got in exchange for their pelts, in the main, was liquor, and cheap liquor at that, often diluted with liberal shots of tea or river water. The Indian quickly became a passionate devotee of firewater and, given a few snifters, was willing to hook everything in sight for more.

Indian bucks and squaws as well, likewise were passionately fond of trinkets and decorative cloth and would toss valuable pelts over the counter in exchange for cheap calico or junk jewelry that was scarcely worth carting home.

His Life Was Lonesome

The free trapper, too, was an easy victim of the traffic, and perhaps understandably so. Although the wild, undisciplined life held a distinct charm for him, for the most part he was lonely at best. He was out with his traps in all kinds of weather and all kinds of country and any moment a Blackfeet Indian might drill him with an arrow or rifle ball. He might go for months entirely alone or with one or two companions.

His fare was of the simplest, consisting largely of meat, and for shelter he had the open air and a blanket.

Small wonder it was, then, when it came time for the rendezvous, that he was chafing at the bit. The rendezvous offered the companionship joviality and departure from routine that his soul craved. It was a carnival, a three-ring circus, a rousing holiday.

He brought with him his year's catch and colossal thirst and he surrendered most of the former to satisfy the latter.

The fur business in Montana did not end with the advent of the gold rush, cattle industry, and homesteading. In the year 1937, Montana produced the following number of furs:

fox	2,872	$143,600
beaver	6,973	83,676
muskrat	4,053	27,476
mink	3,550	31,950
marten	305	2,490
Total		$292,192

The Hudson's Bay Company: "The coat of arms of the company bears the motto Pro Pellem Cuttem, meaning 'We seek the skin for the sake of the fur.' Three trade axes became standard price for one beaver skin from the Indians. Twenty skins bought a gun. One beaver skin secured half a pint of gunpowder, and the price for ten balls to fire in the gun was one beaver skin. The Indians loved chewing tobacco, twisted into long, thin, ropes; one beaver skin bought one foot of the material...The use of alcohol as a trade item was prohibited. The Company men found the Indians reacted viciously to alcohol, brawling at once not with weapons but with physical force that resulted in the biting off of ears and noses and fingers, as well as outright murder."

Ralph Henry, *Our Land Montana*

Last, and certainly not least, was the American Fur Company, founded by John Jacob Astor in 1808. Astor, a German immigrant, began as a fur merchant and later controlled the fur industry from "the trap to the coast — and all steps in between." At his death, the once-poor immigrant was said to have left his son the bulk of his $20,000,000. Astor was a brilliant businessman; his ethics were sometimes questionable, however. He did most anything necessary to achieve his goal of monopolizing the fur trade in the United States.

The Indian, not really understanding the entire situation (fashion, economics, politics), probably observed all this with a large degree of disgust. The next thing he might have thought was "soon they will want the buffalo, and when *they* are gone, who knows what they will *dig up*?"

80

BUFFALO to BEEF... (1850 — 1887)

Chapter One

It was Montana's seemingly limitless supply of fur bearing animals that first attracted the white man to the area. Depletion of the animal populations and changes in styles put an end to all of that. It wasn't long, however, before there was to be an even more irresistible lure: man's eternal aspiration and bane, gold. Gold-Gold-Gold. Get rich quick!

Wait a minute! It (gold) wasn't every man's aspiration. Wealth, to the people who lived here first, was measured in horses. Imagine for a minute the Indians' understandable confusion over gold's appeal. Beaver, which the whites took, could provide life's necessities: food, shelter, and clothing. But to see people facing hardships for which they were often ill-prepared, sacrificing family and friends, for chunks of cold, inedible metal? What kind of people were these whites? They came great distances, sometimes fought and died...for yellow metal?

Prior to these discoveries, little attention had been paid to Montana; it was considered a wasteland. Because of this wasteland notion, few roads or paths had been established for crossing, or even leading into, the vast treeless plains and heavily timbered mountains. The first pathfinders misjudged Montana's extremes in weather. To disregard Montana's winter cold and snow, spring floods, and summer droughts, and, in general, the rather forbidding conditions that *could* exist, is to invite trouble.

The American Fur Company, John Jacob Astor's empire, sought to control the highly profitable trade along the Missouri River by establishing a series of trading posts. (A more subtle way to do this was to *not* dispel the "wasteland" myth, thereby keeping settlers out.) The first of these in the Montana area was Fort Union at the confluence of the Missouri and Yellowstone rivers near the Montana border in North Dakota. Several other forts were built, but many were persuaded, by arrows, to close. By 1846, however, Fort Benton was established as a permanent townsite. Perhaps it was no accident that this site was selected, for even though the first steamboat, the Chippewa, didn't reach Fort Benton til 1860, it was as far upstream as a steamboat could safely navigate.

Many early settlers viewed Montana as that dreaded place that had to be crossed on their way to the Pacific Northwest. As early as 1853, Congress appropriated money for the exploration of railroad routes across the country; the northern route would cross Montana.

In 1853, General Isaac Stevens, governor of the Washington Territory, which included western Montana, sent Lt. John Mullen to check out this northern route. It was two years of remarkable work, crisscrossing the mountains, listing alternative routes, but Mullen proved to be the man for the job. Upon completion of this assignment, Mullen left for Washington, D.C. in hopes of getting more money to continue his explorations. But Jefferson Davis, later the President of the Confederate States of America, of the War Department told him he had spent too much on his first exploration. He could not get more money...unless it was for a military operation. After a lot of political haggling and a few timely (for Mullen that is) skirmishes with Indians in the area in question, (who were understandably opposed to white immigration), Mullen was able to convince Congress of the need for a "Military Road" into the Washington Territory.

"Where the Blackfoot River and the Clark Fork came together Mullan established Cantonment Wright to winter his men in 1861-1862. The Indians extended their own brand of hospitality to the road-builders by stampeding some fifty head of beef cattle and work oxen. Still other animals died by January of lack of forage. These problems did not keep Mullan from establishing work camps along the road to the west of his main camp so that he could resume work as soon as possible in the spring.

"It was cold. One man tried to pass between Cantonment Wright and a work camp. Overtaken by the night, he built a fire. His moccasins, which had become wet during the day, were frozen to his feet, and he could not get them off. Terrified, he returned through the woods to Cantonment Wright where he soaked his feet in a tub of warm water to thaw them out. Not only his moccasins but the flesh of his feet came off clear to the bone. The surgeon saved his life by amputating his legs above the knees."

The most reasonable solution seemed to be a wagon route, connecting steamboat traffic on the Missouri and Columbia rivers. (Remember, the first steamboats hadn't arrived at Fort Benton yet, but it seemed likely they soon would). Due to some violent opposition on the part of the Indians, the road didn't begin until the spring of 1859. Mullen and his men crossed swamps, deep snow, and heavily forested mountains, arriving at Fort Benton in August of 1860, some fifteen months later.

Mullen proved his spirit and stamina by testing the road, soon after its completion, by escorting fresh troops for the Washington and Oregon territories to Walla Walla. The trip took only fifty-seven days. Although it never was a major artery, and some parts of it were really never more than a path, sections of this route are still in use today.

Regular wagon trains travelling north from Salt Lake City and the Oregon Trail came to Montana as early as 1856. They followed the route established by Father DeSmet enroute to the Bitterroot Valley in 1841. One such wagon train brought James and Granville Stuart, who were later to find wealth in the state in the form of gold and cattle. Their gold discovery at Gold Creek would be followed by others elsewhere. Now people wouldn't merely be crossing the state, but instead they would be staying — at least for a while.

Another Oregon Trail offshoot headed *into* Montana was the Bozeman Trail. This was a short route from Fort Laramie to Bannack with easy grades and plentiful wood, forage, and water. However, it also happened to run through some prime buffalo hunting grounds of the Sioux and Cheyenne. Chief Red Cloud of the Sioux along with the Cheyenne made travel very risky along the route. You see, the Indians were well aware of the military preoccupation with the Civil War and the consequent lack of soldiers in the western territories. Three forts were established in 1866 to fortify the Bozeman Trail. But each had so few men that they had all they could do just defending themselves. Later that year, a group of eighty soldiers from Fort Phil Kearney, led by Captain William Fetterman were wiped out while attempting to rescue a wood cutting expedition which was being hassled by a band of Sioux. It seems that the leader of the

Sioux, a brave by the name of Crazy Horse, set an ambush Fetterman should have seen, but didn't. In a short order, eighty soldiers lay dead.

The U.S. government, because of its tenuous position, was forced into negotiations with Red Cloud and the Sioux, the Cheyenne, and the Arapaho. The Indians held firm on their demands for their right to the land. Finally the U.S. government agreed the land should be set aside for the permanent and exclusive use of the Indians. The Fort Laramie Treaty of 1868 is the only treaty between Indians and the U.S. government in which the government acknowledged defeat. White Montanans feared this would affect the development of the territory. They were assured, however, that the completion of the Union Pacific would provide the necessary incentive for another route north.

When the railroad was completed in 1869, the Corrine (Utah)-Virginia City Road became Montana's most widely used access to the outside world. The 550 mile journey, to Helena, was over easy grades and low mountain passes. Heavy snows in the winter months, however, shortened the freight season to only four round trips per year.

Another road into Montana was the "Northern Overland Route." This road was begun by upper midwesterners, many from Minnesota, to facilitate their travel to the gold of the Prickly Pear and Deer Lodge valleys. They felt it to be a logical route (a straight line across the Dakotas and Montana plains). So did Congress. The Sioux didn't agree. Anyway, what became known as the Minnesota-Montana Road followed closely the earlier routes of Stevens and Mullen. The Minnesota-Montana Road carried some eight wagon trains from 1862-1867, four of which were led by James Liberty Fish, frontiersman and organizer. They all travelled under military escort. Even so one was forced to turn back by the not-too-happy, or friendly, Sioux.

Meanwhile, back on the Missouri River, Fort Benton, because of its location, had become a commercial center. It was there that goods transported by steamboat were transferred to overland transportation bound for Helena, some hundred miles away.

This would be a good time to read *Flame on the Frontier* and *Indian Country* both by Dorothy Johnson.

The Missouri was a difficult river to navigate, a muddy, turbulent stream filled with snags and shifting sand bars. It presented a challenge to early travelers in their bullboats and dugout canoes, and the larger mackinaws and keelboats. Then came the steamboats with their shallow draft of only four feet and tall spars or poles with which the crew could "grasshopper" over sand bars. It was said they could "sail on a heavy dew and navigate a muddy road," but, really, even they could travel the Missouri only during the months of spring runoff and high water. They were wood burners, utilizing the mighty cottonwoods which grew along the banks.

Several enterprising groups tried to get a share of the action by competing with Fort Benton. An unbeatable combination of the elements, the Indians, and the influential merchants of Fort Benton prevented their success. One town, Gallatin City, was built upstream near present day Three Forks, ignoring the fact that steamboats could not get past the Great Falls of the Missouri. Good planning, huh? Grasshopping a sandbar is one thing; waterfalls is another.

Some prominent Helena merchants really didn't like "giving" money to the "go-betweens" at Fort Benton. So...they hatched a plan to unload the steamboats down river from Fort Benton. Poof! The town of Carroll was instantly established. This "promising business venture" lasted all of two seasons. From the beginning it was plagued with problems. First of all, the steamboat line proved unreliable. Quartz ore, brought there for shipment east, was delayed for a year. Secondly, the route south through the Judith Basin traversed areas of gumbo, which, after a rain, is similar to wet concrete. Also, a prairie fire destroyed the forage necessary for the draft animals. Thirdly, the route went directly through Indian territory. Military escorts were needed to protect travellers. The Fort Benton merchants, flexing their political muscles, blocked reassignment of troops to that area, thereby leaving overland traffic vulnerable to attack. And, finally, the town of Carroll itself was washed into the river, thereby ending the "promising business venture."

In addition to sending supplies to the gold fields of Montana, one-third of Fort Benton's freight went north to Fort Whoop-Up, on the Oldman River, in Alberta. At times, whiskey, for illegal sale to the Indians, was the biggest trade item. It was sold for tremendous profit, not only because of the Indians' willingness to pay outrageous prices for even a cupfull, but also because of the "watered-down" version that was sold.

GRASSHOPPING IS ONE THING, BUT THIS IS RIDICULOUS!

84

Railroads provided a cheaper, more reliable mode of transportation. With the completion of the Northern Pacific in 1883, and the Great Northern soon after, the steamboat era faded rapidly. By 1890 it was no more.

The area north of the Missouri River was wide open and lawless. Because of this, and the fact that the Hudson Bay Company didn't appreciate competition, Canada organized the Northwest Mounted Police, later the Royal Canadian Mounted Police, or "Mounties." Their job, among other things, was to enforce laws regarding the treatment of Indians written by the U.S. government. With small numbers and an *enlightened approach* they were able to successfully accomplish what the U.S. Cavalry could not. The lucrative trade on the Whoop-Up Trail ended abruptly in 1885 with the completion of the Canadian railway.

Within the Montana Territory, stage lines were set up between such points as Bannack, Virginia City, and Helena. Wells Fargo had a good foothold in the territory in the 1860's. By far the largest and most famous of the freight operations was the "Diamond 'R' Freighting Company, Receivers, Foreworders, and Freighters." At one time they employed hundreds of men and thousands of draft animals. The owners and operators of the outfit were C. A. B. Broadwater and his partners, E. G. Maclay, George Steel, and Matthew Carroll, the same fellows who unsuccessfully attempted the "promising business venture" of draining trade from Fort Benton. The arrival of the railroad ended these lines as large scale enterprises. Some shorter runs continued into the early 1900's.

'Tis hard for we practical people of the present day, ever busy in our search for the almighty dollar, to realize that less than fifty years ago this state was the home of the buffalo and the Indian, that our well tilled fields had then never felt the hoof of horses or oxen nor the bite of the plow shear. Now we have every comfort and convenience that modern civilization can suggest, while in those days a man's hands made all of his luxuries and comforts. We travel quickly over the state in an auto or a Pullman while our fore-bears made the tedious journeys in prairie schooners drawn by oxen. It is easier for us to go to New York now than it was for them to go from Bozeman to Helena. Those were days of hardship and struggle, days when death shot his arrows all too freely, yet they were days that made men, and it was these men who laid the foundation for the Montana of today.

The following interesting story of early Montana, was told me by John McDonald, one of the early settlers of Gallatin valley.

"We left Des Moines, Iowa, early in the spring of 1864. In our party there were 120 wagons, all told, but they were not much like such a train would be at the present day. Some of us drove horses, four to the wagon, others had oxen and still others had a mixture of both. Not a few of the party had a yoke of oxen, then a yoke or two of cows and then another yoke of oxen in the lead. Some of these cows were dry, others fresh. In Nebraska we followed the Platte river, crossing it twice on the journey. These crossings were slow tedious affairs, always fought with more or less anxiety on account of Indians."

"Many members of the party were killed by the Indians from time to time on the way west. After leaving the Platte we started out through Wyoming striking the Yellowstone river not far from where is now the town of Billings. We followed the Yellowstone west, and finally came upon Shields river. About this time we met John Bridger going east with a party of settlers who were entirely discouraged and returning to former homes. This party going east was larger than ours going west. We were very discouraged, but Bridger cheered us up, leaving the eastern bound train and offering to guide us to the Gallatin valley. We went down the Shields river and entered the Gallatin valley through what is now known as Bridger Canyon. At Bozeman there was already a small settlement. The trip had consumed about four months from the time we left Des Moines."

"Some of us got to work and raised a few things that late summer and as there was an abundance of game we got through the winter very nicely. Deer and elk were everywhere and there still were a few buffalo. By the next spring we had all gotten fairly well located.

"We never had a great deal of trouble with the Indians in the valley. At one time a band camped near where Logan now is located. They rounded up all the loose horses in the valley and after killing a couple of ranchers, they left in the direction of the Madison. Other parties were seen from time to time, but they rarely molested us."

"When we arrived in the Gallatin valley it had not be surveyed and so we were free to take what land we wanted up to 160 acres."

"We raised oats, wheat and hay, the latter being very thick in the natural state. The freighters bought most of the grain and hay that we had to sell. Prices then went up even higher than at the present day. I have known flour to be $100 per sack and butter $1.50 per pound. I traded one of my teams of horses for a yoke of oxen and a yoke of cows. Land could be bought very cheap, especially after the railroad had picked out its odd sections of railroad land for varying prices that would not average over $2 per acre. This same land is selling at $100 today."

Northwestern Stockman and Farmer

BENEATH the LAND

This would be a nice time to watch *Gold: Finders and Seekers* from Preservation Ventures, Inc.

87

Chapter Two

The presence of gold in Montana streams was known prior to the great gold rushes of the 1860's. This fact, however, was overshadowed by the "finds" in California, Colorado, and other areas of the West. Montana actually had to *wait its turn* to be exploited! But not for long.

In the spring of 1858, brothers James and Granville Stuart found traces of gold at, where else, Gold Creek, between present-day Drummond and Garrison. The real Montana rush, however, began with John White's discovery at Grasshopper Creek. It was the summer of 1862, and they came. From the crowded fields of California, Colorado, Nevada, from Lewistown, Idaho, and from goodness only knows, but come they did. The town of Bannack sprang up overnight, some twenty miles west of today's Dillon.

With this rush, the stage was set for discoveries of Montana's golden treasure throughout the state. Prospectors ranged all over and over all the mountains of Montana in hopes of striking it rich. Many did; gold was found in numerous areas. The richest and largest of these finds was in Alder Gulch, discovered somewhat by accident in May, 1863. A small party of prospectors were turned away from their original destination by Crow Indians. En route back to Bannack....Alder Gulch. Thousands of prospectors flocked there, causing Virginia City and Nevada City, among others, to spring up. The next five years saw an estimated 30-40 million dollars' worth of gold produced.

The Helena area saw discoveries at Prickly Pear, Last Chance Gulch and Confederate Gulch, the second richest concentration of gold in the world. Last Chance Gulch, around which present-day Helena grew, was second, only to Alder Gulch in gold produced. Ranking third was Confederate Gulch. Central Montana got into the picture with strikes in the Judith, Absaroka, and Little Rocky Mountains.

Placer mining was the most common method for mining the gold. It worked by allowing gravity to separate the gold from the dirt and rocks. As mountains gradually eroded due to wind and water, gold, once hidden in veins deep inside, washed downstream. Of course, with the gold was dust and rock; hundreds of tons of it. Prospectors removed the dirt from the gold by washing away the lighter materials. (You see, gold is quite heavy.) The least complicated method was simply to use a pick and shovel to loosen dirt, then wash it with a stream of water in a small, flat-bottomed pan and wait for the gold to drop to the bottom, providing there was any in the pan to begin with. This method was used by many because it required very little investment. The only drawback was that it allowed a prospector to work only a small area at a time.

During the first five years, mining operations at Alder Gulch produced between $30 and $40 million in gold. During the following years, Alder Gulch produced: 1875, $424,628, 1885, $270,000, 1900, $55,232.

Last Chance Gulch operations, in Helena, produced over $3 million in gold from one vein alone during the years 1864-1876.

Confederate Gulch produced in estimated $12 million in gold during the most active years of its operations.

Cedar Creek gold mining produced between $4 and $5 million in gold.

Copper magnate W.A. Clark estimated in 1876 that Montana's mines to date had yielded over $90 million in gold.

Within days after Alder Gulch was discovered, a "Town Company" was organized to provide a form of government. A short time later, over 20,000 people had flooded into the area.

In order to work larger claims, one had to invest more time (like 30 hours per day) or money, in order to buy the necessary lumber and hardware to construct a "rocker." The rocker was loaded with dirt, then rocked while water was added. The dirt washed out; hopefully the gold stayed. A still larger operation was the "sluice." It required, in most cases, more water and manpower. It was a trough of varied lengths (some up to 1,000 feet) with sheet metal at the lower end containing small holes. If loaded up and washed out, with luck, gold appeared.

The last method was used in only a few areas such as Confederate Gulch where the concentration of gold brought back enough to make the investment worthwhile. The method was hydraulic mining, whereby high pressure hoses were incorporated to blow away large areas of stream beds, causing quite severe environmental damage. The water separated soil from rocks and pushed it through a series of "sluices." This method, when used in dry areas, called for diverting water for great distances through ditches and flumes. The investment was great. The return was greater.

Undoubtedly Montana's gold rush would have been greater had not the U.S. been involved in a Civil War. But it would never have been like California's rush of '49, simply because of its location. Where's Montana? Even so, by 1866, Montana had enough people mining to place it second in U.S. gold production, bowing only to California. Soon, however, Nevada's

Comstock Lode dropped Montana to third. Montana produced millions in gold for several years to come   bottoming out in 1883. The subsequent increase was due to gold mined as a result of the copper and silver operations.

More important to Montana than the gold that was extracted was the fact that the gold rush brought the first significant influx of whites to the area. The great hope of tracing a few dust particles to a "mother lode" or vein of gold was a pretty strong attraction.

The typical mining town was a real "mix bag." That is, they were made up of people, mostly young men, from all over, north, south, east and west. Their common denominators were: they usually weren't skilled in any particular craft (thus explaining the quality of construction in many towns); they were poor; they were constantly on the move for "easy diggin's" (due to a lack of skill and equipment); and, they worked long hours.

Because they were out to make it big, they were a group more interested in what *they* were doing than what their neighbors were doing. This, and the fact that they constantly moved brought about an interesting facet of Western folklore: the nickname. It wasn't unusual to know people only as One-Eyed Pete, Peg Leg Tom, Whiskey Bill, Old Ned, Itchy, and Blackie. To verify the use of such colorful names in mining towns, one need only keep an ear open in present-day Butte.

Men predominated on the mining frontier. Early in the winter of 1862-63, out of a total approximate population (white) of 670, 59 were "respectable" females. But women came in appreciable numbers after 1865 as more "family men" moved to the area.

No study has been made of the important role played by the Chinese in the Montana gold fields. Practically all the Chinese who arrived at that time left, leaving no records of their existence. They reworked the claims from which the whites had already taken the surface gold. As elsewhere, there was considerable hostility toward them because of their willingness to work hard and long for "a pittance." There were thought to be about 800 Chinese in Montana in 1869. Laws were passed which restricted their activity, and taxes were levied specifically on them. For example, a tax was levied on "men operating laundries." Since the only men operating laundries were Chinese, this was obviously discriminatory.

A History of Montana, *Merill Burlingame and K. Ross Toole, New York, Lewis Historical Publishing Company, 1957*

Bill Fairweather, who led the mining party which discovered Alder Gulch, one of Montana's richest claims, died penniless at the age of 39.

The miners tolerated most everything and everyone. Most everyone, as long as they weren't black, or red, or yellow. There really weren't many newly-freed blacks around. Indians not only weren't appreciated because they didn't understand gold fever, but also because they had a tendency to deter the miner's progress at times. (It's hard to "mine" and defend yourself at the same time). The Chinese were a different story. (Chinese in Montana?) Not only did the Chinese "look different," but they had strange, "foreign" customs. What was worse, they worked for less money than anyone else in the camps. (Maybe it took less money to be "rich" in China?) In the majority of cases they were allowed to engage in what the whites considered degrading, non-mining jobs. Some opened restaurants; some opened laundries. Others worked claims that had already been "worked over," another example of working for less.

There's no doubt that the displeasure shown the Chinese by whites was due to conscious racial prejudice, but underlying that was the fear of the "beginning of the end." The Chinese, not known to be wasteful, would come into a "washed over" area to pick up what was left. To those whites still left in the area this meant that the diggin's were getting slim. Time to move on. To blame the Chinese for the lack of gold remaining was as crazy as blaming them for the sun going down. No one likes to see a good thing come to an end but....Maybe the whites viewed them as vultures who picked the bones of skeleton claims, while they in turn were hoping for them to spring back to life.

The Chinese, establishing laundries, panned the dirt washed from the miner's clothes to recover gold dust.

Our Land Montana, *Ralph Henry, Helena, State Publishing Co., 1963*

This would be a good time to read *Montana Pay Dirt* by Muriel Volle.

Where there is money to be made, there are those who come to work, and those who come to steal. Montana being a big place, there were people who came and did things in a big way (they still do), outlaws included. One such character was Henry Plummer, a good looking, intelligent sort of fellow. He was liked by all, , with the possible exception of those whom he killed. Due to his occupation (murderer and robber), he moved around a good deal. He drifted from California and Nevada to Idaho and finally Montana (note these locations are all mining states) where he decided to stay permanently. His gang of "road agents;" (known to each other as "the Innocents" because of their password, "I am innocent" — also a style of beard and a type of knot in their neckerchief) arrived in force in 1861. This band of road agents found their share of gold and silver in the pouches of unsuspecting miners or on the stages between Bannack, Virginia City, and Salt Lake City. People on the road between Virginia City and Bannack from mid-1862 through December of 1863 literally placed their lives in the hands of the agents. During this time, the Innocents killed over one hundred people.

These "easy diggin's" were made even easier after none other than slick-talking, good-looking Henry Plummer became the sheriff of Bannack, *by election,* in 1863. Quite naturally a "respected lawman" would know inside information concerning shipments of gold and such. Plummer hired as deputies two of his agents and one honest man, D.R. Dillingham. Dillingham was killed less than a year later after exposing the other two as "road agents." The deputies were "tried" and set free. They fled immediately.

To fully understand the "road agent business" it is necessary to look at the situation on a different scale. At the time of all these goings-on, Montana was not yet even a territory. Many of the mining towns of the western states were plagued with lawlessness. It was due in part to "the system." Federal authority didn't reach the remote towns that dotted the mountains of the West. Justice in these rough mining camps was the "miner's court," which began in the California camps. The citizens of a "mining district" would elect a "judge," a "recorder," (for mining claims), and a sheriff. Trials could either be heard by a

jury or decided by a vote of all present, and, of course, the "judge" presided. Attorneys were permitted. Sounds good! But...because a jury was more easily intimidated, trial by jury was the preferred method of accused persons with "Innocent" backing. Bannack and Virginia City had trouble with this system from the beginning. The "judge" (understandably) was as frightened as the jury; justice was a farce.

Finally, honest men had their say at the trial of George Ives, a Plummer man accused of a brutal murder. At the four-day trial (December 19-23), 1863) in Nevada City, people witnessed an able and brave prosecutor, Colonel Wilber Sanders (no, not the chicken man). He convinced the jury not only of Ives' guilt (which carried the death penalty), but also to carry out the sentence on the same day so as not to allow the people's "minds to be changed" through intimidation. Ives was hanged less than an hour later, in full view of a crowd of innocent-and "Innocent"-men.

Soon after the hanging, another secret organization was founded. This one, too, was based on California precedent. Its purpose was to find a quicker and safer method (as opposed to the court system) of *eliminating* the road agent problem. The fact that it was the "off-season" for the miners (ice doesn't work well in sluice boxes) aided in getting men involved; the miners normally preoccupied with work could participate. The super-secret group set up regulations and by-laws and an executive committee to determine its actions. The group was so secret that even now much of their activities are still clouded in mystery and legend. It *is* known, however, that according to their by-laws "the only punishment that shall be inflicted by this committee is death," (which didn't leave a lot of alternatives).

The Vigilantes, as they came to be called, were faithful to their by-laws, for between January 4 and February 3, 1864, twenty-four men, including Plummer, found themselves at the end of a rope, all having neglected to flee the "territory." By "territory" is meant the areas the vigilantes travelled to "get their man" which was as far away as Hell Gate (Missoula).

Controversy surrounds the actions of these men, who took justice into their own hands (by no means the only time in Montana's history). For over a hundred years Montanans have

This would be a nice time to watch *Her Last Hope* from MSU Film and Television Center.

sung the praises of these unknown few, for they saw the problem and provided the solution. Even today, the Montana Highway Patrol wears their secret symbol, (3-7-77) on their shoulder patches and cars. The controversy lies in deciding whether their "solution" was the right one. They by-passed their own legal code, the miner's court. In doing away with the "bad guys," they inadvertently hanged a few men who *really* were "innocent."

This would be a good time to read *Shallow Diggin's* by Jean Davis.

Gold Discovery Followed Jest

GRANVILLE STUART BELIEVED JOKE ABOUT ORIGIN OF NUGGET

MORMON WAR FORCED PARTY INTO MONTANA

Montana Pioneer Witnessed Christmas Presentation in 1857 and Then Went to Gold Creek in Spring and Made Great Discovery.

A frontiersman's jest at a Christmas gathering in a cabin in the Beaverhead valley in 1857, brought the discovery of the first real gold field in Montana, which turned the eyes of the world to the then vague hand of the shining mountains. It was related by the widow of the pioneer, whose party unearthed the first yellow metal at Gold creek.

Likewise, the mormon war, in Utah, spreading terror among immigrants, was a factor in the discovery, for it sent the Stuart party, on the way from California to Virginia, into Montana. Winter set in and they were forced to remain in Montana, then Idaho territory.

Camped in Beaverhead valley at a place which is near where Dillon is now located, the few nappers and traders of that valley gathered at the cabins of Captain Richard Grant, a former trader of the Hudson's Bay Co., to celebrate that memorable Christmas of 1857.

Mined in California

It was during this meeting that the incident which led to the discovery of the first gold field in the state, was enacted. Robert Hereford gave to Captain Grant a piece of gold with a value of about 10 cents as a Christmas present, saying that he had mined it on a certain creek in the Montana territory. This was the incident which led the Stuarts the following spring to the stream later called Gold creek, where they discovered gold in great quantities May 26, 1858.

SUN RIVER GOLD RUSH OF 1886

EXTREMELY COLD WEATHER DID NOT STOP HUNDREDS OF PROSPECTORS IN STAMPEDE

Thirty-five degrees below zero and a foot of snow on the ground could not stop the Sun river stampede in January, 1866, which started on a gold strike rumor and netted many gold seekers severe suffering as its only reward.

It all started when John McClellan, the discoverer of the diggings on "McClellan" gulch, after selling his claims, set out to find another. Whether he made a strike is not known but the impression of many miners at Helena in January, 1866, was that he had. McClellan had come to town for supplies from his camp in the Sun river country about 140 miles away. After paying his bill in gold he casually mentioned to a friend that he had just found what he wanted or words to that effect. Others made the interpretation that "Mac" had hit it again and the stampede started.

On a typical "wild goose chase" went between 1,200 and 1,500 men in quest of gold even though the weather was around zero. No gold was found and to increase the hardship of the miners, many of whom had come practically unprepared, a blizzard set in. With the temperature between 35 and 40 degrees below zero, a rush was made by several hundred miners for St. Peter's mission, among the Blackfeet, where the Rev. Father Imoda threw open the mission buildings.

Food, shelter and medical attention were given by the Rev. Father Imoda and the Rev. Father Ravalli.

But two deaths were reported and those were due to exposure.

Chief Little Dog of the Blackfeet nation was also busy offering help and shelter to a few stragglers who reached his lodge.

BOLD PROSPECTOR SCARED TO DEATH

Old Highland Road, Between Alder Gulch and Silver Bow, Once Much Traveled Scene of Strike, Made While Digging Grave of Coyote Bill.

"COYOTE BILL" ESTLINER FOLLOWED HIS HUNCH ALONG SHUNNED TRAIL

When "Coyote Bill" Estliner, in 1872, permitted his desire for gold to overcome his superstitious dread of a shunned mountain trail, the way was paved for the discovery of one of the many rich gold deposits of Montana. But "Coyote Bill" did not claim the reward. Some say he was frightened to death.

The old Highland Trail ran between Alder Gulch and Silver Bow, and served as an artery for the stream of goldseekers and trade that passed between these spots when Highland Gulch attained prominence as a gold camp, soon after Alder became famous as a producer. Today among old-timers and their descendants, the Highland Trail is not thought of as one of the early avenues of travel; it stands out as a gloomy mountain corner where many black murders were committed, and where swift vengeance overtook many outlaws.

The trail traversed hills and valleys and passed through gorges and clefts, attaining lofty elevations and then dropping through dense forests under frowning rocky peaks. It was in one of these woods that a series of brutal murders was committed. Here the Vigilance committee met in secret conclave, and here murderers expiated their crimes. So black was the history of this trail that a cut-off was built and travelers shunned the old passes. Worst of all was the spot called Bone Ridge.

John Estliner, who soon became known as "Coyote Bill" came with the crowd that crossed the plains from Missouri in 1871. He went to Virginia City. His prospector friends tacked his nickname to him because they insisted he didn't mine as a white man should, but bored into the ground coyote fashion. "Coyote Bill" had his own ideas about mining. He never put in timber props in his tunnels.

"Coyote Bill" got to studying over the situation in Montana as time rolled on and he failed to make a strike, and he decided that the reason gold had never been found on the Highland Trail was that no one ever went there. He tried to interest some of his friends in joining him in a prospecting expedition to Bone Ridge. One day he disappeared. He never came back.

Tom Benjamin, his partner, became uneasy after a time and rode over to Moose creek to make inquiries. Finding no information he set about to organize a rescue party. It was hard work, as soon as volunteers learned that the party was to search for "Coyote Bill" on Bone Ridge, they resigned. Finally Benjamin and "Brockey Jake," the only man who stuck, went into the hills and hunted for weeks. A few joined them for a time, but when winter drove them to shelter, "Coyote Bill" was given up for lost.

The following summer a party of prospectors pitched camp on the old Highland Trail at the "Upper Fork," so called by reason of the abandonment of the "Bone Ridge" trail at this point, and the intersection with it of the cut-off.

One of the party had found indications of a lead just below the tall cliff that casts a shadow across the narrow gulch at this point, and the others agreed to remain a few days to try their luck, in following the "float rock" to the lead.

Two of the number, James Truesdel and Ike Parker, bent their energies in the direction of the cliff, and by slow stages worked their way through brush and boulders to the base of the sentinel mound, and there they discovered "Coyote Bill's" body. It was in a sitting position, braced against a tree, face towards the base of the rock. In front of the closed eyes was a heap of human bones, including three skulls. It was the verdict of the jury that Bill had met his death in fright.

"Let's get the other boys, and we'll bury poor old Bill right here," said Truesdel, and his partner agreed. Accordingly the men set to work digging a grave, intending to bury the bones of the other unfortunates with Bill's body.

The men worked in relays and soon were down to bed rock.

"What's that?" cried Parker, who picked up a piece of rock thrown out of the hole.

The work ceased that all hands might inspect Parker's discovery. It was a piece of quartz literally peppered with gold. Another piece was picked up, and another. Forgetful of the melancholy duty they had begun, the men gave vent to their exuberance and shouted in joy, for they had "struck it."

The hole was driven down to the rich croppings of a gold lead, one of the richest ever discovered in Montana, the records of the county clerk designating it as the "Bone Ridge quartz lode claim."

"Coyote Bill" rests under a marble shaft in the cemetery at Virginia City.

Chapter Three

At this particular point in Montana's history most people were concerned with the mineral resources the state had to offer. However, prospectors, like everyone else, needed food, shelter, and clothing. Due to this simple "fact of life," Montana's secondary resources experienced at least limited development.

Abundant timber in the mining areas was a boon to the miner. Wood was used extensively in the mining process: rockers, sluices, and flumes (aqueducts), not to mention the rough-cut planks that made up the miners' shacks. Seeing the opportunity to put gold into their pockets *indirectly,* some miners jumped into the lumber business. Whether they were shrewd businessmen or just crumby miners isn't known. Anyway, the first sawmills should have been successful, especially after mining evolved into the ore-gathering phase, which required timbers as supports in the shafts. Even if the lumber industry wasn't involved in the mining business, in every settlement throughout the territory the demand for lumber existed for use in homes, businesses, and churches.

As for food, most of it was shipped in from other territories. Vegetables, a mining camp scarcity, were grown locally. It was during this peiod that Missoula acquired its nickname, "The Garden City." It was so-called because of the enormous vegetable and flower gardens in the then   center of town, today's East Front Street. Grass was grown in limited amounts. Native grasses provided adequate forage for cattle and sheep.

The agricultural riches of eastern Montana had barely been touched. Range cattle fed on the rich grasslands, as did the draft animals of the wagon trains hauling supplies along the trails. The rather spare timber along these routes was used up, as firewood. The cottonwoods along the riverbanks fell prey to the steamboats, as fuel.

Despite the territory's rapid growth, it was an urban growth. Miners were "town folk." Farmers didn't provide the bulk of the first population as they did in settling much of the country. For this reason treasures beneath the land, were, at this time, more sought after than those growing out of the land.

Food in the mining camps — staples were bread, bacon, beans and coffee. Eggs, butter, fruit, fresh meat and fish were available in the summer. Prices tended to be high since most things had to be shipped in from the Salt Lake area.

Recreational activities included horse racing and prize fighting, which usually provoked gambling, as well as card playing and drinking.

Churches, Masonic organizations and social clubs were also in existence. Sunday was the day when many of these activities would take place. Stores were open on Sundays.

Dwelling units included cabins, tents, brush wiliups. As mining activity continued and some prospered, frame houses were built.

J.K. Miller, a 17 or 18 year old growing up in Virginia City, kept a diary which is part of the Montana Historical Society manuscript collection. From his viewpoint, the mining frontier was not so much a place of violence and disreputable activities as it was a place offering French lessons, dances, sleigh rides, and clubs such as the "Literary Association."

Chapter Four

Although a great portion of eastern Montana's legacy has been the cattle industry, Western Montana was its birth place.

The essential element in the early growth of Montana's cattle industry was "free grass." That's *free* grazing. The idea that there was "something for nothing" was the lure of eastern Montana. (Any economist can tell you that nothing is "free," e.g. fresh air costs X amount of *no* industry or, conversely, polluted air costs whatever it takes, in dollars, to clean it up.) The exceptions to the rule were John Owen, Bitterroot Valley trader, and the Jesuits. Each kept a small number of livestock.

The first one credited with recognizing a good deal (free grass) when he saw one was Richard Grant, a fur trader. Together with his sons Johnny and James, they amassed a substantial herd by trading cattle with the "tourists" on the Oregon Trail in the early 1850's. The going rate was a couple of trail-weary head from the tourists for one, healthy Montana-grazed head from Grant. It didn't take long to double a herd at that ratio. And all due to free grazing. Needless to say it wasn't long before others jumped on the bandwagon and began cattle businesses of their own. The "free grass," man's greed, and ignorance or arrogance concerning the weather and climate were to spell disaster in later years.

So...as you can see, the cattlemen were here before the miners. In fact, James Fisk (the fellow who brought immigrants to western Montana from the upper Midwest) mentioned that in 1863 the Grant spread had several thousand head of beef.

For some, notably Conrad Kohrs and Phillip Lovell, mining just wasn't their "thing." The cattle business was. Kohrs had been a butcher prior to his "gold fever" days, so the transition from cutting beef to raising beef came relatively easily. It must have, for in 1865 he had bought out Johnny Grant at Deer Lodge.

What was it that drove these men to raising cattle in a remote part of the country? Demand, pure and simple. At the time, thousands of miners were flooding into Montana. Just as the lumber industry grew with mining, so did the cattle business. Miners had to eat. So did the soldiers that occupied forts in the area. It was the right time and place to be in the cattle business. Thousands of people were coming in, everyone with a mouth and a stomach. To make things even better, there was little competition....But this wasn't to last long.

Word of free grass and hungry people passed quickly among outside cattlemen. One of the first was the partnership of Poindexter and Orr out of California. By the late 1860's they maintained one of the territory's largest cattle-sheep outfits. The year 1865 saw Montana's first influx of Texas Longhorns, a lanky breed first raised for leather and tallow rather than beef, but with free grass, raised for meat. They were brought in by one Dan Floweree. The next year saw Nelson Story bring more. Even with these Longhorns the Montana stock was primarily shorthorn from the Pacific coast. By now there were enough cattle in Montana for the 1865 territorial legislature to, by law, require outfitters to record and use "brands."

This growth continued til a combination of departing gold-miners and increasing supply drove prices down. This in turn made it necessary for Montana cattlemen to seek other buyers for their beef. Where would they go? North, up the old Whoop-Up Trail. (Mounties ate, so did the men working on the Canadian Pacific Railroad.) South, to lower Wyoming to the camps of the nearly-completed Union Pacific Railroad. (American railroad workers ate also). East (later in the 1870's) to the miners in the Black Hills or railroad workers working on the Northern Pacific, and west...either they didn't eat beef or they had enough of their own.

What made open-range cattle grazing so profitable in the early years was that eastern Montana prairie grew two lush native grasses: tall "blue joint," in the more fertile areas, and shorter "gramma" or "bunch" grass in the more arid regions. These grasses had sustained millions of buffalo for hundreds of years; unfortunately, the over-grazing which took place from 1880-1887 in many areas seriously affected the growth of this native grass.

Early Cow Camp in Present Day Dawson County

Courtesy Montana Historical Society

Trailing the Herd in Winter

Courtesy Montana Historical Society

This would be a good time to read *Before Barbed Wire* and *The Frontier Years* both by Mark Brown and W.R. Felton.

Anyway, by the early 1870's cattlemen were feeling the pressure from farmers and dairy people also in competition for land. This *encroachment* on *their* once "free" grass caused overcrowded and overgrazed conditions on the land remaining. Where would they go? Well...first they went north to the Sun River, a move pioneered by Conrad Kohrs, but soon followed in 1871 by Robert Ford who settled near Fort Shaw. Pressure continued, so did the cattlemen, across the Missouri, Smith, and Judith rivers, on to the Musselshell. Robert Coburn set up his famous Circle C Ranch on Flatwillow Creek in 1877. Kohrs and partner John Bielenberg were again soon on the scene. Next section to come under the hoofs of cattle instead of buffalo was the forage-rich Judith Basin. The cattlemen were angry at the thought that President Grant might lock up the Judith Basin as a non-productive reservation for the Crow Indians. President Grant dropped his plan. The Crows stayed south and east of the Yellowstone River. With that "problem" solved, the Judith Basin quickly filled. Some of the "biggies" in the area were Conrad Kohrs (of course), Granville Stuart, and James Fergus.

Hey, wait a minute! What about the "woolies," you know, sheep? When did they get here? Well, as with the cattle, Jesuits had the first, at St. Ignatius during the 1850's. The first flock of consequence was brought by a partnership of John Bishop and Richard Reynolds in 1869. It was they who herded some 1500 sheep into the Beaverhead Valley from Oregon. From this flock came the fleece that composed Montana's first wool shipment.

Montana's sheep industry was rather insignificant in 1870 with only some 2,000 recorded. It remained this way four or five years, but then...Baa, Baa. Enter A. W. Kingsley, Charles Cook, and William and John Smith. Montana investors also saw the potential in the woolies, and soon jumped into the picture. Men like John Healy, Thomas Cruse, and J. T. Murphy put up the money and let "sheepmen" take care of the actual sheep end of the business. With this "explosion" in the industry, by 1880 Montana had over 275,000 sheep. By 1886 "the peak" of the pre-barbed wire boom, there were nearly 100,000,000 sheep. One could probably guess that kind of growth had to mean the cattle and sheep industries worked well together. For the most part this was true, but it wasn't at all unlike Granville Stuart and a few others to send the cow-hands out to poison sheep dogs. In Stuart's case, it wasn't so much that he disliked sheep but rather that he loved cattle. Whether it be sheepmen, sheep, redmen, buffalo, or white settlers he didn't want to see any of them get in the way of his beloved cattle. And if they did...he'd take care of the situation quickly, thoroughly.

Say, how did these fellows all know the grass land would be suitable for herds of cattle and sheep? Easy...if the northern Great Plains could handle countless millions of buffalo for thousands of years, certainly cattle and sheep could thrive, there, too. And this on the area Major S. H. Long had called the "Great American Desert!"

Say, what about the buffalo? Where did they go? There couldn't have been enough room for cattle, sheep, and buffalo, too. Exactly! Something had to go. Let's see, the cattlemen owned the cattle. Sheepmen owned sheep. And, even though the Indian was totally dependent on them, they did not *own* the buffalo. (Maybe they should have registered buffalo herds or domesticated them.) It was easy to see that the buffalo's days were numbered.

It can be said that the Indian did not "lose" his battle with the whites; his food supply was wasted, making surrender unavoidable. Whether this was a conscious effort on the part of the white man merely another game of making a "quick buck" was never really decided. What we do know is that the buffalo, or, more properly, the American Bison, the magnificent shaggy beast of North America, sometimes called dumb or ornery, was slaughtered unmercifully. Call it business, call it sport, call in an environmental tragedy, call it what you will. The one-time symbol of the Great Plains raises dust no more, except within the confines of places such as the Moiese National Bison Range, other government refuges, and some private livestock concerns interested in marketing them.

There is a degree of irony in the slaughter of North America's largest mammal. The Indian never went hungry with buffalo available. Neither did they have to put up hay for winter feeding. The buffalo was the ideal plains animal. In an attempt to make cattle more suited to the range or create a new beast that would be, cross-breeding has taken place with the results being the "cattelo" or "beefalo." This cross is a sort of strange looking beast, and, as with everything else, it is controversial.

97

As to the actual number of buffalo killed it is impossible to say. It can be reasonably stated that in 1870 there were still ten to twenty *million* of the perhaps sixty million that had lived in North America in 1500. By 1883 the number was down to between one and two *hundred.* That means a daily average of roughly 3200 animals killed per day, for 12 years (or five per minute of daylight).

Meanwhile, as the plains emptied of redmen and buffalo, more and more grasslands opened to the cattle/sheep industry. There was a twist, however, for by 1880 "outsiders" and even "foreigners" were investing in the "free grass" lands of the West. These new investors brought with them the *corporate system.* That is to say that they had many investors in each outfit, which made for greater herd size. The majority of these corporations came from the Southwest (Texas, Nevada), and the Midwest (Missouri and Nebraska), but a few came from as far east as New England. Foreign investments came mainly from the British Isles. However, the most prominent investor from abroad was Pierre Wibaux of France. Pierre, born of wealthy parents, decided to try his hand at ranching in the "Great American West." Anyway, in Montana in 1883, he accumulated a sizeable spread along Beaver Creek. Nearly wiped out once, he rebuilt his herd to seventy or eighty thousand. The town of Wibaux still appreciates him, for without him their town might still bear its earlier name of Mingusville.

Another interesting Frenchman was Antoine-Andre-Marie-Vincent Manca de Vallombrosa, or, simply, the Marquis de Mores. After marrying the daughter of a wealthy New York banker at Cannes, France, he began working in his father-in-law's bank. While at the bank he learned a lot about the cattle business, a lot, but not enough. He founded the town of Medora, North Dakota, naming it after his wife. (It lies thirty miles east of Wibaux.) He didn't care to ranch, just slaughter and send beef to market in refrigerated cars. After three years of this and many other schemes (some ingeneous, some so-so), he ran himself and his father-in-law into debt to the tune of one and one-half million dollars. Oh, well, back to France for the Marquis.

Anyway, to the Montanans, the majority of the "foreign" investors were American, and they were Texans. Texans were those people who ran those lank Longhorns. You see, most Montanans were raising shorthorn stock, many with graded bulls. They saw the Longhorn as an oddity. Skinny, but they soon fattened up on Montana grasses. The Montanans didn't like the idea of these low-grade cattle overgrazing the plains, much less the problem of interbreeding, which lowered the quality of Montana beef.

From the moment Texas cattle set hoof on Montana soil Montanans and Texans were at odds with each other. In a way it is understandable, but in other ways the Texans can't be blamed. Not only did the Texans have a strange breed of cattle, but they were here to "graze and get out." They didn't breed them up here, but merely fattened them up for the market place. Their investment in Montana was neglibible. (In terms of permanency, how much investment does a person make at a campsite today, while on vacation?) They made no bones about it. They were in it for the money and were here for the free grass. However, they had "different ways" and "dressed different." And, to boot, they wanted a permanent right of way from Texas to Montana put aside from settlers, Indians, whatever, so they could use Montana as the "North 40." Shoot! They never got their right of way, *formally,* but continued to drive cattle to Montana until the mid-1890's. The open range of Montana continued to fill at an amazing rate. From 1880-1886 the peak of the open range era, the number of cattle increased by over 50% to 675,000.

If the comparison could be made, it was kind of like the Montanans were in a rowboat they didn't own. They were comfortable and had room left when 25 Texans wanted to get in. What could Montanans say?...They didn't own the boat. It wouldn't be long til the boat would sink. So "free grass" didn't always prove to be a good deal. There was no real control over who would use what land to graze which herd, except of course the age-old method of "first come, first served."

This open range stuff was an amazing business. Just think, cattle from dozens of outfits intermingling over millions of acres. How did they keep it straight? Twice a year they would have a roundup. The spring roundup consisted of gathering the cattle, separating them according to brands, branding new calves, and making notes of increases in herd size. After that was taken care of, they were brought back to their "home" territory. During these roundups a seventy-five mile day wasn't unusual for the cowboy.

The fall roundup was another story. This one was to cut out the cattle ready for market. The end of this roundup brought the beginning of a season of unemployment for many "hands."

Say, with all of these cattle scattered about, weren't there people illegally altering brands or stealing outright? Yep! "Mavericking," a practice of branding strays, occurred with certain regularity. (By the way, the practice got its name from an honest and trusting Sam Maverick of Texas who didn't brand his cattle. Sam didn't keep 'em long, either.) Indians sometimes killed cattle due to the growing absence of their mainstay, buffalo.

The biggest problem faced by the "before barbed wire" crew was rustling. Both cattle and horses fell victim to a rather effective group of outlaws whose home was the Missouri Breaks. (A movie based on the events of this time was made in Montana a few years ago, starring Marlon Brando and Jack Nicholson. It's name, understandably, is "The Missouri Breaks.")

Not to be outdone by the miners of the 1860's, the cattlemen proceeded to organize a "vigilance committee." Under the guidance of Granville Stuart, the same man who poisoned sheep dogs and later became the Butte city librarian, a group of cattlemen decided to take the summer off from ranching and went after *human* varmints. By the fall of 1864 rustling was way down. So were the bodies of some estimated 60-75 men whom "Stuart's Stranglers" either shot up or hung up. As was the case earlier, the taking of justice into the hands of a mob was generally disapproved. However, the problem *was* solved to a great extent. Everything was under control.

Nature wasn't under control, though. Grass fires caused problems for the cattlemen as did the various predators, mainly the coyote, wolf, and black bear (who usually confined his troublemaking to messing up campsites.) Weather was not a problem. Everyone expected the extreme heat in summer, causing occasional draughts and bitter cold and snows in winter. If the buffalo could handle it, why not the cattle? But...a combination of nature's whims and man's poor judgement were to spell disaster on the plains. The winter of 1886-1887 would forever be referred to as "the hard winter."

For nature's part, the winter of 1885-86 was considered to have been very mild. Summer followed with a blazing sun and practically no rain, and the land grew parched. Grazing conditions were poor at *best*. However, man, that magnificent beast capable of great feats and great blunders, had seen to it that the plains were overcrowded. Many were nervous, but few put up hay. They hoped for a mild winter. But it was not to be. Luck had run out for the gamblers. The winter of '86-87 devastated the cattle industry. It began in November, eased a little in January, only to deliver in February a knock-out punch. March's warming trend was much too late. Literally hundreds of thousands of animals died that winter, with estimates of up to 400,000. Blame has been put on the Texas speculators, Montanans, and the U.S. government. But whoever was blamed, it happened. And because of it changes were made. Open range-type cattle business declined considerably, sheep production increased considerably. Those who now raised livestock *also* put some land into hay, at a rate from 56,000 acres in 1880 to 300,000 in 1890.

The Miners needed beef for food during their prospecting, and this became the first market for Montana cattle. A worn-out ox might bring $100 in gold, and fattened animals came proportionately higher.

In the early 1870's, while the mining boom diminished, cattle were fattened in Montana and herded to Wyoming to a shipping point along the Union Pacific Railroad.

In 1880, it was estimated that there were 600,000 herd of cattle, worth over $21 million, in Montana.

Many of the steers that died during the disastrous winter of 1886-87 were what the cattlemen called "pilgrims" — animals unused to the violent climatic changes in Montana, which were brought into the state to fatten on the good Montana grazing land.

One problem of the cattle range was "mavericking" — calves' tongues were split so that they could not nurse. They would not follow their mothers, and would become strays, which were rounded up by cowboys who were building herds of their own.

To the Montanans who had first driven cattle onto the plains in the late seventies and early eighties it was inconceivable that this vast and limitless land could ever be "overcrowded." Had it not sustained buffalo by the millions? Surely the eye alone could testify that it could support almost limitless numbers of cattle for a century. Indeed, it was not really good for anything else. That is what it was made for.

Yet in the shockingly short span of six years the whole empire came crashing down. It took only a brief malevolence of nature and a few years of man's abuse.

During the spring and summer of 1885 there had been plenty of rainfall. The grass was good. The fall was dry, however, and there were a good many range fires. But the winter of 1885-86 was a mild one, with neither severe winds nor heavy snow. The cattle business in the summer of 1886 should have been at a new height. Three things were wrong. The summer was hot, with baking winds. The price of cattle had dropped a little in 1885 and more sharply in the early part of 1886. Believing this to be only temporary, most Montana cattlemen held off on Eastern shipment awaiting a price rise. Thirdly, a bad winter to the south in 1885 had forced some 200,000 head northward to better ranges. The ranges were crammed with cattle.

The fall rains did not come. The grass was thin; the earth baked. And in November the winter howled down out of the North with a vengeance. These storms were violent, and, one on the heels of another, they lasted until the end of November. There then occurred a combination of circumstances that presaged disaster. There was heavy snow in November, then a thaw in mid-December, followed by several months of uniformly low temperatures and bitter winds. The thaw produced a nearly impenetrable ice sheet which was then covered by more snow. The cattle lacerated their noses and legs trying to penetrate the ice. But even when they got through, the grass was skimpy and lacked nutrition. January was bitterly cold. The hope was that February would see a thaw. No one really knew what shape the cattle were in, but it was assumed that the great majority would survive, even though they would be weak, if February proved mild. It did not.

The losses were appalling — so much so that the old cattleman Granville Stuart was sickened and vowed never to ranch again. In every gully, every arroyo, along the stream beds, and dotting the level plains were the rotting carcasses of thousands upon thousands of cattle.

Some idea of the magnitude of the loss can be garnered from individual cattle company estimates. The Hashknife placed its loss, according to one estimate, at about 75 per cent; the Crosby Cattle Company at 80 per cent; J.L. Driskin estimated that he lost two-thirds of his herd; many other estimates ranged between 70 per cent and 90 per cent. When the winter began the E6 and Turkey Track ranches had 27,000 head. By spring they had 250 head.

Montana - An Uncommon Land *K. Ross Toole, Norman, U of Okla. Press, 1959*

Losses from the disastrous winter of 1886-87 were estimated at an average of 60%. The monetary loss was more than $20 million.

A Visual History of Montana; *OSP1, Helena*

Some five to ten years later Montana had considerably more head of beef than before the "hard winter." This time, however, they were on *owned, fenced* property, with hay supplementing the native grass.

WAITING FOR A CHINOOK

It was in the terrible winter of 1887. An open winter range until Christmas, and then snow, two feet on the level. Horses could paw for grass; cattle wouldn't, so the horses got fat, and so did the wolves.

Deep is the snow;
Hear the wind blow.
Cruel is the cold of Winter.
Gone is the warm breath of spring.
No birds to sing.
The Last of Five Thousand are dying
Are dying...

Oh, come soon, Gentle Spring...

—*Charles Russell Suite, 1963; courtesy Francis White, Bozeman.*

101

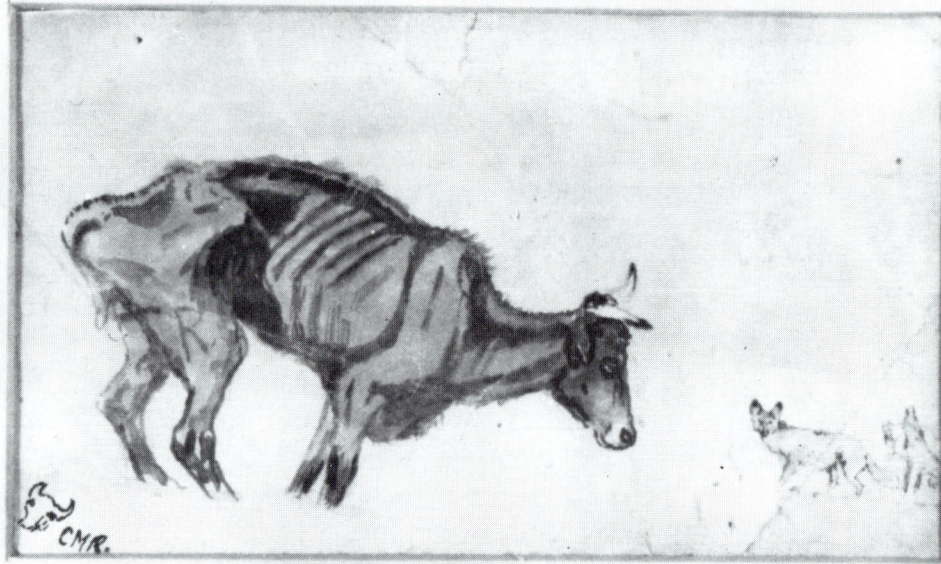

This is the real thing painted the winter of 1886 at the OH ranch

C M Russell

This picture is Chas Russell's reply to ... inquiry as to the condition of ...

During the winter of 1886-1887, word was sent to the ranch where Charles Russell was working, inquiring how its herd was holding up. Russell, instead of writing a report, decided to send the drawing, figuring it would best illustrate the devastating effects the winter had on the herd. Everyone agreed, and Russell's career probably received a boost because of it.

Courtesy Montana Stockgrowers' Association furnished by Montana Historical Society

RULERS of the LAND

Chapter Five

During this particular era it is hard to "nail down just exactly who were the rulers of the land. The Montana scene had suddenly become very complex. Eastern Montana had its cattle and sheep industry, western Montana had its mining and a fledgling timber industry. However, both sections shared common elements: vigilantes or "vigilance committees," businessmen, a newly-founded government, and dealings with the Indian. Having dealt somewhat with the vigilantes already, the thrust of this chapter will be with the remaining three.

Day and night cannot dwell together. The Red Man has ever fled the approach of the White Man, as the morning mist flees before the morning sun.

It matters little where we pass the remnant of our days. They will not be many. The Indians' night promises to be dark. Not a single star of hope hovers above his horizon. Sad-voiced winds moan in the distance. Grim fate seems to be on the Red Man's trail, and wherever he goes he will hear the approaching footsteps of his fell destroyer and prepare stolidly to meet his doom, as does the wounded doe that hears the approaching footsteps of the hunter.

A few more moons. A few more winters — and one of the descendants of the mighty hosts that once moved over this broad land or lived in happy homes, protected by the Great Spirit, will remain to mourn over the graves of a people — once more powerful and hopeful than yours. But why should I mourn at the untimely fate of my people? Tribe follows tribe, and nation follows nation, like the waves of the sea. It is the order of nature, and regret is useless. Your time of decay may be distant, but it will surely come, for even the White Man whose God walked and talked with him as friend with friend, cannot be exempt from the common destiny. We may be brothers after all. We will see.

Seattle, Suquamish, 1853

Editors note:
The Indian speeches used in this book are found in many places, usually government records. All of the versions used here, unless otherwise noted, are taken from:
Indian Oratory: Famous Speeches by Noted Indian Chieftains, by W. C. Vanderwerth. Copyright 1971 by the University of Oklahoma Press.
This is the best collection of such speeches we know of, and contains short biographical sketches of each chieftain quoted. We definitely urge you to obtain a copy for the classroom.

RULERS:
the Merchant Princes

Besides the fur traders, gold miners, and cattlemen who exploited Montana, there was yet another group to greatly profit from the "goings-on" of the era, the merchants. The people in the gold camps were hollering for supplies while the fur trappers, still just finishing up, needed a market place. The establishment of roads and trails into Montana and the development of steamboat traffic on the Missouri made the competition for profits keen. Names such as Worden, Woody and Higgins in Missoula; Maclay and Wall in Virginia City; Steel, Carroll, and Broadwater of the Diamond R in Helena, were synonymous with trade.

Although trade flourished throughout the state, at this time Fort Benton was the hub of activity. Here many steamboat lines developed, as did freight lines and merchandising businesses. Quite often these concerns were financed by eastern backers and, therefore, and as usual, much of the profit left the state.

One such "merchant prince" was T.C. Power, who, with the backing of the brother of the well-known Marshall Field, set up a trading establishment in Fort Benton. Later he convinced his brother John to join him. They did well, in fact business boomed. Together they established the "Black P" steamboat line which, in some years, dominated river trade. They set up posts in numerous Montana towns as well as in Canada. They invested in stage lines, cattle and sheep. Their "spread" was the P Lazy N in the Judith River Country. Their steamboats even carried the railway materials which eventualy "derailed" the river traffic. Although its boom years were the 1870's-80's, "Black P" steamboats appeared on the Missouri into the early 1900's.

T.C. was active in politics as well as business. He lost the state's first gubernatorial election to Democrat Joseph K. Toole in October of 1889. Even so, he was soon chosen as one of the state's first two senators, along with ex-vigilante leader Wilber Fisk Sanders, to represent Montana in Washington D.C.

This would be a nice time to watch *The Pride of the Capitol City* from MSU Film and Television Center.

Looking back into Montana's political past is similar to looking at a plate of spaghetti and trying to find both ends of a single piece. Some have called it confusing, some have called it a mess, while others have said it was impossible to straighten out. Well, somewhere along the way is the truth.

At one time or another, all of present-day Montana had been a part of the Louisiana, Oregon, Washington, Nebraska, or Idaho territories (not to mention the Indian's territory). At best this in itself created confusion. Not to be outdone with all of this, things got even crazier as the present-day boundaries were carved from the Idaho territory. The U.S. Congress, in one of their "looser" moments, actually went "round and round" trying to put a "handle" on the new territory. Suggestions of "Jefferson," "Douglas," and "Shoshone" were pushed by the wayside and finally the name "Montana" became a territory on May 26, 1864.

Something that must be kept in mind is that during Montana's term as a "territory," (some prefer "colony,") the Civil War was just winding down. The division between North and South was very real. Both physically and ideologically, political groups in both the Republican and Democratic parties were at each other's throats.

Now add to this the fact that the miners who streamed into Montana were, by nature, a volatile group whose ideas were well entrenched before their arrival. Although Montanans at the time came from all sections of the country, and a sizeable group from other countries, the Confederacy's ideals were well defended by a very vocal minority in the state.

To make things worse we threw in the type of government under which a territory was run and the result of understandably, and unfortunately mass confusion, frustration, and stagnation. Territories, which did not enjoy the full privileges of states, were run on the "kinda" system. They were capable of running themselves, *kinda.* They knew what was best for themselves, *kinda.* The President of the U.S. appointed the governor, secretary (the sole disbursor of federal funds), and judges making up the Supreme Court. The local control consisted of "allowing" the citizens to elect the standard two-house legislature and a territorial delegate to the House of Representatives in D.C. This delegate, however, could *not* vote, but merely represented the territory's wishes.

Abraham Lincoln, a Republican, was true to his party when he appointed Sidney Edgerton, *also a Republican,* to be Montana's first territorial governor. The problem was that Montana was predominantly Democratic. Putting it mildly, the word "compromise" was not in Edgerton's vocabulary while "abrasive" was written there in bold-face type. Edgerton lasted nearly two years, accomplishing very little. In all fairness, however, it must be pointed out that for most of his term he had no secretary to allocate federal monies. Between the final days of the War and Lincoln's assassination the United States was having other larger problems, and couldn't be bothered with one of its territories.

Prior to Edgerton's removal, President Andrew Johnson, a Democrat, appointed Thomas Francis Meagher, *also a Democrat,* to be secretary of Montana Territory. With Edgerton out, Meagher was "acting governor." Meagher was indeed an interesting part of early Montana. The spring and summer of 1866 saw a convening of the territorial legislature, later termed illegal, and a constitutional convention, whose constitution was lost. By October, President Johnson appointed G. Clay Smith, a Democrat, to the governor's post. Smith arrived in Montana and didn't even unpack his bags before leaving for Washington to push Montana's case firsthand. Great! This again left the reins in the hands of Meagher. True to form, he convened another legislature, which was once again termed illegal by the U.S. Congress.

The Sioux (or their absence) provided Meagher with the reputation which spawned the statue in Helena. The Sioux attacks on the Bozeman Trail in early 1867 caused enough concern for Meagher, the acting governor and Civil War General, to form an army (with federal blessings) to end the threat. The "army" met little resistance due to that fact that it met little opposition. The army quickly disbanded, having spent a considerable sum of money on a "war without an enemy."

Bridge Street, Helena in 1865

Meagher's end came at Fort Beton where on July 1, 1867, he was last seen on a docked steamboat. Speculation has it he fell overboard, but no one really knows. His body was never found.

Just prior to Meagher's death, Smith returned to the state. He barely had time to get things going when Meagher, and his secretarial ability to disburse money, disappeared. Smith ran things as well as expected without money for nearly a year. Exasperated, he left for Washington in mid-1868 to straighten out the situation. Somewhere along the line he decided to just "forget it" and quit.

After a year of no governor, Montana, still Democratic, was awarded by President Grant, a Republican, James M. Ashley, a radical Republican. Ashley's term was to last less than one year due to his hard-line political stance with Montana's Democrats, *and* his mistake of making fun of President Grant.

The saying, "it's always darkest before the dawn" applied at the time. "Dawn" came on July of 1870 when President Grant appointed Benjamin F. Potts to be the fourth governor of the six-year-old territory. Potts was a Republican, of course, but one that fit in well with the majority of both Republicans and Democrats. His administrative ability kept him in office until 1883 when President Chester A. Arthur removed him from office.

During the Potts era Montana achieved political sophistication. The majority of both parties seemed to get its way in terms of reducing Indian reservation size, attracting outside investors (cattle companies from all over), and placing the capitol at Helena. The last achievement took three elections, 1867, 1869, 1874, a legal hassle the U.S. Supreme Court wouldn't touch, and, finally, a Montana Supreme Court decision. So, for the time being, Helena became the uncontested capitol of Montana.

What made the Potts administration work so well? As Malone and Roeder put it in their book *Montana, A History of Two Centuries,* "local businessmen and investors, often ignoring political loyalties, joined forces with leaders of government to gain control of the territory." So by 1883 Montana *businessmen* were already experienced in *running* the government.

Some of Potts' success might also be shared with Martin Maginnis, the Democratic delegate to Washington for the bulk of Potts' term, 1872-82. Maginnis was known for his ability to "land" U.S. government money for Montana. But more importantly he was instrumental in pushing the cattlemen's wish for the release of Indian land for grazing, and the construction of forts for protection from Indian attacks.

Picture yourself on the Northern Great Plains. You're thirteen years old and have been on a thirteen-year long camping trip. You eat, drink, do chores, hunt, and move on! Along comes a man who tells you to worship *his* God. Another man tells you not to cross a certain river "ever again." Your parents now get drunk. Your chance to be a proud warrior is rapidly fading. You've been given *buildings* to live in. You can't roam. Your game is killed off, now you must eat from tin cans (which the government promises but many times sells to traders instead). Your father and some friends cross the river to get fresh meat. Only a few return. Two days after the meat is gone, soldiers come along and drag away the "criminals" who went hunting. (Hunting is a crime?) Some of your friends go to release the "criminals." Most return. A weak later soldiers stream through your village and kill indiscriminately, to "teach a lesson." After much of the grief has passed, your neighborhood has been told it has to move due to the fact that the land was no good for you, but perfect for the white man's cattle.... By now you should begin to the get the idea.

The whites had two legally-recognized ways of dealing with Indian affairs. The first was the treaty; the second was the "executive order," which had to be issued by the President. This method allowed for quick handling of any problem that might arise. You see, treaties had to be submitted to the Senate for approval, and that took a long time.

You said that you wanted to put us upon a reservation, to build us houses and to make us Medicine lodges. I do not want them.

I was born upon the prairie, where the wind blew free, and there was nothing to break the light of the sun. I was born where there were no enclosures, and where everything drew a free breath. I want to die there, and not within walls. I know every stream and every wood between the Rio Grande and the Arkansas. I have hunted and lived over that country. I lived like my fathers before me, and like them, I lived happily. The white man has the country which we loved and we only wish to wander on the prairie until we die.

Ten Bears, Commanche, 1867

Cheyenne warrior chief, Roman Nose, had a special bonnet which, when worn made him invulnerable to weapons made with metal (bullets, knives, etc.) However, the bonnet's powers were useless if, before the battle, Roman Nose had contact with metal objects. If this occurred, then an elaborate ritual had to be performed to restore the bonnet's power. The night before a battle in the Republican River country, Roman Nose feasted with an allied tribe. The woman who prepared the meal, having lived for a time with whites, used metal cooking utensils. When he discovered this, Roman Nose began the restraintive ritual. Before it could be completed, however, the attack began. Taunted by the warriors, Roman Nose agreed to fight saying, "I'll fight, but I'll die today."
As his horse cleared a small rise, a stray bullet struck Roman Nose between the eyes before he even saw his enemies.

This story was related to us by a friend. The closest version we could find as the original source is The Fighting Cheyenne by George Bird Grinnell, Norman: U of Okla Press

This would be a great time to listen to the album, *Bitter Tears*, by Johnny Cash.

The end result of the white man's dealing with the Indians of the West were the same as their dealings with the eastern tribes: "pacification" and containment at *any* cost. If lying was necessary, lies were made. If booze was necessary, booze was served. If bloodshed was necessary, blood was shed, on *both* sides.

It really didn't matter whether the tribes were friendly or hostile to the whites. The results were the same. In fact the methods of dealing were the same; only the degree of severity differed, depending upon the circumstances.

Most of the problems really stemmed from the cultural differences between the whites and the various Indian nations. The Indians led a natural existence which allowed for continuous utilization of the environment in which they lived. The white man called this "primitive." The white man's system was to "use" things for growth, progress, modernization, which were ideas totally foreign to the Indians. In this clash of two such cultures, one seeking to maintain the status quo (the Indian), the other wanting change, having the numbers to achieve their goal, the end was inevitable. The Indians would get shortchanged.

The White Chief says that Big Chief at Washington sends us greetings of friendship and goodwill. This is kind of him for we know he has little need of our friendship in return. His people are many. They are like the grass that covers vast prairies. My people are few. They resemble the scattering trees of a storm swept plain.

There was a time when our people covered the land as the waves of a wind ruffled sea cover its shell paved floor, but that time long since passed away with the greatness of tribes that are now but a mournful memory.

Your God is not our God! Your God loves your people and hates mine. He folds his strong protecting arms lovingly about the pale face and leads him by the hand as a father leads his infant son — but He has forsaken His red children — if they really are His. Our God, the Great Spirit, seems also to have forsaken us. Your God makes your people wax strong every day. Soon they will fill all the land. Our people are ebbing away like a rapidly receding tide that will never return. The white man's God cannot love our people or He would protect them. He must be partial — for He came to His paleface children. We never saw Him. He gave you laws but had no word for his red children whose teeming multitudes once filled this vast continent as stars fill the firmament. No; we are two distinct races with separate origins and separate destinies. There is little in common between us.

To us the ashes of our ancesters are sacred and their resting place is hallowed ground. You wander far from the graves of your ancestors — and seemingly without regret. Your religion was written upon tables of stone by the iron finger of your God so that you could not forget. The Red Man could never comprehend nor remember it. Our religion is the traditions of our ancestors — the dreams of our old men, given them in the solemn hours of night by the Great Spirit; and the visions of our sachems, and is written in the hearts of our people.

Seattle, Suquamish, 1853

Roman Nose, Cheyenne

Courtesy Montana Historical Society

109

The first treaty with any real significance for the Montana area was the Fort Laramie Treaty of 1851. This treaty was written in an attempt to halt the fighting on the Oregon Trail, both Indian vs. white and Indian vs. Indian. The assembled chiefs of the Crow, Gros Ventre, and Assiniboine agreed to reside on reservations of considerable size by today's standards, but still far less territory than they had before. In return, the tribes would annually receive supplies. The Blackfeet, who either weren't asked to participate or didn't want to, were assigned a reservation anyway. It was sort of the nineteenth century version of "sit in the corner" mixed with the old idea of the "great American Desert," after all, the land was worthless, anyway. Actually, when looking at the treaty one could see the longrange plan of "divide and conquer," beginning with the division of the area into separate reservations.

A few years later, in 1855, the Flathead, Kootenai, and Pen d'Oreille of western Montana were given the same business. The Kootenai and Pen d'Oreille agreed on a reservation at the south end of Flathead Lake. The Flathead wanted to stay in the Bitterroot Valley. Late that same year even the once supreme, and still powerful, Blackfeet agreed to a reservation site. Theirs was to be much of north central Montana. Fantastic! All tribes of the area were supposedly reasonably satisfied. The whites were happy. What could possibly mess things up? Gold! And it *did* mess things up.

Putting the whole deal in a nutshell, it kind of went like this (a Montana version of the "House that Jack Built"): GOLD brought PEOPLE who needed ROADS across Indian land, which therefore led to protective FORTS which needed SUPPLIES sold by MERCHANTS who used RIVER BOATS and WAGONS pulled by DRAFT ANIMALS which survived on Montana forage which proved CATTLE and SHEEP could survive here, causing RANGES to be used for grazing, and temptation to RAILROADS, which brought more PEOPLE, who needed more ROADS, etc. This "vicious cycle" on its next revolution demanded more, and still more people. The white man understood this to be "progress." The Indian saw it as an *invasion*. Both sides were equally correct in their interpretation of the situation and to an extent understood each other's feelings. But the white "ethnocentrism" (feelings of cultural or ethnic superiority) was to prevail. But why shouldn't the white man be proud? Hadn't he secured freedom and acquired, one way or another, all of the land that was to be the "lower forty-eight" in just a little over seventy-five years? To do all of this requires strength, wealth, determination, and progress. (Whose progress? White progress, of course. What other kind was there?) Seriously, even today don't we, you and your friends too, measure things by our standards first? It's only natural. But...then walk a mile in someone else's shoes and see the other side...amazing.

The commissioners told us at Laramie if we remained good friends of the whites we would be taken care of for forty years. Since we made that treaty it is only five years. You are in a hurry to quit giving us food. I am a young man yet; my teeth are all good. They told us at Laramie we would get food till we were old, and our children after us.

Some of the Crows went to the Missouri River and got some Crow horses. The white people sent word they were their horses, and we sent them all back. We claim our horses, but they are not brought back.

This is our land, so we told the commissioners at Fort Laramie; but all kinds of white people come over it, and we tell you of it, though we say nothing to them. On this side of the Yellowstone there is a lake; about it are buffalo. It is a rich country; the whites are on it; they are stealing our quartz; it is ours, but we say nothing to them. The whites steal a great deal of our money. We do not want them to go to our country.

Blackfoot, Crow, 1873

I am as a stone, broken and thrown away — one part thrown this way, and one part thrown that way. I am a chief no more; but that is not what grieves me — I am grieved at the ruin of my people; they will go back to the old road, and I must follow them; they will not let me live with the white people. I shall go to my camp, and after a while I shall go a little farther, and then a little farther, until I get as far away as is possible for me. When they show me the big chief they select, I shall follow him wherever he leads. When you take hold of my hand today you have taken it for the last time; when you see me ride away today, you will see Kicking Bird no more. I shall never come back to this place.

Kicking Bird, Kiowa, 1873

GOLD
PEOPLE
ROADS
FORTS
SUPPLIES
MERCHANTS
BOATS
WAGONS
ANIMALS
FORAGE
CATTLE
SHEEP
RANGELAND
RAILROADS
MORE
MORE

Anyway...gold dust did it. Roads such as the Northern Overland Route and the Bozeman Trail were founded for easy access to the gold. These caused the building of Fort Shaw (to keep an eye on the Blackfeet) and Fort Ellis, in Bozeman, to watch the Sioux and Cheyenne. Both were built in 1867 after Thomas Francis Meagher's famous "one-sided" war.

The northern tribes, Blackfeet, Gros Ventre, and Assiniboine, were dealt with first. Between a treaty at Fort Benton in 1865 and a couple of executive orders by President Grant in the early 1870's the northern Indians were nearly pushed out of the country.

A tragic event that occurred during this period was the "Baker Massacre" of January, 1870. Instigating the massacre was bloodshed on the part of both sides. In subzero weather Major Baker led four cavalry companies and two infantry troups into a Blackfeet camp. At the last shot, 173 Blackfeet lay dead, including 53 women and children. And if that wasn't bad enough, Baker had attacked the *wrong* village. He wiped out a *friendly* village. The civilian population "back east" was appalled. Montanans *applauded;* the military called it a *victory* and *thanked* Baker and his men. The Blackfeet didn't fight back, on a large scale, any more. The lesson was taught well. Live on the reservation and accept the supplies we give you in return for your land and *freedom.* What if the supplies didn't come? Starvation, pure and simple.

At about the same time, the Flatheads of the Bitterroot Valley were given an executive order to leave the land which they were granted by treaty some 20 years earlier. The white interpretation of that treaty was that they were there "temporarily." Some left for the Jocko Reservation in the Mission Valley while others stayed with Chief Charlo. Being "contrary" to the U.S. government has been known to be a "mistake." If Charlo didn't know it in 1872 when asked to move, he did in 1891 when he finally did after 20 years of "barely existing" in the Bitterroot. The proud and courageous old man was the last to "fall in line." Undoubtedly he did so sadly, bitterly, but as always proudly as the leader of his people.

As far as the Montana Territory was concerned, the Indians which provided the largest threat were the combined Sioux and Northern Cheyenne nations. (The Blackfeet would have if white migration had been through the north instead of east and south.) The Sioux nation of the upper-midwest was not only large in size, but also in population. They were not about to give up what was theirs without a struggle. (In other words, showing them the receipt for the Louisiana Purchase was not going to convince them that the U.S. government had the right to subdivide *their* land.)

The Cheyenne ranged the eastern slopes of the divide, from the Yellowstone River, south to southern Colorado. It was the Northern Cheyenne that teamed up with the Sioux, both originally having shared the upper-midwest together before the whites began to move west.

During the trouble over the "Bozeman Road" (which miners used to get to the gold sites) Indians constantly raided settlers coming over the trail. The wagon drivers began substituting oxen for horses, since the Indians did not like oxen and seldom stole them.

I once thought that I was the only man that preserved to be the friend of the white man, but since they have come and cleaned out our lodges, horses, and everything else, it is hard for me to believe white men any more.

Black Kettle, Cheyenne, 1865

Remember now, these tribes had already been moved, by the influx of settlers, into their present position. The Sioux staged an uprising in Minnesota in 1862 before leaving to move west. The Cheyenne were engaged in a war in Nebraska and Kansas in 1864. It was the Cheyenne, too, who were victims of the horrendous massacre at Sand Creek, Colorado, in November of the same year, and at that time they were at *peace* with the whites. To say the least, the plains Indians were upset during the early 1860's.

The opening of the Bozeman Road in 1863-64 was too much. It crossed these tribes' prime buffalo grounds. Then a couple of years later, after settlers complained about the Indians' lack of hospitality and abundance of bullets, the government decided to build three forts to protect the travellers. Bad move. The Indians were *on* those forts like *skin*. After the Fetterman Massacre in late 1866, the army decided to send a good size army into the area to beef up the garrisons. This didn't work well either. It only increased casualties on both sides. The choice now was clear to all concerned, either pour in money and many more troops (at a time when the army was occupying and "Reconstructing" the recently-defeated Confederacy), or admit defeat and go home. It was to be the latter. The Treaty of Fort Laramie in 1868 was the *only* treaty with the Indians (or *anybody* else in the *whole world*) in which the U.S. government admitted defeat. Red Cloud, supreme chief of the Sioux, was satisfied enough with the terms to agree to a reservation site (half of South Dakota) with hunting privileges in large areas to the west.

It wasn't but a few years later than an interpretation of the treaty caused problems leading to bloodshed. (The Indians didn't go to Harvard or Yale. Couldn't the treaties have avoided interpretation?) Anyway, the trouble involved the Northern Pacific Railroad coming through their land.

Then in 1874, a surveying group led by Colonel George A. Custer brought back word that the Dakota Territory (where the Sioux land was) was good farm land and that the Black Hills might well be called the Gold Hills. And we know what happened when someone said the word "gold." The people in Washington tried to negotiate the gold fields away from Red Cloud. No deal! (This would be like Christians negotiating away the Holy Land, for the Black Hills were very sacred.) The government decided to put the "stragglers" (those Sioux who didn't reside on the reservation, including both Crazy Horse and Sitting Bull) back on the reservation, by force if necessary. (All this neatly negated the Treaty of 1868.)

Anyway, the Indians were given written orders to get to the reservation "faster than immediately," kind of like being told you had an assignment due yesterday. The time limit really didn't bother the Sioux and Cheyenne for two reasons, first, they didn't wear watches, and second, they didn't plan to go anyway. It was going to be someone's "last stand" very shortly. The Indians felt it was time to dig in their heels; the whites felt it was time to make the Indians "heel."

The old folks are dying off; then who will own the land? I went to Fort Laramie; the old Indians signed the treaty. We came back to the camp and told the young men, and they said we had done wrong and they did not want to have anythint to do with it. All the other Indian tribes fight the whites; we do not do so. We love the whites, and we want them to leave us a big country.

All the other Indians go and talk with the Great Father; you take them to Washington; they are bad; they hide their hearts; but they talk good to the Great Father, and you do more for them than for us. This I want to tell you; yesterday you spoke to us and we listened to you. If you wish to have peace with all the Indians get them all together and make peace with them. Then I will make peace with them, too.

Blackfoot, Crow, 1873

I have thrown away everything. There must be no more bad talk. I will not. I have spoken forever. I want soldiers all to go home. I have given up now and want no more fuss. I have said yes, and thrown away my country.

Captain Jack, Modoc, 1873

This would be a good time to read *The Bloody Bozeman* and *The Perilous Trail to Montana's Gold* both by Dorothy Johnson.

GALL

Gall was one of the greatest of the Hunkpapa Sioux chieftains, and some historians consider him to be the peer of the famous Red Cloud and of Spotted Tail. Gall was one of the leaders of the Hunkpapa Sioux during the time of the fabulous Sitting Bull.

Gall was a superb specimen of manhood, rugged and able. On one occasion he had stolen some ponies and a detachment of a hundred soldiers was sent to his village to arrest him. The soldiers surrounded the village at about 2 A.M., announcing that they wanted Gall. He was aroused, stuck his head out of his tipi, and was promptly shot at by one of the soldiers.

Gall dashed to the back of the tipi, slashed a hole, and started to leap out. Soldiers, armed with rifles and bayonets, were all around, and slammed him to the ground. They clubbed, stomped, and stabbed him, and one soldier had to put his food on Gall's body to retrieve his bayonet. Thinking Gall dead, they left him lying in the snow.

Other Indians in the camp would not touch his body, and they quickly moved their tipis to another location. Gall later revived, and in spite of his terrible wounds and the fact that he was nearly naked in the cold and snow, made his way to the lodge of a friend some twenty miles away. The friend cared for him until he recovered from his ordeal, but one of the wounds remained open for more than a year.

After this affair, Gall carried a lasting hatred for the whites, and finally died December 5, 1894, as a result of his horrible wounds. His birth has been recorded as c. 1840.

His speech here is brief and was made at Fort Rice in 1868 at a peace conference which was headed by General "White Beard"

" The whites ruin our country. If we make peace, the military posts on this Missouri River must be removed and the steamboats stopped from coming up here. Below here is the Running Water, which is our country. You fought me and I had to fight back; I am a soldier. The annuities you speak of we don't want. Our intention is to take no present.

I have been sent here by my people to see and hear what you have got to say. My people told me to get powder and ball, and I want that.

Now, many things have happened that are not our fault. We are blamed for many things. I have been stabbed. If you want to make peace with me, you must remove this Fort Rice, and stop the steamboats. If you won't, I must get all these friendly (Agency) Indians to move away. I have told all this to them, and now I tell you."

Indian Oratory: Famous Speeches by noted Indian Chieftains, by W.C. Vanderworth. Copyright 1971 by the University of Oklahoma Press.

On paper, General Phil Sheridan's three-pronged attack looked great. The "Montana Column" would close the vise from west; the "Dakota Column" from the east, while the "Wyoming Column" would make sure they didn't "get way" to the south.

June 17, 1876 saw the "Wyoming Column" come to a temporary halt due to the Battle of the Rosebud where Crazy Horse gave General George Crook a lesson in strategy. This left the Montana and Dakota Columns to do the job. The Montana contingent was to ensure no escape north or west of the Yellowstone River. (This implied the Indians would run. Bad guess!)

This left the Dakota Column as the outfit which would "teach the lesson." This column was led by General Alfred Terry, and was made up of 600 men of the Seventh Cavalry and an infantry batallion of over 200, plus guides.

A new strategy was cooked up when the Montana Column, some 400 cavalry and infantrymen headed by Colonel John Gibbon, met General Terry near Moon Creek on the Yellowstone River. The idea was to join Terry's infantry with Gibbons' column, with Terry in command. Not only would this make for a somewhat equal striking force of some 700-800 men each, but it would allow the swift Seventh Cavalry, under none other than

George Custer, to cover more ground and more quickly seek out the elusive enemy. The plan called for converging on the Indian village (the whereabouts of which was still unknown) on June 26.

Whatever Custer's reasons, the morning of June 24 saw him break his orders to follow the Rosebud River, in order to follow his hunch that the Little Big Horn was the camp site. This *only* required crossing the Rosebud Mountains, which he proceeded to do. By dawn, after an all-night trip, he was at the crest of the range. It was here he saw the smoke of a *good sized* camp. The elusive enemy was near at hand.

Somewhere around noon Custer divided his command in order to catch them by surprise, before they could escape. (They kept thinking the Indians were going to run away.) Custer's plan was a miniature of Sheridan's, a three-pronged attack with him going up the middle.

In what was supposed to be a lesson for the Indians (the lesson being to get to the reservation when they were told to do so), Custer instead "bit the dust." In the time normally granted for a school lunch period, Custer and his entire contingent of more than 250 men (261 the most commonly-believed figure) lay dead. The other segments were held down with heavy losses.

The "Battle of Little Big Horn" or "Custer's Last Stand" has been immortalized in dozens of books, magazines, and paintings. The number of dead and wounded, and the number of Indians involved varies depending on witnesses. Some say three to five thousand, others as many as 15,000. Whatever the figures, there were definitely enough to do the job quickly and accurately.

One has to wonder how something like this could happen.

For example, the average ratio of horse to Indian on the plains was almost 2 to 1. If this was true and there were 10,000 Indians, could Custer's "blind ambition" have been enough to have him not see the signs that 20,000 horses would have left behind? He must have known, for at least a few terrifying moments before Chief Gall *attacked* him, that it wasn't going to be one of his better days, and it would, in fact, be his last. As the saying goes, "one battle doesn't win the war." The combined Sioux and Cheyenne had their day but Colonel Nelson A. Miles was soon to pop on the scene.

For a short time after the Custer battle the Dakota and Wyoming Columns searched for the elusive Sioux. Without a lot of luck, they disbanded. This left Montana's protection up to Colonel Miles and his infantry. (Foot soldiers versus the mounted Indians that wiped out the now larger-than-life Custer and his Cavalry unit? Ridiculous, not to mention dangerous, or so Montanans thought.) Miles, though arrogant, surely knew his business. When his men were not engaged in battle, they were training. They applied relentless pressure on the "hostiles" summer, fall, and through the winter. In January, 1877, he and Crazy Horse fought to a stalemate.

It was in early 1877 that the "Wyoming Column" rose again under General Crook. Between Miles' boys doing a number on Sitting Bull's camp, causing his people to flee to Canada, it was the ninth inning, two outs, and a three-and-two count for the Indians. And they were down by a hundred runs.

In the spring of 1877 Crazy Horse, after years of bloody dissent, capitulated. Lame Deer refused, and died in battle. It wasn't until 1881 that Sitting Bull, back from Canada, finally resigned himself to reservation life.

According to Ralph Henry in Our Land Montana, *after the Custer massacre, as was the usual custom, Indian women and old men of the tribes went through the battlefield and scalped and mutilated the bodies of the enemy. Only three bodies escaped this treatment: Custer, whom the Indians believed to have committed suicide, which in their eyes made him a holy man; Myles Keough, who wore a medal around his neck, which may have aroused Indian superstitions; and Mark Kellogg, a civilian reporter, who had been known to (and liked by) the tribes of the Sioux.*

According to an exhibit at the Montana State Historical Society, Helena, none of the white bodies were scalped following the battle.

According to some Indian traditions, the bodies were not scalped since the whites, who were considered unscrupulous (they would murder Indian women and children during ambushes) were not deemed worthy of this act of warfare ritual.

MASSACRED

Gen. custer and 261 MEN THE VICTIMS.

NO OFFICER OR MAN OF 5 COMPANIES LEFT TO TELL THE TALE.

3 Days Desperate Fighting by Maj. Reno and the Remainder of the Seventh.

Full Details of the Battle.

LIST OF KILLED AND WOUNDED.

THE BISMARCK TRIBUNE'S SPECIAL CORRESPONDENT SLAIN

Squaws Mutilate and Rob the Dead Victims Captured Alive Tortured in a Most Fiendish Manner.

What Will Congress Do About It?

Shall This Be the Beginning of the End?

It will be remembered that the Bismarck Tribune sent a special correspondent with Gen. Terry, who was the only professional correspondent with the expedition. Kellogg's last words to the writer were: "We leave the Rosebud tomorrow and by the time this reaches you we will have

MET AND FOUGHT.

the red devils, with what result remains to be seen. I go with Custer and will be at the death." Gen. Terry, apprehending danger, urged Custer to take additional men, but Custer having full confidence in his men and in their ability to cope with the Indians in whatever force he might meet them, declined the proffered assistance and marched with his regiment along. He was instructed to strike the trail of the Indians, to follow it until he discovered their position, and report by courier to Gen. Terry who would reach the mouth of Little Horn by the evening of the 26th, when he would act in concert with Custer in the final wiping out.

We said of those who went into battle with Custer none are living — one Crow scout hid himself in the field, and witnessed and survived the battle. His story is plausable, and is accepted, but we have not room for it now. The names of the wounded are as follows:

Tribune Extra, Bismarck D.T., July 6, 1876

This would be a good time to read *Showdown At The Little BigHorn* and *Bury My Heart At Wounded Knee*, both by Dee Brown.

Miles City Story Tells Why Custer Shed Long Hair

Why did General "Longhair" Custer shear the long, curly hair which reached down to his shoulders, and of which he was so proud?

The answer was given recently in the following story which appeared in the Miles City Star:

Several years after he had taken part in General W.S. Hancock's campaign against the Cheyenne Indians in the late 1860's in the southwest, General Goerge A. Armstrong commanding the 7th Cavalry, "long about 1873, came to Fort Abraham Lincoln on the Missouri river, near the present-day Mandan, N.D." as Frank Buffalo White Man, Sioux Indian remembers the story of why Custer "had his hair cut just before he departed from Fort Lincoln on his last march to the Little Big Horn in Montana."

It was widely known among soldiers troops and Indians in the southwest that Custer wore his hair long, falling down on his shoulders and rather curly at "that" Buffalo White Man remarked. The story follows:

Many Sioux Indians during the years from 1873 to the fall of 1875 came to Fort Lincoln, pitched their tepees, did a little hunting to keep up their supply of food, but mainly for the purpose of doing some trading at the fort, "and to look around."

On one occasion Custer enjoyed the opportunity to visit a Sioux Indian village setup near Fort Lincoln. During the course of the visit he sat in a circle in a lodge when the peace pipe was passed around, from which all present took a whiff. He still wore his hair long.

On one particular occasion Custer pledged himself not to fight the Sioux and that he would remain at peace with them. The pledge was made in an atmosphere of solemnity during the passing around of the peace pipe. The Sioux remembered him as the man with long hair, and that is what they named him — "Long Yellow Hair." That was the custom of the Indians. They named Colonel Nelson A. Miles, when he was commandant of Fort Keogh, "Bear Coat."

When Luther S. Kelly, afterwards dubbed "Yellowstone Kelly, Scout for Miles," first came to Fort Keogh to confer with Miles, he, Kelly, sent in his "calling card" which the commandant immediately recognized as coming from the visitor. It was a bear's paw. It was in Bear's Paw mountains where Miles overtook and defeated Chief Joseph of the Nez Perces in early October of 1877.

"In the early spring of 1876, when General Alfred H. Terry, commanding the Department of Dakota, was alerted from the headquarters to meet and conquer the allied Sioux and Cheyenne Indians under the influence of Sitting Bull, he contacted the garrison at Fort Lincoln. Custer, restored to the command of the 7th Cavalry, was ordered to march to the Yellowstone country, to go along with Terry, his superior.

"Before his departure, and remembering the pledge he had made a year or two previously, Custer has his hair cut so that the Indians would not know him in the event he came in contact with them. He had made a vow that he would fight the Indians no more; so he had his curly locks of hair shorn. Otherwise the Sioux and Cheyenne Indians would have recognized him quickly at the time of the fight, on June 25, 1876, on the Little Big Horn river in Montana. But when they looked over the dead on the battlefield the Indians did recognize him and left his body along," according to the story as Buffalo White Man recalls.

On July 27, 1876, in the Helena Weekly Herald, *Bradley made the following statement of what he had found:*

"Of the 206 bodies buried on the field, there were very few that I did not see, and beyond scalping, in possibly a majority of cases, there was little mutilation. Many of the bodies were not even scalped, and in the comparatively few cases of disfiguration it appeared to me rather the result of a blow than of a knife."'

The Indians claimed that no more than 800 warriors took part during the course of the Battle of Little Big Horn. White and Army estimates ran much higher. The Indians claimed further that the total number of Indians camped in the area was only 4,000. Supposedly Gall, the Sioux Chief who helped organize the battle, ordered the Indian women to erect "dummie" tipis, so the Army would think there were more Indians encamped than there were.

One of the interesting sidelights of the battle was that an Indian (Sioux) maiden, Tasina-Man-Win, joined the battle after her brother had been killed. She counted many coups during the course of the battle, and earned the respect of the warriors. Thereafter she was allowed to join other Sioux war parties. She was known to the whites as Mary Crawler.

The Lewistown Daily News, Dec. 23, 1951

CRAZY HORSE

Crazy Horse, the greatest military genius of the Sioux Confederation, was born in 1849. Crazy Horse first came to the notice of writers about 1875, but the name was an old one, and was handed down from generation to generation. His family was highly regarded by the Indians, and had been entrusted with the Sioux history, which was portrayed on buckskin, for some eight hundred years. The buckskin was destroyed by fire many years ago.

Crazy Horse was an imposing figure, about six feet tall. He married a Cheyenne woman, and this resulted in close ties between his band of the Sioux and the Cheyennes. He was also a son-in-law of the famous Red Cloud.

Crazy Horse played an important part in the affairs of the Sioux, and was fearless in battle. He had a superstitious belief that he could not be killed by a bullet, and was disdainful of gunfire. He had lost two close friends and apparently had little desire to live. He is supposed to have told friends he was looking for death.

Indian police suspected that Crazy Horse might be planning an outbreak, and on September 5, 1877, a group of forty-three policemen were sent to arrest him. In the scuffle following the attempt to arrest Crazy Horse, a bayonet was run through his stomach. With police clinging to his arms and his friends trying to help him, Crazy Horse said: "Let me go, my friends, you have hurt me enough." At ten o'clock that night he called Indian Agent Jesse M. Lee to his side and spoke to him, shortly after which he died.

His superstition that he would not be killed by gunfire was good to the last — it was a bayonet thrust which ended his life. He was secretly buried by his parents somewhere in the hills in the vicinity of where he was camped when he was arrested.

There is no authentic photograph of Crazy Horse. He refused to pose, saying: "Why would you wish to shorten my life by taking my shadow from me?"

Crazy Horse's last words to Agent Lee follow.

"My friend, I do not blame you for this. Had I listened to you this trouble would not have happened to me. I was not hostile to the white men. Sometimes my young men would attack the Indians who were their enemies and took their ponies. They did it in return.

We had buffalo for food, and their hides for clothing and for our teepees. We preferred hunting to a life of idleness on the reservation, where we were driven against our will. At times we did not get enough to eat, and we were not allowed to leave the reservation to hunt.

We preferred our own way of living. We were no expense to the government. All we wanted was peace and to be left alone. Soldiers were sent out in the winter, who destroyed our villages.

Then "Long Hair" (Custer) came in the same way. They say we massacred him, but he would have done the same thing to us had we not defended ourselves and fought to the last. Our first impulse was to escape with our squaws and papooses, but we were so hemmed in that we had to fight.

After that I went up on the Tongue River with a few of my people and lived in peace. But the government would not let me alone. Finally, I came back to the Red Cloud Agency. Yet I was not allowed to remain quiet.

I was tired of fighting. I went to the Spotted Tail Agency and asked that chief and his agent to let me live there in peace. I came here with the agent (Lee) to talk with the Big White Chief but was not given a chance. They tried to confine me. I tried to escape, and a soldier ran his bayonet into me.

I have spoken."

Rain in the Face, Sioux — Claimed to have killed Custer

Indian Oratory: Famous Speeches by Noted Indian Chieftains, by W. C. Vanderwerth, Copyright 1971 by the University of Oklahoma Press

Courtesy Montana Historical Society

There is a saying that goes like this: "There is no worse enemy than a one-time friend." Such was the case with the Nez Perce, a tribe that lived in the area where present-day Oregon, Washington, and Idaho meet. They, like the other tribes of the northern Rockies, were receptive to the whites who settled in the area. They were somewhat upset by the gold rush in the territory, however. And really steamed by the one-sided Treaty of 1863 which denied them their choice land. Some went to the reservation, others stayed put, in defiance of the "treaty." Nothing was done about it for a dozen years until finally the number of whites increased, and whites demanded they be put on the reservation. Later a few braves killed some homesteaders.

In the spring of 1877 General Oliver Howard ordered the Nez Perce under Chief Joseph to the reservation. Naturally he didn't want to, but he *did* agree. Some of the younger braves didn't like the idea. Uh oh! The Chiefs decided to split rather than take their chances explaining the murders. Thus began one of the more amazing "wars" in the history of the West.

While hiding out on the Salmon River a few more whites were killed. Howard obviously couldn't tolerate this kind of business. He sent troops to engage the Nez Perce. They did, and wished they hadn't, at White Bird Canyon. You see, the Nez Perce were the kind of shooters who, when asked to shoot a dime tossed in the air at fifty paces, would probably have replied, "which side?" Their marksmen picked off "blue jackets" like blueberries. When they had enough they quit. A similar thing happened at the Clearwater River a few weeks later. This time, chiefs Looking Glass, White Bird, and Toohoolhoolzote were there also. Nez Perce now knew they were being "hunted down." They only wished to be left alone. They did not wish to fight.

From there they made their way across Lolo Pass, causing quite a stir in Missoula and the Bitterroot Valley. In preparation for them, the soldiers of Fort Missoula hurridly built a fortification in Lolo Pass which was later named "Fort Fizzle." The Nez Perce merely went *around* it, avoiding trouble, and headed south through the Bitterroot Valley and into the Big Hole. Here Looking Glass felt his people would be safe. They set up camp for the first time in weeks. Things were about normal for a day or so until Colonel Gibbons from Fort Shaw literally "caught them napping" in the early morning of August 9, 1877. Gibbons stormed the encampment and kept it...for awhile, until those eagle-eyed rifflemen drove them out and kept them pinned down until the rest of the tribe escaped. Their losses were high, with nearly a hundred killed out of a group of 700 or more. The army's losses were some 30 killed and 40 or so wounded. Gibbons' crew was out of action.

General Howard took up the chase again. Meanwhile the Nez Perce decided to flee to Canada to join Sitting Bull. They caused a commotion going through the newly-established Yellowstone National Park, and were headed for Crow and Shoshone territory to find help. The Crow and Shoshone, like the Flatheads of the Bitterroot Valley, said "no way." From there the Nez Perce headed up the Yellowstone River doing a good job of side-stepping Colonel Sturgis of the Seventh Cavalry.

The tribe was now in central Montana, way ahead of slow-moving General Howard. Howard was slow, but he wasn't completely stupid. He called for Montana's best foot soldier, Colonel Nelson Miles. Miles was quickly on the trail with his now-famous infantry.

Much to the dismay of the people of Fort Benton, the Nez Perce decided to stop and *shop* for supplies. After scattering the troops guarding some recently-arrived supplies they helped themselves and moved north. Knowing General Howard's speed and not knowing the irrepressible Miles was tracking them, the Indians, exhausted, stopped for a breather in the Bear Paw Mountains.

We are true when we look you in the face.

Blackfoot Crow, 1873

This would be a nice time to watch *Red Sunday*, available from the North Dakota Highway Department.

On the last day of September, Miles caught up. He attacked the camp, capturing their ponies. The Nez Perce, in return, however, charged them sixty soldiers' lives. Seeing his men being picked off as though part of a shooting gallery, Miles opened up with cannon fire. The battle went on for a few days. Howard finally caught up. Meanwhile the chiefs argued over surrender. Looking Glass was dead; so was Toolhoolhoolzote; and White Bird had made it to Canada. Chief Joseph, the most influential chief left, surrendered along with the remaining 400 Nez Perce. The tribe had retreated altogether some 1700 miles, only to be caught some thirty miles from the Canadian border and freedom.

The story of the Indians in Montana from then on was the story of shrinking reservations, cultural shock, and bitterness. They were proud hunters, nomads, who came and went as they pleased. They were now wards of the state, farmers in pieces of what used to be their nation.

The Dawes Act of 1887 allotted land to the Indians on a graduated scale, with a usual portion of 160 acres per head of household. (160 acres for nomanic horsemen?) The act was made in good faith by the government to the Indians, but it might be like getting a dime to make a phone call from the mugger who just stole $1000 from you.

On October 5, 1877, Joseph spoke for the remaining Nez Perce entrenched in the Bear Paws:

"Tell General Howard I know his heart. What he told me before, I have in my heart. I am tired of fighting. Our chiefs are killed. Looking Glass is dead. Toohoolhoolzote is dead. The old men are all dead. It is the young men who say yes and no. He who led on the young men is dead. It is cold and we have no blankets. The little children are freezing to death. My people, some of them, have run away to the hills and have no blankets, no food; no one knows where they are — perhaps freezing to death. I want to have time to look for my children and see how many I can find. Maybe I shall find them among the dead. Hear me, my chiefs. I am tired; my heart is sick and sad. From where the sun now stands I will fight no more forever."

Indian Oratory: Famous Speeches by Noted Indian Chieftains, by W.C. Vanderwerth, Copyright 1971 by the University of Oklahoma Press

The only living thing left from Custer's regiment after the Battle of the Little Bighorn was Keough's horse, Comanche. He was later designated honorary "Second Commanding Officer" of the Fifth Cavalry, and he lived until 1891 at an Army post.

I have heard that you intend to settle us on a reservation near the mountains. I don't want to settle. I love to roam over the prairies. There I feel free and happy, but when we settle down we grow pale and die.

I have laid aside my lance, bow, and shield, and yet I feel safe in your presence. I have told you the truth. I have no little lies hid about me, but I don't know how it is with the commissioners. Are they as clear as I am?

A long time ago this land belonged to our fathers; but when I go up to the river I see camps of soldiers on its banks. These soldiers cut down my timber; they kill my buffalo; and when I see that, my heart feels like bursting; I feel sorry.

Santanta, Kiowa, 1876

This would be a good time to read *The Good Medicine Book* and *The Blood People* both by Adolf Hungry Wolf.

Joseph, Nez Perce

Barry Photo, courtesy U of M Library

119

Chapter Six

Earlier in this book the "open range" cattle industry was discussed. But the whole idea of open range makes for visions of shifting, nomadic horsemen following cattle, while, at the same time the word "industry" brings about pictures of whitecollared, pot-bellied, cigar-smoking old men giving orders and counting their money in terms of thousands and millions. These fellows were around, but were among an elite minority.

For the most part ranching was conducted on a small family operation basis. The rancher had a small sod or log home, usually consisting of just one room. It was heated by a fireplace, cooled by a breeze. Luxuries were family heirlooms from back east (the civilized world), and glass windows. Running water was the nearest creek. Lights were provided by "Big Red" (the sun), or tallow candles. Beds were feed sacks sewn together stuffed with "prairie down" (hay). School (in the strict sense of a building for formal education) was non-existent. However, people spent their lifetime learning, if nothing else, survival skills. This type of operation usually had 25 head of cattle, a few sheep, chickens, dogs, and a small garden to provide vegetables.

A somewhat larger operation would have a few hundred head. This called for the addition of a bunkhouse for the hired hands, also with a cook house, adjoining the bunkhouse, to feed them. There would also be a barn.

The larger the operation, the better the main house. This only made sense. Same as today. As a person makes more money, he or she usually lives in a better fashion. Even the luxuries were only for the wealthy. The average rancher had only necessities. The only thing that remained the same regardless of the wealth of the spread was the bunkhouse. The bunkhouse was sort of the *ghetto* of the ranch. Generally a one-room building which slept ten to twenty hands, it was a place not fit for man nor beast, but *perfect* for the cowboy.

Aside from the sight of bare walls, and buffalo or wolf skins used for bunks, one saw nothing, except maybe a floor, sometimes dust, sometimes wood, full of "already worn but not necessarily dirty" clothes. When the cowboys were at home, the bunkhouse could be located with one's eyes closed. The unmistakable aroma emitted from sweating bodies, cow chips, licorice-flavored chewing tobacco, and work boots combined to give away its location from quite a distance.

This would be a good time to read *Tough Trip Through Paradise* by Andrew Garcia, edited by Bennett Stein.

But let's say a person had his eyes closed and had a cold, which rendered the nose out of commission. It was still an easy mark to find, for the sound of banjos, fiddles, guitars, jew's harps, or harmonicas was often in the air. Also an occasional gunshot sounded when some hand, out of sheer boredom, would send an unfortunate, trespassing spider on to another life by having it try to catch a chunk of lead from a .45.

This would be a good time to read *Trails Plowed Under* by Charles M. Russell.

This would be a good time to read *Log of a Cowboy* by Andy Adams.

BRONC TO BREAKFAST

Hey, Doc, git that bog-spavined hoss outa the stew kettle!
That Roman-nosed cayuse is just kickin' all the breakfast in the fire!
  I'll take his hide... You hear? Doc, do you hear?
I'll skin him alive while he's still kickin'!
  I'll shoot him so full of holes that his hide won't hold hay!
Hey, Doc, dad blast yer hide...Grab his head, Amby,
  Never mind the bacon or Doc; just save the cawfee...!

  You got ev'body just as mad as HEY...

  We got a bronc to breakfast, shure enuff.
We got a knot-head cayuse, an' he's tuff;
  And if you fancy hosses 'round the table,
You kin eat yer grub out in the stable.
  Ther's a daw-gonned, hammer-headed, cactus-bedded mess of bones,
Pig-eyed, devil-critter awful bitter hoss...
  We mean a Bronc to Breakfast...

  We got a hoss to breakfast, shure enuff,
We got a nasty mustang, an' he's tuff,
  an if you like yer hosses on a platter,
Boy, yer jus' too dum' to really matter...
  There's a dad-burn'd swivel-jointed, self-appointed bag of hay,
nock-need locomatic, too emphatic hoss...
  We mean a Bronc to Breakfast...

  We got a 'quake to breakfast, shure enuff.
We got a ache to breakfast, an' he's tuff;
  And if you cook with hosses, as time passes,
You may find his shoes in yer molasses.
  There's a sun-stroked, widow-makin' not mistaken, leather-belly,
Flea-bit, dub-ble-gaited, trubble-baited hoss.
  NO DERN GOOD Bronc to Breakfast.
And we don't like it...!

—Charles Russell Suite,
Lyrics & Music by Francis E. White; 1963.
Lyrics reprinted courtesy of Francis White, Bozeman, Montana.

By now you should see that filth and boredom were major components in the life of *real* cowboys, as opposed to the Hollywood types. Probably one of their bigger thrills was a new mailorder catalogue. They could look at the pictures, and, if anyone could read, read the descriptions of the "toys" of the civilized world.

Most cowboys were young, teenaged and in the early 20's, and single. This meant they were reckless and devil-may-care, while honest and loyal. Loyalty was the key to the whole operation. It was the glue that held the industry together. You see, the cowboy knew the ranch was an establishment based on the care and well being of cows. The cow was a cut above the cowboy. Why else would anyone lead such a spartan existence? Adventure, yes, but mostly loyalty to the owner.

The summer consisted not only of watching the cattle, but performing many other chores as well. Doctoring cattle was all important. Pulling them from swamps, dehorning them, watching for, and fighting, range fires, bringing cattle to new grazing areas, killing off predators. These were a part of normal duties.

Winter was a time of unemployment for many, and, for a lucky few, a time for repairing or replacing equipment. Chopping holes in frozen ponds to allow cattle to drink and leading them to available grass were routine. Cutting a year's supply of firewood or repairing the ranch house and the other out-buildings was done during the "off-season." About the most exciting job was the hunting of wolves, who became more bold at striking cattle as winter wore on. All of any of these jobs, however, were better than the only alternative, riding the "grub line," which was riding from ranch to ranch getting free meals, or doing small jobs.

Even worse was the distribution of women in the west. A fair estimate of the ratio would be ten men to each woman. This made for difficult times for both. For the men a glimpse of a woman, usually the boss's wife, was considered a treat. For the women, at a time when they were considered to be the "weaker sex," it was proof that they could endure the hardships that accompanied the lifestyle. Consider a life without running water, electricity, perma-press clothes, hospitals, communication, retirement plans, cars, etc....

Lost Gold Mine Secret of Indians; Never Leaked Out

It was on Thanksgiving day, 1868, the white man was first told there was gold in the Little Rockies. Just where it came from there is no one now living, nor has there been for many a day, who knows. The secret belonged to the Indians and they, through fears instilled by the early missionaries, would murder rather than to permit it to leak out. In fact it is believed by old timers that at least one white man lost his life in quest of the gold deposit there.

Sixty-nine years ago, so it is said by those who long ago learned the facts, there was a Thanksgiving dinner at old Fort Browning on the Milk river about 50 miles below the present site of Fort Belknap. It was given by the officers to the little command and included several white men.

While the dinner was in progress it is related that an Indian known as Nepee came into the fort with a little bag containing gold dust and nuggets which he showed to Maj. John Simmons, Capt. D.W. Buck, James Stuart, who afterwards died at Fort Peck, and Major Culbertson. Nepee was a fast friend of the whites and gave the sack to Major Simmons. He was taken into the dining room, where the banquet was in progress, and every effort was made to get him to tell where the gold had been found. However, they proved without avail.

It Was Death to Tell

There is no doubt, it is said, that the Indian would willingly have complied, but he knew well that if he did it would mean his life. He stated as much at the time that he was afraid his tribe would put him to death as they all had explicit instructions not to divulge the hiding place of the precious metal.

There were made to him at that time all sorts of offers. He was promised protection from the members of his tribe for all time to come, but while he was ready and willing to perform any other favorable act to the whites he would not give up this secret.

However, it is believed that he did reveal it to at least one white man, and that was Joe Hontus, commonly known as "Buckskin Joe," who was afterwards killed on the Milk river. Joe and the Indian were on the best of terms. They had slept together and had been on the prairies for weeks and months at a time and it was well known there was no one whom the Indian thought so much of as he did of Joe.

Hontus, a few years after the Thanksgiving day the Indian came to the fort, while drinking, stated he knew where the mines were located and that he was going out to find them. Shortly afterwards he left and the next seen of him was when his body was found riddled with bullets. It is the general belief of old timers, and always has been, that Joe started out to find the mine and was discovered by members of the tribe and put to death.

Secret Died With Nepee

Nepee died in 1876 and with him passed the only man, friendly enough with the whites to tell them the place. So far as it has ever been learned, he took his secret with him to the grave.

The story goes that for a long time prior to the Thanksgiving day when Nepee came to Fort Browning, the Indians knew of the existence of gold in the Little Rockies and that they had taken some of it out, after their own fashion. About 1865 they were visited by two French priests and the story has it that they showed these priests some of the gold. Thinking that they would be better able to learn the secret of its location, they are said to have informed the Indians that they must never tell the white men that there was gold there, or it would only be a short time before he would man-

age to take away their land. This schooling was the means of sealing the secret and even the priests were unable to learn its location.

In 1867 one of these priests was put to death by the Indians and the reason for the murder, it is stated, was that he was believed to be possessed with knowledge regarding the location of the gold deposit.

There were in the early days many of the old miners of northern Montana who sought to find out the secret. Weeks of search lengthened into months, and although there have been those who claimed to have found it, no one has been able to bring forth the same class of gold as was exhibited on that Thanksgiving day by Nepee.

Indians Kept Watch

There is a legend connected with this lost mine, but whether or not true no one can be found who will say. It is that after the priests told the Indians what would be the result should they divulge the mine, they put a guard on the mountain pass leading to it. For years afterward this guard was maintained and even as late as 1875 an Indian sentry is said to have been seen in the Little Rockies.

There has been gold found there since that day, but nowhere in such quantities as was told by Nepee, and there are men living who believe to this day that the secret of the tribe is their own.

Because of the recognized temporary nature of placer mining and the short residency of persons who attained financial success, Diamond City and its adjoining gulches operated under a looser organization — if possible — than other mining camps. One account records the following, rather typical, but unusually short, set of articles in its miners' code:

We, the miners of this district, resolve, first, that the district shall be called Confederate Gulch, and that a claim shall be 1000 feet long in the creek, 200 feet long in the gulch, and 50 feet front on the bank, and that a man may hold one of each.

Secondly, that no more Chinamen shall take up claims.

Thirdly, that a white man must stick up a notice at each end of his claim when he takes it up.

Fourthly, that a man may lay over his claim a month by posting a notice and paying the receiver one dollar.

Fifthly, that all disputes about claims shall be settled by a miners' meeting and no lawyers.

Single pans of gold on Montana Bar yielding as much as $1000 were not uncommon, and nuggets worth from $300 to $500 appeared often enough to keep the entire camp working at fever pitch. Only rough estimates can be made of the total value of gold taken in the area. Approximately $12,000,000 from Confederate, and some $5,000,000 from the neighboring gulches is an average guess.

"The Mining Frontier in Montana," Merill Burlingame, in Montana's Past, ed. Roeder-Malone, Missoula, 1973

Consequence of Mining Activity

Due to the influx of miners in the west central portion of Montana, merchants established settlements and stores. Missoula was one such settlement. By 1862 there were enough settlers in Missoula's original site, Hellgate Village, for it to be the scene of Montana's first civil lawsuit. A Frenchman named Tin Cup Joe accused Baron O'Keefe (wealthy local landowner) of killing his horse, which had been eating the Baron's hay. At one point the trail erupted into a fistfight between the lawyers; at another point O'Keefe berated and insulted the judge. Tin Cup Joe was eventually awarded $40 in damages plus court costs, but no one ever collected from O'Keefe.

To depict the life of a gold miner of this era, a selection from the handbook titled *Treasure State Treasure Tales* by J.M. Moore has been chosen. The title of the selection is "The Last Keyes Mine." It speaks for itself.

The Lost Keyes Mine

In the Badlands of Montana, below the mouth of the Judith River, there is supposedly located "The Lost Keyes Mine." Although it is not certain whether the lost gold was taken from rich diggings or taken forcefully from lucky prospectors, there is little doubt that the long sought treasure actually exists.

In 1864, two young men, John Lepley and John Keyes, operated a small ranching business at Silver City on the old Fort Benton road about twelve miles northeast of Helena. They made a good living selling dairy products and garden produce to nearby mining camps, but Keyes became infected by gold fever and wanted to make his fortune faster. In the fall of 1864, he set out in search of it by traveling into territory northeast of Fort Benton, then down the Missouri River.

He bought supplies including mining tools, food, blankets, tobacco, a couple of horses and several bottles of a No. 1 necessity, whiskey, and began his journey into the Sweet Grass Hills, the Bear Paw Mountains and down the river and north into the Little Rocky Mountains. The following spring he returned to civilization accompanied by a beautiful Gros Ventre squaw and carrying a poke filled with over $2,000 worth of gold dust which he proudly exhibited in "The Golden Nugget Saloon" in Fort Benton. This was the last time he was seen before going back into the Little Rockies.

Several years later the squaw told a white man that she and Keyes, two men he had picked up with at Fort Benton and one of the men's squaws, had attempted to re-locate the gold when Keyes was killed. According to her story, she had asked him how much farther it was to the end of their journey and he had replied, "Two more sleeps," meaning two more days of travel. The next evening there was a sharp report, the little party was surrounded by Sioux Indians and Keyes was killed and scalped.

Keyes' squaw was badly wounded, but because she was recognized by one of the Indians her life was spared and she managed to get to the thick timber along the river where she lay in a semi-conscious state for several days. She finally gained enough strength to struggle on west in search of her own people. She existed on roots and grasses and during her journey gave birth to a baby which lived but a short time. She located her people, later married a white man and lived on the Fort Belknap Reservation. When she was a very old woman, she attempted to point out the site of the massacre but was unable to do so. It is claimed that many lives were lost in the search for "The Lost Keyes Gold."

One of the most persevering and optimistic hunters for this lost treasure was a long, lanky red-headed prospector called Alexander who arrived in the Badlands in the spring of 1895 and camped on Big Dry Creek during the wild gold rush to Big Dry Creek. He announced often to all who would listen to him that he was searching for the Lost Keyes diggings and wouldn't stop until he found them. He had had, he said, a wonderful dream in which a beautiful Indian maiden had appeared to him and whispered softly over and over in his ear, "Two more sleeps," then laughed softly and disapeared into the air.

The second day Alexander was on the creek he found an old rubber boot, and a piece of rotten plank with a pleat nailed across one end. Although he didn't attach too much importance to the articles at the time, within a few weeks the objects were displayed with great reverence in a mine's shrine.

A few days after he had found the boot Alexander was panning for gold along the creek and had carefully panned down a shovelful of gravel until there was a thin line of fine sand. Mingled with the sand were three fine particles of gold. He was busy examining the gold under a magnifying glass when a cowboy who was much interested in Alexander and his ambition to find "The Lost Keyes Gold" took a look at the pan. Seeing the small particles of gold his imagination ran away with him and he visioned them as large nuggets of pure gold.

This would be a good time to read The Old West Series by Time-Life Books (e.g. *The Cowboys, The Gunfighters.*)

"This here gold sure satisfies me," he shouted. "How fer does this dam go?" Already urging his horse on he called back, "I'll stake out a claim fer you too!" He staked out his claim and then rode of in the direction of Glasgow, the county seat.

The cowboy's reaction to the gold dust in Alexander's pan caused the prospector to become concerned about his own claim which was not yet on record. Early the next morning Alexander followed the cowboy's trail to Glasgow where he learned that the cowboy, in an extreme state of excitement, had reported the discovery of the Keyes diggings by him and that the more he had talked, the larger the nuggets had grown. He had verified the discovery by saying he himself had witnessed it.

Before starting on his search for the Lost Keyes diggings, Alexander had made a pact with a friend in Cascade, Montana, to the effect that should he be forunate enough to really find the mine he would notify the friend. He was true to his promise and having convinced himself that he was close to the treasure wrote his friend stressing the discovery of the sluice box relic, the rubber boot and shovel handle, believing that they had indeed been left by Keyes twenty-four years ago.

After Alexander's letter had been read by his friend it was turned over to a reporter on one of the daily papers. The story of the discovery of the Lost Keyes mine was played up with such phrases as "Millions in Sight," "A Second Golconda," "Another Eldorado," and "Keyes Gold Re-discovered."

The papers bearing the discovery news had hardly been printed when one of the biggest stampedes in mining history began. Men from all walks of life, and women too, appeared from all directions in any conveyance they could get. Some, unable to obtain a horse, even came on foot carrying blankets and food on their backs. Many descended the river in boats and homemade rafts and one came in a Red River cart drawn by a mule and a cow. All had but one goal: To get in on the big gold rush in the Badlands and migrate to the famous Big Dry Creek area where an old rubber boot, a piece of rotten plank and three tiny pieces of gold had been found. Even the weather, which so often contributed to the hardships of gold seekers remained unusually warm and clear for late fall.

The desolate country surrounding the Big Dry was a bedlam of activity. Named Alexander City, it was supposedly destined to become a metropolis of a busy mining region with avenues stretched out into the Badlands, but it was built upon a foundation of foolish hope and imagination.

In the center of Alexander City a large tent was used as a shrine and housed the Keyes relics which were kept in a glass case. Newly arrived men were escorted to the shrine by older residents where they were allowed to stand with awed respect before the old rubber boot, the round, weather-smoothed stick and the rotten pieces of plank.

Prospect holes were sunk to bedrock on either side of the creek and miners watched anxiously for the rich pay dirt that was never found. In less than two weeks after the big stampede to Big Dry Creek the miners folded their tents like the Arabs and almost as silently stole away.

The beginning of the end came when a newcomer from Missouri viewed the sacred relics. He picked up the piece of plank and proceeded to scrape away part of the heavy incrustation from the head of a nail holding the cleat with his pocketknife. As he did so he laughed gleefully, for the cleat was nailed to the plank with wire nails and wire nails had not yet been invented in 1871!

This shocking expose spelled "finish" for the Big Dry boom. The men immediately began to pack their horses and wagons and by the next day a regiment of disillusioned miners took the trail back to everyday reality. All that remained of the dream city of Alexander was a row of pegs which marked the course of Main Street and the avenues which were to have led to its beautiful residential section.

A few miners left momentos to their short stay before their exodus. On one discovery post of a claim was left the following message by the owner...

"The Big Dry was our only hope.

Our only hope is gone, we're broke!"

Another disgusted miner left this notice on the trunk of an old cottonwood tree...

"To all whom it may concern:

I hereby locate the right-of-way

up and down this tree!"

A German who had walked from the railroad, a distance of about 100 miles, arrived in Alexander City with his blankets, food and other provisions on his back just in time to see the residents packing up to leave. As he was wearily treking back to the railroad a man in a buggy stopped beside him and offered him a ride. The German shook his shaggy head in refusal, then by way of explanation said, "Nein, I vant no ride. I'll learn dis crazy Dutchman someting yet!"

Chapter Seven

WEALTH

Pinning down the wealth of the land for this era is an easy enough thing to do. Attaching a dollar-and-cent price tag or even a set of values is something altogether different.

You see, to extract the wealth there must be a trade off, or give-and-take. Generally, the smaller the give, the smaller the take, and vice-versa. It would be fair to say that a lot of the "vice-versa" took place because of outside investors. Huge sums of money were invested in Montana in order that even larger amounts could be taken out. This is a very favorable balance if you are the taker, the investor, but a position of dependance and loss for the area of investment, the giver.

A few examples might be in order. Say a Texas cattle outfit brought 1,000 head to Montana at $10 a head. This would be an investment of $10,000. Two years later, after eating free grass, the cattle are driven to the railroad and sold for $20 each. A sum of $20,000 is received. $10,000 is the "take," or profit. We now see $10,000 or more than we did two years earlier. How much did the grass really cost? This, of course, is over simplified.

How about the prospector who invests $100? He takes his equipment and food and takes to the hills. A few months later he emerges with $1,000 in gold. The investment of $100 got the prospector $1,000. Was the gold "free?" Who gained? Who lost?

A mechant purchases $10,000 worth of material for shirts and dresses. He sells it for $15,000. Who profits? Who loses?

A piece of ground could graze a thousand animals. Would that 1,000 be cattle, sheep, or buffalo? Or a mixture of all? Who loses or wins with each differing ratio? What if someone puts 5,000 animals on the land?

In these examples there are many unknown variables that need, for the sake of accuracy, to be considered. Accuracy is not the main consideration here, however, but rather the general idea. Nothing is free. There are costs, hidden as they may be that must be taken into consideration. If they aren't, profits would be high for all "takers" and losses equally high for the "givers" (they just didn't show up right away).

Example: What if Montana Territory would have charged the Texas outfit in the example $5,000 for a "grazing fee?" Montana (the giver) would have received some money for the "free grass." The cattle outfit, (the taker) would have made less profit. Both share the price of "free" grass.

This would be a good time to read *Montana, Idaho, & Wyoming Ghost Towns* by Lambert Florin.

Gold dust and gold nuggets, weighed on gold scales, was the only medium of exchange in the camps.

Unscrupulous men who weighed the gold permitted their fingernails to grow long; as they handled the gold, they edged a few flakes under the nails, and afterwards tapped them out.

In commercial establishments where gold changed hands the janitors panned the floor sweepings each morning for gold that had been dropped.

Our Land Montana, *Ralph Henry, Helena, State Publishing Co., 1963*

of the LAND

Anyway, Montana has been the perennial giver while interests from outside its boundaries have been the takers. A few exceptions are those came with little, made a lot, and stayed, namely Grant, Kohrs, Stuart, and, to an extent, Wibaux, and an interesting fellow by the name of William A. Clark.

1887

WHOA!

WHEW! THERE GOES THE OLD NEIGHBORHOOD...

This would be a great time to listen to "The Renegade," written by Ian Tyson. It's on the album, *Shades of Time* by the Pozo Seco Singers.

MINERS and MILLIONAIRES... (1887 — 1917)

129

Chapter One

CROSSING the LAND

What good is having money in the bank if you can't get at it? What good is a piece of property if you can't get to it? These are merely examples of the predicament of Montana and other western states prior to the introduction of the railroad. Sure, there were steamboats and freightlines, but they were slow and moved at nature's whims.

The railroad, prior to its arrival, was much sought after due to the prosperity and permanence it would lend to any town it touched. Every city west of the Mississippi wished to become a transportation center for its area, not just for the money but also for the status of becoming the county seat or maybe the state capital.

Competition from the Northern Pacific began the minute the Montana Central pulled into Butte in 1889. Rates dropped immediately. Jim Hill and C. A. Broadwater were heroes. *And* they accomplished this feat without a land grant.

Just as Hill was completing his line to the Pacific the U.S. again went into one of its "tight money" (or depression) periods. During this time the Northern Pacific, the railroad with all of the *land*, and *no money*, fell due to lack of operating money. So Jim Hill of the Great Northern, the railroad with *some money* and *no land*, and some associates bought controlling interests in the competing line. Hill had both the Great Northern and the Northern Pacific by 1896.

In the meantime a Chicago-based outfit, the Chicago, Burlington, and Quincy Railroad, felt that in order to be competitive with other lines, they, too, needed to go transcontinental. They struck up a deal with Hill whereby Hill's railroads could use their tracks while they would use his. The Burlington hooked up with Hill's at Billings. (They were already as far west as Nebraska.) Everyone was happy. Everyone, that is, except the people on the "Hill Lines," for in 1901, Hill and the boys also put the Burlington in their back pockets. The three railroads, the Northern Pacific, Great Northern, and Burlington, all went into Hill's holding company, called the Northern Securities Company, worth some 400 million dollars. Now there was *no* competition in the Northwest. Hill owned all of 'em. Freight prices would be out of this world. President Theodore Roosevelt, the "Trust Buster," with the help of the U.S. Supreme Court, broke up the Northern Securities for its violation of the 1890 Sherman Anti-trust Act. The Northwest was relieved. It sounded good, but in actuality the changes made were only on paper. Rates stayed high.

Help was soon on the way, however, in the form of the Chicago, Milwaukee, St. Paul, and Pacific Railroad, or "Milwaukee Road." They, too, needed a Pacific connection. Starting in South Dakota in 1906, they completed their track to Seattle by the spring of 1909. Competition was restored, for a while. By 1925 the competition of Hill's lines was too much; the Milwaukee, the first railroad in the nation with long-distance electrified trains (across the Rockies) was put into receivership.

Looking back on all of this, what do we have? From the time when the U. and N. first reached Montana in 1880 until the completion of the Milwaukee Road in 1909 people across the state could hear the cold steel ring. Mainlines numbered as many as four with dozens of spur lines. Thousands of miles of track crossed the state giving rise to towns and cities. The states' major industries, mining, lumber, and livestock, all benefitted immensely with the presence of the railroads. The world had shrunk a little bit. Montana wasn't so removed from everywhere. However, it wasn't without cost to Montanans. Because of lack of competition on the "Hill Lines" (later renamed the Burlington Northern) freight charges have remained high in the state. Instead of huge government subsidies to build, the railroads inflated their rates to customers in areas of no competition (like Montana) and gained "mini-subsidies" from each person using its services. This led to a boom in trucking, busing, and air freighting in recent years. The high freight charges are a familiar tune throughout the West. But this is a book about Montana so our concern lies here.

At the same time construction began for the Northern Pacific in 1870, the group of Mormon businessmen who were doing quite well trafficking goods on the Corrine-Virginia City Road saw the Northern Pacific route as a great threat to their economic well being. Within one year John W. Young, son of Brigham Young, along with other Mormon investors got together with some eastern money men and put together an offshoot of the Union Pacific to southwest Montana. The line was to be called the Utah Northern. They, too, felt the crunch of '73, laying very little track in their first year. In fact, they, too, came to a halt, still inside the Utah border.

Money loosened up, banks were lending, and tracks were moving competitively by 1879. It was the N.P. moving from the east and the U. and N. (recently bought out and renamed by the Union Pacific) battling to reach the mining areas of southwestern Montana. The U. and N. won the race, reaching Butte on the day after Christmas, 1881. The N.P. completed its task on September 8, 1883, with a golden spike ceremony at, appropriately, Gold Creek, Montana. Portland, Oregon, was now connected to the Great Lakes, nearly 20 years after the N. P. charter was issued.

The situation was fantastic. Montana now had two railroads competing for business; freight costs would be reasonable.

Wrong! The railroads agreed to stay out of each other's territory. Prices would stay high until *real* competition arrived.

The year 1866 was interesting for Montana railroading for it marked the beginning of the Montana Central Railroad. It was a venture involving C. A. Broadwater, a long-time freighter, and financed by Jim Hill of the Minneapolis and Manitoba Railroad Company. Hill had every intention of punching another northern route through to the Pacific Northwest. In fact, his railroad stood poised at the Montana border awaiting the Congressional greenlight to run through Indian reservations in northern Montana. The green light came in early 1887. Now the Montana Central was racing from Helena to Great Falls while the Manitoba was racing west from near Wolf Point to Havre, then on to Great Falls. The Manitoba worked at a breakneck pace and made some 100 miles per month reaching Great Falls in October of 1887. The Montana Central met them there from Helena shortly thereafter. By 1889 the Montana Central was in Butte and the Manitoba was pushing through the newly rediscovered Marias Pass. But now these two railroads were under one man, Jim Hill. The name of the line was the Great Northern. By 1893 the Great Northern reached Puget Sound and the city of Seattle.

Psychologically, the railroad was going to cure a lot of ills. It was going to end, to a degree, the feeling of being totally removed from the rest of the world. Jump on a train in Missoula one day and get off in Chicago the next. It would be great. People would come out, business would thrive, cattle and precious metals could be shipped to eastern markets. More growth! Bigger! Better! Maybe if we are real good and sit straight they (the powers that be in Washington D.C.) will let us be a state. So you see it was more than just wanting to ''see'' and ''hear'' a train that caused the people of Montana and the whole West to want the railroad. It was the chain reaction of the growth and progress cycle that would make the ''Great American Dream'' a reality in the West.

The idea of a transcontinental railroad was a hot item long before the Civil War, but it took that war to make it a reality. You see, before the actual split by the Confederacy, the Senate and House of Representatives were divided into northern industrial interests and southern agricultural interests. When it came time to decide anything Congress was constantly deadlocked. As for the rail route to the Pacific, obviously the South wanted a southern route, the North a northern route.

With secession and the outbreak of war, the Union Congress pushed through the legislation necessary to enable the Union Pacific-Central Pacific transcontinental railroad to begin construction in 1861. The line was completed with the driving of the golden spike in 1869 at Promontory, Utah. The spot is a National Historic Site and should be, but the West is a big place and one line across it hardly would do. So, with enough griping and complaining, mostly legitimate, the people of the Northwest got their way when in July of 1864 Congress authorized a rail line from the upper Great Lakes to the Pacific. The Northern Pacific Railroad was on its way. They didn't get the fantastic loans that the first transcontinental railway received (the first always gets the better deal) but they did receive, as an incentive, the railroads' largest land grant. In other words they didn't get money to build, they received land (worth money) instead. (This might be compared to the difference between getting an allowance for doing chores or getting ''a piece of the Rock.'') If you've ever seen a U.S. Forest Service map of your area and noticed the ''checkerboard'' look   about it, this is why. The federal government gave the Northern Pacific forty sections per each mile of track through Montana. It was given in this checkerboard fashion probably to maintain a degree of control in the area. Actual construction didn't begin until 1870 when crews began in Minnesota and headed west. Because they received land instead of money the burden of paying wages and buying materials became too much. Construction ceased in 1873 at Bismark, Dakota Territory. The nation was in a period of ''tight money'' due to bank failures started by the outfit that was trying to finance the railroad.

Chapter Two

BENEATH the LAND

The year was 1863. The place, Bannack, Montana, a booming gold camp whose sheriff, one Henry Plummer, was less than a year away from being hanged along with the rest of his "road agent" friends. Into this town came a skinny little dude by the name of William Andrews Clark. He had been born on a Pennsylvania farm in 1839, when the U.S. consisted of only 25 states, and totaled less than half of its present-day size. This was the time of great fortunes, a time to "go west, young man" and make your fortune. Clark would, and did. He attended schools in Pennsylvania and Iowa, long enough to become a country school teacher in Missouri. At the age of 23 he set out for Colorado in hopes of finding riches in mining.

In 1863 at a time when he could have been making a name for himself in the Civil War like so many others, he was out to make money. He and a few buddies made their way to eastern Idaho Territory (now western Montana) to a new strike, Bannack. In Clark's possession upon his arrival in Bannack were a team of oxen, some mining equipment, five dollars in gold dust, and three books, one dealing in geology, another in law, and the last a collection of poems by Robert Burns.

Clark, who later was to be worth tens of millions of dollars, made his first money in Montana by selling a pair of elk antlers to Cy Skinner, a saloon keeper (and road agent, soon to be hanged), as decoration for his place. He soon made several thousands of dollars working a gold claim on the area. This he invested into shipping goods from Salt Lake City to the mining camps. In 1865 he made handsome profits selling mules and livestock. By 1869 he moved to Deer Lodge and was into merchandising. By 1872 he was a partner in a Deer Lodge bank. Mr. Clark, with a keen mind for business, a lust for power, and a wish for prestige, was on his way to the top.

In the meantime, gold miners had fanned out across the mountains of Montana. In late spring of 1864 G.O. Humphrey and William Allison expanded a hole apparently dug by use of the elk antlers found inside. They panned their diggings and not only discovered gold but also what was to be dubbed by Marcus Daly "the richest hill on earth," Butte.

Soon Butte's placer gold disappeared; silver was the abundant precious metal. That was okay except for one simple problem: silver mining was a completely different operation. Instead of the simple placer business (which, incidentally, wasn't all that easy in Butte because water was scarce), silver *required* underground mining, which required skilled labor, heavy machinery, and lots of capital. Only a few men, those with the necessary funds, men like Samuel T. Hauser and William A. Clark, could get into the game. Mining in Montana was evolving from a small-time, low investment business into company operations with sizable payrolls. Miners were no longer their own bosses, but rather they were employees.

Samuel T. Hauser was the money man behind Montana's first silver smelter, outside Bannack, built in 1866. The following year saw Hauser and the St. Louis and Montana Mining Company (one of his interests) begin operations in what was to become Phillipsburg, a booming silvertown. By the way, the town got its name from one of Hauser's engineers. Phillip Deidesheimer. It's a good thing they used his first name. Could you imagine a town called Deidescheimerburg?

Meanwhile, money wasn't burning a hole in Clark's pocket. He established a mail-carrying business from Walla Walla to Missoula but there were no "big bucks" in it like there were in mining. By 1872 Clark had purchased controlling interests in four mines in Butte, only some forty miles from his Deer Lodge base of operations. He bought at low prices from hard-pressed miners whose small placer operations panned out and whose capital wouldn't allow them to go underground.

An interesting story about Clark which was used by U. of M. Professor K. Ross Toole in his book, Montana, an Uncommon Land, was that of Clark's arrival in Butte. When he arrived, he carried three books with him: Robert Burns' Poems, a textbook, Elements of Geology, and Parsons on Contracts, a law book. Only a man with foresight and ambition would have chosen the last two. Poetry was Clark's hobby.

Now, with a chunk of property in Butte ready for mining, Clark split for New York and the prestigious Columbia School of Mines to "cram" the latest techniques before making his big move. (Clark was no dummy.) He was gone for several months, but when he returned he was ready to do it up right.

In 1875 a fellow by the name of William L. Farlin needed some money to work his Travonia Mine and build his Dexter Mill. The bank he went to was the "Donnell, Clark, (good old William A.) and Larabie." With the opening of Farlin's Dexter Mill and John How's Centennial Mill, in 1876, Butte was on its way.

With the capability to not only mine the silver but now to smelt it, Butte grew rapidly, for better or worse. The population shot from fifty to a hundred times than number. The year 1876 was a biggie. It was the year of the famous Crazy Horse and Gall vs. Custer bout southeast of Billings. It was the Centennial of the United States. It was the year of W. Farlin's inability to make good his loan on the Travonia Mine and Dexter Mill, allowing W. A. Clark to secure them. It was the year the telephone was invented. It was also the year Marcus Daly arrived in Butte.

Marcus Daly was born December 5, 1841, in County Caven, Ireland. At age fifteen he found himself in New York where for five years he worked on the docks. San Francisco was his next home, then on to Calaveras County, California, for what was to become his path to fabulous wealth...mining. Virginia City, Nevada, was his next stop. It was here that he struck valuable friendships while learning the mining business at the famous Comstock Lode.

By 1870 he was supervising mines at the Emma Mine in Utah. The next year the Walker brothers, Salt Lake City bankers and investors, hired him as a roving prospector and mine assessor. It was the Walker brothers who sent him to Butte. His job there was to assess the Alice Mine as a possible investment in the booming camp. *On his word* they purchased the mine, setting up Daly as the manager. That was nice, but Daly wanted and needed to be on his own. In 1880 Daly did just that. Getting $100,000 for his share of the Alice, he immediately paid Michael Hickey $30,000 for his sixty-five foot hole in the ground, the Anaconda. The purchase was a gamble for the stocky, likable Irishman. It was a gamble that would pay off in unbelievable wealth. This not-so-promising piece of real estate was to become the foundation of multi-million, multi-national conglomerate that *could* and *did* bring governments tumbling to their knees.

137

Daly now had the Anaconda silver mine but needed financial backing to get rolling. The Walker brothers told him to "take a walk." It was then he turned to his old buddies, some of the wealthiest mine investors in the country, George Hearst, James B. Haggin, and Lloyd Tevis. Daly had provided this "syndicate" of friends with millions. On Daly's urging they had jumped into the Ontario Mine in Utah. They invested a mere $30,000 and took out $17,000,000 in silver. Not bad! So when Daly said he had a hot number in Butte, Montana Territory, they didn't hesitate. Maybe the fact that Hearst had just begun to get returns on his Homestake Mine in South Dakota helped also. (By the way, the Homestake was the greatest gold mine in world history, with more than $80,000,000 going to Hearst alone.)

Anyway, old Marcus was on his way. He (with his friends' aid) dropped millions for development into the Anaconda. The deeper he went the less silver he found. The silver had given way to copper, copper as the world had never seen it before. But this was a silver mine! What good was copper? In the 1870's copper was used for pots and pans. Copper was almost worthless. But, Marcus Daly was no fool; uneducated, yes, but not foolish! Only a few years earlier, the same year he arrived in Butte, a dude by the name of Alexander Graham Bell invented the telephone. Three years later another fellow, by the name of Thomas A. Edison, invented a practical light bulb. These inventions had something in common: both would need that inexpensive red metal known as copper. Butte, dubbed by Daly as the "richest hill on earth," was now going to prove it.

Like the jealous fisherman protecting his favorite hole, Daly let his neighbors know how poorly his mine was producing silver (what they, too, were looking for), *somehow* neglecting to tell them how rich it was in copper. Daly was now turning all of his attention to copper while his neighbors continued to look for ever-shrinking supplies of silver. Naturally as their disappointment grew it was not difficult for Daly to buy them out, at low prices, *before* the copper market took off. While others were looking for thousands of dollars in dimes (silver), Daly was looking for millions of dollars in pennies (copper). Chalk one up for Daly's foresight! A clearcut cast of the right time, plus the right place, plus the necessary knowledge equalling success.

Daly wasn't into only mining, for in 1882 he was also starting the Montana Improvement Company, a lumber operation run by A.B. Hammond, C.L. Bonner, and R.A. Eddy. In 1883-84 Daly saw the completion of his smelter, the world's largest, just over 25 miles west of Butte. Around it grew his own town, Anaconda. Anaconda was "spared" when Daly found that Montana already had a town with his chosen name, "Copperopolis." (It was located near White Sulphur Springs. Today a lone cabin claims the name.) To connect his mine and his reduction works and smelter Daly began his own railroad, the Butte, Anaconda and Pacific. (Pacific? It didn't make it that far. It didn't even get as far as Idaho!) It was completed in 1894. Daly continued to buy more mines, smelters, lumber, and coal.

The 1880's saw both Clark and Daly going "great guns" in the mining business. The town of Butte was *the* mining town of the West. Millions of dollars in precious metals were being extracted and shipped out. Montana (via the Anaconda Company) and Michigan (via the Calumet and Hecla Company) were locked in economic warfare over the copper market. Montana "won" in 1889. The character of Montana mining was changing, as these statistics show:

The 1880's were the years in which Montana experienced its most rapid growth. In 1880 the population was 39,159; 1890 saw that figure grow to 142,924. There was work for all who came. Up until the mid-1880's most investments were local with profits spent in the area, causing further growth. Everyone was happy. Butte was a wide open town. Its tender moments could match its toughest. But toughness was its calling card.

Whether it was the loud singing from one of Butte's pubs or possibly the mineral wealth, we'll never know, but something began to attract outside investment. It came in the form of the Boston and Montana Mining Company and the Butte and Boston Consolidated Mining Company. These companies were formed by a combination of New York financiers and the Boston copper elite, who probably had their fingers in the business since Paul Revere invented Revereware. Anyway, these companies invested huge sums of money in both Butte and Great Falls.

Value of Metals Extracted, in Millions of Dollars

	Gold	Silver	Copper	Lead
1879	2.5	2.5	??	??
1885	3.3	10.0	10.0	.5
1890	3.3	16.5	16.5	2.0

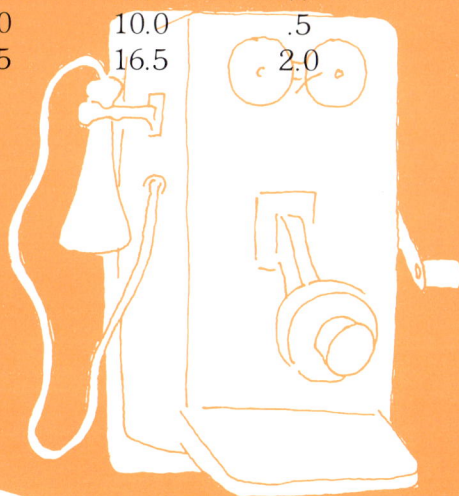

In September of 1889 the Boston and Montana Mining Company hired a new engineer to do some underground survey work for them. Their new employee, though only twenty, was a graduate of the Columbia School of Mines in New York. He had spent his summers working in the mines of Michigan, Pennsylvania and Colorado. The Boston and Montana got more than they bargained for when they hired Fritz Augustus Heinze, especially since they were paying him only $5 per day.

Fritz probably didn't mind the wage, for *he knew* he was going to do better. This tall, muscular, well-educated "boy from the East" was, in just a few years, to rise to become Montana's third "copper king," along with Marcus Daly and William Clark. Heinze's legal battles against Standard Oil, the most powerful trust in the world, was to leave not only Butte and Montana but the entire nation, and, to an extent the world, awed by his energy, his intelligence, and his gall.

140

Yes, Fritz took the job and did it well, all the while recording notes for his future reference. For the next few years he worked "on and off" for the firm. When "off" he was drumming up support back East and in Europe to finance a scheme of his own, the Montana Ore Purchasing Company. It was incorporated in the spring of 1893, with production beginning early in 1894. Heinze was a boon to the independent copper companies, for his smelter handled their ore in a reduced rate. They in turn kept their miners on the job. In this way, along with his enormous personal charm, F. A. Heinze won the hearts of many miners. As he was to find out later, hearts are one thing, stomachs another.

By 1895 he owned the Rarus and Johnstown mines, purchasing them from his ex-employer, the Boston and Montana Mining Company. It was the Rarus that began the Heinze versus Bigelow (A. S. Bigelow, president of the Boston and Montana Company) battle that was to set the stage for the real war with Standard Oil. You see, there was written into U.S. mining laws a little-known and seldom-used "Apex Law." This law merely states that if a vein of ore surfaced or apexed on a person's claim, that person could legally follow it regardless of where it went. It was a well written law for places where there was no "faulting" in the ground. And we all know that Butte has "faults."

Anyway...Heinze was brought to court by the Boston and Montana Company for digging into their adjoining property and extracting tons of rich ore. Like gangsters pleading the "Fifth Amendment," Fritz pleaded the Apex Law, a phrase which would become synonymous with his name. To show there were no hard feelings, Fritz offered Bigelow $250,000 for the property bordering the Rarus. Both men knew it was worth $20,000,000. Bigelow was furious. Boston had already lost, through its Michigan mines, a copper war with Montana, and now an insolent youngster of 26, who just a few years before had worked for $5 per day, was trying to steal property worth $20,000,000! No way! Heinze had promised a battle and Bigelow got it. Three years later Bigelow had lost, out of his own pocket, over $10,000,000 and his Globe National Bank. He was broke. The Boston and Montana wasn't, for it became part of Standard Oil.

Meanwhile, Marcus Daly and William Clark had, since 1888, kept Montana citizens, through their newspapers and government "friends," confused, divided, and bitter. All of this was made possible, of course, due to the enormous wealth each had acquired from that hill. Whatever its cause, the Clark-Daly "feud" was, at best, sometimes entertaining for the common folk, but mostly cause for great embarrassment for Montana. The battle ended abruptly when, on November 12, 1900, Marcus Daly, who had been ill for a few years, died in his New York City hotel suite. The *Anaconda Standard*, now a company paper, reported "a mighty oak has fallen." A year later his one-time enemy, William A. Clark, went to Washington to serve as U.S. Senator.

This would be a good time to read *Mile High, Mile Deep* by R.K. O'Malley.

A year and a half before his death, Marcus Daly, already ill, had sold the Anaconda Company to the Standard Oil Company through its "main men" Henry Rogers and William Rockefeller. Daly received $39,000,000. At the same time, Standard Oil and its "Wizards of Wall Street" sold $75,000,000 of stock in the Company, now known as Amalgamated Copper, creating an inflated price. They later deflated the stock, squeezing out the small buyers. It was the same old song for Standard Oil: the rich got richer, and the poor got poorer....

As soon as W. A. Clark obtained his long-sought Senate seat, he sold some of his properties to Amalgamated. This left Heinze alone to cope with the monopolistic giant. Heinze put on a grand show for more than five years. Armed with his two "paid" judges he was able to keep the giant "foreign (to Montana) menance" on the defensive. Fritz fought both in the courtroom and in the mines. If it took lawyers, he hired them. At one time he employed nearly forty to handle over 130 cases. If it took guns and dynamite, he used them, in the Minnie Healy and Davitt mines. His legal finagling was second to none as was the case with his Copper Trust Mine and Delaware Surety Company.

But all of his tricks merely put off the inevitable. No one, not even Amalgamated-Standard Oil would have believed it would take so long to get rid of one man. In February of 1906, F. A. Heinze received $10,500,000 from the Butte Coalition, a Standard Oil subsidiary, for the majority of his Butte holdings. With this sale all court cases were dropped. Standard Oil-Amalgamated finally had wiped out all competition in Butte. But it had cost them dearly, millions in legal fees, ore, and Heinze's final payoff. A year later however, Standard's wizards of Wall Street "retrieved" most of Heinze's payoff.

From then on Heinze was on the skids. His death, due to liver disease, came in late 1914. For a short time Butte again sang his praises, promising building dedications and statues to his mem-

ory. These projects never materialized, however. Montana's most flamboyant "copper king" was dead at 45. He had lived his life as though he knew he would die young.

Amalgamated rolled on, Daly, Clark, Heinze all behind them. It continued to grow and expand, wiping out or buying out any competition. In 1915, however, Standard Oil's affiliation with its mining interests came to an end. The actual mining operations, now renamed the Anaconda Mining Company, took over. For Montana, it was merely a change in paperwork.

The Anaconda Company still had many irons in the fire. Besides the obvious mining interests in Butte, it had smelters in Anaconda, Great Falls and East Helena. Coal and lumber were produced to fire the smelters and build the mines. Stores and hotels owned by the Company provided employees with food and shelter. But most important, and most unfortunate, the Company controlled the state's newspapers.

Revelations in the national press in 1977 of the CIA's use of mind-controlling drugs did not shock Montanans who remembered the days of the Company papers. The Company used its papers to alter opinions and prevent alternative views from being heard. In fairness, it must be said that Company officials did not originate the practice. Clark, Daly, and Heinze all attempted to influence politicians and employees through their own papers. Montana journalism was not known for its objectivity. Montana papers, as well as legislative and judicial branches of state government, had long histories of being mouthpieces of special interest groups. Daly and especially Clark were guilty of influencing legislatures; Heinze's dealing with the judiciary were classic, and, not to be outdone, Standard Oil and Amalgamated Copper openly and defiantly brought the Legislature and often the governors to their knees. Oh, yes, a path was there to follow, but the Company widened it and paved it.

143

Chapter Three

GROWING ON THE LAND

Traditionally, much of Montana's late 19th century history has focused on the mining industry. This, of course, is understandable, for, after all, it was a billion dollar industry. Growing with the metals industry was another, more far-reaching business, one that would surpass mining. This enterprise would depend on a *renewable* resource: trees.

Montana's lumber industry had its beginnings in the early gold mining days when timber was needed for construction of homes, sluice boxes, flumes, and countless other purposes. But as placer mining waned and quartz mining began, the needs of the busines changed considerably. Mining went from a small operation to big business. Thousands of employees, each need-

ing homes, and businesses needing buildings all contributed to its growth, to say nothing of the usual complements of garages, warehouses, barns, stables, and fences, all requiring lumber.

For a moment, let's forget all of this and look to an even greater consumer of wood. Remember all of the railroads that were so eager to come into Montana? Hmmm...Let's see, the rails rest on something. Ah, yes, *wooden* ties, all eight to ten feet in length, placed some six to eight inches apart, stretching for thousands of miles in Montana alone. Wooden trestles needed to be built for gorges or canyons, of which there are a *few* in Montana.

The flames, fanned by the wind, developed also their own air currents, rolling ahead of them so that there were times when a fiery sheet moved with almost locomotive speed. The smoke was so thick that everywhere the sun's rays were blotted out and even at noon temperature of the air reached far down towards the frost point; the sun peered through the mist like a faint, red ball.

Scores of people were burned to death. In Montana, the fire moved in or around the towns of Taft, Saltese, Deborgia, Haugan and St. Regis. Special trains on the Northern Pacific railroad, which rolled out just as flames were burning some of the wooden trestles, brought a thousand refugees to Missoula.

Many of the settlers back in the forest had no chance of escape. Some parties managed to move through the flames, escaped both burning and suffocation; one of these included a one-legged man who had difficulty walking on his wooden peg. For a couple of days the men and one woman with them wandered among the flames. Eventually they sighted an open park which offered safety, but the fire was moving swiftly behind them and they were driven to a run. The one-legged man was unable to keep the pace, and his companions were forced to abandon him to the fire.

Most notable hero of the 1910 fire was forest ranger E.C. Pulaski who headed a fire-fighting camp back in the forests of northern Idaho. When the flames overtook his crew, he led them into an abandoned mine tunnel; during the following hours many of the men went briefly insane, and Pulaski fought to hold them from running out into sure death.

He was the inventor of a fire-fighting tool known as the "pulaski" — a combination axe and grub hoe. Today, the pulaski is widely used by fire fighting crews when they trench around a flame to prevent further spread.

Our Land Montana by Ralph C. Henry; Helena: State Publishing Co., 1963.

Rebuilding Bridge #7, Tunnel #26 after the 1910 fire!

Lastly and sometimes most easily overlooked by modern-day Montanans was the enormous quantities of timber used in the actual mining and smelting processes. The Butte area's nearly two hundred mines had a total of over 10,000 *miles* of underground workings, *every* foot of which required braces. The smelting of ores, too, used a phenomenal amount of logs.

At one time smelting was conducted by merely piling the ore upon a large base of timber. The whole pile was then set ablaze. Besides extracting the metal, this method gave off a foul and miserable odor, not to mention highly toxic arsenic and sulphur fumes. If when approaching the Butte-Anaconda area one is struck by the barren, stark, and raw landscape, the immediate question is, "what happened here?" A combination of things led to the situation. First of all, it would seem only natural that the closest trees to the mines would be cut for use in either the mines or the smelters. A clearcut policy of "cut and get out" was followed. Secondly, the *wonderful* fumes emitted from the smelting process, contrary to William A. Clark's assertion that it caused Butte's women to have fair complexions, actually killed off not only the remaining trees but also bushes, shrubs, flowers, livestock and humans. But of course it *didn't* harm flies or mosquitoes!

By now one can readily see that the timber industry was to mining as bacon is to eggs. Mining could not have survived without the timber industry. Marcus Daly understood this when in 1882 he, along with the already-mentioned (but worth repeating) A. B. Hammond, E. L. Bonner, and R. A. Eddy, and the Northern Pacific Railway, created the Montana Improvement Company. Aside from making money for these people it provided the much-needed lumber for Daly's mines and smel-

ter. It also provided the tunnel and trestle frameworks for the Northern Pacific. The Montana Improvement Company got itself into federal government "hot water" by cutting thousands of trees on government land. This was sort of western Montana's answer to eastern Montana's "free grass." In fact, Marcus Daly's problems with the federal government over lumber was the main reason for round one in the famous-or infamous-Clark/Daly feud.

The Montana Improvement Company set up shop in the Missoula area with mills both east and west of the city. Because of the troubles with the federal government, Daly decided to make his lumber business a division of his Anaconda Copper Mining Company. This division eventually acquired some one million acres of forest. Its headquarters was at Bonner.

Meanwhile, on the other side of the mountains, events were taking place that were to change the face of the land forever. Remember now, the "hard winter" of 1886-87 did in the idea of the "open range" in Montana. Because of it, land was fenced and some hay put up. The Northern Pacific Railroad, with its super-sized land grant, was, with the exception of the federal government, the largest landowner in the Territory with some seventeen million acres. In Washington, D.C., the federal government was passing land legislation. The industrial revolution was in full swing. The West was being settled, this time by farmers. The *end* of the frontier era was at hand. Some applauded it, others felt trapped. (On the national level it caused the expansionistic tendencies which led to the acquisition of Hawaii and Panama, and got us into the Spanish American War.) And *once again* Montanans were looking for *outside investors.*

The first lumbering in the state took place in conjunction with gold mining. Timber was needed to build mine shafts and supply the miners with building materials and fuel. When the gold camps became deserted, many small mills closed. However, the late 1880's saw the introduction of hard-rock mining, and the mills once again had a market. Between 1845 and 1958, a total of 20 billion board-feet of timber (enough to load 10,000 freight cars) was produced in Montana.

The lumber industry was greatly boosted by the construction of Daly's smelter in Anaconda. The smelter used 300,000 cords of wood per year. Daly and the other mining magnates realized the close tie between the two industries, and eventually took over most of the lumbering industries in the state.

Mineral Independent, Nov., 1958

Average workday in the life of a logger in Western Montana around the year 1900:
Pay was $3 a day plus meals
Work shift was 10 hours per day
Meals included breakfast, two lunches, and supper

June 28, 1963 article in the *Hungry Horse News*

1910 fire that swept most of the Northwest:
By August 15, the main fire was made up of 90 big fires and 3,000 smaller blazes. Flames traveled at 70 miles per hour. Over 3,000,000 acres, mostly of timber, were lost.

Mineral Independent, Nov., 1958

Lumbering — Near Heron c. 1908

Remember, back in Book II, the coming of the white man was compared to a wave. This wave was merely a ripple compared to what was about to happen in eastern Montana in the years 1908-18. It was during these years that many of Montana's "wide spots on the road" were founded. It is interesting how the various elements of nature, government, business, modernization, and the end of the frontier came together to play the tune that could very well be Montana's theme song, "Boom and Bust."

The song actually began back with the passage of the Homestead Act of 1862. Although this Act didn't really affect Montana at the time, it did plant the idea of "free land" into the heads of the people back East. This idea, if nothing else, allowed these people to feel they were able to get away from the rat race of urban living if it became too much. In other words, it was an "escape valve." The industrial revolution, only some 10 to 15 years old, was already giving some people the idea of "getting back to nature." (It is not a new idea.)

In 1877 Congress passed the Desert Land Act, which really didn't bring as many settlers as it did cattle. This Act was the one used by ranchers in order to obtain cheap grazing land by simply attempting to irrigate some of the land. The last major piece of legislation of the 19th century to affect settlers was the infamous Dawes Act of 1877. This Act broke up the Indian land and allowed much of the better reservation land to go to white settlers. The *intention* of the Act was to assimilate Indians into white culture. The *results* were unfortunate. The dawning of the 20th century saw Montana as one of the few places left with any large open expanses of suitable farmland. (The Dakotas fell to the plow during the last two decades of the 19th century.)

One has to remember, now, that the western half of the Dakotas and the eastern two-thirds of Montana form the northern boundary of an area once referred to as the "Great American Desert." Major Long's statement of some eighty years previous kept people away.

The turn of the century brought an entirely different point of view. The Great American *Desert* was now referred to as the Great *Plains*. In 1902 the federal government passed the Newlands Reclamation Act. The Act would enable the construction of large-scale irrigation projects which would, in turn, supply water enough for millions of acres. Some of the projects spawned by that Act were the Sun River Project, the Mill River Project, and the Huntley Project. These projects made it possible to farm in eastern Montana, or at least portions of it. From 1900-1906 farmers slowly began to move into Montana.

The pace at which the farmers moved into Montana evidently wasn't fast enough for the railroads, which stood to benefit from the area's settlement. In a way, they can't be blamed for promoting land, since empty railroad cars don't put money into investors' pockets. But they did have a tendency to overdo things a bit.

Understandably it was the Milwaukee Road that began promoting the cheap but excellent farming opportunities in Montana. After all, the other railroads were owned and run by Jim Hill. The Milwaukee must have felt that if they were to be competitive they had to be innovative. But, predictably, Jim Hill, the "Empire Builder," wasn't to be outdone by his competition. It took a couple of years, but Jim Hill cranked his advertising department into high gear, and by 1909 both he and the Milwaukee were passing off Montana, to the Midwest and New England as well as northern Europe, as the place Adam and Eve were asked to leave. They used every trick in the book and then invented some to get farmers into the area. Probably the most successful were the super low rates to transport people from the East. The newcomers were given a choice of regular coach arrangements or a special economy ride in a boxcar with their belongings and livestock. (Cozy, huh?)

Even the federal government got into the picture. It passed the Enlarged Homestead Act (in 1909) which was more applicable to the western plains. The well-heeled and well-intentioned Congress had the right idea, but 320 acres *still* wasn't a practical chunk of land to farm in the West. But...the doubling of the size of the homestead had an immediate effect on the restless easterners and foreigners who had been bombarded with the railroads' propaganda. They probably thought the government was crazy to be giving away such *prime agricultural land*.

By 1912 the U.S. government had acted again. This time it loosened restrictions on the homesteader by shortening his "prove up" period from five years to three — and it also gave the brave souls a five month-per-year peiod of time to be able to leave their property. The farmer was to be given some time to make some money during the off-season to tide him over *if necessary*.

Anyway, to briefly recap, here's what happened. The industrial revolution took a toll of dissatisfied factory workers. Tenant farmers in the eastern U.S. and northern Europe wanted their own acreage. The U.S. government made it easier to obtain up to 320 acres, free for the asking. The railroads told them how good the land was. The Northern Pacific sold some of its prime land grant. The railroads provided inexpensive transportation from Europe and the East. But something is missing! What could it be? Oh, yes, an *expert*. Of course! Every cause needs an expert. One expert, coming up!

Hardy Webster Campbell was nearly sixty years old when he finally acquired national recognition. Born in Vermont, he landed in Dakota Territory in 1879. He developed a dry farming system that was "totally fool proof." It worked "100%" of the time. In fact, rain got in the way. Rain robbed the soil of its nutrients. Hindsight, historical perspective or whatever causes us to laugh at such talk, but...there were thousands of farmers who listened attentively to his every word or read his articles in various periodicals. Do you get the picture that the man had a great following? He did. What needs to be mentioned also is that Campbell was no doubt sincere in his ideas. The fact that he worked for Jim Hill and the Northern Pacific probably added to his credibility *and* conviction.

By the way, Jim Hill was an exceptional person. He built a major rail line to the Pacific, controlled three railroads, and now set about to make them profitable by settling the areas they crossed. He did so for two reasons: first of all, the obvious but not necessarily most important, money, and secondly, he truly believed that if America was to continue in its greatness, it needed to build on the sturdy shoulders of the American farmer. And *he* was going to be the man who would sell the Northern Pacific's land grant to them. And he did.

With the addition of Campbell's expertise and grandfatherly sermons on "deep plowing and intensive cultivation," the farmers came. Boy, did they ever. The schemes of the railroads, chambers of commerce, bankers, real estate people, and even the state's Publicity Department was coming true. Farmers poured in from all over. Thousands of them. Montana's population increased by 60% from 1900 to 1910. The number of farms increased by nearly 100%

Soon, small towns grew near these new farms. The word "practical" doesn't even begin to describe these towns. Even the term "spartan" doesn't do them justice. Each "wide spot in the road" had as its focal point a grain elevator, bank, and railroad depot. "Frills" were the school and church. No, these people weren't crazy, just conservative, poor, hard working, and, in many cases, inept. You see, many of the new farmers came from cities and had little farming expeience. But the lure of free, fertile land that "scorned" rain was *too much*.

With this type of town one can only imagine the individual houses, or, more appropriately, shacks. If they weren't made from sod then they were a combination of rough hewn lumber and tarpaper. Stories of their comfort, or lack of it, still abound. Ask a friend or a friend's grandparent. That so many people stayed, and succeeded, is amazing.

The arrival of the farmer into the land of the "free grazing" obviously was to earn him and her not only the disdain of the cattlemen, but also various nicknames. Two which are printable are "sod-buster" and "honyoker," a racial slur. The cattleman, atop his favorite horse, literally and figuratively looked down on the farmer as though agriculture was a lesser calling in life. A cowboy, after viewing a farming community as opposed to the "wide open" cowtowns, was convinced that working in dirt drove people crazy.

Anyway, the farmers poured in. Because of this steady and seemingly unending flow, many real estate companies sprang up. Some were honest, some not. Also, the legendary "locator" came into being. He would, for a fee, of course, *assist* the new farmer in obtaining and locating choice land. Again, some were honest, others were crooked.

Another reason for this rush was that the market for grain was unusually high. And it was wheat that the farmers were planting. With the outbreak of World War I, grain prices stayed high. What a fantastic situation these farmers found themselves in. All conditions were perfect for successful farming on the Great Plains. Even nature, that final element that had all but destroyed the cattle industry, was cooperating. Nature made sure everything was booming.... But wasn't the name of the song "Boom and *Bust*?"

PAST, PRESENT AND FUTURE OF EASTERN MONTANA IS DESCRIBED

AGRICULTURAL POSSIBILITIES OF TERRITORY SURROUNDING

MILES CITY HOLDS FORTH MUCH — HOMESTEADERS TAKING THE PLACE OF OLD TIME STOCKMAN — OUTLOOK FOR THE FUTURE APPEARS GOOD.

Native Grasses.

The same wonderfully nutritious grasses that had made this country the favorite pasturage of the buffalo, elk, antelope and deer, enabled the stock men to very rapidly build up large herds of cattle, horses and sheep.

It is an undisputed fact that Montana's native grasses contain more nutrition than the native grasses of most other parts of the country and the very unusual thing about these grasses is, that the food value is but little impaired by the winter snows and the spring rains. I have seen cattle, in the winter, turned onto pastures that had been untouched for three years. The grass all looked dead and dry but the cattle ate it all and put on fat almost as fast as did our northern Indiana cattle on full corn feed. The grass that was two or three years old seemed to contain just as much nutrition as the last year's growth.

Seed Bearing.

The native grasses nearly all bear seed that ripens as the grass is cured by the dry fall weather, and it is almost as good feed when left standing in the pasture as when cut and stacked for hay. No old grass is ever burned in Montana. It is eaten.

The Old-Time Stockmen.

From the building of the Northern Pacific until the Milwaukee built through in 1907-08, the stock men reigned supreme all over this country. They had occasional clashes among themselves, especially the sheep and cattle men, and some of them were killed, but the penalty for killing a man in those days, was less than the penalty for stealing a steer.

A Great Market.

During this period, when the stock men reigned, Miles City became the largest primary horse market in the world. It was almost equally famous as a shipping point for native cattle, principally steers and was but little less famous as a primary wool market.

As stated above, there were few settlers. Only the best camp sites and watering places were scripted, squatted on, or homesteaded, by these stock men. The large herds of cattle and horses roamed over the country almost unobstructed and unmolested. The sheep were kept in bands of 1,000 to 5,000 which were looked after by one or more herders and a camp tender.

Free Feed.

Feed for all this stock cost the owners nothing. The cattleman's and horseman's only expense was a few cowboys to roundup the cattle and horses in the spring and summer to brand calves and colts, and in the fall to bring in the beef and mature horses, for driving and shipping to market. The sheepman's only expense was the wages of his herders and camp tenders. Therefore, in spite of the occasional big losses, many of the old-timers made fortunes out of the business. They all looked upon their winter losses as only an incident that was soon overcome or offset by the rapid increases.

152

No Winter Feed.

They put up little or no hay for winter use, sometimes only enough for their saddle horses. Some few of them put up hay for their hospital bunch (which generally consisted of calves and weak cows), but more often the first cattlemen, the real old-timers, put up no hay or feed whatever, but hauled out from town what little feed they needed for their saddle horses. They planted nothing and kept no milk cows.

The Homesteader.

When the Milwaukee came, the government opened large sections of the country to the homesteader and offered him 320 acres instead of 160 acres, as before. This larger acreage attracted large numbers of settlers and soon the government land was taken up, or homesteaded, back as much as 100 miles from the railroad. The land office at Miles City was a veritable beehive of industry, during that period.

Government Land All Taken.

In the rougher localities these were not all taken and within the last three years the government has been granting 640-acre homesteads where there is not more than 150 or 200 acres of tillable land on the 640 acres. Homestead lands in the entire district are now practically gone. Nothing desirable remains.

The First Crops Raised

When the homesteader came, the stockmen told them this country would not produce crops. Nothing would grow. They were so sure of this that few of them had ever tried to even raise a garden. The homesteader, however, had to plow 40 acres on every 320 or 640 acres (as the case might be) before Uncle Sam would give a patent to the land and since they had to plow anyway, they nearly all planted something, principally wheat, oats and flax, at first.

The majority of the homesteaders or "honyockers" as they are called here, came into this part of Montana between the years 1910 and 1914. These years, together with 1915 and 1916 were good years and what little crops were put out almost invariably yielded well.

All Borrowed Money

In fact, the crops were so good from 1910 to 1915 that all the homesteaders who could do so made proof on their lands and borrowed all the money they could get on them. Those who could not make proof, borrowed on their stock, tools, or personal notes, etc. Practically all of the money borrowed went into extended cropraising operations. Nearly all of them, on account of the government's urgent request for wheat and thinking that the good-seasons would continue and that they would get rich quick, planted wheat and some oats and flax. They did very poor farming, thinking almost entirely of getting out as large an acreage as possible and paid little attention to the condition of their seed beds. The dry years of 1917, 1918 and 1919 came on and their crops, especially wheat, oats and flax, made small yields, or failed entirely and a large number of them, including many of those who had the very best lands, went badly behind. Some of them have deserted their lands and left the country, knocking, of course.

Not Farmers.

Most of the homesteaders who came into this country from 1910 to 1914, were not farmers, but instead they were mechanics, mechanists, clerks, stenographers, bookkeepers, school ma'ams and almost everything else except farmers. There were however, a few among the lot that were real farmers. These few did better farming. They got hold of some cows, and raised some hogs. They also raised corn, millet, Sudan grass, and other feed crops in addition to their wheat, oats and flax. They sold cream and fed their milk to the calves, pigs and chickens. They were not so anxious to get rich quick, but wanted to make good and stick and most of them have made good and are sticking.

HER PRESENT.
A Hard Winter.

The winter of 1919 and 1920 was a very long, hard winter in Montana, as elsewhere. It wasn't so cold but it was long and an unusually large amount of snow fell and laid on almost steadily. This hard winter, following as it did three dry years, with their shortage of feed, will long be remembered, especially by the stockmen.

The Chinook Winds.

This country is subject to chinook winds that take the snow off quickly. During most winters the snow seldom lays on more than a few days at a time, but the chinooks in the winter of 1919 and 1920 were few and far between.

No Feed.

During the past several winters the stockmen have begun to realize the need of winter feed. They have been clearing the sage off of the creek and river bottom lands, especially such lands as are often flooded by the spring rains and melting snows letting these grow up for hay. Some of them can be counted among our very best farmers. In 1919 the meadows and alfalfa had almost failed, the corn was mostly light and there was very little grass on the range in the fall.

No Grass

In more recent years, the stockmen have been buying up the Northern Pacific land surrounding their home ranches and have fenced much of it, but there was but very little grass even in their fenced pastures last fall. On this account the stockmen, and the homesteaders reduced their livestock as much as they thought would be necessary.

HER FUTURE.
Rainfall.

The government records at Miles City and Fort Keogh for the past 41 years including 1919 show an average rainfall of nearly 14 inches with 7½ inches of this coming in the months of April, May, June, July and August, our five crop months. These records also show that there have never been more than three dry years in succession and that following each period of dry years there has always been a period of good, or average years. The records show that out of every ten-year period there are two or three dry seasons. *If you will investigate, carefully, you will find that this compares favorably with the seasons in all other sections of the country.*

Out of the 41 years, shown by these records, 1919 was the next direct year in the period and following as it did two previous dry years, it is safe to say that in 1919 there was less feed produced than in any one year out of the 41 and there was less grass on the range in the fall, as no other three-year period had been nearly so dry as the past three years. Every farming country has its dry years or other handicaps.

Seasons.

The records show that the latest killing frost during the past 17 years at Miles City was May 7th in 1909, and the earliest killing frost was September 17, 1912. This gives us practically a frost period of 113 days. I might add here that our first killing frost in the fall of 1917, at Miles City, was on October 18th. In 1918 it was on October 17th, and in 1919 it was on October 9th. Some localities in Eastern Montana had killing frosts earlier than these dates, but these were about the average.

With a 133 day frost free period and our summer days averaging about an hour longer than those of northern Iowa, Indiana and Illinois, we have practically the same corn growing season that those localities have and with 7½ inches of rainfall, during the crop season, we can produce corn and other crops in competition with those states whenever our farmers get down to proper methods of farming.

Crop Yields.

In 1915, Montana, as a state, yielded an average of 28 bushels of wheat and 55 bushels of oats per acre. This is the highest record ever made by any state in the Union. In 1915 corn raising in this country was an infant industry but one 600-acre field of white dent corn only a few miles from Miles City yielded 55 bushels per acre on sod, without cultivation. Wheat yeilds were recorded as high as 60 bushels per acre. Oats as high as 100 bushels and flax as much as 28 bushels per acre. We admit that 1915 was the banner year, up to date for Montana, rainfall was abundant and so distributed that all the crops made good, but *what a state does in a banner year she can at least approach in a good year.*

A New Country.

It is also to be remembered that this is a new country, agriculturally and in 1915 the majority of the land in crop in Eastern Montana was sod or at least was soddy and any experienced farmer knows that well cultivated and subdued land will produce better than sod, land, under similar weather conditions. The next year after sod is broken it generally yields well, but after that, it becomes foul unless given good care and should be plowed again for the third crop. For example; there is a tremendous difference this year between the crops that are growing on well prepared land and those where the seed bed was poorly prepared, even on sod.

Topography.

There are very few localities where the land is so rough that plenty of good farming land could not be found on which to raise winter feed for the stock that could be summered on the rougher portions. In fact, all of our rougher localities are traversed by rivers and creeks that have valleys. In these valleys can be produced winter feed in abundance thus giving to the rough grass lands much greater value than they would have without the tillable areas. In many cases these creek and river valleys can be irrigated. In part at least. It is in these rougher portions of the country where nearly all our larger ranches are located.

Beef Cattle vs. Milk Cows.

The old cattlemen bred for beef only but now all but the very largest of the cattlemen should breed both for milk and beef. The homesteader should either raise milk cows or cows that are equally valuable for milk and beef. In other words, *the homesteader and small stockman, in order to succeed must raise two crops, cattle, cream and calves.*

Montana Oil News, c. 1920

Chapter Four

During the period from the hard winter of 1886-87 to the end of World War I, life changed dramaticlly for an often-forgotten segment of Montana's living, breathing population, the animals. The 1890's saw the last of the great cattle drives, and many ranchers switched to raising "woolies." Two of the most noteworthy were Charles Bair and Lee Simonsen of the Castle Mountain and Musselshell River areas. With outfits such as theirs, and many smaller outfits, Montana's sheep population soared to nearly six million at the turn of the century, putting Montana at the forefront of the nation's woolgrowers. This was to be short-lived, however, as the plow had a tendency to put the "free grass" upside down, *permanently.*

Meanwhile, back in the mountains, some mules and horses were sent deep into the "richest hill on earth" to pull the ore cars. While some people felt it cruel to send an animal down into the "bowels of the earth" never to come out alive, others insisted the animals had a better deal, for after work the miners *had* to go back up to Butte.

As for wildlife, all sorts of things happened to ensure their survival, *kind of.* What's meant by "kind of" will become evident. Read on.

Montana's first conservation law was passed by the Territorial Legislature. It closed hunting of certain game birds. A few years later, hunting of the following animals was closed from February to August: hares, antelope, mountain goats, bighorn sheep, deer, elk, moose, and buffalo. That was in 1872. So buffalo hunting was closed six months a year. We know *that* law was not enforced. 1877 saw commercial hunting for game birds banned. A couple of years later bounties were established to control predators. In actuality these rules were only paperwork. "Native" Montanans and settlers alike ignored the laws. If that wasn't enough, the Territory didn't enforce them, anyway.

Statehood changed things to an extent. Laws were made more stringent. By 1895 the state legislature established the Board of Game Commissioners. *Immediately* a bag limit was placed on bull elk (3), deer (8), sheep (8), goats (8), antelope (8), and grouse (100). The Board also established a trapping season of October 1 to April 1 and an open season for waterfowl from September 1 to December 1, with no limits. To enforce these rules, Governor Robert B. Smith appointed W. F. Scott State Game Warden in 1901. He was assisted by eight deputies. *Nine men* for the *whole* state meant that each had more than 16,000 square miles to police. Seasons and limits became more and more restrictive, with a goal of increasing the animal populations. Transplanting became a reality, with the first elk moved from Yellowstone Park to Montana in 1910.

With the ever-increasing flood of settlers moving into what had been the natural range of many animals, it became increasingly necessary to establish game preserves. The first of many came in 1911 at Snow Creek in Dawson County. So conservation, never a hallmark in the state, was at least followed in the field of wildlife management. By 1913 the Montana Fish and Game Commission was organized and began collecting data and introducing new species to many areas. Birds had their own preserve when the Flathead Lake Preserve was established in 1917. Their preserve was two islands, thusly saving the Commission the expense of erecting fences. (That was a joke.)

the LAND

SHOOTOUT IN THE SWAN
The Story of CHARLES PAYTON
by Lee Nelson

It was about 8 a.m. Sunday morning, October 18, 1908. Game warden Charles Payton and Herman Rudolph were approaching Flathead camp on Holland prairie about 60 miles from Ovando, Montana. Peyton had been at the camp the day before to inspect the Indians' hunting licenses. He had been sent there from Missoula by his superiors who had received reports that the Indians were hunting illegally. The Indian camp consisted of three men, three women, a thirteen-year-old boy, a young girl, about 18 horses, several dogs, and a number of slain deer and elk. Upon inspecting their credentials, Peyton discovered that one of the men did not have a license, but only a paper that gave him permission to leave the reservation. The Indian, named Martin Stuee, did not understand English, and gave the appearance that he thought the permission paper was his hunting license. Peyton informed Martin through the 13-year-old boy as interpreter, that he was under arrest and would have to come with Peyton to Missoula.

Upon receiving this unpleasant information, Martin reached for his rifle, but before he could do anything with it, Peyton pointed his Colt revolver directly into the brave's face, who quickly acquiesced by dropping the rifle. The Indian's squaw then reached for the fallen rifle in the hope of defending her man, but before she could get the drop on Peyton, the wiley warden wrenched it from her grip. Peyton retreated alone, informing them that he would be back tomorrow to take Martin to Missoula.

Peyton spent the night at the nearby ranch of Joe Waldbillig, and returned the next morning with the Russian ranch hand and hunter, Herman Rudolph. They left the ranch before daylight so as to reach the Indian camp by sunup. Peyton was armed with two Colt revolvers and his .405 Winchester carbine. Rudolph carried a smaller caliber rifle.

When they reached the Indian camp, Peyton instructed Rudolph to remain at the edge of camp, ready to offer assistance, if needed.

According to Rudolph, Peyton approached Martin Stuee to make the arrest. As he did so, the Indian grabbed Peyton by the throat. Peyton broke the grip and shook the Indian free, who then pulled a rifle from a scabbard on one of the horses. Before Martin could raise the rifle to his shoulder, Peyton shot him between the eyes with his Winchester.

Immediately after this initial shooting, Rudolph saw the boy, Martin's son, pointing a rifle under the belly of a horse directly at Peyton. Rudolph aimed his own rifle at the boy and pulled the trigger, but the gun misfired and nothing happened. By the time he could eject the bad cartridge and replace it with a good one, the boy had fired, inflicting a fatal wound two inches below Peyton's naval. Rudolph finally got away his shot, killing the boy instantly. Seeing that Peyton had been shot down, Rudolph beat a hasty retreat into the woods and headed back to the ranch as fast as his legs could carry him.

Several hours later, when Rudolph returned with reinforcements, two Missoula hunters and Joe Waldbillig, they found four dead Indians laid neatly in a row with rolled up blankets tucked under each of their heads. A growling dog was laying protectively by one of the braves. Some of the horses were still tied to the nearby brush. They found Peyton about sixty feet away, stone dead. In addition to his belly wound there were two bullet holes in his chest. His empty carbine lay on the ground touching his right hand. His eight-shot Colt automatic revolver was touching his left hand, cocked, but not yet fired.

Investigators of the shooting believed the two chest wounds were inflicted by the Indian women after the gun battle was over and Peyton was already dead or dying.

When news of the story reached the outside, Peyton became an instant hero, a brave warrior who died valiantly enforcing the laws of his state. Some of his closest friends from the Bitter Root Valley, Frank Prince of Victor, Dick Vance of Grantsdale and Wesley Fales, headed for the Swan to set things right and to help bring the remaining savages to justice — three widowed squaws and a little girl.

Rudolph related the above account of the warden's death. The Indian women, who returned to the reservation several days later of their own free will, gave a different account of the killings. Following is their description of what happened in their own words:

"On Friday morning, October 16, about 10 o'clock, the white man, who was afterward killed, came to our camp with another white man. Holland, they think; our men were out hunting, but while he was there, the boy, Pelasoway Stuee, came in, and, as he talked English, the man asked if we had any papers for hunting. The boy told him if he would wait a little while the men would be back and he could see the papers, as the men had them with them. The white man said all right, and went away. On Saturday, before noon, he came back again with Rudolph and went into both lodges and turned everything over. Our men were gone, but had left their licenses with us and we showed them to him. While he was looking at them the boy and Martin came back and the boy told him what game they had killed. The white man wrote on the back of the license the number of animals the men had killed and wrote something in a book of his own. The deer and elk hides were in sacks. There were three dogs with the two lodges, but the dogs stayed in camp while the men were hunting.

"About sundown on Saturday the white man came back to our camp together with the man who was with him in the forenoon. Our men were in camp and it was the first time Stuee and Camille had seen the warden. The white man told Camille to stop hunting and Camille said all right. He told Stuee and the boy they could hunt. He told Martin, your paper is no good. I will be back in the morning; I have a right to kill any one, white man or Indian, who has no paper to kill deer. Martin never said a word to the white man, as he could not understand what he said. There were no angry words passed or trouble of any kind between the white man and our men while they were in the lodge.

"After the white man left, Camille said the white man had told me to stop hunting and we will go back over the mountains, and we all decided to go home. We got up early to start back, but we had lost three horses by straying, and it was near sun up before we found our horses and we packed right away. The sun was just up when the same two white men who had been there Saturday came to where our camp had been. Just before the white man came in sight there was a shot fired, which we think was fired by one of them. When the white man got to where we were, the men that got killed asked what we were going to do, and Camille told him we were going home, as he had told us we could kill no more deer. Stuee was standing by the white man and said "Good Morning," at the same time smiling and patting him on the chin. The white man said nothing, but shook his head and pushed Stuee's hand away. Stuee was not armed. The white man asked a second

time, "What are you going to do?" And Camille again told him we were going home across the mountains, as he (the white man) had told us to do. After the white man had pushed Stuee's hand away, Stuee turned to one of the horses and was fixing a rope on the pack. There was 21 head of horses, including four colts. Nine of the horses were packed, the other eight head were for us to ride — three men, one boy, three women, one girl. The horses were all bunched together and the white man that was killed stood near the outside of the bunch. The other white man, 10 or 12 feet away.

"After the white man asked the second time where we were going, he pointed to Martin and said, "this man is not going." Martin at this time was helping his wife get on her horse. Camille was tying a rope on his horse before mounting and had his gun under his right arm. The other three guns were standing against a tree 10 feet or more away. The white man was on the left and opposite side of the horse from Camille. Camille again told the white man that we were going home, and the white man said, "No, no, no," and shaking his head, at the same time raising his gun. Camille's wife called to him to look out, the white man was going to shoot and Camille stepped toward the head of his horse. The white man did the same, and turning around the head of the horse shot Camille in the left arm, the ball passing through and entering his side. As Camille fell he called to the women to run and we all ran off. off.

"When we came back in a short time we found Stuee just breathing, and when his wife raised his head, he died. Stuee was shot in the back, the ball entering between the shoulders and coming out above the hips, tearing a hole along the backbone like a knife cut. Martin was shot through the left arm, the ball passing through the body and coming out through the right arm. Pelasoway was shot, through the heart; also three bullets had passed through his hat. The men were all evidently shot with a rifle of large caliber and the boy by a revolver or small caliber rifle, from the nature of the wounds.

"When the women got back to where the men were dead, Martin's and Stuee's guns were still leaning against the tree as they had been before the shooting commenced, and undischarged.

"Mary Stuee   "Clara Paul
    Her   Her
    X   X
    Mark   Mark

Who was right? Peyton or the Indians? Who

were the "bad guys" and who were the "good guys?" After Peyton's death, State Game warden Scott said of him, "Pleasant and affable, quiet and unassuming, yet one of the most untiring men I have ever known, his continued rides of from 60 to 75 miles a day over the mountains being remarkable, not only to me but to all residents of that section. His vitality was perhaps unequaled, while as for bravery, I doubt if the man knew what fear meant. Personally, I feel as if I had lost a brother, so intimate had our relations become. While as an officer, he was one of the best I have ever known. Sympathetic to a degree, yet a terror to evildoers, the department has suffered an irreparable loss."

Those from the reservation who knew the Indians involved in the fight described them as peaceful, industrious citizens of the reservation. The Flatheads, unlike their neighbors the Blackfeet, had always taken pride in their ability to get along with the white men. In fact, there seems to be no recorded account anywhere of Indian-white conflicts where Flatheads were aggressors.

The killings at Swan Lake had nothing to do with "good guys" and "bad guys." The Indians were merely getting meat to feed their families through the winter. They were taking game in a wild land where their ancestors had been taking game for innumerable generations. A white man, an outsider speaking a strange tongue, shows up at their camp and says they must have papers from other white men in order to hunt. They show him the papers they were given at the reservation. After examining the papers, the white man says one of the Indians doesn't have the right paper and must come to Missoula with him as a prisoner. What man walking in that Indian's moccasins would not feel resentment and anger?

On the other hand, Charles Peyton was hired by his state to protect the game by enforcing game laws. As more and more people moved into Montana the importance of protecting the game became more important. Game laws had to be enforced if the game was to be preserved. Peyton had spent most of his life in the hills, hunting, trapping and packing. He loved the land as it was and did not want to see the animals vanish. His job was to protect them. One of the Indians at Swan Lake was hunting without a license. It was Peyton's duty to arrest the Indian and take him to justice. When he entered the Indian camp, he was merely doing his job, as he thought best.

When two civilizations as different as that of the white man and red man are forced to intermesh, the resulting friction destroys many of the best people of both civilizations, as happened in the Swan in 1908.
End

The Bitterroot Journal, Oct. 1976 (published in Hamilton by Lee Nelson)

RULERS of the LAND

Chapter Five

To fully understand the situation surrounding the "War of the Copper Kings," and its aftermath, one must take a moment to project himself/herself back into the last quarter of the nineteenth century and must really try to feel what it would be like to be able to "go west," obtain free land and work it with the hope, and slim chances, of striking it rich. Both the dreamer and the well-born had a chance to make it.

The times were simple compared to today's instant, plastic, electronic times of easy credit. It was a time, more so than any other in this nation's history, that the term "laissez faire" was closest to reality. Laissez faire meant that government should leave business alone. Government shouldn't place restrictions on business because of the "free market system," where supply and demand determined prices and profits. During this age, these were enough to keep business in line. That sounded reasonable. Besides, businessmen had the American dream of "rags to riches" on their side. But, as we all know, there are those who took advantage of free anything, and these few altered the free market system.

The other side of the coin was the labor movement, which also justifiably felt that the wage earner, or employee, should get a fair piece of the "pie." The trouble came in determining the size of that "fair piece." It varied depending upon who held the knife, labor or management.

Anyway, our story began during a time when the government pretty much allowed business to take care of business. There were no federal officials around telling mine owners to pay the miners a certain wage, or charge a certain price for their products. To keep things that way, successful businessmen ran for political office so that they could make sure that new regulations would not be passed. If that businessman was influential or wealthy enough, he might find himself a spot on the most exclusive club of them all, what was then a "Millionaire's Club," the United States Senate.

Hoping for Color

Courtesy U of M Library

As the curtain rises on our story, William A. Clark had already established himself as a financial and mining power in the Montana Territory. Marcus Daly had just entered the Territory, in the employ of the expanding Walker Brothers firm of Salt Lake City. One story has it that Clark, disappointed that Daly beat him to the Alice Mine, refused to recognize Daly's authority as an agent for the Walker Brothers, thus signaling the beginning of their feud. Another equally credible story has Clark selling his water rights, vital to Daly's Anaconda workings, to Daly for an outrageously high price. Still another has Clark insulting one of Daly's business partners. Whichever, if any, of these stories is true, the consequence of their animosity toward one another kept Montana in constant turmoil.

As mentioned earlier, the dream of many successful businessmen was to be elected to the U.S. Senate. To say the least, William Andrews Clark was successful. Here was a man who came to Montana practically penniless and successfully amassed a fortune of such magnitude that he was included in Senator LaFollette's list of the one hundred men who "owned America." The other had used corporate muscle, but Clark did it alone. He relied on his keen business mind and his total lack of scruples. He was a cold man capable of anything, including occasional philanthropy. It was Clark whose thirst for money and power could not be quenched. He *would* be Senator, but it would have to be over Daly's dead body.

The year was 1884. Montana politics were understandably the concern of many special interest groups — cattlemen, railroaders, bankers, merchants, and miners. The people running these organizations felt it was less than satisfactory to be a mere "territory," or colony of the United States. Montana wanted and deserved statehood, which would bring local control (including the ability to tax — business included).

Montana was, at the time, a heavily Democratic territory. The "Big Four" of that party and, consequently, the Territory, were Samuel T. Hauser, C.A. Broadwater, William A. Clark, and Marcus Daly. What was good for them was good for the Territory. In fact, it was in that year that William A. Clark, president of an unsuccessful state constitutional convention, had the firm support of Marcus Daly in the matter of mine taxation. (You can bet they didn't want taxes to be very high!)

Meanwhile, on the national level, Grover Cleveland, a Democrat, was serving a term as the nation's twenty-second President. Among Cleveland's good points was the fact that he was a confirmed conservationist. One of his supporters, L.Q.C. Lamar, Secretary of the Interior, was out to "get" people who were stealing timber from public land. This was being done on a large scale throughout the country.

For some reason, perhaps that they were the most obvious illegal operation, or maybe just the largest, the Montana Improvement Company was singled out. This brought Hammond, Eddy, and Daly into court on civil and criminal charges. What would Daly (and his mines and smelter) do without the timber? At this point he was locked in a price war with the Michigan copper industry. He *had* to keep his source of timber. By 1888 Daly and the Montana Improvement Company were up to their necks in lawsuits. They needed some political clout in Washington D.C. to help them out of the jam.

The "handwriting was on the wall" in Washington that Cleveland was out, and a Republican, Benjamin Harrison would be "in" as the next President. Being shrewd, and quick to tap any power source in the area, Daly put his influence, which by then was considerable in Butte, Anaconda, and lumber towns like Missoula, behind an ambitious, intelligent, but unknown Republican by the name of Thomas H. Carter. Daly's strategy, even though he was a Democrat, was that Carter, being Republican, might be able to convince the new Republican administration in Washington to take some of the heat off the Montana Improvement Company.

Meanwhile William A. Clark felt that by securing the state's Democratic nomination he was a shoe-in for election as Territorial Delegate in the U.S. Congress. (Remember, Montana is not yet a state.) After all, he was better known, more wealthy, and more powerful than Carter. Had he not represented Montana in Philadelphia at the nation's centennial celebration in 1876? Had he not proven himself a leader in 1877 when as "Major Clark" he led a Butte Brigade to intercept the renegade Nez Perce? (Wasn't he also lucky they were retreating and purposely avoided contact?) So too, wasn't he the man who led the state constitutional convention in 1884? If nothing else, he *knew* that Montana *always* chose a Democratic candidate. So, in November 1888, with bags packed, Clark waited out the *mere formality* of the vote count before his trip to Washington D.C. He should have packed Carter's bags. Carter, with a little help from his "friends," handed Clark a humiliating defeat. Mr. Omnipotent was defeated by Mr. Unknown. Clark was furious. There was only one man who could have pulled enough strings, influenced enough people, and *perhaps* purchased enough votes to have caused his defeat. That man was Marcus Daly.

Clark was down but not out. In his own words, "For the *time being* I retire politically." At the end of the first inning, the score was Daly 1, Clark 0. By the way, the Montana Improvement Company got off its legal hook in 1889, the same year Michigan (with its Boston backers) cried "uncle" to Marcus Daly. Daly was really flying high.

The following year saw President Cleveland, with less than two weeks remaining in his term before Republican Benjamin Harrison took office, sign the Omnibus Bill. It was this bill that eventually led to Montana's admission as a state on November 8, 1889. In a nutshell, the bill said, "make up a suitable constitution and we'll make you a state."

Ten weeks and one special election later, Montana's third state constitutional convention began its work at drafting a suitable document. At the position of presiding officer was William Andrews Clark. His political retirement was brief. It was a double-take of the Constitutional Convention of 1884. In order to achieve statehood, the various interest groups decided on a very non-controversial document. All sides made concessions to speed the process. Two questions left unanswered by this group, because they were hot potatoes, were: women's suffrage (the right to vote), and the location of the state capital. The document was whipped out in six weeks. Montana voters couldn't wait to get to the polls. They approved the constitution by an 8 to 1 margin.

It was on October 1, 1889 that the people of Montana proclaimed their desire for statehood. Who was going to lead them was another question. In an area *supposedly* Democratic a rare thing occurred. The same election that passed the constitution also provided a proverbial "house divided against itself." Joseph K. Toole, a Democrat, nosed out Republican T.C. Power for governor. The state senate split at 8 senators from each party, the tie-breaker being a Republican lieutenant-governor. The house of representatives also split, at 25 apiece.

To top the whole mess, there were five seats disputed due to some *problems* at the polling places. True to political form, both sides claimed a victory and seated five additional representatives. This marked the beginning of a finely tuned, well-oiled political machine which was to sputter for quite some time. Both political parties acted ridiculously, never really wanting to get down to essential state business. For its final, and most absurd, move *each party* elected two U.S. Senators to represent the new and obviously confused state. The Republicans chose Wilbur Fisk Sanders of vigilante fame and T.C. Power, the unsuccessful gubernatorial candidate. The Democrats elected Martin Maginnis, long time politician and territorial representative to Congress, and none other than William A. Clark. Finally, Clark was going to Washington.

So, while most states sent (and still send) two Senators to Washington, D.C., Montana, still young and crazy, sent four. For obvious reasons, the situation wasn't going to work. As for Clark, his and the others' fate would be decided by the U.S. Senate itself. Unfortunately for Clark, and Maginnis, a Republican President brought with him a Republican Senate. The Republican Senate of course seated Montana's Republican would-be Senators, Sanders and Powers. Clark and Maginnis were told that as long as they were in town, there were many beautiful sights to see. It wasn't a terribly unforseen defeat for Clark, but it was a defeat. The score at the end of two innings remained Daly 1, Clark 0.

Next came the summer of 1892. Clark was in Chicago as head of Montana's delegation to the Democratic National Convention. Their plan was to get Grover Cleveland, who four years earlier was bumped from the White House by Harrison, back into office. Cleveland was nominated and later that year elected   the 24thPresident, the only President in history to serve two non-consecutive terms.

The same year Clark was again chairman of a Montana constitutional convention. Among other things it dealt with the still-thorny issue of the location for the state's capital. After weeks of arguments, for each town in the state wanted the prestige of being the capital, an election was scheduled immediately. The top two vote-getters would then face each other in a run-off election in 1894. The two towns were Clark's choice, Helena, and Daly's town, Anaconda. It was a good year for Clark, but the score after 3 innings was still Daly 1 and Clark 0.

Nevertheless, Daly felt it was time for a direct appeal to the people. His paper, the Anaconda *Standard*, was soon recognized as not only the rival of Clark's Butte *Miner*, but also as one of the top newspapers in the Northwest. It was through their newspapers that Daly and Clark leveled libelous accusations at each other.

In 1893 the state of Montana had its second Senatorial election. Sanders' term was up, and he was running as the incumbent Republican. William A. Clark, naturally, ran, along with a few others. Since U.S. Senators were at this time elected not by the people but by state houses of representative, in Montana it would take 25 votes to get elected. Clark began with only fifteen, against Sanders' 33. During the next six weeks, Sanders' support vanished, leaving Clark facing a few others. Time was running out. The legislature had a deadline. Clark had an acceptance speech all set, but he couldn't wrestle enough votes from the opposition. When it was over, Montana had only one Senator. The deadlock couldn't be broken. Soon then-Governor Richards appointed *Lee Mantle,* owner of the Butte *Inter Mountain,* and a popular vote-getter, to fill the vacant Senate seat. The score still remained Daly 1, Clark 0.

By 1894, the year of the final vote to decide the capital, the stage was set for an all-out, knock-down, drag-out fight. The year had two. One was an episode of Butte's then favorite pastime — a riot. The American Protective Association, or A.P.A., riot on July 4, 1894, proved false the city's "melting pot" reputation. There were many nationalities present in Butte, but each survived in its *own* neighborhood. Melting or blending meant giving up "the old ways." No way! The A.P.A. disliked Catholics and in a town like Butte (with its Irish Catholic miners) it was bound to cause trouble.

The second fight had no less intensity, though less bloodshed, and involved more money. It was the showdown at the polls for the selection of the state capital. For the past two years Daly's Anaconda *Standard* had referred to Helena as the "temporary capital." By now each side had numerous daily and weekly papers, and the whole state could "enjoy" the battle. When Daly handed out custom-made "Anaconda-for-capital cigars," Clark effectively countered with the statement that the cigars were made by non-union workers, or "scabs." Butte and Anaconda were then, as they are now, synonymous with the word "union." Add this to the fact that all across the nation labor was having its troubles, trying to get its piece of the "pie," and you have the idea that Clark was fighting back with a good weapon.

Daly and Clark literally passed out money on the street corners to influence the election. Whiskey flowed freely. Clark had a big advantage in that Daly literally ran the city of Anaconda. It was his, lock, stock and barrel. Because of this, people all over the state were hesitant to put their government in one man's "backyard," if no pocket, even if that person was the benevolent Marcus Daly. Clark *capitalized* on this by handing out hundreds of *little copper collars* that effectively made his point.

It has been said that millions were spent on this election, millions of corporate dollars to change votes. Partisan politics, though sometimes unreasonable, were at least bearable, but Montana politics began to take on the foul smell of *bought* politics. In the final analysis, it was Daly's Anaconda Mining Company's image and the threat of a "company town" running a "company state" that brought about the resulting vote of Helena, 27,028 votes and Anaconda, 25,118. Less than 2,000 votes decided the winner.

Clark was triumphant. Helena went wild with joy. Clark was now the "main man." Booze flowed freely. There was a parade through Last Chance Gulch and fireworks galore. The word "temporary" could now be laughed at and forgotten. The score was now tied at one each, after five innings. In the bullpen, "warming up" for Clark, was none other than Fritz Augustus Heinze. He'd have plenty of time to warm up, for the next inning wasn't until 1900.

Capital Celebration — Helena — Clark & Ladies

Courtesy Montana Historical Society

Heinze's warmup really consisted of making a name for himself. He did that by first quitting his job with the Boston and Montana Copper Company, and then travelling to New York City and Europe to gain support for his next venture. With a well-timed inheritance and the backing of his brothers and friends, Fritz began the Montana Ore Purchasing Company in 1893. Late that same year Heinze bought his first real copper mine, the Glengarry #2. The purchase of the Glengary was made possible through what later became his calling card, the lawsuit.

It seems that Henize's first victim was Jim Murray, a well-known and well-liked Butte gambler and land speculator. Murray owned the Estella Mine and was receiving a flat 20% of all takings from the fellow who had leased it. When the lease lapsed, Heinze quickly jumped in and offered the gambler 50% of the takings on all high-grade ore, and *nothing* on the low grade. Murray couldn't lose, for the mine was into a rich vein. Surprisingly enough, after Heinze signed the lease, the mine apparently stopped producing high-grade ore. Murray never saw another dime. Something obviously was wrong, in Murray's book. His suspicion was confirmed when he found Heinze's men mixing rock with the ore to lower its quality. Murray immediately sued. The action dragged through the courts for five years. All the while Fritz made money on the claim. Naturally, Heinze won.

Old Fritz was off and running. By 1894, the year of the capital battle, Fritz's Montana Ore Purchasing Company processed huge quantities of ore from his Estella and Glengary mines, and independent mines; because of this he was becoming a hero of sorts to the miners. Soon he leased two additional mines, the Rarus and the Johnstown, from his old employer, Boston and Montana. Just to be sure he kept busy, Fritz built a smelter in British Columbia, in Canada, and began construction of a narrow-gauge railway, which he eventually sold, for considerable profit, to the Canadian Pacific Railroad.

Although Clark wouldn't use F. Augustus Heinze as a relief pitcher in his game plan for the U.S. Senate until 1900, Heinize was cocky and bold enough to "show his stuff" in 1896 when he *simultaneously* took on the Boston and Montana Company

and Marcus Daly. How could Heinze lose when the "umpire," Judge Clancy, called all of his balls "strikes?" Blind justice is good; a blind umpire is not. What was going on in Butte wasn't really justice.

Fritz's curve balls came in the form of the Apex Law, discussed in Chapter 2 of this book. From his Rarus Mine he attacked A.S. Bigelow and the Boston and Montana Company. In an even more incredible move, F. Augustus Heinze founded the Copper Trust Company.

One day, while searching for technicalities, his speciality, he stumbled on an amazing oversight, a small chunk of unclaimed land on the Butte hill. Although it was only a large enough spot for two cars to be parked today, it was definitely in a good location. It bordered Marcus Daly's Neversweat Mine, as well as the St. Lawrence, and the cornerstone of Daly's empire, the mighty Anaconda Mine. What a find! Heinze was beside himself with joy. A secret weapon inside enemy territory. Fantastic! However, Heinze did not use this weapon until after Daly sold out to Standard Oil. But the threat was there, and Daly didn't appreciate it.

It was in 1898 that Heinze proved to Clark that he would be a valuable ally. At least for a while. The action began with a controversy over mining rights between the by-now consolidated Boston and Montana Mining and Butte and Boston Mining Company's Michael Davitt Mine and Heinze's neighboring Rarus Mine. The case was heard by a truly impartial though some say pro-Boston judge by the name of Hiram Knowles. The judge decided that the Boston claims were correct. In an unusual move, the jury went against the judge, thus causing a retrial in 1900. Fritz was popular. A well-loved and followed leader was just what Clark needed in his bullpen.

The election of legislators in November of 1898 went as everyone had expected, with the Daly Democrats cleaning up. Although Clark tried, he couldn't shake the powerful grip of Marcus Daly on the mining towns of Butte and Anaconda. What could be expect? By then Daly employed three out of every four workers in the area! End of six innings. The score was still Daly 1, Clark 1.

It was the legislative session of 1899 that really proved unbelievable, *even for Montana*. This book doesn't do justice to the details, and right now we recommend C.B. Glasscock's *The War of the Copper Kings* to give you a better view of the situation. Anyway, the main task of this legislative session was to elect a U.S. Senator. Already you probably have asked, "Who's Clark running against this time?" It didn't matter. Even while under grand jury testimony for bribery, W.A. Clark won the election at the last moment. Immediately, many legislators who had come to Helena found their pockets lined with thousands of dollars. Coincidentally, *all* had voted for Clark. This goes to prove that Chicago isn't the *only* place where elections are *somewhat irregular*.

The score at the end of the seventh inning of play now read Clark 2, Daly 1. Clark, for the first time, is ahead, but there *are* two innings left. Clark was finally going to Washington. His ticket cost approximately $1,000,000.

Daly's team was shocked by Clark's "go-ahead" run, but they were ready to tie the score. Daly's plan was to prove Clark's election was bought outright. A committee was formed immediately. The Daly forces were joined by other anti-Clark forces. Clark was in hot water with other people. There was a libel suit pending against his Butte *Miner*, and disbarment proceedings were pending against one of his lawyers. A list of prominent Montana citizens, including the governor, a few dozen legislators, and nearly a hundred others, were witnesses to Clark's "buying power."

All of this was presented to the U.S. Senate Committee on Privileges and Elections. Along with their testimony was other evidence, including the attempted bribing of two state supreme court judges. All of this involved eleven months' investigation, much of it accomplished through underhanded methods. Daly would do most anything to stop his arch enemy. All of this material would take some time to read through and digest before a decision could be made.

John B. Wellcome, Clark's lawyer, was disbarred, or prevented from practicing law. It looked as though the axe was about to fall on William A. Clark. Finally, after three months of reading, examinations, and cross-examinations, the Senate Committee reached a verdict. Clark was guilty of bribery,

attempted bribery, and other corrupt practices. Clark's stay in Congress was a short one, for on May 15, 1900, before the Senate could act as a whole and force him out, he resigned. He went down lashing out at Daly.

But Daly could do nothing but laugh. He had tied the score at 2 apiece. It was now the end of the eighth inning. Daly couldn't laugh as loud as he would have liked, however, for the Senate's committee had said, in essence, sure, Mr. Clark cheated and bribed, but *your* stealing of mail, using newspapers to alter public opinions, and your own vote-buying are just as bad. The committee had also expressed shock at the kind of politics that Montanans had put up with since 1888.

After such commotion, most men would be crushed. But then again, how many men have turned elk antlers into tens of millions of dollars? Clark was down, but not for long. Even as he gave his resignation speech, a letter was in transit to Montana containing a plan of action for the Clark team.

The plan worked. It called for luring Governor Smith, the man who had signed the charges against Clark, out of state. Smith didn't want to leave, due to the fact that his absence would leave the state in the hands of a Clark man, Lieutenant Governor Spriggs. But Spriggs, too, was out of the state. Smith left the state in the hands of state senator Ed Norris, a Daly man. No sooner did Smith leave the state than Spriggs returned. Then, in a move that still leaves political observers everywhere dumbfounded, Spriggs, as Acting Governor, appointed *Clark* to fill the empty seat that *Clark* had vacated because of the bribery charges. Only in Montana! Good grief! You can imagine how Daly and Smith reacted when they got the news. Naturally Clark's newspapers were thrilled. But not for long. Smith sped back to Montana and *dis*-appointed Clark. Clark was able to retire twice in one month from the same Senate seat. That *has* to be some kind of record.

Anyway, Clark was now 61 years old. He had everything that any man could *ever* want. But he wasn't just any man. He *had* to have that U.S. Senate seat. He had millions, but he wanted more. He had power, but he wanted more. It was the ninth inning. It was time to pull out all of the stops. It was time to use his ace relief pitcher, Fritz Augustus Heinze.

165

It was truly amazing to think that a man *totally* discredited could even consider running for office again while sentiment was still against him. It was unthinkable! Heinze was loved. He was rich. He was powerful. But was he loved *enough*, and powerful *enough* to get Clark, the perennial election loser, into office? Their first tandem move came only a few weeks after Clark's second removal. They sat together in the lead carriage in the Miner's Union Day Parade, June 13, 1900, and were *cheered*. The people loved them. How could this be?

Let's take a look back on the events of the past year. There had been a few lineup changes and strategy changes that were to make this ninth inning closer than one might expect. In simplified form, the story is what follows. Montanans, as much as they disliked the "little copper collars" associated with the Anaconda Copper Mining Company, felt as though they worked for a benevolent monarch, Marcus Daly. Daly, as well as Clark and Heinze, was known to treat his employees well. They all respected the unions which had been active in the area since 1878.

But Marcus Daly wasn't in the best of health. And even though he remained at the helm of local control, Daly had sold his Anaconda Company to Henry H. Rogers and William Rockefeller of the notorious Standard Oil Trust. All of a sudden *Montana's* business that had done so well was the foundation of a "copper trust" controlled by "foreigners." With the signing

over of the Company, Daly and his top men became the "visitors." Daly's prestige dropped a couple of notches. He was now the manager for a bunch of "out of staters" who, to Montanans, looked like a rogue's gallery. Perhaps not a bad observation.

Standard Oil now effectively controlled the combined Boston and Montana and Butte and Boston companies as well as the enormous Anaconda Company. They combined these under the holding company known as the "Amalgamated Copper Company." It was the beginning of Standard Oil's realization of its long-awaited dream of a world-wide copper trust.

Actually, things couldn't have worked out better for the combined Clark and Heinze forces. Now Heinze could effectively lash out at Anaconda without fearing a Daly backlash. After all, Daly had sold out. Montana journalism had been colorful for quite *some time*, but Heinze's idea of a newspaper, the *Reveille* was an amazing piece of pulp. Through the acid pen of his editor, P.A. O'Farrell, Heinze opened an unending attack on Standard Oil and the Amalgamated. His paper made the Butte *Miner* and the Anaconda *Standard* look like Psalm books.

Meanwhile, Clark was loving every minute of it. Heinze was out in the forefront, fighting in the courts, the newspapers, and in the streets. But wait a minute! What did Heinze stand to gain? Clark needed Heinze, but did Heinze need Clark?

Territorial Capital Moved   To Helena 87 Years Ago

By LaVerne Kelly

Eighty-seven years ago this month the records and equipment of the Montana Territorial capital were moved by freight wagons from Virginia City to Helena.

The capital had first been located at Bannack, when the territory was created in 1864. Less than a year later, in February, 1865, the capital was moved to Virginia City.

And a year after that, Helena began to cast a covetous eye on the capital. The residents of Last Chance Gulch waged a strenuous campaign to have the seat of government moved from Virginia City, but it wasn't until 1874, when the people approved the move in the general election, that the change was authorized.

The deep resentment of Virginia Citians at los-

ing the capital is evident in this sparse news report carried in the *Madisonian* on April 13, 1875:

"...a mongrel outfit of poor mules and lank kiyuses, said to belong to the Diamond R Co. of Helena, cavorted, swaggered and switched their tails as they entered this city. The outfit came to freight the movable furniture of the capital up to Helena, the county town of Lewis and Clark County. After the wagon boss had loaded his teams, he left."

Naturally, the Helena newspaper, the *Herald*, gave the event a little more coverage. Even so, judged by present-day standards, the news reports were sketchy.

The *Herald's* first account appeared on April 6,

1875. It employed much prettier figures of speech than would ordinarily be used to report the departure of a wagon train:

"The Capital paraphernalia was taken aboard of Diamond R schooners at Virginia City on Friday last, and on Saturday the fleet sailed out of that harbor and down Alder River with a favorable breeze. No salute was fired on their departure. With average fair sailing, they may be expected at the Capital about the 12th.

Actually, the overland trip was not exactly like sailing down the river. Here's the *Herald* report to Helena residents on April 12, 1875:

"The Diamond R train, transporting the capital archives and effects, passed Gaffney, en route to Helena, on Thursday last. The teams travel by

way of the Crow Creek divide and are probably today in the vicinity of Radersburg. They will likely roll into town on Wednesday, making all due allowance for delays occasioned by deep mud and hard pulling on portions of the road at this end of the trip."

The report of the *Herald* on April 15 of the arrival of the capital effects the previous day was most matter-of-fact:

"The archives of the Territory, together with the office furniture of the Secretary, and books and papers, belonging to the Chief Justice, Auditor Clerk of the Supreme Court, etc., were delivered here yesterday afternoon and stored in the Blake building, Broadway."

Heinze was more clever than anyone had imagined. Sure, he would spend Clark's money campaigning for him, but at the same time he put in a good word for Edward Harney to be appointed district judge. Old Fritz was thinking of his future. A person never can tell when he might "need" another judge. Pretty slick! Now he would have two blind umpires. The visiting team wouldn't have a chance.

Clark, though, wasn't taking any chances. Partly out of his love for children and partly out of his love for their parents' votes, he had a *grand* design for a recreation spot which would serve the miners and their families. The result? Columbia Gardens. It was a fantastic place where one could get away from the city, its problems and its *scandals*. It was a smart move, politically and philanthropically. (Better look up *that* word!)

So, things were going well for the Clark-Heinze team. The same legislature that tried to elect Clark in 1899 passed a bill which enabled the Amalgamated to transfer stock with the consent of two-thirds of its stockholders. Although this bill caused Heinze some problems in his court battles, it also served as the ammunition for future attacks. Among other things, this "two-thirds rule" allowed Amalgamated to transfer its stock to its New York operations. This *really* made the company "foreign." By the way, this was how laissez-faire business worked. The rule rather than the exception was that corporations would expand, buy out their competitors, and monopolize business.

Think of it this way. What if the Safeway store in your town buys out all of the small neighborhood grocery stores. Then it buys out all the Buttrey's, Super-Save, Albertson's, and other big stores. Then it does the same for the whole country. The only place where you can buy food is at Safeway's. They can charge whatever prices they want, because you can't go anywhere else. Do you think they would lower prices? Fat chance!

Meanwhile, let's get back to this "two-thirds bill." It was supported by the Northern Pacific Railroad, the First National Bank of New York, Standard Oil, *and* William Andrews Clark. The same legislature which elected Clark was bound to pass the bill. Standard Oil figured this bill would help them get richer. What it didn't know was that Clark and Heinze would use it to gain advantage over them.

Last, but not least, Daly was unable to do any personal campaigning against Clark in this election. His health was so bad that he couldn't leave his hotel suite at the Netherlands Hotel in New York City. His power and charismatic appeal were far away from Montana. His papers continued to spread his messages; his final appeal went out to Montana voters on November 5, 1900, just two days before the election.

On November 7, solidly pro-Clark state legislators were elected. They seemed a sure thing to elect Clark as U.S. Senator. It was the bottom of the ninth, and Clark had put the winning run across the plate.

On November 12, 1900, Marcus Daly died. Some say he died of a broken heart. It seemed as though the ball game was over. But wait, the Amalgamated Company was out for blood. That the nine innings were over didn't matter. Standard Oil never played by the rules, why start now?

Clark, after being elected, made a move that General Custer would have appreciated, if he had been around. He sold his equipment to the enemy to avoid a fight. The boys from New York didn't seem likely to be graceful losers. Besides, Clark's game had been against Daly. So instead of taking Heinze off the hook by taking his ball and bat home, Clark sold them to the New Yorkers. Clark sold some of his better mining facilities to Amalgamated. Poor Heinze was alone on the pitcher's mound.

The teams were no longer Daly versus Clark, but rather Amalgamated Copper versus Heinze. Amalgamated was certain it would score a run in the tenth inning and go home. But what about the umpires? Good old Judge Clancy and newly-acquired (as of the 1900 election) Judge Edward Harney might still make a game out of it. And they did.

Heinze, having every reason to feel betrayed, outdid himself with blasts through editor O'Farrell and the *Reveille*. The difference was that now his attacks were directed at Amalgamated *and* Clark, his old ally.

Daly Statue at Montana Tech Campus

Courtesy U of M Library

Clark, however, went off to Congress in 1901. He served until 1907. He didn't seek another term. Ironically, or maybe as a part of some stroke of poetic justic, Clark found his much sought-after Senate seat somewhat to his disliking. Here was a man who worked hard. He never asked for a nickel, and he never gave one. He had controlled thousands of employees and many businesses. He owned beautiful homes. But the long-elusive position had made him a public *servant*.

After his term of office, Clark was seldom in Montana, let alone in the public *eye*. A few years after his death in March of 1925 the bulk of his remaining Montana interests were sold to the Anaconda Company (the "new" name of the Amalgamated.) He left a large sum to charity and the rest to his family. Most of Clark's Montana legacy is gone. His Montana home is currently being restored. His favorite concern, Columbia Gardens, his only money-losing venture and, by his own words, his "monument," closed its gates for the last time at the end of summer, 1974.

Meanwhile, back in 1900, Heinze, during Clark's ninth inning campaign, had decided that it was time to use his secret weapon, the tiny Copper Trust claim which bordered the Neversweat, St. Lawrence, and Anaconda mines. In the spring Fritz claimed that the rich veins of ore from the three large mines "apexed" on his property. Judge Clancy, the "blind" umpire, obligingly placed an injunction upon mighty Amalgamated until proper ownership of the ore could be determined. Amalgamated closed down the mines immediately. It looked as though Fritz had them where he wanted.

Because of the closed mines, however, three thousand miners were out of work. The Company told them that their unemployment was due to Judge Clancy. They didn't have to hear another word. Clancy would have been hanged if he did not revoke the injunction. He did, the next day. Through all of this Fritz came out without a blemish on his relationship with the miners. However, Fritz, though he had won the *hearts* of Butte's miners, could not win their stomachs. That was impossible since Amalgamated employed 4 out of 5 workers in the area.

To ensure that he hadn't ruptured any ties with the men, and to help Clark get elected (remember, we've backtracked a little), Heinze and Clark had put their men on an eight-hour day, with their pay the same as it had been for a longer shift. The Amalgamated miners were working twelve hour shifts. Next, Fritz hammered at the theme of the "company store," referring to a system used by companies in the eastern U.S. to control their workers' lives. A company-owned store would allow workers to buy (at high prices, of course) on credit, and then would collect payment directly from their wages. This kept the workers indebted to the company. Heinze's reference was to the Hennessey store in Butte and the Mercantile in Missoula, both owned (or controlled) by the company. Heinze hammered away at Amalgamated. The miners loved it. Amalgamated didn't.

Why didn't Amalgamated "buy out" Heinze? They had already tried — twice. The first time was in 1898 when they offered a mere $500,000. Only three months later the offer was raised to $5,000,000. Heinze's confidence soared. He knew he was making the "biggies" nervous. It was at this point that Clark left the game.

Clark's departure embittered, but didn't slow, Heinze. Less than a month after Clark's election and deal with the Company, Fritz was back in court. This time he was claiming that his Minnie Healy Mine, for which he held a shaky title, was the apex point of Amalgamated's newly-acquired (from Clark) Piccolo and Gambetta mines. Heinze fought with lawyers in the courtroom, miners with rifles in the streets, and dynamite underground. He never slowed down his ore production, and he continued to quickly and efficiently drain the rich veins of the neighboring mines.

Judge Clancy (being interviewed by Dimsdale)

The case went before Judge Harney. Harney called Heinze's new "curve ball" a strike. Amalgamated immedaitely appealed to the Montana Supreme Court. Heinze kept digging. His crews were not only loyal, but they were fast. Court proceedings could take much time, even years. Before the court decision in July, 1903, Heinze kept Amalgamated "hopping" and the legal staffs of both sides working long hours. The Supreme Court returned the case to a lower court. That lower court was presided over by none other than Judge Clancy, Heinze's other legal "expert." Was there any doubt what ruling he would deliver?

On October 22, 1903, Clancy called *two* "strikes." The first dealt with the Parrot Mine, another Heinze-inspired thorn in the side of Amalgamated. The second was the all-important Minnie Healy Mine case. The ore belonged to Heinze. At the same time, Amalgamated not only reappealed to the Supreme Court, but also pulled out all stops to fight Heinze.

By now it was around the fifteenth inning. No one knew for sure. The Company was so furious they probably didn't even know the score. But what they *did* know was that they were losing to *one man*. The largest, most feared, most unscrupulous corporation in the whole world was losing to a single person and in *Butte, Montana*. How? They knew how! Heinze controlled the courts. So, in what must be one of corporate America's lowest points, the Standard Oil/Amalgamated trust did the ultimate in blackmail. It shut down *all* of its Montana operations. Everything. Not just the mines but the lumber business as

well. Everything except the newspapers. Within one week, 20,000 people were out of work. This meant that between 70% and 80% of the state's workers were jobless. Unemployment is an unpleasant prospect at any time of year, but with winter approaching, this situation was as bad as it could be.

Naturally the Company's papers blamed Heinze and his judges. Sure, Fritz had won their affection, but, as in 1900, the work stoppage turned their stomachs. It was evident that Amalgamated had been considering this move for some time. They had set aside a surplus of copper which was enough to get them through a long drawn-out battle. Had the miners put aside any money to tide *them* over? After only four days the miners turned against Heinze. Fritz agreed to meet with them at the Butte Courthouse.

By the appointed time over 10,000 miners assembled. They were angry. In what became his most famous speech, F.A. Heinze, in a little more than one hour, had changed their minds. He laid it on thick, attacking the Company. The miners were again his. But...they had only been out of work for four days.

The Company papers shifted into high gear, putting pressure on the state's governor, Joseph K. Toole. Toole, in turn, along with the state's U.S. Senators, William A. Clark and Gibson, and James J. Hill, president of the Great Northern, tried to mediate the situation. By October 31, they admitted that they were powerless to help.

Immediately, William Scanlon, Daly's successor, announced Amalgamated's idea of a solution. It was simple. If Montana, a sovereign state, wrote a ''change of venue'' law, the whole mess would be cleared up. That was it. This new law would allow the Company to have its court cases heard by a different judge. Of course, this law would also mean the end of Heinze's stranglehold on the Company.

The plan split the workers. Many wanted to go back to work, but more asked Governor Toole to hold fast against the Company's demand. Toole told the Company that he would call a special legislative session to *consider* the proposal *if* they would put their men back to work. There were no guarantees. On November 10th, Toole called for a special session. On November 10th, the Company resumed its operations. It was that simple.

The special session began in Helena on December 1. By December 10 it recessed. The ''Fair Trials Bill' was now part of Montana's state law. The Company won.

For Heinze, it was as though he were a television whose plug had been pulled. The once bright picture was gone and only a little dot remained, but not for long. His power was gone. Amalgamated had found a way to play without using his umpires. They were still losing, but it didn't take long to catch up. They controlled nine out of ten newspapers in the state. They now controlled the legislature as well as their employees.

The ''Company'' was now all powerful in Montana. The whole deal made William Scanlon, Daly's successor at Amalgamated, so disgusted he couldn't take it anymore. Scanlon resigned. His replacement was a man by the name of John D.

Ryan. Now there was a man who could take it. He ate power for breakfast.

1904 witnessed another round of action. Things got hot for Heinze. War was going on in the press and underground. The courts were still backlogged with Heinze cases. At the polls both Clancy and Harney were voted out. Heinze began secret negotiations with Ryan. By 1906 an agreement was reached. The Company, in return for Heinze's main Butte interests plus the dismissal of all court cases, paid Heinze $10,500,000.

So, the man who only seventeen years earlier earned a $5.00 per day salary walked out with several million. He had wrestled it away from a giant. The ball game was over. The ''visitor'' quit while Heinze was still winning.

The visitors quit while Heinze was still winning? Why did they do that? Who knows? All that *is* known is that one year later, Heinze was ''robbed.'' Standard Oil's ''wizards of Wall Street'' were waiting for him. With his pockets overflowing with Standard Oil money he was easy to find. They tricked him into a fraudulent stock deal and he lost $10,000,000. He did have some money left, but he never recovered. He died in November, 1914.

Less than a year after Heinze's death, Standard Oil, under tremendous pressure from the federal government, broke its affiliation with the Amalgamated Copper Company. There was a shuffling of paperwork and from it emerged the Anaconda Copper Mining Company, a company with such immense and diverse holdings that it would continue to control the entire state of Montana.

173

Chapter Six

Before the copper era, Montana had few people who could wield enough power and wealth to attract international attention. Sure, the Territory, and later the state, had many wealthy and locally powerful men, but none that could compete with James Hill, William A. Clark, Marcus Daly, and F.A. Heinze. In fact, the only other truly big names associated with Montana were Lewis and Clark, who had just *passed through,* and General Custer, who had *passed away.*

Written history, for the most part, omitted mention of the common man. Yes, there *are* novels written which depict, sometimes very accurately, the "average" Joe, but in general the larger portion of Montana society remained anonymous. Because of this, oral history, you know, "Back when I was a boy..." or "I'll never forget when my mamma said...," the traditional "hand-me-down" history became very important. It was the stuff of which people were made. Every "wide spot in the road," and larger town shared this tradition.

Everyone in the state, people of all nationalities, and races, and occupations share a justifiable pride that *even today* we are a young state. Stories from the past therefore became very important. There is one place in Montana that probably relished the oral tradition of history more than any other. As you might has guessed, that place is Butte. It is (and was) a town of extremes. It is a mile high and a mile deep. A person either loves it or hates it. The poeple of Plentywood and Hardin and Chester and Yaak all have their tales to tell, but the difference is that people all over the country (and maybe the world) have heard stories about "Butte, America."

Like it or not, Butte was Montana's only cosmopolitan city. It is this quality which gave (and still gives) it a unique flavor and color. It was here that some of the first unions were formed. It was here that the greatest performers of the time came to entertain the wealthy. Presidential candidates made it a regular campaign stop. What other Montana town can boast of throwing a tomato in the face of Wall Street king J.P. Morgan? It was Morgan who had helped finance Jim Hill's railroad. It was Morgan who had provided the funds for a wheat operation in the Big Horn basin which was the world's largest. But all this meant nothing to at least one man with a "good arm" in Butte's Dublin Gulch.

Daly's new smelter, built in 1902, could smelt 5,000 tons of copper ore per day. To construct it, over 10,000 train carloads of building material were needed. 20,000,000 board feet of lumber were used in constructing the smelter's buildings, 5,000,000 more were used to construct the flume which carried the smelter's water supply. 5,000 gallons of water were used every minute during part of the smelting process.

Miners during this period were paid $3.50 per shift; engineers received $4 per shift.

The smelter consumed 75 train carloads of wood per day, or 180 cords every 24 hours.

Clark's Butte mines included the Colusa, Parrot, the Black Rock, the Elm Orlu, the Acquisition, the Original, the Travona, the Black Chief, the Mount Moriah, the Morning Star, the William Penn, the Neptune, the Stewart, and the Fraction. The Colusa mine alone produced 30,000,000 pounds of copper in only 2 years.

In 1891, the following dollar amounts of metals were produced in Montana's mines:

gold	$ 2,891,386
silver	24,029,572
copper	14,377,336
lead	1,229,027
total	$39,635,986

(all from James A. MacKnight, *The Mines of Montana: Their History and Development to Date,* Helena, C.K. Wells Co., 1892)

174

Butte's cosmopolitan character began with the mass importation of laborers for the mining industry. Irish and Cornish miners were already there in sizeable numbers, having come from other mining camps in the West. Daly and Clark brought still more. The Irish ("Micks") and Cornish ("Cousin Jacks") were constant rivals. There were many contests, pranks, and fist fights.

As the mining operations expanded Butte saw the arrival of Germans, Finns, Chinese, Italians, and Slavs. Each group brought with it its own language, food, clothing styles, and other customs, which became the source of jokes as well as prejudice. The "neighborhood" was created. Each independent entity helped make up Butte, which in turn was often considered to be part of "the Company."

One might ask, "Well, if there was all of this divisiveness, what kept the town together?" Well, with a few exceptions, like a big riot in 1894, it wasn't all that bad, even if Daly, Clark, Heinze, and the Company all at one time or another tried to alienate the miners from each other. After all, working twelve hours per day, six days a week didn't leave a lot of time for *anything*, much less fighting and arguing.

There was one unifying factor. The union. First organized in 1878, the Butte Miner's Union wasted no time in flexing its muscle. That very same year a strike shut down the Walker Brothers' Alice and Lexington mines. The manager at the time was Marcus Daly.

Daly, Clark, and Heinze made life really quite pleasant for the Union organizers. All realized the need for healthy (except for the severe air pollution) and happy employees. In comparison with other mining towns, life in Butte was "fat city." Wages were good. Hours were the same or better. Both Clark and Daly treated their men paternalistically. Clark even supplied the people with a playground, Columbia Gardens. For these reasons the Unions grew and prospered in Butte. These "Copper Kings" knew what (and who) was making them rich. Standard Oil also knew, but the 1903 shutdown proved that they didn't care.

For the sake of brevity, and not a lack of material, this book, rather than continuing with this description of Butte, will instead highly recommend a few of the many books that have been written about that city. The *Butte Memory Book* by Don James and C.O. Smithers contains wonderful photographs as well as an interesting text. *Butte Commemorative 1864-1974* by Mary Ann Carling is also good, as is a book which was mentioned earlier, *The War of the Copper Kings,* by C.B. Glasscock. A Works Project Administration writer's project produced another interesting book, *Copper Camp.* Finally, the recently published *Butte Heritage Cookbook* contains interesting stories about Butte's many immigrant communities, as well as examples of the best recipes you'll find anywhere.

Last but not least, the best method to learn about Butte is to see it for yourself. Visit Butte and its museums. Stand overlooking "the pit" and look down "the hill." Repeat words like the following; pasty, lunch bucket, Mick, mucker, headframe, gallows, Neversweat, Granite Mountain, Gamers' Bakery, Meaderville, Centerville, Walkerville, Cabbage Patch, Venus Alley, the Winter Garden, and "Fat Jack" Jones. Just remember one thing. When you say any one or more of these words, remember you're in Butte, a place where one might expect any kind of answer including a fist fight.

"LEACHING"

Jim Ledford, a miner who lived in a cabin below the Anaconda mine, noticed that mine water running through discarded cans and iron junk made the metal disappear and left a heavy sludge. He was curious and had the sludge assayed. It was 98 per cent pure copper. He got a one year contract for water flowing from the Anaconda and earned $90,000. The company refused to renew the contract. They called it "precipitating" and this was the first plant. Today they refer to it as "leaching."

From *Butte's Memory Bank,* Caldwell, Idaho, Caxton Printers, 1975

THE ROLL CALL

Rhymes of the Mines, Bill Burke & Sons, Bill Jr., Vancouver, Washington, 1964

"Lannigan, Madigan, Kelly,
Pengally, Blascovich, Bates!"
Saint Peter was calling the roll-call,
As he stood in the Pearly Gates.

"Bonino, Sullivan, Swanson—
First names, Guisippe, Dennis and Knute!"
He studied his book, and he murmured,
"I see you're all miners from Butte.

"Lannigan, Madigan, Kelly—
All three rode a runaway cage,
Hm-m — hard workers, hard drinkers—"
And Pete scratched with a pen on the page.

"Next Blascovich — Serbian, married,
Stepped in a fifty-foot chute—
They've you down as a number one shoveler,
In fact, the best mucker in Butte.

"Bonino, Sullivan, Swanson—
Names that ring stalwart and brave;
Buried deep in a stope at the Gagnon,
The three of you caught in a cave.

"Albert G. Bates and Richard Pengally
Are the last names marked on the roll—
You'd both be alive and still mining
If Pengally had seen that missed hole.

"Well, boys," said Saint Peter, "Stand muster,
Answer your names, then be mute.
'Twas a bad night for hard-working miners,
Nine men from that one town of Butte.

"Un truth, lads, your records are spotty;
You could have done better — and, well,
The head-devil has sent me an order—
He's needing nine shovelers in hell.

"Now, I may be a fool, I'm a thinking;
But a miner, somehow, makes me sad.
You're a wild, whooping bunch, no denying.
But down in your hearts, you're not bad.

"You've all had your hell in hot-boxes;
My word I don't think you'll dispute.
There's always room up here for a miner,
If he hails from the old town of Butte.

"So life up the gates, ye arch-angels,
Tell the cherubs to strike up their lute,
Make way for these nine hard-rock miners;
The best in the House — They're from Butte!

Miners and Lumber Workers, Garnet

BUTTE DURING THE DAYS OF COPPER MINING AND SMELTING

One afternoon, Granville Stuart and an English friend got off the train at the Butte depot. The depot lights were "barely discernable through the window, obscured by volumes of yellowish smoke thick with the fumes of arsenic and sulphur. It was like a pall enveloping everything in midnight darkness, and almost suffocating. We could not see and we could scarcely breathe. My friend grabbed my arm and gasped, "What is this to which you have brought me?"

from Granville Staurt, *Forty Years on the Frontier*

"By 1890 practically all the vegetation in the town and surrounding hills had disappeared. If inversions dominated the valley, carriages had to be driven slowly for fear of knocking pedestrians down. Railroad engines collided with one another in the switching yard. Trolly cars had to creep through the streets ringing their bells constantly; at night the conductors walked ahead of them with their lanterns in their hands. Many people experienced bleeding from their noses and vomited in the streets. Workers would lose their way going and coming from work."

According to William Andrews Clark, smoke was "a disinfectant which destroyed the microbes that contribute the germs of disease... I must say that the ladies are very fond of this smoky city... because there is just enough arsenic there to give them a beautiful complexion, and that is the reason the ladies of Butte are reknowned wherever they go for their beautiful complexion."

The winter of 1890 was one of the worst periods — between July and October, 192 deaths, most due to respiratory ailments, were recorded. The greatest mortality was among miners. Women hanging their clothes on the line noticed that they "turned green and were completely ruined." In 1891, between January and March, there were 246 deaths. The average age of the dead was 38 years; these were not elderly people who probably would have died anyway.

Two examples:

William Kurz was a bachelor, 50 years old, who worked at a brewery. He lived upstairs over a bar and restaurant. In March, 1891, he took off twelve days from work, complaining of a respiratory ailment. When an air inversion took place later in the month, his condition grew worse. One evening he went downstairs to get a glass of water. He collapsed. Friends propped him up in a chair. A while later, his head dropped. When a friend went to check on his condition he was dead.

Walter Webb, 30, had been complaining of a cold. His wife had been nursing him at home with various home remedies. He died very suddenly, the night of the worst of the March air inversion.

EFFECTS OF THE ANACONDA SMELTER ON THE DEER LODGE VALLEY

A few months after the Smelter was opened in 1902, livestock in the Deer Lodge Valley began to die. The smelter refined 7,000 tons of ore per day, and spewed as much as 59,000 pounds of waste per day into the atmosphere. Most of the waste was arsenic and sulphur. Between 1902 and 1903, one farmer alone lost 1,000 head of cattle, 20 horses, and 800 sheep. The farmers began to bring lawsuits against the Company, and in 1902 alone, over $330,000 was paid in damages.

When the plant was to be remodeled, the mountainsides surrounding the smelter, now totally denuded of all animals and plants, were swept of their debris. This was re-smelted — the result was over $6,000,000 worth of copper!

(all of this information, including that about Butte, is from Donald MacMillan, unpublished PhD dissertation, "A History of the Struggle to Alleviate Air Pollution from Copper Smelters of the Far West, 1885-1933," University of Montana, 1973)

177

THE SEVEN STACKS OF THE NEVERSWEAT

Before the advent of electrical hoists, the Neversweat mine probably was the most photographed and famous mine in Butte. Although it stood high above Irish-named Dublin Gulch on the west side of the hill, it was a favorite mine for Cornish "Cousin Jacks." One legend asserts that many a Cousin Jack was "ticketed in England with a tag reading 'The Seven Stacks of the Neversweat' and that Ellis Island employees would know where to send the new settlers."

The mine won its name because in its early development it was unusually cool and comfortable for workers. As the mine deepened, this advantage gradually disappeared. So did the famous stacks when electricity took over.

from *Butte's Memory Book*, by Don James, Caldwell, Idaho, Caxton Printers, 1975

Courtesy William Farr

178

DISASTERS IN THE MINES

The history of mining is heavily accented by disaster. All men who mine the earth for minerals accept the challenge of falling rock, fire, deadly gas, injuries, and death.

The mines of Butte have offered no exceptions. Their history is marked by disaster, sometimes massive in scope, and tragic in consequence. Nothing could strike more terror to the people than the ascending wail of the camp's many mine whistles as one by one they joined into a cacophonous alarm that announced disaster in a mine. Terrified women whose men worked underground grabbed children and ran toward the mines. Anxious crowds gathered at the gates. Emergency vehicles rushed toward the big hill. Newsboys raced through streets with hastily printed extras.

Finally details became known, bodies were brought up, names listed. Miners became heroes. Some died trying to save others. Death, mourning, and burial hung heavy over the city, and once, after the Granite Mountain and Speculator fire, 166 miners were buried in a mass funeral. Those who could not be identified are commemorated in bronze at the cemetery site.

November 23, 1889 marked Butte's first major mine calamity when fire in the Anaconda killed six. In 1893 a fire in the Silver Bow killed nine. On April 24, 1911 the Leonard hoist ran out of control and dropped 14 men 1500 feet to the sump. Five died. On September 3 in that year six young Black Rock nippers were killed in a hoisting accident.

Sixteen mine bosses stood around the Granite Mountain shaft, October 15, 1915, waiting for the after-lunch whistle signal to go below. Twelve cases of dynamite waited beside them. The big whistle sounded. The dynamite exploded. No one knows why. Parts of the 16 bodies were found as far as a mile away. On February 14, 1916, fire on the 1200-foot level of the Pennsylvania asphyxiated 21 men.

In 1917 the U.S. entered World War I. Mines operated around the clock. On the evening of June 8 hundreds of men had been lowered into the adjoining Speculator and Granite Mountain properties and were hard at work.

Earlier that day workers had been lowering a heavy cable down a Speculator air shaft. It had become fouled. Now an assistant foreman inspected the frayed insulated cable. His carbide lamp accidentally brushed the cable. In moments, aided by a strong up-draft, the entire 3,000 feet of timbered shaft became a raging furnace. Deadly smoke and gas crept back through mine tunnels.

Some miners escaped into adjoining mines. Gas trapped others. Eventually helmeted rescue crews could begin the search for the living or the dead. They found the dead — 166.

On June 10, before the search, while those on the surface waited for the fire to burn out, a signal suddenly flashed in the Speculator hoisting house. A startled engineer sprang to controls of the huge engine. A cage dropped to the indicated level far below. A brief wait. A signal to hoist. The cage surfaced and nine exhausted men stepped off. Sixteen others waited below. A young miner, Manus Duggan, had supervised construction of a bulkhead against gas, but he had died with three followers in an attempt to find a way out.

Men have always found death in Butte mines and probably always will as long as the mines are operated. But men who work in the mines accept the challenge.

from *Butte's Memory Book*, by Don Jones, Caldwell, Idaho, Caxton Printers, 1975

This would be a good time to read *The 1897 Sears-Roebuck Catalogue* edited by Fred Israel, Chelsea House Publishers.

A MINER'S TREASURE CHEST

by Bill Burke

Just an old wooden box that's been battered by time,
Itself and what's in it wouldn't bring o'er a dime;
But to me it's worth more than money, or treasure or loot—
It's a miner's collection gathered-up while in Butte.

From late in the eighties up to the time that he died,
You'll find the story of Butte from the things that's inside.
There's a hammer and drill used in sinking the Con,
Alongside a pallbearer's glove wore for a partner that's gone.

There's a flower from his coat, worn the day he was wed—
Withered and dried — at one time it was red;
A tattered old hat, with a hole in the crown
That came from the time he forgot to bar down.

Here's an old candle-stick, well rusted by time,
And pink slips galore from near every mine.
There's a badge from the union, displayed at parades,
Stuck down in the pipe he smoked for decades.

There's a package of Peerless made stronger by years
And two chips from Walkers that were good for two beers.
There's a sample of ore from every mine on the Hill,
From slopes and from cross-cuts, from raises and rill.

A high-toned looking wine glass gleams up where it's lain
Since the days of Clark-Daly, when it was filled with champagne.
A band from a stogie that once cost a buck—
It's a relic from Heinze, and the days of his luck.

Of papers and pamphlets, you'll find near a score—
The Standard, the News, the Miner — and more;
Votin' cards by the dozen and an old dinner-pail,
A receipt from the jailer for a night spent in jail.

Bills from Brophy's and Connell's and other places of trade—
But on the bottom of each, you'll see they're marked Paid.
Here's a star from the war, when the kid went away;
Of medals and badges there's quite an array.

An old rustlin' card that's near worn through
And something in writing about making home-brew,
A steel bolt from the blast that shook up the town,
A brick from the night they blew the Union Hall down.

Here's a bid to a shindig, and a card for a fight,
A bit of cake from a wedding, and an old carbide light.
There's a badge boosting Bryan and Wilson and Taft,
And a chunk of pure copper from the West Greyrock shaft.

There's a dried bit of shamrock, right from the old sod,
A bankbook from Yeagan's that went broke with his wad.
A blue chip from faro, the night he made his big stake,
And a clay pipe he smoked at Mrs. Callahan's wake.

There's photos galore and other things more,
    far too many to name;
Yet, most homes in Butte could if they would, show you the same.
It was all that they owned, not being noted for thrift.
'Twas all that they left when they finished the shift.

Just an old wooden box all battered by time,
The treasure chest of a miner who gave his all to the mine.
It tells the tale of our city, although it is mute,
And we close it up gently — It's the story of Butte.

This would be a good time to read *Rhymes of the Mines* by Bill Burke. This book is hard to find, but requests for a new edition can be sent to:
Mrs. Wm. Burke
311 West 25th Street
Vancouver, Washington

Rhymes of the Mines, Bill Burke & Son, Bill Jr., Vancouver, Washington, 1964

During the second half of Standard Oil's stay in Montana, people on the other side of the divide were also digging into the earth for a living. The difference was in terms of depth. Butte dug through thousands of feet; central and eastern Montanans dug through only inches. Though it was only inches, it was the "deep plowing" method of "dry farming" espoused by Hardy Webster Campbell that was the rule. Combined with "intense cultivation" and of course his handy-dandy "subsurface packer," the new farmers were supposed to put the humid farmlands of the Midwest to shame. Or so they were told. They heard this from not only Campbell but the railroads, real estate people, chambers of commerce, and some government agencies. The propoganda was of such intensity that it reached people all over the country and in Europe.

The tendency has been to make these people look somewhat foolish. This has been easy to do with the advantage of hindsight and historical perspective. Foolish no, but they *were* dreamers. But this nation was *built* by dreamers. Dreamers who *succeeded,* such as Columbus, George Washington, Thomas Edison, Susan B. Anthony, and others, are called *heroes*. Those that didn't succeed are called *fools,* and at best relegated to footnotes in history books, or back shelves in libraries awaiting revival in scholarly dissertations.

Such was the fate of the "honyocker" or "plow chaser." But that fate would not be realized until later. During the influx of homesteaders the feeling was strictly one of "boom." The farmers saw themselves as just another group that could strike it rich in Montana. The others had made it. The fur industry, gold, silver, and copper mines, cattle business, and lumber enterprises had all succeeded. Why couldn't wheat? It was only right that the "yeoman farmer," the man most praised by greats like Thomas Jefferson, would now get his chance, with a little help from Jim Hill. And Hill's new farming methods claimed that wheat would grow without water. In fact, some "experts" claimed that water "robbed" the soil of its fertility.

Most of the newcomers brought with them some agricultural experience. Part of the problem was that their experience usu-ally was with another type of farming. Switching from farming in Indiana or Illinois, where there was much rainfall, to farming in Montana, was like going into a Chinese restaurant for the first time. Sure, you know how to eat, but with chopsticks? Montana dry land farming was sweet and sour pork and fried rice to those who were used to steak and eggs.

America as a whole was going through a period of such confidence that it might be called "cocky." Why not? Great things were happening all over. The Wright Brothers had literally "gotten off the ground." President Taft was pursuing Teddy Roosevelt's policy of "trust busting," and even Standard Oil was in trouble. In 1909 the passengers and crew of a sinking ship had been saved due to a new device, radio. In 1912 Alaska became a Territory, and New Mexico and Arizona became states. The 17th. Amendment to the U.S. Constitution gave the people the right to directly elect their Senators. The Federal Reserve System was created. And a great invention called the "horseless carriage" was starting to catch on.

Montana was the scene of an interesting item which could be added to this list. In 1913 a man named Charles Jasper Glidden, who regularly made cross-country tours to promote the construction of better roads, made a trip from Minneapolis to Glacier National Park. He and his party were escorted by a special Great Northern Train, compliments of L.W. Hill, Railroad president. Hill and a band of Blackfeet added a bit of "Old West" flavor to the group by "attacking" it at Poplar. The town of Havre gave them the royal treatment. Glacier Park was theirs when they limped in on their ninth day out.

Also in the realm of transportation, the Panama Canal was completed, in 1914. World War I sent Europe into turmoil. The war effort demanded all sorts of supplies, including food. President Woodrow Wilson was reelected in 1916 on a promise to keep the U.S. out of the war. A Federal Farm Loan Act was passed setting up banks to provide cheap and easy credit for farmers. Everything was running smoothly. What more could a person ask for? How about 320 or 640 acres of land in Montana? Many of them asked, and came.

Barbers from Cleveland, postal workers from Chicago, farmers from Iowa, blacksmiths from Germany, coal miners from Scotland, real estate agents from North Dakota all were welcomed. There was plenty of room beneath the "Big Sky." They came to make a lasting impression on the land. They were not looking for free grass or free success. They were willing to work, and work hard.

After ridding themselves of the real estate people and "locators," they were really on their own. As many a present-day eastern Montanan knows, when you're out there, you're not at the end of the world, but you *can* see it.

Obviously the first things that they needed were food, shelter, and clothing, followed by a water supply and fuel. Having brought food and clothing enough to last for a while, their first task would be to build a home and find water and firewood. But this was the Great Plains, not the Black Forest. So some built sod homes (have you ever tried mowing a house?), but most built tarpaper shacks. Whichever they chose, the "houses" shared common deficiencies, like no windows and one-room construction. The constant wind made it impossible that these structures be kept clean. The tarpaper shack was by far superior in appearance, at least from the inside. This was due to the fact that newspaper wall coverings were much more in vogue than the plain, black mud of its nearest competitor.

182

Montana Squatter 1910

Courtesy William Farr

GRAPHIC STORY OF THE FAT AND LEAN YEARS IN MONTANA

(The following, an account of Eastern Montana and of the present-day farm opportunities there, is written by Congressman Carl W. Riddic, who is one of the real "dirt farmers" in Congress.)

Montana is an empire of unrivaled agricultural possibilities yet undeveoped. A conservative narration of the agricultural history, and presentday farm opportunities of the State will contain facts so remarkable and unusual as to read like a romance.

Many Wrong Impressions

Because of its great size, the diversity of its interests, and the variety of its soil, altitude, climate, farming conditions, and character of crops raised, I find on every hand many misconceptions regarding the State. Many of the reports remind me of the blind men who went to "see" the elephant. The one who felt of its legs described it as like a tree, the one who felt its sides though it like a wall, while the one who felt its trunk likened it to a snake. To correct some of the commonest errors let me say right here that the winters are less rigorous than in the States of Wisconsin and Michigan.

While Montana is regarded as a pioneer state, the people, the schools and the business places are as up-to-date as in the States of the east and the middle west. If there is any difference at all in the stores, it is that the Montana stores carry a better grade of goods than eastern merchants because Montana people demand the best the market affords. A recent official survey of the common school systems of all States in the Union placed Montana first. There are good towns everywhere, and good roads.

Wonderful Crop Yields.

Montana has thirty millions of acres of farm land, a territory as great as the State of Illinois or Wisconsin, and less than one acre in every six is being farmed. Is this because the crops are of a poor quality? No indeed. Montana's crops have been entered in competition with the products of other States and the world at national and international shows, and hold first prizes for the best wheat, oats, barley, corn, flax and timothy. In addition to that remarkable fact, Montana land holds the record for producing larger yeilds per acre, according to official government reports, of wheat, oats, rye, potatoes and hay than any other State in the Union for the ten-year period from 1909 to 1918. Remarkable as those records are, I think the following fact even more interesting and

of practical value, that good farm land that will raise those kind of crops can be bought in Montana from $20 to $50 per acre, and on easy terms.

Where The Trouble Lies.

"How do you explain that — there must be something the matter?" I imagine I hear some practical, hard-headed farmer inquire, who has read thus far. Yes, there is something the matter, and to my way of thinking, it is the most interesting and significant part of the whole story, and I will try and tell it exactly as I have seen it with my own eyes during the past ten years.

When I was a boy the school geography taught me that Montana was a part of the great American desert, occupied by roving herds of buffalo and bands of Indians. Gold seekers and fur traders first occupied the country. Then about fifty years ago enterprising cattle men from Texas drove their herds to feed on the luxuriant grass on the Montana plains, where they took on new growth and size. Some of these cattle men settled on the creek bottoms, and raised hay to feed their stock during the stormy periods of the winters, but it was believed the greater part of the land was worthless for farming because of the light rainfall, except where irrigation was possible from the frequent streams carrying the run-off of snow water from the mountains. Roosevelt spent his cowboy life on one of these Montana cattle ranches.

The Pioneer Grain Farmers.

In 1900 a few daring pioneers took up government homesteads on portions of these cattle and sheep ranches, and while only small patches of grain were planted, the yields attracted attention. In 1909-10 there was a great back-to-the-land agitation in the press all over the nation. Western railroads brought samples of the grain grown in Montana to the eastern land shows, and published alluring accounts of the large yeilds and wonderful opportunities to make a living upon a farm which Uncle-Sam would give free to all who would accept. Excursion rates of $30 for the round trip from Chicago induced tens of thousands of prospectors to go west to investigate the opportunities, and thousands filed upon government homesteads, erected 10 by 12 shacks, fenced in their 160-acre claims with two-wire fencing with posts two or three rods apart, and called themselves farmers. As a matter of fact, there were comparatively few actual farmers among the

number. There were clerks, book-keepers, barbers, salesmen, and mechanics, and of these there were few who had sufficient capital to more than make a bare start. In fact, many had to go in debt or work by the day to buy the wire to fence their claims.

Careless Farming Methods.

The sole thought of the "average homesteader was to plow as much ground as possible and sow it to wheat. Much of the plowing was poorly done. A very small part of the ground plowed was properly worked down. Little care was taken in selecting or cleaning seed. Winter wheat was often planted late in December. After the first crop was harvested it was a common custom to disc the stubble and sow a second crop of wheat without plowing. Often a third crop was planted on the first plowing, and sometimes without the discing. There were, of course, a few good farmers here and there. They knew that farming was a science. They scoffed at the sloppy farming going on all around them and said no crops could be expected from such operation. But they were mistaken. Crops not only did grow, but abundantly, wheat yielding 20, 30 and in some cases as high as 40 bushels to the acre. There were actual cases that came to my knowledge where poor farming seemed to yield larger returns than good farming. It appeared like a waste of time to plow deeply, or to work down the ground carefully, when the same amount of work would plow more acres, and everybody was mad to get in every acre possible. Good farmers began to be careless with everybody else.

Old Timers Were Bluffed.

Old timers who saw tremendous crops on land they had theretofore regarded as all but worthless, declared the seasons had changed, and that the planting of crops was cuasing it to rain more frequently. The scientists at the Agriculture Department at Washington, who had kept records for Montana and other States for years, said that was mistaken theory, and warned that deep plowing, and summer fallowing, and clean seed, and prevention of weed growth were essential to permanent success in that semi-arid country, but everybody scoffed at the warnings of the scientists, for we had the evidence that the Agriculture Department was wrong in the abundant rains and successful seasons that followed one after another. Secretary of the Interior Lane made a visit to the

State, and proposed a feasible irrigation project north of Great Falls, and at a great mass-meeting of farmers he told me that only one person, a slip of a girl schhol teacher, agreed that irrigation was desirable. All the rest said: "Why irrigate, when we have abundant rain to raise 30 bushels of wheat and 60 bushels of oats to the acre, as we are doing year after year?"

But Finally Trouble Came.

Then came some dry years. Where the ground had not been well prepared and the seed well planted, the crops did not grow, but the weeds did. Those who farmed well, raised crops, but had small yields on account of the dry weather. But even many of the good farmers had forgotten their cunning in their zeal to plant a big acreage and get rich all at once with one big crop. The next year was again a dry year, worse perhaps than the preceding year, and people began to recall what the scientists of the Agriculture Department had told them. With a gambler's spirit many took another chance on shoddy farming, and prayed for rain and bumper crops as of old, as the only thing that could now save them from failure, but again came little rain. In 1920 even many of the good farmers suffered, for it was the dryest year in the history of the State.

Many of the ameteur farmers became discouraged with their farm operations. Farming did not appear to be the get-rich-quick method they had hoped it would prove. With two years of crop failure staring them in the face, and with a mortgage on their land and bills unpaid, many abandoned their places to the banks of eastern loan companies who held the mortgages, and, attracted by the high wages and demand for help on the railroads and in the cities, went back to their old trades or occupations.

How Good Farming Now Pays.

Last year, in 1921, good farming, in those sections adapted to farming, produced fair crops. The low prices for all farm products however hit Montana farmers as they injured farmers everywhere.

But through a period of twenty-years it has been well demonstrated that in the farming sections of Montana, land that today can be purchased at from $20 to $50 per acre, will produce year in and year out larger yields than can be produced on the best farm lands of the Middle Western States that sell at from $100 to $300 per acre.

Medicine Lake, April 7, 1922

Proving that what they lacked in farming skills was made up for by their enthusiasm, the homesteaders tilled the soil according to the prescribed methods. They worked long hours. Maybe that way, at the end of the day, even a tarpaper shack looked good.

At any rate, they planted, cultivated, and harvested their way into semi-prosperity. Beautifully bleak (or bleakly beautiful) farming communities sprang up around the grain elevators, banks, and general stores. Every one of these "whitewashed cases" hoped to last longer than the mining communities which had folded to the west. It was this desire for permanence that drove earlier towns to vie for the title of state capital. Since that contest had been decided already, the best these new towns could hope for was the title of county seat.

Politically, things seemed to go crazy for a while. For nearly fifteen years, intense small-town rivalry continued while the number of counties in the state increased from 28 to 56. Since then these counties have at times experienced difficulty in trying to finance government in such sparsely populated areas; wheat and cows can't pay taxes.

All during this period, the rancher reacted with both amusement and anger toward the new "sod-busters" or "plow chasers." Places such as Lewistown, Miles City, and Chinook were typical "cowtowns," complete with saloons and "shady ladies." The homesteaders were really "straight" by comparison. The cowtowns, after all, catered to the cowboy, who seldom came to town, and when he did, was ready to "have some fun." The farming communities catered to the needs of a different type of folk, the practical, usually-married, stable, industrious family man. Towns of both types dotted the plains.

While many ranchers remained dead set against anyone who would "plow under" the native grasses, many others jumped on the bandwagon and plowed up their acreage, too. From 1908 to 1917, nature cooperated. Abundant rain fell, and crops were good. Besides, because of the War, the price of wheat was fixed. Even though an open market price would have been higher, the farmers had a "sure thing" in raising wheat.

In April, 1917, the United States joined the War. Montana became a twentieth-century version of the Salem "witch hunts" of the seventeenth century. Super-patriots cast a suspicious eye on anyone who spoke with an accent. (Since many homesteaders had been immigrants, there were *lots* of folks who spoke with accents.) The Irish, Scandinavians, Poles, and especially the Germans were singled out. After all, the War was against Germany.

A typical case was that of A.L. Zimmerman, a homesteader who had located some 13 miles east of Ledger. Zimmerman had recently moved to the area with his new wife, Alice, a nurse. She was a city girl, born in Kentucky and raised in Illinois. He was born in Minnesota, but raised in Aberdeen, South Dakota when his parents had moved there to homestead in the 1880's. In fact, much of Aberdeen was built on Zimmerman land.

Anyway, soon after Zimmerman's tiny three-room home was finished, some neighbors came by for what the couple expected was a welcoming call. Instead, Zimmerman was called "Hun" and questioned about his position concerning the war and his loyalty to the U.S. Zimmerman was not a big man, physically, only 5'8", but his inner strength won the day. He told them that yes, he was German, but German American, with emphasis on the latter. Between the couple's sincerity and Alice's willingness to aid sick neighbors in a time of few doctors, they encountered few additional problems.

Others, however, weren't as fortunate. Hundreds of people were rounded up because of mere gossip. The super-patriots organized a "Montana Council of Defense," which operated on both state-wide and county levels. These councils "checked out" suspicious persons and monitored their activities for possible prosecution. In fairness, it must be mentioned that organizations like this sprang up all over the nation. But one wonders about the intensity of Montana's efforts to prevent "enemy infiltration." The German Army could hardly mount an attack in Montana without going through the rest of the nation first. Yet there were Montanans who constantly reported German airplanes flying over the Bitterroot Valley.

Socially, Montana was a "bust." Oh, well, at least the crops were good.

Chapter Seven

WEALTH

When a person asks for the name of a cool, fruit-flavored, wiggly dessert, the automatic response is Jello. When a person asks for facial tissue, again the response is automatic, Kleenex. Obviously other products are available, but these names are used most often, probably the result of good advertising. The same holds true when naming wealthy Montanans who lived during the later years of the nineteenth century. Clark, Daly, and Heinze pop up instantly. They were not the only wealthy citizens, but they were the best known. Besides, they all owned newspapers.

Clark was first in the wealth category. He had to be. His hunger for power and wealth fed upon money, which in turn increased his appetite for still more power and wealth. He was the epitome of nineteenth century American capitalism. Just one of the hundreds of thousands of people who heeded Horace Greely's famous advice to "Go west, young man," Clark was one of the lucky few who really struck it rich. But luck alone didn't do it. Clark *made* his own luck. Never one to pass up a chance to make a profit, his entire business life was a many-faceted operation of merchandising, banking, railroads, and mining. Though he was fair with the people he employed, it just wasn't his style to be "one of the guys" and share a chew or drink beer at a neighborhood tavern. He maintained a "cut above" image.

Like many other wealthy people of his time, he not only knew how to make money, he knew how to spend it. It wasn't his fault that when he spent it, usually on another investment, he made still more money. Aside from his purchase of a Senate seat a good deal of his money went towards the construction of two homes, or, more fittingly, mansions. The "little" one is still standing, in Butte. From the frescoes on the ceilings (by European artists brought over especially for the job) to the floors made of imported wood, the place is impressive, to say the least.

The other "house," in New York City, is also still standing. It is on Fifth Avenue, one of the most exclusive locations in that city. It is a place where one could "get away from it all" without ever going out-of-doors. To say it was big is an understatement. Let's put it this way: if a person spent 3 days in each room, it would be a year before he would have been in all of them. Plus a person could use a different shower every day of the month. There were 31.

Probably the greatest single undertaking by Clark, or almost anyone in those years, was the construction of a railroad from Salt Lake City to Los Angeles. Railroads were built before and after that one, but never financed from *one* man's wallet. To Montanans, however, Columbia Gardens was Clark's most worthwhile venture. He spared little in ensuring that everyone in Butte would enjoy visiting there. Its ballroom, picnic grounds, pool, and amusement park were among the finest in the nation.

In the final analysis, Clark's success started with that tiny Deer Lodge bank, founded in 1869. That bank enabled him to accumulate the capital necessary for further investment. Who would have thought that first small enterprise would help make him one of the richest men in the world?

This would be a good time to read *The Old Copper Collar* by Dan Cushman.

the LAND

"WHERE W.A. CLARK PLAYS"

**Former Resident Tells Inter-
estingly of His Great
Art Collection.**

The following article, entitled "Where W.A. Clark Plays," was written for the Sunday Missoulian by a former resident of Missoula, whose home now is in New York. Senator Clark is one of the best known art connosseurs in this country and his private gallery is one of the finest collections in the world.

"Next corner to the right, the home of W.A. Clark, the Montana Copper King! shouts the megaphone man as the sightseeing car approaches 902 Fifth avenue. Every stone and every bit of metal in the building came from his own mines."

Another version of the story was heard in a Fifth Avenue bus recently. A New York woman, pointing out to a visiting friend the residences facing Central Park announced, "Now here is the home of Andrew Carnegie."

A few minutes later she corrected, "No, this is Carnegie's house; that other belongs to Calrk."

Whatever New Yorkers may or may not know of the places where Mr. Clark works, there is one thing they cannot ignore — the place where he plays. Some people play with race-horses, some with gold-sticks or garden tools, but W.A. Clark plays with art treasures. And so persistently and successfully has he played that his gallery is recognized as one of the best private collections in the world.

And now he enjoys seeing other people enjoy it too. As he expresses it, "I have lots of thrills in buying them; I like to have others get thrills out of seeing them."

A short time ago, it was my good fortune to be present, with 700 others at one of his receptions. The two lower floors of the house were thrown open to visitors, the family rooms being above.

On the first floor are the reception room and halls, the private office and library, the billiard room and two salons.

The reception room is finished in Circassian walnut and the office and library in American oak, the furniture being of the Empire period. Above the mantel in the office is a portrait of Washington by Sir Joshua Reynolds which seems to dominate the entire place.

The billiard room has a floor of teakwood inlaid with ebony and four immense pillars of Numidian marble. In the western end of the room is a window from an old monastery, in those marvelous deep colors of Thirteenth century glass. For these walls a series of paintings depicting the life of Jeanne d'Arc were made by the famous French artist, M. Boulet d'Monvel, whose death occurred soon after he had finished the work, in 1911

Just beyond the alcove, in the center of the cross formed by the three galleries, stands Mr. Clark receiving the congratulations and thanks of the enthusiastic crowds.

"Yes, I selected them all myself," he says.

He is one of the best judges of paintings in New York. As one man puts it, "You can't fool him on a picture."

On the second floor are the *main* galleries and the state dining-room, which might well be called an art gallery in itself. On an easel across one corner stands a huge canvas by L'Abbey, "Trial of Catherine Aragon." The rays of a spot-light, reflected from the gorgeous robes of cardinals and nobles, throw a soft glo over the walls of dark, old English oak — oak that grew in the Forest of Sherwood 1,200 years ago. The fireplace in the dining room is of such great size that one expects to see the Yeomen bringing in the Yule log with appropriate ceremonies. The curtains here are not of Venetial lace, as in the rooms below, but are a reproduction of the famous curtains of the palace of Fontainebleau, picturing the four seasons.

But it is not the modern painters alone that are hero. Raphael, Titian, Rembrandt, Vandyck, Tenier, Leonardo de Vinci, Valesquez. Ruben's fat women and Boucher's chubby babies, and many more have their place. There is also a fine display of portraits by the English masters, their massive gilt frames standing out against the background of soft-toned red velours mellowed by the light and shade of three hundred years.

"What do you consider your most valuable painting?" one woman asked. Then without waiting for an answer, she rambled on. "I like that Rembrandt," indicating the well-known portrait of Rembrandt's pleasant friend.

"Well, I suppose that is the most valuable," Mr. Clark agreed. (It cost him almost a half-million.)

But wonderful as are the galleries, they could not detract from my admiration of the halls and grand staircase.

The story of the building of that stairway doubtless accounts for the extravagant announcement of the megaphoning guide. It is so characteristic of the way the energy of the west overcomes the obstacles of the east, that I cannot refrain from repeating it here.

When the bronze factory could not fill his orders fast enough to keep the building going, Mr. Clark *bought* the factory outright — and he still operates it, for profit now.

Then a strike cut off the supply of marble, and held up the work again. This particular kind of marble could be obtained only in this one locality. When the strike was over the owners of the quarry demanded two or three times the usual price for necessary material to finish the job. Mr. Clark refused to pay their price, but bought a parcel of ground adjoining theirs, where he opened up a quarry of his own and obtained the identical marble he needed. And he continues to operate that quarry, much to the regret of the would-be-profiteers.

Missoulian, April 14, 1922

Clark was one of the first ten billionaires (real property plus value of his holdings) in the United States.

Courtesy U of M Library

W.A. Clark's Last Gold Panning Trip; Once A Cow Ate His Only Mattress

The *Mineral Independent*, Sept. 1925

(By Bryon E. Cooney)

Generally considered an extremely practical man, the late Senator W.A. Clark had one weak spot in the armor of his reserve. He was decidedly sentimental about the past. He was soft hearted about the pioneers and he loved his memories and the associations of his early struggles. In close touch with the early placer mining days of both Bannack and Deer Lodge, he had a comprehensive knowledge of the mining and handling of placer gold. His last placer mining occurred a few years before his death and was an informal experiment to see how well he could still wield a pan.

The senator was en route in his private car from Butte to Los Angeles over the San Pedro road, which he had built across the trackless desert. The train was stalled for several hours by a washout and W.A. suggested to his auditor, James Phillips of Butte, that they take a little walk up a canyon, as there was plenty of time.

Following a stream they encountered two placer mines, working with pan and rocker. The senator stopped to talk and was greatly interested in their work. Finally he asked if he might pan a little to see if he could find "colors." Selecting a point where the bed rock emerged at a sheer bank he filled his pan and was soon swashing the gravel around in veteran style.

"Get any colors, pilgrim?" inquired one of the miners.

The senator came back with the pan triumphantly. He not only had found colors but there was a neat little circlet of golden gleams emerging from the black sand which accompanies nearly all free gold.

It wasn't a sensational streak but it showed good ground — better than the miners were working on and they moved their rocker over to the "Clark prospect." The incident tickled the old man immensely, merely showing the old timers that he knew how to pan.

"When did you birds eat?" asked one of the miners. "If you're hungry there's some grub up at the cabin. There's some flapjack batter and bacon. Help yourself."

The senator eagerly accepted the invitation. In the spick and span little one room cabin the coffee pot was soon humming and one of the miners came over and handed them a couple of trout he had caught in the morning. The senator did the cooking and made a piquant lunch of hot cakes — or rather flap jacks — bacon and trout with fragrant coffee. Phillips says the senator ate the heartiest meal in weeks and when he finished he washed up the dishes and put everything back in its place. The miners did not know they were entertaining a multi-millionaire nor did Clark disclose this identity. What pleased him most was the fact that the miners moved to the spot where he had prospected and that he had shown Phillips a few things, especially the trick of flipping a flapjack in the air and catching it on the uncooked side.

Bidding his pioneer friends goodby they were surprised to find that he left a $20 gold piece in each palm, while complimenting them on their true frontier hospitality. According to Phillips the incident seemed much more important and interesting to the senator than the deal involving millions, which had occasioned the trip.

While the senator was naturally a busy man, he was extremely punctilious about his correspondence and answered every letter no matter how trivial. Indeed he managed to see everybody who had actual business with him. I never had any business with him but he used to tell Phillips to tell me to come up and visit with him, when he was in Butte. When he talked of the "old days" or his youth, everyone in the outside room could wait or postpone their business to another day. When he had a spare hour he liked to drop into the commissioners' office in the courthouse. The commissioners would suspend official duties while the old man would tell stories and before he finished he would have an interested audience.

Once, visiting with him in his office I asked: "Senator, were you ever a school teacher?"

He laughed.

"I'll tell you a funny story about that," said the senator, "and you can write it any time you want to. You know I came west from Collinsville, Pa., pretty young and went to Missouri. I stuck a settlement where there were quite a few children but no school facilities so the settlers offered me the job teaching. I was rather modest but they said the three "R's" were all that was needed and they dug up some school books they had brought with them.

"I batched in a cabin and taught school in a sort of barn all that summer. On account of the great distances there was no winter school, just from May to October. I think I gave satisfaction and my dozen pupils were anxious to learn which is a great help in teaching. Later I went to Colorado where I worked at day labor, though I was always looking for something better. From Colorado I came to Montana and learned to swing a gold pan at Bannack and never forgot how.

"When I started my school I had no furniture, but I made it after a primitive fashion. I had no bed and I made my own mattress out of freshly mowed grass. There is quite a trick about making a good mattress with a wool sack. A little sweet clover makes it a perfumed couch as long as you use it. I was very happy there and learned to be a good cook. The nearest town was 32 miles away and every two weeks they had a dance. Saturday mornings I would start off in the saddle, take a bath in the creek near the town and stay until the dance was over. Some of the boys and girls rode 50 miles to those dances. The folks were kind of religious and as Sunday dancing was not approved of we used to stop the clock at 12 o'clock and dance until morning. After a nap I would ride back to my school and bachelor quarters.

"One Sunday I got back quite late and found an inmate in my cabin. A cow had pushed the door open and had raised the dickens. First she went after the bacon because it was salty and then she upset the table with the dishes and knocked down the stove. The door had closed on her and she couldn't get out, and would you believe it, that darned cow had eaten my nice mattress to the last straw. The cabin was so disordered and dirty I had to sleep on the board floor of the school with my saddle for a pillow. Next day the pupils helped me clean up and gather another mattress full of hay so we didn't have much class that day.

"Children have their own sense of humor and got a great kick out of the cow eating up the teacher's bed and I was teased about it as long as I remained in that part of Missouri." The old man's eyes grew pensive. "They were good children. I wonder what became of them. I've often hoped to run across some of them later in life but I never did."

Such memories threw a glamor over the old gentleman's sunset days and I could tell he was happiest when he recalled the way things used to be.

MARCUS DALY OWNED HOTEL BUT COULDN'T GET ROOM IN IT WHEN ANACONDA WAS NEW

by Byron B. Cooney

Shortly after the opening of the Montana Hotel in Anaconda, Marcus Daly stepped into the lobby unexpectedly and the new clerk who had never seen Daly and didn't know him except by reputation, politely told him that there wasn't a room to be had in the hotel. Anaconda was booming, housing facilities were unequal to the demand and out at the race track many of the horsemen were sleeping in the quarters originally intended for stable boys and apprentices.

Here was Daly in the town his vision virtually created, the head of his only industry, the owner of the Anaconda *Standard*, virtually the owner of the race track, potentially the owner of the Montana Hotel, dismissed with a curt "Sorry, Mister, but we can't do anything for you."

Daly didn't storm and rage — quick-tempered though he was — nor did he disclose his identity to the clerk. "I should have reserved rooms," he said half to himself as he paused at the desk.

Lou Lammers, one of Montana's pioneer printers, had a room at the hotel and a job on the *Standard*. He had been working only a week and though the hotel was rather expensive it was the only place he could get a room.

Overhearing the conversation he turned to Daly and said:

"I'm on night shift and don't go to bed till morning. You can use my room if you want to."

"Thanks," said Daly, "I'll be out and away before 9 a.m. or earlier. I appreciate this very much and before I leave I will fix it up with the manager."

"Don't mention it," said Lammers, "It isn't anything; I rent my room here by the month."

Lammers did not know Daly and he walked over to the composing room of the *Standard* conscious of having done a kindly, gracious act to an elderly stranger and having no idea that he was entertaining an angel, unawares or otherwise. Lammers told me last year that he never saw Marcus Daly before or since, though he worked on the *Standard* for several years after He cor

roborated the story which I had heard many times before and which is pretty well known in the printing fraternity in the Butte and Anaconda district.

When Lammers returned to the hotel about noon the next day; Daly had checked out, but Manager George Reynolds was on the job.

"Lou, you're pretty lucky," said Reynolds.

"How so?" asked Lammers.

"Marcus Daly just left and he gave orders that your room rent is to be charged to him as long as you're a guest at this hotel."

"For the love of Pete," said Lammers, "was that Marcus Daly? I sized him up for a whisky drummer and thought he might leave me some of his samples."

Daly was as good as his word.

Lammers lived at the Montana nearly three years and never got a bill for room rent. He was the envy of all the craft and was the object of much goodnatured kidding about his good fortune.

Finally, an attractive offer in California and an over-powering migratory instinct made him leave Anaconda and his much prized free room. After world rambling, he returned to Anaconda in 1927 and once more worked on the *Standard*. But he made no effort to re-establish his old prerogative. Daly was dead — there were strang faces around the old Montana, so he rented a modest room down the street.

I met him a year ago last summer in the Eagles Club in Butte and recalled the story which up to that time had always been heresay.

"The story's true, all right," said Lammers, "I was Daly's guest for nearly three years. Actually it didn't save me a cent. I felt so elated about not having to pay any room rent that I used to celebrate every day in the bar room. I was a pretty good customer, if I do say so myself, and when I left for California all I had was my ticket and a very thin bank roll.

"It's still thin and I'm still traveling. I'm leaving tonight to go to work on the St. Paul *Dispatch*."

Philipsburg Mail, Dec. 23, 1927

187

Clark's house in Butte:
designed by C.H. Brown, famous architect of Los Angeles
has 24 rooms
has 9 fireplaces imported from France
ballroom on third floor
built in 1884 at a cost of $250,000
French woodcutter stayed in Butte for 4 years working on the mansion's woodwork
23 chandeliers
many of the windows were of stained glass encrusted with precious stones. Front door window panels
alone worth $2,500.
all doors were solid, 3 inches thick, with oak on one side and mahogany on the other
fire and burglar alarms connected directly to the fire and police stations.
Clark's son Charles built a mansion two blocks away. Called "Charlie's Castle,"
it had a moat and drawbridge.

188

The Clark mansion in New York was made of white marble, had four art galleries to display Clark's impressive art collection, and had 31 bathrooms.

When W.A. Clark died, his heirs paid a total of $1,745,189 in estate taxes to the state of Montana.

What Clark did for Butte:

Built Columbia Gardens, a beautiful public park.

Every summer, every child in Butte could ride the streetcar, free of charge, to Columbia Gardens and back on Thursdays, courtesy of Clark.

Clark Park, which had the best outdoor athletic facilities in the state.

Paul Clark Home for Children, built in memory of Clark's son.

(all the above information is from an article by Helen Clark in Old West, *which appeared in Spring, 1973)*

Marcus Daly was a man altogether different from Clark, except for his keen business mind. He was a warm and genuine person. He knew many of his employees by name, and he treated his workers with dignity. Though he amassed great personal wealth, he never forgot his days as a laborer on the New York docks and in the Nevada mines. He was an *extraordinary common man,* if that combination is possible.

By no means a saint, as some believe, Daly could match Clark in dirty tricks, bribes, and vote buying. But Daly became a Montana folk hero due to his common taste. While Clark spent thousands of dollars on art work unseen and not understood by many Montanans, Daly poured his money into horse raising. When his horses won everyone in Montana shared his pride. He also built a large mansion near his horse farm in the Bitterroot Valley.

The last of the "Copper Kings" was F. Augustus Heinze. The expression "last but not least" fits him perfectly. Heinze's character was an annoying blend of both Clark's and Daly's. At first appearance one could tell there was something special about him. No one said *good,* just special. He was an opportunist's opportunist. If he had found the elk antlers, as Clark had, he'd have tracked down the elk, sued it for not leaving a better rack, and *then* sold them for $20 to the condemned man to whom Clark had sold them. After the unfortunate man's execution, Heinze would have reclaimed them for resale.

Heinze's formal education surpassed that of Clark and Daly. His personal magnetism was phenomenal. Due in part to his physical size and handsome appearance, both men and women admired and loved him. His lifestyle was as fast-paced as his legal and mining enterprises. He carried on each with an eye for detail, sparing them no expense at conquests in either area. His parties were the talk of Butte. And, to boot, he was very wealthy.

When Daly's widow died, her heirs paid to the state of Montana a total of $1,200,000 in estate taxes. (Remember that both Clark and Daly had extensive holdings in many other states, so their heirs paid taxes to states other than Montana. In both cases, however, more estate taxes went to Montana than any other state.)

Daly's philanthropic ventures in the state included the Montana Hotel, in Anaconda, which was built at a cost of $200,000; the founding of the race track association on the state; newspapers in Anaconda; and the city water supply for Anaconda.

One of Marcus Daly's horses, Montana, was involved in a particularly close horse race. The jockey did an unusually good job of maneuvering the horse to the winning position. As a reward, Daly paid the jockey, for that race alone, a "bonus" of $10,000.

(from an article in the Poplar *Standard,* Feb. 27, 1941)

Daly's home outside Hamilton (completed by his widow after his death):
40 rooms
15 bathrooms
swimming pool
duck pond
private lake
built on part of the 22,000 acres M.D. owned there
decorated by a Baltimore firm
bathrooms had nickel-plated brass trim; bathtubs were decorated with gold leaf strips
nearby was a covered, all-weather race track, and stables used by Daly to pursue his hobby, raising racehorses.

Why did Daly first become interested in the Bitterroot Valley? "Daly moved to the Bitterroot in 1888, lured by the prospect of unlimited timber supplies for his Butte mines, which used 40,000 board feet of timber per day."

He settled near Hamilton, which was named for one of Daly's foremen.

(the above information all from an article which appeared in the Great Falls Tribune in January 21, 1968)

190

Courtesy Montana Historical Society

Aside from his looks, smooth talk, education, and parties, F. A. Heinze was the man who dared stand up against Standard Oil. He was the classic underdog. He would have made the Christians in the lion's den an even bet. He was the neighborhood store fighting the national chain. He was the Montana Robin Hood who robbed from the rich and *kept it*. Heinze came to Montana "wet behind the ears." He worked as a wage earner, studied hard, and waited to make his move. Seventeen years later he walked out a very wealthy man. He was both a good engineer and a good businessman. He had to be better, or maybe more devious, to match the challenge of the bigger companies. He died at 45, burned out, leaving an estate clouded with mysterious investments.

These three men, Clark, Daly, and Heinze, were products of their time, a time of little government interference in the realm of business. But also a time that offered little for those who lost the race to succeed. There were no insured bank accounts, no social security, no welfare, no Medicare, no food stamps. It was a time when a person stood on his own two feet and made the best of the situation. Those who fell were gone. Those who stood remained. Clark, Daly, and Heinze not only stood but walked, and eventually they ran everything and everyone fortunate or unfortunate enough to be near them.

This would be a good time to read *Memories of Columbia Gardens* by Frank Quinn.

"The Great Chief in Washington sends word that he wishes to buy our land. How can you buy or sell the sky — the warmth of the land? The idea is strange to us. Yet we do not own the freshness of the air or the sparkle of the water. How can you buy them from us? Every part of this earth is sacred to my people. Every shiny pine needle, every sandy shore, every mist in the dark woods, every clearing and humming insect is holy in the memory and experience of my people.

"We know that white man does not understand our ways. One portion of the land is the same to him as the next, for he is a stranger who comes in the night and takes from the land whatever he needs. The earth is not his brother but his enemy, and when he has conquered it he moves on. He leaves his father's graves and his children's birthright is forgotten.

"There is no quiet place in the white man's cities. No place to hear the leaves of spring or the rustle of insect wings. But perhaps because I am savage and do not understand — the clatter only seems to insult the ears. And what is there to life if a man cannot hear the lovely cry of the whippoorwill or the arguments of the frog around the pond at night."

191

"The whites too, shall pass — perhaps sooner than other tribes. Continue to contaminate your bed and you will one night suffocate in your own waste. When the buffalo are all slaughtered, the wild horses all tamed, the secret corners of the forest heavy with the scent of many men and the view of the ripe hills blotted by talking wires. Where is the thicket? Gone. Where is the eagle? Gone. And what is it to say goodbye to the swift and the hunt, the end of living and beginning of survival."

Chief Seulth (Seattle) of the Duwanish Tribe in Washington
wrote these words in a letter sent to President
Franklin Pierce in 1855

Montana Outdoors, January-February, 1975

BOOK VI

WATER and WELFARE... (1917 — 1950)

193

Chapter One

CROSSING

Time, like an ever-rolling stream,
Bears all its sons away;
They fly forgotten, as a dream
Dies at the opening day.

Isaac Watts, 1674-1748

As America rolled into the twentieth century, it did so on the iron wheels of the railroad. The railroad was the primary carrier of people and goods. There was, however, a wonderful invention being manufactured in hundreds of livery stables and warehouses around the nation and the world. This "wonderful invention" was the horseless carriage, or automobile. At first, the automobile was viewed by many as pure folly, a mere curiosity. Soon, due to its limited accessibility it was condemned by many who agreed with Woodrow Wilson when he said that it was a symbol of the "arrogance of wealth."

It wasn't long, however, before Wilson and others who felt as he did, changed their minds and saw the automobile for what it potentially was. It was the vehicle that would change the face of America. Not only would Americans be noted around the world as a people who enjoyed *social mobility,* but they would now also be known as a people who enjoyed a *mobile society.*

This would be a good time to read This Is Series, a collection of clothbound books (e.g. *This Is Pioneer Motoring)* published by Bonanza Books, a division of Crown Publishing.

the

LAND

194

At the onset, the railroads didn't view automobiles as a threat. Why should they? Although they were comparatively simple machines, they were also unreliable. But say a person had an extremely reliable machine. That still was *no* guarantee that the owner was going anywhere. You see, the roads, or "ruts," as they were more accurately described, left a lot to be desired. Not only that, but gas stations and other automobile-related industries were obviously either at the beginning stages, or were nonexistent. The railroads had a firm grip on the transportation business. Their tracks connected all major cities. Who would be crazy enough to risk life and limb travelling across the country?

Enter one Dr. H. Nelson Jackson and chauffeur, in a Winton touring car. Whether it was the need to be "first" or the need to dramatize the U.S.'s lack of roads isn't clear, but Nelson made it from San Francisco to New York in an incredible 63 days. What could a person expect in 1903 when these statistics were true: there were 2.2 million miles of roads in the U.S., only a little more than half of which had any improvements at all; the rest did not even have a thin layer of gravel.

Nelson's dramatization obviously carried little weight in Congress, for it took another 13 years to get any action. Three years to the day, after Charles J. Glidden and party started their Minneapolis to Glacier Park excursion, President Wilson signed the Federal Aid Road Act. This act was to provide matching funds for "any public road over which the U.S. mails now are or *may hereafter* be transported." That was definitely good news for the drivers of America, who already owned 3.6 million cars

and trucks.

It was at this juncture that our story resumes. World War I saw a tremendous jump in the production of trucks and automobiles of all kinds. In fact, a fairly common sight at railroad depots across Montana was that of the homesteader unloading from the cheaply-rented boxcar not only his reliable team of horses, but also a "Model T" or some other car.

The railroad hauling cars and trucks was similar to the steamboat hauling components necessary to the railroad. They both brought the devices which undercut their own positions. In the short run it was good business, in the long run, it was "goodbye."

It was inevitable that trucking would become a fierce competitor of the railroads in Montana. After all, by maintaining high rates, the railroads proved that there were great profits to be made in the transportation business. And, as has been seen before, when the profits are high, people are willing to take risks. Early motoring in this state was indeed a risky business. Roads were merely the natural paths taken by animals, then the redmen, covered wagons, and finally the automobile. Improved roads were merely heresay. The pattern the roads followed was similar to those taken by the railroads. That is, the most widely travelled roads are those which stretch from east to west. Remember, remote Montana was a place to *cross,* not to stay. Montana has been the rural area between the industrialized Pacific Coast and Midwest. Traffic patterns north and south didn't call for as many roads.

Cars became more affordable, passenger service on the railways decreased dramatically. At the same time, trucks were taking a huge bite of the frieght business. Trucks were able to get into areas that could not, for economic reasons, be served by railroads. After all, grading and laying track was also expensive. If the market wasn't big enough, the rail service didn't bother with it. Not only accessibility, but also the fact that trucks could handle small cargoes and still make a profit, led to their widespread use.

The railroads were set back a few notches by the new competition, but they knew they'd always be needed in Montana. How? Simple. Take a look at the kind of products that Montana had (and has) to offer. Lumber, coal, grain, beef, and metals lent themselves to bulk shipping. There was enough business for both industries to prosper.

The rise in train and automobile traffic gave rise to one of Montana's "cleaner" industries, tourism. Actually, tourism got its start long before the car came on the scene. In 1889, C.A. Broadwater opened his Broadwater Hotel and Natatorium (fancy name for an indoor swimming pool) just outside of Helena. It was by far the most elegant of Montana's resorts. It may have been the most elegant, but it certainly was not the *only* one, for numerous dude ranches soon became popular. Other Montana resorts included the numerous hot springs and mineral baths. Many felt, and still do, that these would cure many ailments. The result was instant popularity for such spots. But by far the state's most prominent attractions were (and are) Yellowstone and Glacier national parks. After the bans on automobiles in the parks were lifted, tourism increased incredibly.

This rise in tourism was made possible by the prosperity enjoyed by most Americans during the "Roaring 20's." It was during this time that the automobile became a middle class vehicle. America was on the move. This movement in turn spawned new businesses, such as the *motor hotel,* or motel, roadside cafes, campgrounds, and gas stations. These businesses, however profitable, were based on prosperity. That is, as long as people had money, they'd travel. Vacations and Sunday drives were luxuries.

The Great Depression all but destroyed tourism, not only in Montana but across the entire country. Ironically, this time of poverty and heavy unemployment was also a time of great improvement for Montana's roads and highways. You see in order to get money into people's pockets, President Franklin Roosevelt started a "New Deal" of "make-work" projects. One such project was the improvement of roadways across Montana and the whole country. This was done by the Works Progress Administration, or W.P.A. Finally Montana had some decent roads. Unfortunately, most Montanans were too poor to use them.

World War II brought an understandable rationing of gas and tires. People were asked to curb vacations in order to conserve resources needed in the war effort. Vacations were taken a couple of hours at a time by allowing one's *mind* to travel while attending a movie or listening to the radio.

Fourth of July Parade, Winnet, 1916

Courtesy William Farr

Chapter Two

BENEATH the LAND

Hopefully one of the underlying themes of this book, cause and effect, has been successfully carried out thus far. However, if that's not the case, here goes an obvious example. Remember back in Book I somewhere around page 9 when the formation of Montana's vast mineral deposits were being described? If you don't, take a second to thumb through and recapture the mood (Go on, DO IT!) Now that you're back, you're probably wondering why all the mention of coal then, and none since. Well, read on.

First mention of Montana coal was made by, of course, Lewis and Clark. Those fellows didn't miss anything! Coal was also used in the gold camps of southwestern Montana during "the rush." However, the first genuine "big time" operation came in the Bozeman Pass area in 1867. Why then? It was in 1867 that the U.S. Government chose to build a military installation to protect the miners and cattle ranchers from the not-too-friendly Sioux and Cheyenne. Actually the federal government was also answering the cries for help from the Montana Territory. Anyway, Fort Ellis was built.

The first cold morning of September, 1867, gave at least one person, probably a private, the idea that heat would be nice. There was a knock at the gate. As the gate opened, the shivering soldiers saw a black man with a cart of coal and a sign that said,

"Coal — $9.00 per ton — you buy it — you burn it." As the man entered the dust fell from him and...poof! It was not a black man after all, but Colonel James D. Chestnut. He knew there was a market for coal, and he made money selling to the fort. At that price, however, the people of Bozeman burned wood.

Another clear case of supply (coal) meeting demand came in 1882 when the Northern Pacific was rushing across the Bozeman Pass on its way to the Pacific. Again, Bozeman area miners were called upon to supply a need. Changes in smelting technology, and railroad construction were great for the Bozeman area. Next, the mighty Anaconda Company joined the coal rush. Anaconda needed coke, which is made from bituminous coal, to use in their smelters in Anaconda, Butte, and East Helena. A bunch of little towns sprang up and dug down. One of them was appropriately named Cokedale.

By 1905 the Bozeman area fields were on their way out. The terrain was steep, which made further mining difficult. Over the previous forty or so years the better and more easily mined coal had been removed. The death knell, however, was ironically what had been the earlier wedding bell. Technological changes in the smelting process again changed. Only this time, less coke was needed. The little "one resource" communities folded into history books, under the heading, "ghost towns."

After 1920, the Anaconda Company had such power over politics and the economy in Montana that the famous writer, John Gunther, wrote, "Anaconda has a snake-like gripe on much that goes on in Montana, and that state is the nearest thing to a 'colony' of any American state."
(From Gunther's Inside U.S.A..)

In the meantime, the meantime being 1877, coal had been discovered in the Great Falls area. Here the discoverer was a man by the name of John K. Castner. It was Castner's idea to haul the coal to Fort Benton, because they needed heat there, too. His biggest buyers, however, were the steamboat people. After all, there were only a limited number of cottonwoods to be used as fuel. Castner, finding some success, then went into the coke business. Again the Anaconda Company liked what it saw. It bought out Castner.

To add to the area's success, Jim Hill and his soon-to-be Great Northern came rumbling into Paris Gibson's Great Falls in 1887. Guess what he needed to run his trains? Then, to top things off, the Anaconda Company opened a smelter and refinery in the town five years later. The coal industry thrived. The following year, the Great Falls area exceeded Bozeman's output of coal.

But...as had happened in Bozeman, the boom didn't last. Again, changes in technology spelled the end of the line. During the 20's and early 30's not only did the Anaconda Company, and its various subsidiaries, switch from using coke and coal to natural gas, but the railroads also switched from coal to oilburning steam engines. The area lingered for a number of years, catering to domestic users.

Another of Montana's bituminous "boom and bust" towns was Red Lodge. Here in 1884 one Walter Cooper, founder of the town, began to extract coal. Five years later the Northern Pacific pulled into town, and the boom was on. The N.P. turned to its subsidiary, the Northwest Improvement Company, to extract the coal needed to operate the trains. Besides serving the domestic needs of Billings, and, of course, Red Lodge, this area also provided fuel for the energy-hungry Anaconda Company.

At the same time, a few miles to the east, the Bearcreek mines were starting to produce. They did well until the early 20's when labor disputes, Anaconda's switch to gas, and another coal field robbed them of their business.

The next roller-coaster coal town was Roundup. People there knew about the coal there since the 1880's. They must have felt that it should be left alone, because it was, until 1907. Then they changed their tune. The sleepy little cowtown was instantly transformed into a coal town. What changed their minds? The whistle of the Milwaukee Road, and knowing they had the Milwaukee where they wanted them. You see, the Milwaukee Road was laying track between the Great Northern and the Northern Pacific routes, with the hopes of exploiting the Musselshell Valley. By taking this route, however, there was but one major refueling area between the Midwest and the Cascade Mountains of Washington. That place was Montana's Bull Mountains, or, more specifically, Roundup. Once again, the area prospered until the 1920's, when technology claimed yet another victim.

Lastly, not because it is the last coal operation, but rather the last covered here, we have the Fort Union coal deposit. This deposit covers the eastern quarter of the state. The coal is found in relatively horizontal seams of considerable and varying thickness. It was easy to mine. And people had known of its existence for quite some time. If all of this is true, why hadn't the Fort Union coal been mined before? Well, the catch was that it was lignite and sub-bituminous coal, and it couldn't be made into coke. Besides, the place where the Northwestern Improvement Company first found it was in the middle of nowhere. But, the same technology that doomed the other fields brought this one to life. Enter the power shovel. With these large machines the N.I.P. could strip mine the rich seams of coal from the earth quite easily. Immediately the Northern Pacific layed a spur road to the site. Its name, appropriately, was Colstrip.

From the N.I.P.'s point of view, the situation was ideal. Not only could they produce coal at five times the rate of production of the Red Lodge operation, but the power shovels eliminated many jobs. This in turn eliminated many union hassles and costly payrolls, which for them reduced the cost of extraction by a phenomenal 80%. Colstrip was in full swing by 1924. Ten years later they were producing 40% of Montana's coal.

Montana's metal mines produced over $20,000,000 in 1922, but paid only $13,559 in state taxes.
(From Michael Malone and Richard Roeder, Montana: A History of Two Centuries, *Seattle, University of Washington Press, 1976.)*

But this is a deceiving statement since 40% of not very much is not very much, indeed. What that meant is that Montana, like the rest of the country, was converting to oil, gas, and other electric alternatives for power and heat. This, in turn, spelled "shutdown" for coal until World War II caused a temporary boom. That short boom included a tragedy in the Red Lodge district at Washoe. It was there in late February of 1943 that 74 men died in an explosion at the Smith mine.

Montana's coal industry had followed, geographically, the same path the open range cattle industry had followed. It began in the southwest and moved north and east until it peaked. Unlike the open range cattle industry, however, the coal industry was to experience rebirth later.

Meanwhile, let's take a look at the young upstart fuel alternatives that knocked coal from its number one position, namely oil and natural gas. With the invention of cars and trucks and dozens of other motorized contraptions many people immediately began thinking about the empty gas tanks that would need filling. As the farmer cares for mankind by producing food to fill their stomachs, the oil man cares for the machines by producing the gas to fill their gas tanks. Spurred by the thought of empty gas tanks, or full wallets, the scramble was on, worldwide.

Elk Basin, near Warren, was Montana's first oil discovery of any size. It was opened in 1915. A few years later there were strikes near Roundup and Cat Creek. These formed a nearly north and south line. In 1922 Gordon Campbell continued his "hot streak" and developed the Kevin-Sunburst field. The word "boom" was now being used in reference to the area. It wasn't long before the Conrad area got involved due to the newly-discovered Pondera field. By 1931 the highly productive Cut Bank deposits were being tapped. Now the "biggies" moved in. Texaco and Montana Power understandably wanted a "piece of the action," and they got it.

As a general rule, Montana's oil industry boomed in the 1920's, but didn't do much in the 1930's. Also, the word "boom" must be explained. When the term "boom" is applied to the Montana oil business, it really is deceiving, for when compared to oil-rich states such as Texas and Oklahoma, our boom was small. By comparison with the total U.S. production, the boom was very small. In terms of Montana only, though, it *was* a boom. Along with oil came its natural partner, gas. Found primarily in north central and east central Montana, the Montana Power and Montana-Dakota Utilities companies were quick to see the profits for home heating and industrial uses.

Before getting into the copper industry it must be stated that numerous underground treasures were known to exist, and were produced. Time and space demand that they merely be listed here. Their stories are undoubtedly as interesting as the others, so please find out more about them on your own: gold, silver, lead, zinc, vermiculite, phosphates, magnese, chromium, iron ore, and gemstones.

The year is 1918. It is Christmastime in Butte. A certain strain of flu had just gone through the town. It still lingered in a few neighborhoods. Some 300 residents were moved to the cemetary in its wake. A few months earlier the librarian had died. His name was Granville Stuart, the famous iron-fisted cattle baron of earlier years. Just six weeks before, the Great War (that's what World War I was called then) had come to an end. A month previously, martial law, which had lasted some sixteen months due to labor problems, came to an end. Feelings were somewhat mixed about how things were going. And, to boot, Butte, with its wild reputation, was one week away from the Montana Prohibition Law going into effect.

Now that the mood is set, it's time to get into the copper business once again. Over the previous 18 years the Anaconda Company had garnered immeasurably strength in Montana. Names like Daly, Clark, Heinze, and the Butte Miners Union, once synonymous with power and influence, were gone. The first three had sold out, and the last was stamped out. During the days of Daly, Clark, and Heinze, the miners were treated comparatively well, thus making the labor union's use of strength unnecessary. But now it was a different story. For all practical purposes, one company ran the whole show. It robbed the union of what strength it had. But that didn't stop the men from voicing their disapproval.

Butte, from 1910-1920, could very well have been a military installation. Troops were called out so many times that "S.O.S.," a military "delicacy," almost replaced the party. Seriously, the National Guard and federal troops were called in often to break up labor disputes. Martial law had been declared on a few occasions. With the advantage of historical perspective we can readily see that issues concerning the mines got thoroughly confused, sometimes on purpose to benefit one side or the other.

On one level we have the miners, genuinely and rightfully upset about wages and working conditions. After all, the Granite Mountain Spectacular Mine disaster of June, 1917, created a hero in the form of Manus Duggan, who died while saving 25 men, but it also killed some 175 others. There were numerous other incidents and tragedies of lesser proportion. Pitted against this we have the image of "The Company," wishing to make profits by keeping its operating costs (including wages) down. (This is, after all, the goal of every business.)

On another level there was the confusion over the miners' loyalty to the United States, due to the presence of the Industrial Workers of the World, the I.W.W., or "Wobblies." The I.W.W. was a radical left-wing labor union. As is the case with any extreme organization, they were open for attack from both sides. The side the Company chose to use was the "pinko" side. The same year the U.S. entered World War I, Russia pulled out due to its own internal problems. These became known as the Russian Revolution, or the Bolshevik Revolution. It was then that the Communists took over Russia. The feeling that this might happen elsewhere was known at the time as the "Red Scare."

O.K....now, the Company labelled the I.W.W. as a group out to subvert the U.S. Looking at it today that was like saying that an upset five-year-old was going to overthrow the whole Montana school system because his or her kindergarten didn't have a see-saw. But during war in 1917, it was not a threat taken lightly. Any slowdown, strike, or union organizing was labelled "red," or Communist, sometimes *blood* red. One I.W.W. leader was beaten and hanged outside Butte. The criminals were never caught.

Wartime production was high. Copper and other metals were in great demand. Butte, full of unrest, kept working, proving itself again as the "richest hill on earth." But then the war was over. The price of copper dropped. By 1921 Butte had a surplus. The mines and smelters shut down for over nine months. Butte was hurting. Starvation was knocking on many doors.

By early 1922 many of Butte's workers were back on the job. That's been the problem with mining; it's always subjected to the whims of the world trade market. The 20's was a generally prosperous decade in Butte, however, and in most of the country. It was during this time that the Anaconda Copper Mining Company, following the lead of many other American firms, decided to expand. This they did, and in a big way. Let's take a look at some possible reasons for expansion, other than the most obvious, money.

When a company such as the Anaconda is dealing in a raw material, it is at the mercy of the world market to set a price. To maintain a decent price, one at which a *reasonable* profit can be made, there are relatively few options. Some of them are: ask the government to limit the amount of competing products that could be imported; stockpile the product and wait for the right price (this would create a storage problem as well as put men out of work); or create a demand for the product by spending money to develop a new use for it.

In 1922 Anaconda bought the American Brass Company, which happened to be the world's largest copper deposit, located in the Andes Mountains in Chile. It was an open-pit mine requiring fewer workers. It was also safer than underground mining. In 1928 it acquired the remaining property belonging to the estate of W. A. Clark. In 1929, the Anaconda Copper Mining Company created the Anaconda Wire and Cable Company, with plants in various locations. One was Great Falls. The year 1930 saw a huge copper deposit in northern Mexico taken over by Anaconda. Whew! One thing was certain, this Anaconda knew how to expand and constrict.

The 30's are another story. If the 20's boomed, the 30's definitely busted. The entire nation was locked in the depths of a worldwide depression. Money was not just tight, it was scarce or non-existent. The speculative 20's were taking their toll. Suffering was immeasurable. It was a time, however, that spawned, by necessity, homespun innovation and ingenuity. The stories that come out of that period are captivating, not only because of their total contrast to today's prosperous times but also because of the valuable lessons they contain.

To get an idea of price fluctuation, try this one for size: In 1916, copper was 28¢ per pound; in 1928, 18¢ per pound. By 1931 the price had dropped to 8¢ per pound, and by 1933, 5¢ per pound. Anaconda and the other mines were hurting, causing widespread hardship for all employees. Its production in 1933 was 10% of what it had been in 1929.

The 30's were not good. Both labor and management were in difficult positions. It would take drastic action to get things going again. Franklin D. Roosevelt was the man to do this; his New Deal was the solution. He asked in 1932 the now-popular question, "How do you spell relief?" His response to that question was spelled, N-E-W D-E-A-L. This plan was exactly what its name implied. It was a new plan, but while, like Rolaids, it didn't cure the ailment and only treated the symptoms, it did get things going again.

Part of the New Deal was a law called the Wagner Labor Relations Act, which *encouraged* unions. One has only to guess how "The Company" felt about that, seeing as though only the year earlier the Butte unions ended a 20 year "power drought." The "Great Strike" of 1934 achieved not only a 40-hour work week, a wage increase, and full union recognition, but also the return of the "closed shop" in Butte. However, what good were all of these when the Butte miners constantly heard rumors that the Company would shut down for good in Butte, and rely on its mines "south of the border." Although these plans were never *officially* announced, the fear these rumors generated was enough to keep the neighborhoods uneasy.

World War II and its demands on industries stimulated mining throughout the war years. But, just as the post-World War I era had witnessed, when the war ended a recession began. There were a couple of strikes, some violence, and a decreasing number of jobs.

The "Greater Butte Project" was supposed to get things going again in 1947. The project didn't work as anticipated, and was discontinued on a losing note. Maybe an open pit would work? But, by doing that, Butte would disappear! Was this private industry's answer to urban renewal?

By 1916, the mining industry, which controlled the wealth of Montana, was paying fewer taxes than any other group. Farmers paid 32% of state tax revenues and the mines paid only 8%. A University of Montana economics professor, Louis Levine, recommended that the mining companies pay more taxes. He was fired. The newspapers in Montana, many of which were owned by the Anaconda Company, called Levine a "radical." Several national magazines and New York newspapers, such as the New York Times, *took a great interest in this issue. Levine got his job back, although he took another job elsewhere. He later became a famous economist for both the League of Nations and the United States.*

In 1919, three million tons of coal had been produced in Montana, worth over $7,000,000. The coal companies, mostly owned by the Northern Pacific Railroad, paid only $682 in taxes for that year. The Anaconda Co. had paid no taxes at all on the net proceeds of the mining industry.

When Joseph M. Dixon took office as governor in 1920, he proposed laws which would require industry to pay more taxes. Company representatives known as "lobbyists" were sent to Helena to meet with legislators and "advise" them how to vote. "Not often, but occasionally, they were caught off guard, and a bill would hit the floor and come to a vote without the House or Senate having been briefed. It was then a source of great amusement to observe the heads swing toward the gallery, where Company men were always seated, so that the signal could be given how to vote."

(The above is all from K. Ross Toole, Twentieth Century Montana: A State of Extremes, *Norman, University of Oklahoma Press, 1972).*

Chapter Three

GROWING ON

As stated in Book V, the lumber industry was a vital part of both the mining and railroad industries. Therefore, it only stands to reason that when hard times befall one, it naturally affects the others. With this in mind, figure out for a second how the lumber industry did during the years 1917-1950. Remember to include any other developments that might have helped or hindered its progress.

Now that you've given that some thought, here goes. The timber industry, depending on which side you were on, was plagued with the problem of (some say negligent with) pay and working conditions. Seeing as though workers in the lumber industries had needs similar to those in the mining industry, namely food, shelter, and clothing, they used similar tactics to get their "fair share" through the unions. However, "The Company" had been successful in the mines and therefore had reason to believe it would prevail in the wood industry, too, which they did. How could they lose? They were the largest lumber operation in the state. Between "The Company," the Northern Pacific, and the J. Neils Company in Libby, the state's lumber industry was all locked up. Most of the small operators were on contract to the Company. With that in mind, the executives slept well.

Early in 1917, the I.W.W. was busy organizing a general strike of the lumber-related industries in the Northwest. Remember, they were the Industrial Workers of the World. They were not limited to a particular industry, or even one country, for that matter. What did matter was that there was a war going on, and we were going to win no matter what the "red" I.W.W. radicals were saying. It was unpatriotic to strike during wartime, wasn't it?

The newspapers owned by the Company made it sound as if the men were on strike for the purpose of undermining the American war effort. Separating fact from fiction sometimes is difficult even in times of tranquility; during wartime, emotions flare, and doing this is almost impossible. Such was the case in Montana's wood industry. Federal troops were brought in. The status quo prevailed. The lumber camps remained unfit for human habitation, but, after all, working the woods was at least a job. The I.W.W. or Wobblies became victims of a federal crackdown. They were soon out of the picture. Some people in Butte and Bonner rested a little easier.

The lumber industry dragged along during the 20's, 30's, and 40's. At least, if nothing else, as the trees grew, so did the inventory. Seriously, the logging industry provides a most fascinating story of man versus nature. Logging prior to mechinization was incredibly dangerous and difficult. It still is...but....Do yourself a favor and get out into the forests of this state and let your mind wonder. Then get the real story from those that have logged and are logging now. Or, the next best thing, read up on it.

To offset the power of the Company, Butte's miners and Anaconda's smelter workers formed strong unions. Butte for many years was known as the strongest union town in the country. There were so many different unions that there was even one for chimney-sweepers; it had two members.

The Montana Power Company was started in 1912 by the President of the Anaconda Company, John Ryan. The Montana Power Co. was never officially part of the Anaconda Company, though Ryan served as president of both for twenty years.

the LAND

Tragic Inferno Brought Death to 13

By Ann Conger
IR Staff Writer

Black Destruction

A raging four-day blaze of crown fire left black destruction on Mann Gulch on the Missouri River in 1949 and 13 firefighters lost their lives. Deer were reported running in circles near the blaze and a lioness appeared to be dazed and confused by the inferno.

Aug. 5, 6, 7, 8 and 9 here in 1949 are days scared with the memory of 13 charred bodies and 6,000 acres of scorched forest.

An inferno that slumbered on a Wednesday leaped into flame on a Thursday and became a raging monster, fought, but not beaten until the following Tuesday.

It was the Mann Gulch crown fire.

Five hundred men fought the holocaust in the Gates of the Mountains area. Twelve smokejumpers and one fire prevention guard lost their lives.

The bodies of all but two of the young victims were brought out of the blackened, steep forest by helicopter and rescue workers.

Small Dunkirk

Two others died of burns at St. Peter's Hospital where they were taken by ambulance from Hilger Landing, which a reporter said "looked like a small Dunkirk."

Fifteen smokejumpers from Missoula parachuted into Mann Gulch, enclosed by rocky cliffs on the Missouri River, on the afternoon of Thursday, Aug. 5.

By Friday, five persons were known dead, four were injured and seven were missing.

The smokejumpers were dropped in front of the fire and immediately started to fight it, but in the words of one victim, "the fire made its own wind and was coming at us fast."

The men appeared to be caught in a draw. The foreman, Wag Dodge, of Missoula, "threw a match into the grass to burn out an area for us but I guess the boys didn't understand. They began running up the side of the mountain with the fire behind them." the smokejumper said.

"I got out alive. Another fellow and I made it over the ridge and got in a large rockslide. I don't know how many others got to the top. Flames burned around and over us."

When the foreman made the burned out area it was with the intent of eliminating fuel for the leaping flames and with the hope that the fire would crown over that area. Only one man remained with him there. That man, the foreman and one other smokejumper survived. All the others died.

By Sunday there were 11 known dead and two missing.

By Monday the death toll reached a final 13 and the rampant crown fire which caught the smokejumpers had been diminished to a creeper which crawls along the ground.

The fire was started by lightening in record heat. It was fought with bulldozers, shovels and a 21-mile long fireline. It had a perimeter of 2.4 miles. Men operating from Meriwether Camp turned that area into what reminded some observers of an operation station in World War II.

It was from Meriwether Canyon that the prevention guard left his post to fight the fire. The body of J. C. Harrison, 20 of Missoula was only identifiable by his key and key chain. His clothes, like those of the other victims, were completely burned off.

Men of all ages fought the fire, many of them coming from northern Idaho and Missoula.

Most of the smokejumpers were college students and most had seen military service.

All Joined In

There were also young and old, clerks and construction workers and others from Helena who left their jobs to battle the roaring flames.

Boats piled up and down the Missouri River bringing firefighters to Hilger Landing and back and Forrest Retz waited there with an ambulance for injured firefighters.

Dr. Amos R. Little directed rescue operations. Dr. Thomas Hawkins and a visiting friend, Dr. Ronald Haines of Phoenix, Ariz., joined rescue workers to give blood transfusions and first aid, clambering up the steep hillside.

Dr. Little recalls that the bodies of the smokejumpers who didn't make it up the hill, were found in "what you might call an attack position." He said the men were asphyxiated and their bodies were badly charred. He recalls a scene of grey ashes from bodies, brush and everything touched by the dragon of fire.

Dr. Little said there was much criticism of his friend Wagner, the foreman, who, he said, died later of cancer when he was still young. But Dr. Little notes that the smokejumpers panicked and didn't obey the foreman's order to stay in the burned out area. He said he attributes the fact that they lost their lives to inadequate training.

Worst Tragedy

It was estimated that it cost about $125,000 a day to fight the fire which was the worst tragedy in northwestern forests since 1910 and the smokejumpers were the first to die since establishment of the training school at Missoula 10 years before.

Only flashlight light and the light from the crackling flames aided rescue workers on Friday night.

The reporter George Remington, now the editor of The Independent Record, recorded the names of the victims, and borrowing a camera at the scene of the fire, he took a picture that was used in the coverage of the tragedy by Life magazine.

The Independent Record
Sunday, August 3, 1969

Does this story sound familiar? A similar one was used in the movie "Red Skies Over Montana," which was filmed in Missoula in the 1950's.

Meanwhile, the homesteaders were halfway through *their* version of "Boom and Bust." The year 1917 saw the grain farmers enjoy a price for wheat set by the government. They couldn't lose. Although they felt that they could get more than the government offered, which was $2 per bushel, it was a nice figure. Over the previous few years many of them had followed the national business of expansion. The set price of wheat allowed a farmer to put a down payment on additional real estate and plow away. Additional money might be placed in one of the many commercial banks that mushroomed up overnight in many farming communities. With the creation of the Federal Reserve System in 1914, loans were easier to obtain. In the war years, Montana farmers had a right to smile. Many proudly sent their sons off to fight in the "war to end all wars," while they stayed home and raised the food that would help win the war, at a good price. Everyone was doing his or her share.

The homestead decade of 1910-1920 had the opposite effect on counties in Montana. As the farms expanded, the counties contracted, or more accurately, split up. Montana's not the smallest chunk of land around. As the farmer prospered, he found it increasingly bothersome to have to travel great distances to do business at the county seat. After all, the counties were rather large, and transportation wasn't any faster than a trot. There was a demand for counties in Montana. Presto! The 1915 Montana Legislature, through the Leighton Act, created the carving knife which was used time and again until the state's number of counties doubled. This, in essence, meant, and still means, twice as much government. Some might have considered it a somewhat surprising move for a conservative state. But the lure of being the county seat was pretty strong. Oh, well, with the *good crops,* they could afford the *extra* taxes.

Sometime in mid-June of 1917, Theodore Kenfield, a homesteader near Inverness, felt something was wrong. He knew good and well what it was. It had created a housecleaning problem for his wife. Dust was everywhere. A good rain would keep it down and bring crops up. Where was the rain? Almost hauntingly the words of the old cowboy song came back..."and

the skies are not cloudy all day." There hadn't been a cloud in the neighborhood for quite some time. It was right then and there that Theodore Kenfield realized that without any clouds at all, it was truly the "Big Sky Country." He knew, too, that the year's crop might not make more than a dozen loaves of bread. He was wrong. It didn't make any.

If consolation rested in the saying "misery loves company," Ted Kenfield had plenty of consolation. From Cut Bank east, all across the "High Line," crops were a total loss. Maybe S.H. Long's Great American Desert idea was closer to the truth than anyone had guessed. But, what the heck, one bad year does not a desert make. Some packed their bags and went to California, others to Canada. Most, however, gritted their teeth and borrowed money for the following year's seed. The banks were *quite* willing to oblige.

Many of the farmers felt the disaster was their own making. Maybe they should have plowed deeper. After all, the farmers near Great Falls averaged 25-30 bushels per acre in 1917. But, in 1918, the idea of the "Big Sky" spread across the entire eastern two-thirds of the state. Temperatures were often above 100° while the humidity was often below 10%. It was so dry that wells coughed. A weather report of "partly cloudy" would have brought tears to people's eyes. By July, 1918, any clouds were reported as UFO's.

Seriously, as it was serious, crop damages amounted in the millions of dollars. Montana's roads were dusty not only from the searing winds, but also from the wheels of carts, wagons, and "tin lizzies" filled with whatever they would carry. For some people, the second year was too much.

Sherman's infamous "march to the sea" during the Civil War could not match the Montana drought for total destructiveness. Draft animals and livestock died. The one-time stubble of wheat plants had long since turned to dust and blown away in the wind. It wasn't enough that the *sun* beat down man, beast, and vegetation; the *wind* aged or killed all with its constant slap in the face.

Newspapers across the state echoed the pleas and cries for help that fell on seemingly deaf ears. The Legislature empathized, but nothing materialized. Some Chambers of Commerce, obviously irked by the complaints of the farmers, felt that all this talk about the drought would damage Montana's *image*. Farms were lost, acres of topsoil blown away, animals died, and the little guy with the cigar was thinking of billing the whole tragedy as "dehydrated farms, just add water." Good grief!

By early 1919 the heat wave swept across the divide to the western valleys. The state of Montana, not just isolated areas, was now an openair kiln. The Chambers of Commerce now knew the extent of the tragedy. One really can't blame them for clinging to the idea that "it would go away." After all, a decade or more of hard core promotion, investment, returns, more investment is a cycle no one wanted to see slow down, much less grind to an absolute standstill.

Farming may have been at a standstill, but thousands of farmers weren't. Many new Montanans became even newer Californians or Canadians. The way the winds screamed across the plains it was amazing their tarpaper homes didn't follow them. To make matters worse, all of that "deep plowing" enabled the neighboring states of North and South Dakota to obtain, free and *delivered,* some 2,000,000+ acres of topsoil. The Black Hills got blacker. Then, as though things weren't bad enough already, with bankruptcies, no food, and no seed for crop, the grass fires started. It's a wonder that anyone stayed. Maybe, just maybe, the ones that did, those courageous thousands, did so to prove they could outlast the final onslaught.

Final onslaught? What else could possibly have happened? Well, when the sun didn't burn out the crops, grasshoppers ate them out. That's right, they, too, could totally destroy the crops. Descending out of the sky in millions, they made the U.S. Army's 82nd and 101st Airborne divisions look like amateurs. It was truly the grasshopper that invented the "search and destroy mission." Farmers believed that if hungry enough, those little devils would even eat rocks painted green.

Not all of the farmers hated the grasshoppers. A.L. Zimmerman, the fellow from Book V, actually went out of his way to feed them. His recipe was really quite simple, for it contained only three ingredients, bran for roughage, banana oil for flavor, and arsenic to discourage wheat eating permanently. The results often were good.

This agony of poor or no crops went into the mid-1920's when once again the rain began to fall. By then it was too late for over 50,000 people. They were forced to leave the *land that had scoffed at rain.* Some 11,000 farms went "belly up" in those awful years. Along with them went over 200 of those "instant" banks that extended the easy credit. With all of the millions of dollars lost, that amount, no matter how staggering, couldn't compare with the human suffering endured by the people of the plains.

To make economic matters worse, all the time the crops were failing, the price of wheat was dropping in market value. The same bushel of wheat in 1921 received less than half of the 1917 price of $2.20 per bushel. The value of land was halved. Europe was again producing its own food, and, consequently, the demand for American products dropped. However, most of America wasn't hit as hard as Montana. The one-two punch of drought and recession kept Montana reeling for years.

Those who stayed on through the lean years now wore (and still do) the name "homesteader" proudly. They were seasoned veterans of Montana's ugliest moments. To aid in their chances of never seeing a repeat of the late teens and early 20's drought, many changed their farming methods. Nature and the land do not change; the farmer had to. Many diversified their crops, growing not only wheat but also barley, sugar beets, and other cash crops. The idea of summer fallow and strip farming caught on also. To protect the soil from the wind, trees were planted in long rows as barriers to lessen its intensity. These were known as "shelter-belts." Some fertilizers were introduced.

About the most revolutionary change came by way of mechanization. Tractors were few and far between in the early years, but by the mid and late 20's, almost every farm had at least one. With the tractors came new implements designed to

Agriculture and "Honyokers"

Between 1910 and 1922, homesteaders took up 93,000,000 acres of Montana land, mostly in the east. This was 43% of Montana's total area.

Wheat acreage increased during these years from 250,000 in 1909 to 3,417,000 acres in 1919. (The war greatly increased the demand for wheat, and Montana profited enormously from this demand. The price of wheat soared to $2 per bushel, and in 1918, Montana produced 50,000,000 bushels. The prosperity would not last, however.)

James Hill, President of the Great Northern Railroad, promoted an extensive campaign to lure settlers to eastern Montana (so the Railroad could sell its land, and the railroad would have traffic and goods to carry). In one day alone, in 1913, a Great Northern train carried 500 settlers bound for eastern Montana.

These new settlers were called "Honyokers," a derisive term which came from the name "Hunyaks," which is what Slav immigrants had been called in the Dakotas.

To reach eastern Montana from the Minneapolis area, settlers could rent an entire freight car for $50.

Few settlers really settled on the land for free (as they could under the provisions of the various Homestead Acts). Most had to hire "locators" to help them find a desireable farmsite; such men usually charged between $20 and $50 for their services.

The homesteaders enjoyed good harvest from 1910 to 1916, which increased their numbers, but then a long period of drought began. For example, Shelby, in the good years, had received well over its average 15 inches of rain per year. But in the following years, its annual rainfall was as follows:

1916 — 15.26 inches
1917 — 9.96
1918 — 8.88
1919 — 6.86

The result of these dry years was that over 60,000 settlers left the state.

(The above all taken from Joseph K. Howard's Montana, High, Wide and Handsome, published by Yale University Press, New Haven, Ct., 1943.)

At the 1915 Panama-Pacific Exposition in San Francisco, Montana won more agricultural awards than any other nation.

The total value of Montana's eleven major crops during these years was:

1918 $122,000,000
1919 $65,000,000
1920 $83,000,000 (notice the decline after World War 1)
1921 $88,000,000
By 1926, the value was back to $118,000,000.

—Taken from an informational booklet published by the State (courtesy U of M Montana Collection)

December Draftees, Columbus, 1917

Courtesy William Farr

Because agricultural hard times had begun in Montana by 1917 and men were out of work, a disproportionately (in comparison to other states) high number of Montanans enlisted in the army. Due to the higher-than-average number of enlistments, the War Department erroneously listed Montana's population as 950,000 when it was actually 496,000. A total of 40,000 Montanans served in the Army during the war, and 1,500 were killed. Montana, proportionately, provided more soldiers, and lost more, than any other state.

(from J.K. Howard's Montana, High Wide, and Handsome)

In 1919, the drought in Montana, which began before World War I, was so bad that gophers and grasshoppers swarmed the farms and ranches. Montana farmers imported 100,000 turkeys to eat the grasshoppers, but they did not help.

During the period of 1919-1925, 11,000 farms (20% of all in the state) were vacated. 20,000 farm mortgages were foreclosed, and over one-third of the state's farmers lost their land. 214 of the state's banks, over one-half, failed. Montana had the highest bankruptcy rate in the nation. 60,000 people left the state during the 1920's.

Sod House, East of Judith Gap, 1910

Montana was the first state to enact an old-age pension law.

The Great Depression was so bad in Montana that the amount of wheat worth $100 in 1920 was worth only $19 in 1932. Even the Anaconda Company suffered. Copper cost 18¢ per pound in 1929, 8¢ in 1931, and only 5¢ in 1933. Production in the mines was cut back from 300,000 tons per month to 30,000 tons per month.

Fort Peck was financed entirely by federal funds. It cost $75,000,000. It provided irrigation for 180,000 acres of farm and ranchland. The dam itself was filled with 90,000,000 cubic yards of dirt. It was 3,000,000 tons of rock and 5,000,000 tons of gravel. The reservoir behind the dam is 175 miles long, and 16 miles wide at its widest point. The lake is as deep as 200 feet in places, and takes up over 250,000 acres.

During World War II, Montana lost population. Many residents moved to the cities of the west coast to work at war industry plants. In 1940, the state had about 560,000 residents. By 1943, it had only 470,000.

(All of the above is taken from Michael Malone and Richard Roeder, Montana: A History of Two Centuries.)

allow one man to farm large amounts of land alone. The farmer, to keep up in competition, *had* to buy this equipment. Farming efficiency was greatly increased. So were the headaches. Many men, excellent with draft animals, found mechanical farming less "romantic." Those gas burners just didn't have the feel for the land the "oat-burners" had. Some got out of the business entirely; for others, the transition was indeed painful.

From 1925 to 1929 the Montana farmer, for the most part, did pretty well. The crash of the stock market in late 1929 again sent prices to the basement. This time, however, it was different. The price of *everything* went down. Millions across the nation were out of jobs. For that matter, tens of millions around the world were suffering. For Montana it was, "Oh, no, not again."

Then, however, the weather took another turn for the worse. Once again the rain ceased to fall. Once again it was only the brim of a hat, not the clouds, that kept the sun out of people's eyes. Once again the farmer was in trouble. It was like seeing a scarey movie for the second time. Sure, they were scared, nervous, and they hoped it would end. But this time they knew it *would* end. They didn't know when, but it could end. This thought alone probably stopped the stampede out of state that had been a reality a few years before. That, coupled with the fact that things really weren't any better anywhere else kept most of the people in place.

The people of the Northern Great Plains, which includes eastern Montana, finally were beginning to realize the truth of the situation. Before the homesteaders arrived, no one had ever *cultivated* these semi-arid rolling hills and flatlands. No one ever stayed in one place long enough to become dependent on one chunk of real estate. Therefore, no one had known that both Lewis and Clark's *and* S.H. Long's descriptions of the Great Plains were accurate. It was both lush *and* arid. These stories did not conflict with, but rather followed one another, in an unending, irregular cycle.

Whether the 30's were worse than the 20's is still debated in many areas. It depended on where a person was located. Some

things changed for the better, however, such as the rural electrification project brought on as a result of the New Deal. Not only did this provide light and refrigeration, it also provided power for more efficient, more maintenance-free electric water pumps for irrigation. The 30's weren't fun. In many areas the decade was worse than the 20's, but this time there was massive federal aid. The 1932 election of Franklin D. Roosevelt changed fiscal ideas 180°. The idea was no longer to balance the budget and ignore the suffering that went with economic hardship. Instead, the philosophy was "full speed ahead" into a plan of aiding people as much as possible.

For the farmer, it was the return of rainfall, in adequate quantities in the late 30's and early 40's, coupled with the increased demand for grain brought on by World War II, that really got him back on his feet. At the war's end, fixed prices remained, underwriting, in part, continued success for the farmer.

For those who lived on and tilled the land through the years 1917-1950, neither this book nor any other can possibly capture, accurately, with mere words, the feelings, the lasting impressions, the hope, and the helplessness they encountered. These people rode the national and worldwide economic roller coaster which sent prices both soaring and dropping. They also rode the still more deadly climatic cycle of the Northern Great Plains and learned to adapt to it. While some fell off, many hung on and made it.

With justifiable pride, and many time — and wind-worn wrinkles, many of these people have written first-hand accounts which appear in county and regional memory books. They are available across the state. At this time it might be appropriate to read the words of the real homesteader. Or, better yet, talk with, but *mostly listen* to them as they tell their own stories. A book you may wish to read at this time is entitled *Letters of a Woman Homesteader,* by Elenore Pruitt Stewart. The letters are all genuine and speak for themselves.

Chapter Four

The money and drought problems of Montana in the 20's, and the nation as a whole in the 30's, had similar impact on both farming and the cattle industry. Who lost more or suffered more is still debated whenever farmers and cattle ranches get together.

For the rancher, though, the drop in prices and the lack of rainfall had nowhere near the effect of the "Hard Winter" of 1886-87. From that time on ranching was undeniably different. For many, the "open range" system *was* ranching. There was no separating the two. When one died, so did the other. The men and women who stayed in the ranching business did so using totally different methods to raise the same product, beef cattle. Cowboys on horseback had kept the cattle where they needed to be. Now, three strands of barbed wire did the job. Slowly but surely, bales of hay were stacked inside the bunkhouse. The downward cycle of fewer cowboys, fewer people to carry on the tradition, and, therefore, fewer ranches, coincided with increased mechanization.

As the "larger than life" cowboy disappeared, the "no-life" machine took his place. Sure, the machinery added a new meaning to ranching as far as efficiency goes, but the thought of a "shoot-out" with grease guns in a used-tractor lot leaves some element of the "Old West" missing.

With the influx of homesteaders onto the plains, the Montana rancher found himself in difficult straights. He knew the lesson that had been learned from the winter of 1886-87, that

overcrowding, could not be ignored. If herds were to expand, the ranches would have to expand, too. With these enthusiastic "dry landers" (farmers) moving in, the price of land was skyrocketing.

By the late 20's, a group of Montana cattle outfits, under the watchful eye of both state and federal governments, joined together to form a grazing corporation. What? A *grazing* corporation? At first glance, this looked like a good idea, and it was, but there was more than met the eye. Sure, ranchers had shared rangeland before, during the open range days, but then they each had their "own" chunk that wasn't really theirs, and yet was, due to the "customary range," which had been divided on a first-come, first-served bases. Each outfit operated with a lot of pride. They were proud not only of their product, but also of their _independence_. With each new calf branded, that pride grew. Friendly and not-so-friendly rivalries had developed.

This grazing corporation, the Mizpah-Pumpkin Creek Project of 1929, was different. It was an experiment being conducted so that the cattle industry could *survive*. The ranches, once again a highly independent sort, now *had* to band together. This project, in southeastern Montana, proved to the nation that cooperative grazing could work. By 1933, the Montana legislature opened the door to increasing the number of these districts. The federal government followed a year later. Grazing on leased land was a lot more reasonable than having to buy the land.

Relief for the rancher came in another form, too. In 1934, the U.S. Government, trying to kill a few birds with one stone, began a policy of buying up large numbers of cattle. It was hoped that by so doing the government would aid the rancher not only by putting dollars into his pocket but also by making cattle "scarcer," which would increase the price. Rangelands were opened to more stock. Besides this, the slaughtered beef would provide food necessary to feed hungry people. It was a good idea, but things don't always work out as they are planned.

A major shock came to the cattle business when the Chicago Livestock market, of Carl Sandburg fame, began to break up. It was like the fall of the Roman Empire. Good grief, generation after generation of cows from all over the west "looked forward" to that one lasting fling, and one *last meal,* on Chicago's South Side; the bright lights, the night life, and the crowds. It was *exciting.* But now the thought of a last meal in Montana didn't do much for the ones in the herd who longed for adventure.

Ranchers also felt the bite of the grasshopper, locust, cicada, and Mormon cricket plagues that ravaged the Rocky Mountains during the 30's and 40's. During their stay, these pesky eaters destroyed some $400,000,000 worth of crops. These little dudes would eat anything that grew, and *some* things that didn't.

An interesting story dealing with these miserable munchers comes from the Cowan clan, who at the time lived in the Fromberg area. The story took place at Ted Cowan's ranch near Edger. But it could just as easily have happened at Bill's farm near Fromberg, or in any number of other places. Ted and his wife Violet were having his brother Bill and *his* wife Hazel(who was Violet's sister) over for dinner. While the four ate dinner, Violet got up to get something, and by chance looked out the window. What she saw she couldn't believe. The ground was moving. Immediately, the others went to the windows to take a look. Upon closer inspection, it was discovered that it wasn't the ground that was moving at all, but a thick mass of black, Mormon crickets.

They ate everything in their path. This black, slow-moving, but never-stopping horde proceeded through the southern half of Ted and Violet's forty acres of irrigated alfalfa. They moved closer to the house with each bite. Too startled to believe what was happening, too outnumbered to do anything, they watched the black tide approach and go not around, but *over* the house. The advancing column made an abrupt turn and proceeded to devour the rest of the alfalfa. By nightfall, the crop had disappeared as though a giant Gillette Trac II had shaved the field. To add insult to injury, a couple of the more spiteful critters got inside the house and ate part of the kitchen curtains. Needless to say, Ted had to buy some hay that year, and it was "curtains" for Violet.

213

Between the overgrazing, drought, and the grasshoppers, the rangeland was not in the best shape. With hopes of improving it, the Federal Government spent a bundle of money reseeding 1,500,000 acres of Montana grazing land. If they spent money to replace grass, this time it obviously wasn't the "tree grass" it was once thought to be.

Besides all of the other things going on, a far more basic change was taking place in the cattle industry. The change was in timing. That is, ranchers used to let their cattle graze until the age of four before sending them off to market. Somewhere in the 20's, people's tastes changed. They wanted younger, more tender beef. The ranchers were now selling stock at the ripe old age of 2 years. Feedlots, because grain prices were low, would fatten up the calves. All of a sudden the rancher was *dependent* on the price of grain, because the American public felt grain-fed beef was the only kind to eat.

The cattle business was changing dramatically. There was a time when the rancher needed to know only three things: horses, cows, and the weather. He was independent; he took care of his cattle, and they, in turn, provided a living for him and his family. But things had changed. Besides three initial ingredients, the rancher now needed to understand and deal with machines of all sorts, grain prices, tax structures, health codes, diseases, and hundreds of other unromantic aspects of the business. And then, even after learning all of that, he still had no control over the price of his product. *That* was established in the market place. Ranching had, indeed, entered the complex twentieth century.

In the meantime, questions were being raised about the state's wildlife population. Montanans, being the free spirits they are, were sometimes skirting the Fish and Game Department's directives on limits and seasons. If they didn't like the enforcement officer in their district, they'd simply get another one to replace him.

With the arrival of the homesteaders, problems multiplied phenomenally. One problem in particular was that the farmer, having spread out across the entire prairie, took up the winter range of many species. The wildlife needed a place to winter; the farmer couldn't afford to allow game animals to feed from hay set aside for his livestock.

The problem was partially solved with the landmark Rathbone case in 1939. In this case, a landowner killed an elk out of season. The kill was made on his ranch while the elk was eating food meant for the livestock. The case involved defending one's property versus the right of the state to preserve game animals. The state won the case, and after review by the State Supreme Court, guidelines were set up for similar cases.

The year 1941 was a good year for the Montana Fish and Game Department. Four years earlier, the Federal Aid in Wildlife Act provided funding for state and wildlife management programs. The funding came by placing a special tax on all guns and ammunition. In 1941 the Montana Legislature provided the authority necessary for the Commission to put some teeth in these regulations. Not only that, it provided long-sought-after teams of trained wildlife specialists to record valuable data so as to protect both man and wildlife. The idea of the individual animal's position in the ecosystem was beginning to replace the idea of merely setting up limits and "blasting away."

As with domestic animals, the care and welfare of the state's game animals grew. The men and women of the Fish and Game Department were finally getting more money and scientific data that would, in turn, enable them to ensure proper management of the state's wildlife populations.

Chapter Five

Back in Book IV we stated that identifying rulers of the land was difficult for that time period, due to the complexity of the era. Well...that era was kid's stuff compared to the one we are now covering, 1917-1950. However, the chore of identifying the rulers was made considerably easier. How could that be? Simple, it's merely a case finding the rich who got richer, and the powerful, who became more so.

In the rulers department, the *federal government* came out number one. Second was *nature.* Last and by no means least was the *"Dynamic Duo"* of the Anaconda Copper Mining Company and the Montana Power Company. At times, these three and their various branches provided enough hot air to melt all the glaciers at Glacier National Park. Then, too, they could reverse themselves for some beautiful "snow jobs." But then, still, there were times when they all worked together to create the environment *they* personally felt was best for Montana.

Taking things chronologically, it was nature that first proved itself worthy of the title "ruler." By 1917, people in Montana knew what to expect from the Anaconda Company, but it was the *weather* that caught them off guard.

The drought during the late teens and early 20's genuinely caught the homesteaders by surprise. After all, Montana, for the preceding few years, had been so good to them. Why the hassle? Besides plowing up the land, what had they done wrong?

It wasn't as though they planned to plow up the land and leave. *They* were here to stay. They were here to raise food for the nation and the world. Those who left before the rain came back never really understood the area. Those who stayed found out that to make it on the Great Plains, one has to adapt to nature. Life and death are in the balance, and the balance *was, and still is,* delicate, to say the least.

Most Montanans proved that they could work with nature, and even harness it, but to try to subdue it or ignore it was strictly suicide. With the return of the drought in the 30's, and intermittently ever since, man has made great progress heading off some of the devastating effects of these unavoidable cycles. In a state that depends so heavily on agriculture, common sense coupled with applied science and technology seem to be the only alternatives. Luckily, Montana has a good supply of both, in the form of experienced farmers, rancher, foresters, and others involved in these professions. Then, too, there are the new generations, better-educated and more highly skilled, field technicians, and agricultural and biological experts sent to universities and vocational training by the dollars made during the post-World War II years. The "new crop" is already influencing Montana's agriculture.

Coming in first in the ruler's "power poll" was none other than the government of the United States of America. Good grief! As for *lasting* effects on the state of Montana, and all the other states, the federal government won (and probably still wins), hand down.

During this period, the federal government went from being "those white marble buildings back in Washington" to "Oh, yes, the couple next door both work for the 'feds.' He works at the Post Office. She works at the Forest Service." The federal government and its bureaucracy grew (in some people's eyes) from "guarding of the nation" to "babysitter for the states." Others have looked upon this federal growth as the best thing since sliced bread.

Back in 1917, the major efforts of the federal government in Montana were the federal court system and the federal troops, which were used to quell labor disputes in the mining and lumber industries. Twice the Montana Legislature prevented the U.S. Government from looking like the "bad guy." They did this by beating the "feds" to the punch with controversial legislation, the famous, or infamous, Sedition and Prohibitions acts. Both were later rescinded when more reasonable sentiment prevailed.

The Montana Sedition Act was passed during the highly emotional years of World War I. In essence, it greatly curtailed freedom of expression. No one was allowed to utter anything, much less write anything, that the everpresent Montana Council for Defense thought was anti-American or pro-German. Montanans weren't the only people to do this, they were just the first. The following year similar laws were passed in all forty-eight states.

The same was true of Prohibition, the banning of alcoholic beverages. Religious groups, even before the turn of the century, had been trying to outlaw booze. With the influx of thousands of "super-straight" midwesterners, the homesteaders, Montana was ready to pass a referendum concerning the "dreaded spirits." Boy, did it pass! By nearly a 30,000 vote margin, Montanans climbed "on the wagon" in 1919.

During World War I, the Montana legislature passed a "Sedition Act" to protect the war effort from German spies and others who might wish to disrupt the United States; probably there were none in Montana. But people in Montana were very suspicious of everyone's behavior during the war, and often their suspicions had tragic, though sometimes comic, consequences. Here are some of the things that happened.

Burton K. Wheeler, the U.S. District Attorney in Montana, received many reports of enemy airplanes operating out of a secret hideaway in the Bitterroot Valley. Wheeler remarked, "Just how and why the German high command expected to launch an invasion of the U.S. through western Montana, 6,000 miles from Berlin, never made the slightest bit of sense to me."

People frequently thought they saw German airships flying over Montana, always flying south.

Labor unions were frequently singled out as being radical "puppets" of the German government.

Laws were passed which made it a criminal offense for any person to write or speak out against the war or the draft. Doing so was punishable by a fine of not more than $20,000 or imprisonment for up to 20 years.

A "Montana Council of Defense" was organized to help find "traitors" in Montana. It was also in charge of selling Liberty Bonds, which provided the federal government with money to fight the war.

A schoolbook entitled The Ancient World *was barred from use in Montana schools because it stated "the great contributions to civilization in the West were Roman and Teutonic (German)." This was said to be "German propaganda."*

Because speaking German was against the law in Montana, many Montanans of German ancestry, who still spoke German, left the state. This included a large group of Mennonites, who had been among the state's best farmers.

The Council encouraged all to buy Liberty Bonds. One farmer in the Bitterroot Valley, who was deeply in debt and on the verge of bankruptcy, was called in to explain why he had not bought any. When he explained that he would contribute when he was out of debt, the Council accused him of "looking toward your own comfort all the time."

The Sedition Law which made action like this possible is no longer enforced, but it is still a state law.

(All of the above information is taken from K. Ross Toole's Twentieth Century Montana: A State of Extremes, *Norman, Oklahoma, University of Oklahoma Press, 1972.)*

216

Famous Political Figures

Thomas J. Walsh, who was elected U.S. Senator from Montana, discovered the "Teapot Dome" scandal in 1924. This case involved President Harding's Secretary of the Interior, who had leased, at favorable rates, federal oil lands to his personal friends. Walsh discovered this, and the Secretary was sent to jail.

Walsh was named U.S. Attorney General, a Cabinet post, by President Franklin Roosevelt, in 1933. He died before assuming office.

Burton K. Wheeler, one of Montana's best-known politicians, never meant to settle in Missoula. A graduate of the University of Michigan, he was en route to the west coast when he stopped in Butte. He lost all his money in a poker game there, so he decided to stay.

Toole, *Twentieth Century Montana: A State of Extremes.*

Jeanette Rankin of Missoula was the first woman ever elected to serve in the U.S. House of Representatives. A month after taking her seat in Washington, she was among 50 Representatives who voted against U.S. entry in World War I.

Her platform (she ran as a Republican) included the following:
national women's suffrage (not all women had the right to vote yet)
protection of childhood (probably child labor laws and compulsory education)
state and national prohibition (no liquor anywhere)
farm loan law (so farmers could borrow to buy land and equipment—remember Montana's farmers were in less than good shape)
equal taxation (perhaps aimed at the mining operations, which paid very little in taxes at that time)

—Taken from Campaign Brochure, 1915 (courtesy U of M Montana Collection)

"Mike" Mansfield Goes to Congress

Professor Leaves Campus For Service in Capital

Mike, One of Youngest World War Veterans, Sees Service in Army, Navy, Marine Corps Before College Days

Mike Mansfield, who still insists on being called Mike in spite of the fact that he might well be addressed as "The Honorable Mr. Mansfield," has gained national prominence by sweeping through the November elections to win a seat in the House of Representatives. Mike, long one of the most deservedly popular teachers on the University faculty, won a close race against Howard Hazelbaker, '36, to be the representative for Montana's district No. 1 for the ensuing two years. He ran on the Democratic ticket.

He and Mrs. Mansfield left Missoula in December for Washington to begin establishing themselves in the nation's capitol. Both are graduates of the University, he in 1933 and Mrs. Mansfield, the former Maureen Hayes, in 1934. He has been on the faculty since 1934, during which year he also attained his Master's degree in history and political science. He has been granted a leave of absence from the University.

Before his collegiate days, Mike had one of the most exciting "soldier of fortune" careers imaginable. He is a veteran of the first World War, one of the youngest in the nation. He had to lie about his age to enlist in the Navy way back in 1916, at which time he was only 14 years of age. After serving thirteen months overseas, he was honorably discharged in 1919, whereon he enlisted in the Army.

Enlists in Marines

After his Army hitch, he still wasn't satisfied that he had served his country enough, so he enlisted in the Marine Corps in 1920.

Mike's service in the Marines took him to such fascinating far eastern places as the Philippines, China, Japan and Siberia. It was during this time that he picked up his first-hand knowledge of the oriental situation. His understanding of Far Eastern affairs today, therefore, has as its background a personal perspective.

Returns to Montana

His enlistment in the Marines having ended in 1922, he returned to Montana, his native state, to work in the Butte mines. But with innate farsightedness, Mike decided that a career underground was not for him, so he laid plans to attend college. Having had no formal education past the eighth grade, he enrolled as a special student in the School of Mines in 1927 and '28. During the summer of 1928, he transferred to the University still as a special student.

In his senior year at the University, in 1932, he became a regular student, having made up through hard study his high school work and pushing on at the same time toward his degree. January 31, 1933, he was granted his B.A.

"I owe a great deal to Montana State University," Mike said, "and feel indebted for the opportunities it has given me."

When asked if he intended to abandon entirely his teaching, he replied that politics fitted in with what had always been his first love, the teaching profession.

Montana State University
(Missoula)
Alumni News Bulletin
Jan. 1943

218

Mike Mansfield, long time Senate Leader — Currently U.S. Ambassador to Japan

Courtesy Montana Historical Society

Mansfield Credits Education to His Wife

By Sen. Mike Mansfield

Gus Erickson was one of the strongest men I've known. For most of 1926 we stayed in the same rooming house in Butte, Mont. We ate together, loafed together, talked together. And together we sweated in the dust-filled air of the copper mines.

Gus died of silicosis that year. The dust had gotten into his lungs. I watched his weigh and muscle disappear. I saw him doubled over in bed, coughing and choking until his face was deathly white. At his funeal, I kept thinking: this could be me...this could be me.

I was 19 when I went down on my first shift as a mucker (ore shoveler) at $4.25 a day. That was big money in 1922, but men paid a hard price for it. I spent the next nine years watching many like Gus cough their lungs out.

This was a world I might still be in — struggling to stay alive — if it hadn't been for a vivacious copper-haired girl who taught high-school English in Butte and showed me the way out of the mines. Maureen Hayes had been raised in the mining camp and started teaching in Butte in 1928. Her sister introduced us. Suddenly, I had a new friend — perhaps the only genuinely close friend in my life.

I had always been a loner who kept his thoughts to himself, but Maureen brought out the talk in me. I told her about my early love of history and adventure books and how, at 14, I'd run away from my home in Great Falls, Mont., to join the Navy. We talked about school. The fact that she had a college education while I'd never gotten beyond the eighth grade troubled me.

Correspondence Study

"Mike, if it bothers you, do something about it," she finally said. "I'll help you study for a high-school diploma." Within days she had me enrolled in a correspondence course. From then on I spent most of my free hours studying.

But in 1929 and 1930 the depression hit Butte, and the mines began to lay off workers. I was scared; mining was the only work I knew. So when two friends working in South America told me their company was offering the security of three-year contracts to experienced miners, I quickly shared the news with Maureen.

She was thoughtful for more than a minute. Then she said in a soft, serious voice: "Mike, are you sure you really want a career in mining? Since you've always loved history and reading, why don't you take the money you've been saving and go down to the state university at Missoula and study for a degree?"

"But what about us?" I interrupted. "We couldn't afford to get married for years." Maureen smiled. "The most important thing is for you to find yourself; we'll talk about marriage later."

College Bound

The idea was absurd, and yet I knew I disliked my life as a miner. Maureen argued on. Finally, in the spring of 1931 when people were crying for jobs, I quit the mines and went to college.

Maureen continued to teach in Butte; our only contact was through letters. But by 1932, the separation was becoming too painful. So one day that autumn Maureen gave up her job and drove down to Missoula, where we were married. She had waited three long years for me.

Bad Bargain

There were other couples living on the campus, but I doubt if any were poorer than we. I recall one time when I saw hamburger selling at three pounds for 25 cents. This seemed like a bargain, so I bought 25 cents worth. But when Maureen saw the meat she began to cry.

"What's the matter?" I asked. "We haven't any place to put this meat," she said. "We haven't got an icebox." The meat was distributed to friends, and from that moment on I let Maureen do all the buying.

But no matter how much we scrimped, we could not make ends meet. Aain, it was Maureen who found an answer. One evening she picked up the latest rent bill and said: "Mike, I think it's time I cashed in my insurance policy."

I started to protest, but she shook her head angrily. "Be sensible, Mike — keeping you in school is our insurance for the future." Her logic was unanswerable. I could only promise myself that someday I would repay this wonderful girl.

Several weeks before my graduation, the chairman of the history department asked me to drop in to his office. His first question was: "Are you taking your master's, Mike?" I told him how worried I was about my finances. He nodded: "That's why I called you in. I can give you two history classes at the University next year. They won't pay much, but they will at least take care of your rent and a few other problems. You'll be able to go on for your master's."

Real Joy

I've never been a man given to expressive emotions. But even today, after years of dealing with momentous affairs in Washington, I can still vividly recall the joy and excitement I felt at that moment. Here was the goal for which Maureen and I had been striving. At last, I was truly a part of the world of books and ideas.

Maureen was working in the kitchen when I arrived home. "Tonight, Mrs. Mansfield," I said with a mock severe voice as I untied her apron, "we are going out for a steak dinner." It was my first payment on a long overdue bill.

The Missoulian
Oct. 9, 1962

CONGRESSWOMAN JEANNETTE RANKIN EXPLAINS HER "NO" VOTE ON WAR

Miss Jeannette Rankin, member of congress for the first district of Montana, voted the only "No" against war with Japan.

The Montana representative has been criticised severely by labor unions, and American Legions, whose organizations have requested an explanation.

The following is a letter received by the Silver State Post from Miss Jeannette Rankin, Wednesday:

"Washington, D.C., December 8, 1941. Today I voted against the resolution declaring war on the Japanese Empire. In as much as my vote was the only one cast against our entry, I feel I owe the people of my District a statement.

"As those of you who listen in over the radio are aware, I tried repeatedly to get the floor to ask some questions. I felt there were not enough facts before us — especialy since most of them were based on brief, unconfirmed radio reports — to justify such hasty action. The address of the President did not give us any additional facts.

"After a speech of little more than 500 words and a debate which lasted only 18 minutes, the roll was called in the House and the die was cast which hurled our country into the conflict.

"Before we entered the last World War, four days were consumed in debating all phases of the issue before the vote was taken. Every argument used today was the same as in the last war, except this time the speed was so great that it prevented any answer or questions. Had the vote to go to war been unanimous, it would have been a totalitarian vote, one not in keeping with our American way of life."

Silver State Post
Dec. 11, 1941

As in the rest of the nation, which went "dry" a year later, Prohibition created a huge demand for illegal liquor. Presto! Enter such terms as "whiskey road," "rum runners," and "bootleggers." The only *real* difference was that instead of drinking at local pubs, people drank at home, or somewhere on the "sly." Later, prior to the 1933 repeal of the well-intentioned, but overly optimistic law, violations became open and totally outrageous. The ironic part of the repeal was that the anti-booze people had nowhere to drown their sorrows.

The federal government's involvement in Montana really didn't begin until the election of 1931 when the Democratic candidate, Franklin D. Roosevelt, was elected President. Roosevelt was ushered into the Oval Office on the promise of a "New Deal." People, after three years of the "Great Depression," were groping for just that. Remember, President Hoover, a conservative Republican, felt that relief for the poor should come from private sources. The government should stay clear and play the role of spectator. At first, many agreed with Hoover, but many more put the blame for the whole mess on his shoulders.

This is fairly common political thinking. If something bad happens, get the person in charge out of office. Montanans saw this happen in 1924, when Joseph Dixon, a progressive Republican, was ousted from the governor-ship because he was, unfortunately for him, in office when Montana's "mini-depression" struck. Luckily for Dixon that President Hoover recognized his talents as an able administrator and appointed him to the Department of the Interior as Assistant Secretary. Then just four years later, Hoover went "down the road" to be forever known as the President who let the bottom fall out of the economy.

Anyway, F.D.R. was in. His "New Deal" really consisted of one plan, spend money. The people *knew* they were broke. They needed jobs and money. F.D.R. created "makework" jobs and spent money, billions of dollars, in all directions. The "kicker" came when the bureaucracies necessary to dispense this money greatly increased the size of state and federal government. At first, no one really complained, because, after all, jobs were jobs. And people needed jobs, desperately. Some people, mostly arch conservative Republicans, saw this as gross federal meddling in states' affairs, due to the "strings attached" to the federal money spent in each state. The overwhelming response to this criticism was, "Quiet, it's money, isn't it?"

As time went on, more and more money was spent. At the same time, the bureaucracy grew. The deficit spending (spending more money than you take in) and added governmental agencies caused many a heated debate, not only in Washington and state capitols, but across America.

As of 1974, federal expenditures for the state of Montana were a mere .4% of the national total (which, by the way, made Montana rank 45th). But .4% is a deceptively small figure. When translated into dollars and cents, the figure is $1,044,541,000. That's right, over 1 *billion* dollars of federal money came into the state in 1974.

Rather than bore you with a few statistics taken out of context, a trick many people use to prove whatever they wish to, this book will give you the source of its information. The publication is entitled *Federal Outlays in Montana*, and the most recent one was for 1974. The publication is compiled for the Executive office of the President by the Office of Economic Opportunity. It is not an easy publication to find. Because of this, a partial list of places to look is: The Governor's Office, State Economic Opportunity Office, offices of mayors of cities over 25,000 population, and principal county officials in all U.S. counties. So, county offices would be the best bet. It seems that in 1974 the publication's circulation was *cut*, to *save federal spending?*

Seriously, it is an amazing publication. Although, for sure, you couldn't check it out for home use, it makes an interesting hour's study. After all, the federal government spent an average of $1300-1400 *per person* in Montana in 1974. It's interesting to see how, why, and where.

Anyway, all of this spending began with programs designed to not only stop the country's downward economic spiral, but also to get things started again. From the New Deal's beginning until 1939, Montana received a massive transfusion of nearly $400,000,000. This didn't count over $140,000,000 in loans.

Immediately, Montana was filled with those funny government acronyms: A.A.A., F.C.A., C.C.C., W.P.A., and others. But each provided necessary relief, so no one was laughing. The Agricultural Adjustment Administration (A.A.A.) went to work paying farmers *not* to raise crops. It was felt that by making grain less plentiful, the price would increase. If nothing else, some farmers were getting a couple of nickels to rub together, the first such occurrence in a while. To prevent the farm foreclosure which crippled the 20's, the feds came up with the Farm Credit Administration (F.C.A.), which allowed easy farm loans.

The Civilian Conservation Corps (C.C.C.), under the guidance of the U.S. Army and the U.S. Forest Service, employed young men to assist nature in meeting man's needs. This ambitious outfit proceeded, among other things, to construct mountain roads, built lookout stations, fight fires, and plant trees. It was this group that reseeded much of the barren plains of eastern Montana.

However, it was undoubtedly the Works Progress Administration (W.P.A.) that made the largest overall contribution to Montana. This program, through the employment of many Montanans, supported over 40,000 people. W.P.A. people were all over the state repairing roads and highways, building bridges and public buildings, and constructing sewers. The projects included all sorts of jobs, some extremely necessary, others kind of "goof-offs," boondoggle-type jobs. It was this latter type that caused many people to scream "government waste," whenever the W.P.A. was mentioned. So as not to discriminate against the rural population, the W.P.A., after having built city sewers, proceeded to construct over 10,000 small but well-built structures. Each housed flushless facilities. They were truly tax dollars well spent!

As far as choosing one project which caught the eye and imagination of Montanans, as well as the nation, the Fort Peck Dam claims the title. It was a project of massive proportion. It was definitely the "pet project" of the Montana New Deal. By its completion in 1939, it was the world's largest earthen dam. Thousands were employed during its construction, and it cost millions. It was a remarkable project with lasting value.

It was during the New Deal also that Social Security had its beginning. Basically, it worked by people paying into the program for a specified number of years. On retirement, they could use the money, receiving a certain amount each month. It seemed to be the answer to the problem of the many poor, elderly people of the nation.

But such was not the case for Andrew Hansen of Bonner. He and millions like him were victims of the "cut-off date." That is, Hansen retired from the Anaconda Lumber Mill in Bonner less than a year before the Social Security program went into effect. The result, of course, was that he received no benefits. He moved to Hamilton to live on the small piece of property where he had lived prior to taking a job in Bonner. Hansen died in early 1952, never having received any of the direct benefits of the "New Deal."

This was no fault of the government. This was merely a case which dramatized the transition between a time when people "stood on their own two feet" and the time the government would begin a retirement program for all. Today, the Social Security System has, like many other agencies, widened its scope, to the extent that a person needs to give them a call or stop by a local office to fully take advantage of what they have to offer.

Many other pieces of legislation led to numerous programs, all with the idea of ending the troubled time. Check into some U.S. history and make the connections yourself.

Our final entrant in the "rulers" category is a joint effort. The first half of the "dynamic Duo" had been around for nearly forty years, while the other half was still "wet behind the ears." This combination was, of course, the Anaconda Copper Mining Company and the Montana Power Company.

It was the combined team of the A.C.M. and M.P.C. that used all of Montana as a stage for their Wall Street "hit musical," entitled "corporate domination." It played to sold out, "captive" audiences across the state for many years. The newspapers (owned by A.C.M.) acclaimed their act as a powerful melodrama that pitted free enterprise against radical labor organizations, and men versus the harnessing of power. Funny thing, though, although they played to sold-out audiences, they seldom received applause, much less standing ovations. Much of this changed, however, when major changes in their cast and a change of tune greatly altered their public image. No longer did they wish to play the part of the menacing young street fighter. After all, "The Company" was grown up. It sought after, and attained, a new degree of sophistication. *Now* Montana applauded.

221

Now, how about going through all of that again and explaining the A.C.M. — M.P.C. era? O.K. Read on.

First of all, seeing as though the A.C.M. was covered in Chapter 2 of this book, the main thrust of this chapter will be with the M.P.C. No one is ever going to deny that at the turn of the century, the business community in the United States consisted of some rather unscrupulous individuals. Time after time decisions affecting millions of people were made in little "smoke filled rooms" by the "biggies." Each one of these men had started out as a little kid with big brothers, sisters, moms, and dads, just like most people. Somewhere along the line, whether on purpose or by accident, these men became engulfed in the business of making money, as is the case with most people.

This in itself was no big deal. The big deal came at the next step: making *money* make more money. That is, the accumulation of additional money by putting the money *first* earned to good use. For some, it was a sort of real-life monopoly game. For others, though, it was an obsession. They *had* to make the right deal. They were in the public eye. Confidence in the system rested with each move they made. To some extent, they were correct.

Anyway, along with Anaconda's purchase by the Standard Oil Company in 1899 came new tactics proven effective on the "eastern front." The 1903 ultimatum to the state still remains as a classic in corporate depravity. From then on, anything the Company did at least "wasn't as bad as back in '03."

The "star" of the melodrama was A.C.M.'s president, John D. Ryan, a man who definitely knew his lines. Besides being a good actor, John D. Ryan was a superb businessman. It was Ryan who decided that A.C.M. was finished as a solo act. He was the "talent scout" who gathered together a few ragtag utility outfits near Great Falls and molded them into the new east coast sensation, "The Montana Power Company" of New Jersey. New Jersey? Yes, until 1961, the Montana Power Company was legally incorporated in New Jersey.

Good grief! That doesn't sound right. Well, think of it this way: the last time you went to an Italian restaurant for pizza, were you disappointed that you weren't in Italy? Just because it said "Montana Power Company," didn't mean it had to be a *Montana* power company. As long as the lights were on, few people cared. In fact, if Montana incorporation requirements would have been more flexible, they may have incorporated here.

There *were* reasons for such titles as "Standard Oil Company of *New Jersey*." Evidently New Jersey was a good place to

incorporate. Close to the Wall Street gang. Fifth Avenue. Coney Island. Maybe they had heard of the impressive home-run hitting pitcher about to move up to the majors in Baltimore, George (Babe) Ruth.

Meanwhile, back in Montana, audiences were held in awe by the new act. They worked together in certain areas, such as lobbying in Helena for favorable legislation. They had legal staffs to present a common defense, and a publicity outfit to make sure no one got the idea that they weren't really the same company. It wasn't *their* fault that John Ryan was president of *both,* until his death in 1933.

It worked like this: John D. Ryan was, as stated, a superb businessman. Early in the game he recognized the value in the up-and-coming utilities business. So, with the necessary capital, he got together a few minor power firms and established the Montana Power Company. His plan was to have his newly-founded private utility company provide power for his other interests, namely, A.C.M. and the Milwaukee Road. You see, he was also on the Board of Directors of the Milwaukee. (Remember, he was a sharp dude, no getting around it.) Remember, too, that the Milwaukee used *electric* engines to cross the Rockies. It had nearly 450 miles of lines to power these trains. It was the U.S.'s first long distance electrified railroad.

By 1916, the M.P.C. was picking up steam, literally. In that year they picked up a steam heating contract in Butte. During the 20's both the A.C.M. and the M.P.C. showed the knack for quick expansion. One major difference in the type of expansion was that A.C.M. did much of it out of state, seemingly to avoid putting all of its eggs in one basket. M.P.C., on the other hand, was making itself known around a considerably large area of the state.

In 1929, M.P.C. acquired some half-dozen dams in central Montana, each with the appropriate water rights. Their system then contained more than 2,500 miles of transmission lines connecting over 100 communities. Even then, A.C.M. still used more power than all of these combined, by a wide margin. The next year saw a M.P.C. subsidiary, the Rocky Mountain Power Company, get the go-ahead for the Kerr Dam, so named after Frank M. Kerr, M.P.C. president from 1933-1940. The project was completed in 1938.

1935 probably was not the best year for M.P.C. The New Deal, in its efforts to aid the ranchers and farmers, created competition for M.P.C. by establishing the Rural Electrification Administration. It was as though a rival newspaper had sprung up in a little town. The R.E.A. proved to be a boon to the rural family. Between electric lights, refrigeration, and electric pumps, for irrigation, the farmer was instantly "spoiled."

The R.E.A. also gave low-interest loans to rural co-ops for the purpose of allowing farmers and ranchers to put up their own wires and generating their own electricity. All of this sped up the process of moving the farms into the twentieth century. If left to private industry, rural electrification, because it wasn't profitable, probably would not have occurred for quite some time.

By 1939, the Fort Peck Dam, to which the Montana Power Company had been supplying power for construction, was completed. Once in operation, the federally-owned dam provided cheap electricity for a large section of east central Montana.

Some historians have gone to great lengths to show, and convincingly so at times, that the combined A.C.M. and M.P.C. ran the state of Montana for a number of years. Although this statement is definitely false, it does need elaboration. A.C.M. and M.P.C. beyond a doubt carried an amazing amount of "clout," (a Chicago word meaning political power). There is no doubt that when the Company backed a candidate, he or she usually won. Besides, the tremendous payrolls they controlled, the money thrown into campaigns, and coverage in the "friendly" press, plus a loose alliance with *large* ranchers and

farmers almost always generated a victory. To beat the Company, its opposition had to approach the people as a moderate, or "middle of the road" candidate.

As a final thought concerning this section, it might be interesting to speculate what might have happened in Montana's past if the 17th Amendment to the United States Constitution had not been ratified. By the way, that amendment deals with the election of U.S. Senators by the people, instead of by the state legislatures. Would the rich and powerful corporations have followed the example set by William Andrews Clark and tried to "buy" a seat in the U.S. Senate? There are arguments for both answers.

Maybe it wasn't an accident that the public relations departments for both the A.C.M. and the M.P.C. looked for a different image at about the same time the radio brought the outside world to Montana. The fact that the first radio station was sponsored by the Great Falls *Tribune,* one of the state's few independent papers, may or may not have had something to do with it.

Regardless of the reasoning, by the mid-30's, the "terrors of the neighborhood," the separate-but-equal A.C.M. and M.P.C. had grown up a bit. So had Montana. The irony in the whole situation has been that the problem for the one side was, and is the solution for the other. Montanans have *long* memories.

Wild West Going Full Blast in Town Near Ft. Peck Dam

By Earnie Pyle

WHEELER, Mont. — You have to see the town of Wheeler to believe it.

When you drive thru, you think somebody must have set up hand-painted store fronts on both sides of the road, as background for a western movie thriller. But it's real.

Wheeler is today the wildest wild-west town in North America. Except for the autos, it is a genuine throwback to the '80s, to Tombstone and Dodge City and Goldfield.

Wheeler is a slopover from the Government-built city at Ft. Peck dam. It is not on Government property, hence is free to go its own way. These boom towns always mushroom up around a big construction project. There are 18 of them around Ft. Peck.

The are shantytowns proper. They have such names as New Deal and Delano Heights. Their houses are made of boxes and tin cans and old boards and tar roofing. They look just like Hoover's famous Bonus Army camp of 1932 on the Anacostia Flats.

All except Wheeler. It is the metropolis of the mushroom villages. It has 3500 people, and real houses and stores. It has 65 little businesses lining either side of the main street. Such places as "Buckhorn Club" and "Rooms — 50¢" and just "HOTEL."

It has nearly a thousand homes scattered back behind the main drag. It has half a dozen all-night taverns, and innumerable beer parlors. The taverns open at 8 in the evening and run till 6 in the morning.

At night the streets are a melee of drunken men and painted women, as they are called in books. Gambling, and liquor by the drink, are illegal in Montana. But Wheeler pays no attention. You can sit in a stud game, or keep ordering forty-rod all night.

The taverns don't have floor shows. You just drink and dance. The music goes 'till long after daylight. You don't have to pay to dance with the girls, but they get a nickel a glass for all the beer and whiskey they induce the boys to buy. Back behind Wheeler is a separate village where the women of easy virtue live. This town has an unprintable name. It has no other name. Everybody calls it by this name. They say a thousand women have heard the call and drifted in for the easy reapings among the dam workers.

* * *

Wheeler is two-and-a-half years old. It started with Ft. Peck dam, when some guy brought in a trailer, built bunks in it, and rented them to dam workers at $4 a week.

Ruby Smith was the first real settler. She started an eating place along the road, and within 30 days

the town had sprung up around her almost to its present size.

Ruby now runs the Wheeler Inn, one of the biggest all-night hot spots. She goes to bed at daylight and gets up late in the afternoon. She's coining the money.

Joe Frazier is the enterpreneur of Wheeler. Twenty years ago he homesteaded a large batch of practically worthless land here on the bare Montana knobs. It never did pay its way. Joe Frazier became a barber in Glasgow, 20 miles away.

Then God sent Ruby Smith and the Army Engineers, and they say Joe Frazier will come out of it easily with $100,000. He owns all the land Wheeler is built on.

Wheeler won't exist six months after the dam is finished in 1939. So Joe Frazier doesn't try to sell lots. He just rents them. His income, they say, is $2500 a month.

* * *

Wheeler is all wood. There isn't a stone or steel building in town. It has no water system. They have had 16 fires since New Year's. One side of the town has wells. The other side hasn't any. There has been, fortunately, no epidemic.

Prices are typical boom-town prices. Rents aren't bad, but food is high. There is one small wooden church and there are two gospel missions.

Quite a few of the boys indulge in holdups. Motorists on the road, and cashiers behind the cash register, have looked many times down the barrel of a six shooter.

There has been considerable gun waving, but little pulling of the trigger. The thieves take their swag and beat it. Wheeler has not developed any spectacular individual bad man, such as "Curley Bill" of old Tombstone.

And whereas the cowboys used to get drunk and ride down the main street yelling and shooting up the town, nowadays the process is to get drunk and drive down the main highway at 70 miles an hour. They've killed and maimed as many people that way around Wheeler as the tough characters used to with their bullets.

It was the wild criminal driving that finally brought a little law and order to Wheeler. They have a deputy sheriff and two constables now. They don't go to extremes, of course, but they pull in the drunken drivers. They say the two justices of the peace have a very good thing.

Wheeler will be gone in three more years. There may never be another one. Somebody had better record it for prosterity, before it's too late.

The Washington Daily News
Friday, September 18, 1936

223

Chapter Six

AT HOME

While the bright lights of Broadway heralded such names as Fanny Brice and W.C. Fields, a war was going on in Europe. A war in which U.S. would eventually participate. The year 1916 saw Congress authorize the Council of National Defense. The Council's job was to get Americans "psyched up" about the war. Farmers had to grow more food. Production had to increase. In this way, the "war to end all wars," as it was billed, would be over that much sooner.

By 1918, the legendary Irving Berlin had definitely changed his tune to stay in touch with the times, as a partial list of his "hits" from 1918 shows: "Dream On, Little Soldier Boy," "I'm Gonna' Pin a Medal on the Girl I Left Behind," "Oh, How I Hate to Get Up in the Morning," and "They Were All Out of Step but Jim." Meanwhile, George M. Cohan was "Yankee Doodle Dandy"-ing across the stage. America went blind with hatred for the Germans. German-Americans, needless to say, had a rough time during World War I, and for a time after.

At the beginning of American involvement in the War, German-Americans numbered in the millions. Over 2,000,000 alone had emigrated. People who just a few years before had been looked upon as ideal citizens were condemned. Across the U.S. the anti-German sentiment spread like a plague. Washington had employees check their personnel rosters and ensure the loyalty of their workers. Many people with German last names were fired or laid off. Instantly, German-Americans all over were subjected to public ridicule. Some had to crawl on their hands and knees and kiss an American flag as proof of their loyalty. One German-American narrowly escaped being hanged, in Omaha, but one in Illinois wasn't as lucky.

While Wisconsin citizens burned books with mere references to Germany, Henry Ford's foreign-speaking employees were forced to learn English. Their first sentence in English was "I am a good American."

The insanity didn't stop there. Congress passed laws that sent a movie producer to prison for showing the British killing Americans in the movie version of "The Spirit of 76." How would a person go about depicting the American Revolution *without* showing that? Then the ultimate in suppression came when current historians were instructed to write that only Germany was responsible for starting the war. Lying is bad. Perpetrating lies in the guise of history is totally unjustified.

Montana, too, shared in this madness. Encouraged by President Wilson, Montana followed the example of other states, and set up a "patriot program." Understandably, the program's name was the "Montana Council of Defense." It was set up at both the state and county levels. Montana soon joined Delaware and Illinois in banning use of the German language in schools, church, or *anywhere*. Books with references to Germany or German civilization were removed from libraries.

These were highly emotional times. Prejudice overruled common sense. It was during this time that people on all sides suffered wounds to egos, aspirations, and in some cases, their bodies. Some of these wounds healed, in time. Some were carried to the grave. Some have been kept alive in hopes of preventing a recurrence. Unfortunately, later wars brought similar responses. It must be a product of war's propaganda.

Anyway, in Montana the lines, in many respects, were clearly drawn. For the conservatives and super-patriots, the lineup was the A.C.M. and M.P.C. and its newspapers, the state and county Councils of Defense, and many lesser groups, as well as individuals. For the liberals, radicals, and anti-war pacifists, there were the Industrial Workers of the World (I.W.W.), and the Non-Partisan League (N.P.L.). The people caught in the middle, obviously, were the German-Americans.

As has been the case in all wars, there are people who oppose fighting and killing for various reasons. This one wasn't to be any different. But, in a way, it was, for, indeed, people believed, *really* believed, down deep that this would be the last war. Mankind was civilized enough to put an end to the need for conflict on the battlefield. Also, knowing that it would be the cause of eternal, worldwide peace brought many people otherwise against war into conservative ranks.

Beet Growers Accept Jap Field Labor

Valley Represented
At Helena Meeting
Called by Gov. Ford

State Senator R. S. Nutt of Sidney, President Gerald Wells of the Montana-Dakota Beet Growers Associations, I. R. Alling, representing the Fairview Commercial club, and Nels Back of Sidney, were delegates in attendance at the meeting called by Gov. Sam C. Ford at Helena on March 26 to take action on the proposition of bringing Japanese evacuees from California and other west coast sections to work in the beet fields.

Governor Ford presided at the meeting and James E. Harrington of Los Angeles presented a message to the group from General DeWitt, in charge of evacuation of Japs from the west coast.

J. P. Brennan of the U.S. Employment service gave the information that 6,000 Japs will be required in the beet fields of Montana in the face of the present labor shortage.

Final action in the meeting was to bring the required number of Japs into the sugar beet areas and keep them for the duration of the war only, when they would be removed from the state. Two motorized caravans of Japs will be escorted by the Army to these beet sections and those brought in will be under the observation and protection of the FBI and police agencies.

President Gerald Wells of the Montana-Dakota Beet Growers association, President Blaine Ferguson of the Western Beet Growers association, and H. A. Williams, representative of the Hardin Beet Growers association, with two others to be appointed, will go to California in the near future to make selection of Japs to be brought to these areas, based on adaptability to the work they will have to do. Their families will be brought with them.

Following are the recommendations of the Montana-Dakota Beet Growers association, Chambers of Commerce of the City of Sidney,

City of Miles City, Commercial clubs of the towns of Savage and Fairview, Richland county, Montana, relative to the use of Japanese labor.

Need and Facilities:

Twenty thousand acres of sugar beets will be produced in this area in 1942 if labor is available. Two thousand five hundred workers will be required. Houses are available for approximately five hundred families. Of these not more than three hundred fifty would be suitable for winter occupancy. We therefore make the following recommendations:

1. That the CCC camps at Ridgelawn and Savage, Montana, be used as placement camps.

2. That a permanent concentration camp be established at Fort Keough, Montana, adjacent to Miles City.

3. That five hundred beet workers and one hundred fifty farm laborers be made immediately available.

4. That we (The Montana Dakota Beet Growers association) insist upon the privilege of selecting our own labor.

5. We recommend that for permanent and temporary camps doctors, dentists, and so forth of Japanese blood be furnished by the government.

6. We recommend that moderate protection by the army or some government agency be furnished for the Japanese residents.

7. We recommend that local housing of reputable and satisfactory families be used as far as possible.

We urge that the federal government and all its agencies cooperate with each district at the termination of the war in removing Japanese laborers and their families when they are no longer needed.

Sidney Herald
April 2, 1942

Senator Murray Urges Prison Camps In Montana

Washington, D.C. — Senator James E. Murray today before leaving Washington for Montana called upon the War Department and urged that immediate steps be taken to establish prisoner of war camps in Montana. In view of the large number of Italian and German prisoners being taken by the Allied armies in Sicily, Senator Murray urged that provision be made to house these prisoners at camps at Sidney, in the Billings area and at Havre, where they may be available for use on farms and ranches and in the furtherance of reclamation projects.

"Some weeks ago, I called upon the War Department to take action to establish prisoner of war camps in Montana," Senator Murray said. "The Soil Conservation Service and the Reclamation Bureau both have recommended the establishment of such camps. I was advised at the time by Colonel I. B. Summers, Director of the Prisoner of War Department, that there were not sufficient prisoners of war in this country to warrant an extension of camp facilities. Conditions have changed and are changing rapidly. We are now capturing thousands upon thousands of war prisoners, and it is my hope that Montana will be granted two or three camps.

"The agricultural labor situation in Montana is acute," Senator Murray pointed out to Colonel Summers. "Montana produces huge quantities of vital foodstuffs, yet its farm population is lower than other states producing much less. Harvesting has been done in the past by transient and migratory workers. Now that these workers are no longer available, it is absolutely necessary that the Government provide sufficient agricultural workers to harvest Montana's fod crops. The establishment of prisoner of war camps is an essential contribution to the agriculture of my state."

Senator Murray said that he has been advised by the War Department that immediate attention will be given to his request.

Sidney Herald
Sept. 29, 1943

The Japanese-Americans interned in the camps were mostly from California. When they returned home after the War, most of their homes and property had been confiscated. Interestingly, Hawaii, which had the most Japanese-Americans did not react this way. Many Hawaiians of Japanese descent served in a famous Army battalion, including Senator Daniel Innoye who was on the Watergate committee, and who lost his arm in battle.

This would be a good time to read *Fabulous Century* by Time-Life Books, a collection of facinating glimpses of American life, bound in decades (e.g. *This Fabulous Century: 1920-1930.*)

The problem in Montana came about when the more radical minority of the I.W.W. and the N.P.L. (and they were just a few), made it known that they didn't like the war or the war effort. The I.W.W. and N.P.L. each had a few members who were socialist or communist; consequently, these groups were attacked directly by the conservatives. In the shuffle, loyalty became confused with working conditions and wages. The conservative press, owned by you-know-who, labeled any and all work slowdowns or strikes as unpatriotic (which they may have been), not as workers seeking better pay and working conditions.

It was *this* confusion that labeled patriotic Montanans "slackers" and traitors because they sought well-deserved pay increases and improved conditions. By the same token, this hostility undoubtedly allowed some on each side to vent their hostilities toward the opposing sides. It was under this kind of tension and pressure that the era 1917-1950 was begun. Montanans were understandably confused about what they should believe and how they should act on most issues. They did not want to be unpatriotic.

There were a few bright spots in these otherwise troublesome times. They came in the form of Burton K. Wheeler, U.S. District Attorney for Montana, and Butte district judge George M. Bourquin. These men, even during the worst possible barrages of personal threats and attempts to unseat them, didn't allow the hysteria to sway their sense of fairness. Time and again Wheeler was called upon to prosecute "traitors," which had been rounded up by over-zealous citizens. Time and again he remembered the rights granted all Americans by the First Amendment to the Constitution.

Judge Bourquin was an instant enemy of the patriots when he found a Rosebud County rancher, Vess Hall, innocent of charges made against him due to the fact that his opinions on the war differed from those of some of his "neighbors." Because of this ruling, conservatives got together and lobbied the 1918 Legislature to pass some regretable legislation, such as the Montana Sedition Act, which curbed "abusive talk," and the Criminal Syndicalism Act, which was a plan to "get" the I.W.W. Even the war's end didn't stop the conservative forces. However, it *did* slow them down a bit. The hysteria passed. The memories didn't.

Next came the post-war depression, which caught the already-confused state in an economic squeeze. It was bad enough to be bitter and divided, but now people were bitter, divided, *and* bankrupt.

In Butte and elsewhere miners were laid off due to extended shutdowns caused by the declining demand for copper. Meanwhile, nature "shutdown" agriculture for a few years. Montana was definitely hurting. Many left the state. Because of this, Montana was the only state in the Union to *lose* population during the supposedly "roaring" 20's.

This would be a good time to read *One Man's Montana* by John Hutchens.

Because of improvements in technology and farm machinery the number of farms in Montana decreased as fewer men could perform more work. The size of farms increased at the same time. Between 1920 and 1974, the size of the average farm or ranch increased from 608 to 2,510 acres. The number of people employed in agriculture dropped from 82,000 to 36,000.

In 1974 only about 3,000 employees worked in Montana's oil and natural gas fields, but they produced over $203,000,000 worth of oil and $17,000,000 of gas.

Montana has about 108 billion tons of mineable coal. In 1974, 14 million tons were mined.

Those who stuck it out did so under conditions that were so bad that we might wonder whether it was the smart ones who had left. But that thought is quickly put to rest when we remember that most of these people were strong, and believed in themselves and their land. Then, too, the fact that moving wasn't economically possible perhaps forced them to stay.

The romanticized view of the little farm home, set out in the middle of nowhere, without the advantages or frills of city life (such as plumbing, electricity, neighbors, a corner store, etc.) has always filled the minds of the city dweller. To actually have lived under such conditions brings about an entirely different point of view. This romantic look at the past was "cashed in on" in 1976 when Alex Haley searched for his "Roots." The phenomenon may be explained by the fact that no matter how bad it was, our existence today is living proof that our heroic ancestors pulled through. It is with this kind of pride that Montanans of this generation can remember those earlier generations.

Some of the "hardships" might surprise us today. Those who lived through that time probably laugh when they hear that word applied to their lives, since they did have the choice of living with or without a certain thing. Either you did without, or you did the work yourself. If a person wanted butter, he or she had to churn it, or do without.

Knowing about, or, better yet, actually doing "chores" in the old way is particularly fascinating to today's generation. This is true probably because most of the methods used to accomplish anything in those days before electricity required a lot of hard, physical labor. In today's world of push-button appliances, it is sort of "fun" to do something that requires some work, once in a while. Today, things are sometimes the opposite of how they used to be. Many jobs have been made easier, and often the only physical "work" a person does is his or her leisure activities, such as jogging, bicycling, tennis, backpacking.

To get a better picture of the situation, following is an account of life on a small farm during these early years of the twentieth century. This account first appeared in a local publication entitled the Grime, Gut, and Gumption, put out by the Pondera-Toole Extension Homemaker's Club, printed by the Shelby Promoter. It was written by A.L. Zimmerman's daughter, Margaret Zimmerman Brabeck.

At first the new life was an adventure for my mother. Relatives from the East loved to visit in the summer. But with poor crops, fast dwindling bank balance, and children added to the family things became more difficult. Our home was the same as most with the necessary furnishings and no luxuries, other than a phonograph and radio. This was used sparingly since it was operated by batteries. Noontime news and market report and a few carefully selected evening programs meant much to us. The Morris chair, square oak table and chairs, oak combination bookcase and desk, and brass bed steads would be valuable antique collector's items today. Then they were just old furniture. The floors were covered with linoleum with rugs by the beds to absorb part of the shock of stepping out of a warm bed onto an icy floor. Heat was furnished by a cookstove in the kitchen and a coal heater in the living room. When it was very cold in the winter time we could see our own breath in the bedrooms and sometimes find frost on the quilt's edge near our faces.

In the summertime we enjoyed the trips to town, usually to Conrad, with a five gallon can of sour cream and a case of eggs to help pay for the groceries. We always got an ice cream cone to eat on the way home when we picked up the empty cream can, and before that had stopped at the bakery to by penny candy — boxes of licorice cigarettes being a prime favorite. On a hot day a glass of cherry phosphate served to us in a booth at Drakes Drug Store was a special treat. Occasionally we would have lunch in a restaurant where we would eat a bowl of oyster crackers while waiting for our meal. We did not go to Shelby often even though it was our County Seat, because we either had to ford the river where the "F" bridge was later built, or go through either Fowler or Ledger to reach the highway with a bridge across the Marias. This latter route would be a forty mile drive each way. Trips to the dentist and doctor were infrequent and always dreaded because we only went if we had a tooth that needed attention or had a health problem my mother could not treat without the doctor's attention and prescription. Since she was a nurse, she not only cared for us, but also neighbors who sought her help especially in winter. She even delivered two babies.

In the wintertime we often would be snowed-in for as long as two months. We were prepared as an ample supply of coal had been hauled from Fowler by wagon in earlier years and by truck from Ledger or Conrad later on. Sugar was purchased in 100 pound sacks and wheat taken to Yeager's to be milled into flour in 100 pound sacks. Eggs would be put into crocks and covered with water-glass to preserve them for winter baking when the hens didn't lay well. A beef was butchered every winter as well as several pigs and lambs. Butchering was an important winter job, for not only did it provide fresh meat then, but also meat to be canned and preserved for summer use. My parents rendered lard and cured hams and bacon, and my father made several kinds of sausage and even dried beef. He had the small smokehouse full every winter. Some meat would be roasted and canned as well as the smoked pork sausage. The hams and bacon would be stored in barrels of oats and needed to be parboiled to remove part of the salt before frying. But they were a welcome change from the canned meat, eggs, and homeade cottage cheese in the summertime.

Holidays were fun. We shared them with friends. A decorated tree complete with candles awaited us on Christmas morning. The candles were carefully placed and before they were lighted a bucket of water was set nearby in case of fire. What a thrill to see the lighted candles if only for a few minutes! We had toys and a few games. Two that stand out in my mind were a steam engine sent to my brother by our Illinois grandparents. The engine burned wood alcohol and whistled when steam built up. The other was a large doll with curls and a wardrobe made for it by my mother complete even to coat with a fur collar. After a delicious dinner had been eaten and the dishes cleared away the adults would visit and play cards (500 and auction bridge) and the children played games like dominoes, checkers, or parchesi until supper time. You expected guests to stay for two meals and usually they started for home about 9:15 P.M. after everyone had listened to Amos' n Andy. World renowned British playwright George Bernard Shaw was quoted as saying "Three things which I shall never forget about America — the Rocky Mountains, the Statue of Liberty, and Amos' n Andy." Then there was a six mile or so trip home in the sled but no one seemed to mind it.

Mail service was tri-weekly. In the summer delivered by car and, when the roads were snowed-in, by sled. We took the *Great Falls Tribune* and *Pathfinder* for news and several magazines for enjoyment. Letters from out-of-state relatives and friends were always eagerly read. In the wintertime the mailman occasionally would bring a much needed food item from the store in Ledger if someone on the route requested it. No one was more appreciated or deserved it more than the mailman.

A Home Demonstration Club was organized in the community sometime in the 1920's. The County Agent's wife, brought a starter to make bread to one of the meetings that was excellent and used by several of the families — ours included — for years. Another project was the making of dress forms for the women who sewed for their families but had difficulty fitting themselves. I can remember my mother getting together with a friend using glue-backed paper tape over a long cotton shirt. It was a messy job but the result was successfully used for fitting dresses thereafter. During the winter months the meetings were held in the evening in different homes and whole families were invited; other times we would go after school and get there in time for refreshments.

While we were growing up there were not many good years as crops go. We had grasshoppers, drought, wind, hail, and low prices for the grains raised. Farmers were beginning to adopt the summerfallow method of farming but winter wheat had not yet been tried. And power had been transferred from horses to machines. A J.I. Case was our first tractor, later a John Deere which boasted an umbrella for protection from the sun. I don't remember my parents considering moving because conditions were bad. Someone once said that we had the best "next year" country in the world, and that feeling and the fact that credit was extended got people through somehow.

My mother passed away in September of 1932 just after we had rented an apartment in Conrad and I had started high school. The next four years were difficult ones made somewhat easier by good friends as our father's unlimited patience and good sense of humor.

Another example of the problems faced in the transition from buggy to Model "T" is this excerpt from Margaret Coleman Fowler's account of her father, Charles Coleman, who was one of the original homesteaders on the Marias. "In the early 20's, Charles bought a Model "T" car. He had driven horses all his life, so when he came to a gate, he would say, 'Whoa' instead of stopping with the brake. As a result, there were many gates to be fixed." The last account in the excerpt tells of the irony and personal loss suffered not due to a drought or flood, but due to "progress." Progress, in this case, came in the form of a dam that even today is surrounded by controversy. The story is of the

Mayette and Isa Denson place on the Marias as told by their son Shadrach (Shade), through Eldora Coover. "The Densons lived through many hazards on the river, such as the floods of 1908, 1947 (caused by an ice jam), and 1948, bad winters and droughts... The original Denson place on the Marias River bottom was flooded in the mid 1950's when the Tiber Reservoir filled up. Shade tells how he had to burn the old home and buildings before the water rose. This was not easy for one to do who had loved their old home so much." The "one-horsepower" plow was replaced by the 100 horsepower ski boat.

True story Dempsey — Gibbons fight emerges
by J.W. Johnson

Independently
OBSERVING

by Chet

Sports Illustrated recently published an article by James W. "Body" Johnson on the true facts of the Dempsey-Gibbons world heavyweight championship fight which was held in Shelby July 4, 1923. The essence of this article is printed elsewhere in this issue because many from here, can still recall this most remarkable incident in fight history.

The spectacle of such a small town aspiring to seek publicity for its oil boom and offering such an astronomical figure as $300,000 for the opportunity is well beyond the ken of modern day folks. That amount of money then would represent more than a million dollars of our inflated coin of the realm in this day and age, and so of course to put it mildly, most persons thought Shelby was "nuts."

The excitement was more a frenzy. I didn't know about such things as financial matters which would make or break the big fight. All we knew was that we were suddenly amidst such a sup-posed bonanza that there wasn't time to half keep up with all the things that were going on.

What was going on? Well, my gosh, there were tents and cabins and makeshift buildings springing up like mushrooms all over. There were tent shows and boxing gyms, eating houses and flop houses all around. There were gypsy fortune tellers, small carnivals and rodeos and stories in my

Dad's paper about new golden oil gushing out of the ground in the Kevin-Sunburst field.

The sportswriters who came to Shelby, including such greats as Ring Lardner and Damon Runyun were accorded no fanfare (because the citizens were too busy trying to raise the money for Dempsey's guarantee) that they had to occupy tents or anything they could sleep under, so they mostly wrote bitter articles about the town and the unlikely prospects of a fight.

But they were dignitaries in their own bailiwicks and not used to being ignored. So they — along with Doc Kearns (Dempsey's manager) destroyed a valiant effort.

After years of fanciful stories by sportswriters about the famed Dempsey-Gibbons worlds heavy-weight championship fight held at Shelby on July 4, 1923, the truth about it has finally come to light nationally.

James W. "Body" Johnson, former Shelby resident who now lives in Spokane has presented the true version of why and how the championship battle was fought in the July 4 issue of Sports Illustrated, the popular national magazine with over one million circulation.

Johnson, who was well known here for oil development near Gallup City in the discovery days of the Pondera oilfield, reveals that the offer of $200,000 to Jack Kearns, Dempsey's manager, was intended to bring publicity to Shelby and enable his company to attract more people for the benefit of his real estate firm.

But what started out as a publicity gag, snowballed throughout the national press and was so enthusiastically real to Shelby residents, that before long the offer became an actual bona fide bid for the fight and through a chain of reactions and errors finally evolved into a $300,000 guarantee to Kearns and Dempsey, which was mainly responsible for the financial fiasco.

The original backers and those responsible for money raising to meet the purse of $200,000 were astounded to find that Loy Molumby, then state commander of the American Legion, had gone to Chicago and "on his own" had signed a contract for $300,000.

Jack "Doc" Kearns, Dempsey's manager, KNEW according to contract that Dempsey had to fight Gibbons, whether he received the final $100,000 or not, but he would never announce it publicly. That fact and stories that the fight would never be held at all, caused fight fans throughout the country to cancel plans to attend the bout.

The promoters had nearly $500,000 in advance reservations and more than 26 special trains and parties lined up.

The Johnson realty firm did not sell one single lot — from the time of the signing of the contract in Chicago until the company dissolved that fall.

James A. Johnson, who because he was Shelby's leading citizen had with reluctance accepted the job as treasurer and finally became general manager of the promotion, lost over $50,000 of his own money.

Kearns not only "busted" the fight financially, but actually outfoxed himself in the end. Because it was agreed that he was to have all the gate receipts up to the amount of the last $100,000 and if he had announced in plenty of time ahead that the fight was to be held, he would probably have gotten the full amount.

Instead the Internal Revenue Bureau stepped in and assumed the proceeds from the last of the ticket sales. This amounted to $54,000 and Kearns somehow "conned" that amount from the government, although it was explicitly designated to pay the tax.

12,000 people saw the fight but many of them crashed the gate just before the main bout was to be held because the revenue agents left their ticket selling posts to go inside the arena to see the action.

The oft repeated story that Tommy Gibbons got nothing out of the fight was erroneous. In addition to a purse of $7500 he was furnished a free house for himself and family with all expenses paid. He was also built a complete training camp and his manager was allowed to collect the daily fees for his workouts, which amounted to a considerable sum. After going the route with Dempsey his publicity enabled him to go on a 20-week vaudeville tour and later resulted in a remunerative fight with the Frenchman, Georges Carpentier.

It was a good fight and Tommy Gibbons proved a worthy challenger.

Editor's note

At this point you may be getting a feeling for those who tightened their grip on the land and stayed. We did. We read a lot of articles and personal anecdotes from this time period before selecting those printed in this chapter. Throughout our research I was amazed by the feelings and values shared by the homesteaders. They seemed to reflect a common character flavored with optimism, acceptance, strength, and compassion.

We offer the following poem as a case in point. The author begins with thoughts of a hard childhood I can scarcely visualize. He ends with a feeling of forgiveness and understanding I would recognize anywhere — he is *my* little boy's *grandfather*.

FHC

Dark and cruel — my Grandfather.
Slanted almond eyes — probably a gift
bestowed, by the raping conquering horde
of Gengis Kahn.

A hard man from a harsh land—
Sevestopal on the Black Sea—
Conscripted to the Army at age six.
"Walk straight," he said, "or I will make
a collar with an iron spike under your chin."

He never put his arm around me.
He never held me on his lap.
Get on your knees little seven year
old and with two wooden blocks, squash
Those throngs of potato bugs.
Spring out of bed at dawn little
seven year old and drive that
team on the header barge.

Shock that grain, and when the
little boy fell asleep by a grainshock

and didn't come home till the moon was up—
He was awakened by a clout on his ear.

Pull the bellows in the blacksmith shop—
Too small to reach the handle—
Stand on a box — Jump off the box
and on a red hot iron with barefeet.

A hard hand grabbed and a hard
hand spanked — Teach you to cry
over little things.
Eight year old, drive a binder and
fourhorses — My God — Looking at my
grandchildren — could I be having
a dreadful dream?

Did he resent and try to break this
Scottish heart my dead father gave me?
(He didn't know the strength of the
Highlanders.)
Or...was he molding a man The
only way he knew.

—I.G. Atchison, 1976

For the man sound in body and serene of mind there is no such thing as bad weather; every sky has its beauty, and the storms which whip the blood do but make it pulse more vigorously.

Chapter Seven

George Gissing, 1857-1903

The first chapter of Book VI began with a quotation, so why not the last? Gissing was an English novelist who dealt in social realism, and although he spent some time in America, it is apparent the man never spent any time on the Northern Great Plains. Either that, or Mr. Gissing was a city kid who never came to realize that "bad crops" are often the product of "bad weather." Maybe, though, it is the wheat and barley that don't understand the difference between good and bad weather, but then *they* don't read.

Thus far, the seventh chapter of each book has dealt with the theme of wealth. Unfortunately, this particular period of time doesn't cooperate with the outline of this book. In fact, maybe to be spiteful, it turned 180° to make the theme of this chapter the enormous loss of wealth. Much of this was due to a mere change in the weather. Whether the weather was "bad" or not is academic today. Take the word of the thousands who lived through the era.

Maybe it was fact that Montana was forty-first in line for statehood that made it seek out "firsts" were: first state to have a woman assistant attorney general, E.L.K. Haskell in 1892; first woman in the U.S. Congress, Jeanette Rankin in 1917 (she set other "firsts" by voting against U.S. entry in both World War I and World War II), and, the first state to have free Bibles placed in its hotel rooms, in Superior in 1908.

Well, it was also Montana that first suffered from a major depression, coming ahead of the rest of the nation's in the 1920's. Sure, the nation in general had a general recession after World War I. But they snapped back. On the other hand, as was already mentioned, Montana was also the only state in the union to *lose* population during the decade.

Some people have speculated that this loss of people was actually good for the state. It was a sort of culling process, or a type of natural selection where only the strong survived. On the other hand, those who survived did so with an entirely different attitude. Gone were the days of the devil-may-care, optimistic even naive, homesteader. Gone was the myth of the land that "scorned" rain. The "seasoned veteran" of the drought understandably cast a doubtful, even pessimistic eye to the future. After all, not only had nature betrayed him or her, so had the historically sound land investment and banking industry.

During the first half of the 20's, Montana banks fell and the rain didn't. A combination of things contributed to a situation similar to the hard winter of 1886-87. Just as there had been too many cattle on the plains, there were too many banks. Montana towns with populations of 200 had banks, some even had more than one. Many of these banks overextended themselves by

"The earth was created by the assistance of the sun, and it should be left as it was... The country was made without lines of demarcation, and it is no man's business to divide it... I see the whites all over the country gaining wealth, and see their desire to give us lands which are worthless... The earth and myself are of one mind. The measure of our bodies are the same."

Chief Joseph, Nez Perce

231

extending credit to people with poor or little collateral. But, what the heck. Things were working out well. Prices were high. Crops were good. Besides that, it was patriotic to lend in order that farmers might grow the crops needed to win the war.

The drought and low prices for crops due to Europe's rebound after the war caught some 200 or more banks in Montana off guard, and out on a limb.

By the Great Depression of the 1930's, Montanans were "pros" in the field of bank failure. This time it was the rest of the nation's turn to experience devastation. This time it was different. F.D.R.'s New Deal ushered in programs to salvage not only the banking business but also the individual farm or homeowner. The Federal Deposit Insurance Corporation, or F.D.I.C., set up insurance to guarantee savings accounts. In this way, confidence was restored in the banking system.

At the same time, the Home Owners Loan Act provided the means to refinance homes of millions of people caught in the economic squeeze. A similar bill to aid the farmer created the Farm Credit Administration. Through these agencies, millions of people across the country, including many Montanans, re-

tained their property. The hidden cost of all this was the enormously increased role of the federal government. It is this ever-increased role that continues to separate "conservatives" and "liberals" in this country. While conservatives brand this expansion as "socialism," liberals refer to it as a "more responsive government."

In any case, no one, regardless of his or her political persuasion, can deny that without continued federal support, Montana, like many other states, would be in a bad position. The subject of money always casues an interesting debate. What do you think?

THERE GOES THE OLD NEIGHBORHOOD...

TECHNOLOGY and ECOLOGY (1950 — AND BEYOND)

Chapter One

Without a doubt Montana today is going through its most critical period. This is true not only because of the many and complex issues that confront us, but also because our objectivity is lessened due to our closeness to the issues. Our emotions can deceive us. For example, the Teapot Dome scandal of the Harding Administration back in 1923 raised as many doubts concerning government corruption as did the Watergate scandal of the early 70's. Now, the Teapot Dome business can be looked at objectively by most, whereas tempers still flare over the different issues raised by the Watergate investigations.

Obviously, then, history, an imperfect science to begin with, needs perspective, or time to allow "events to run their course." Today is merely a scene, in an act, in a play, in a very complex world. Finding patterns without the benefit of some perspective is difficult, to say the least, because current history is alive and constantly changing. In other words, it is only after the dust settles (and not always then), that we can clearly see where we've been.

It is the dust cloud of uncertainty surrounding us that makes the future so doubtful. Maybe if we knew *who* was kicking up all of the dust, and *why*, we would not fear, but rather eagerly await the future. We may even shed the reputation of being somewhat cynical about the future. This pessimism might better be replaced with the cautious optimism of people who understand the existence of unavoidable natural and economic cycles that affect the state. With this understanding, Montanans can prepare themselves and their children for a more pleasant "ride" in to the future. Montanans now confront the choices which will determine which path the state will follow for a long time to come.

The reality of the situation is that the high-powered, fast-paced world greatly affects Montana's economy, and therefore its people. It has been stated by some historians that Montana could, if necessary, stand on its own. Admittedly the statement makes one feel more independent and secure, but is it a false sense of security? How long could Montana stand alone without outside markets for its products? Without importing manufactured items? In today's complex society of economic interdependence, how long could any state, or nation, stand alone? Like it or not, Montana is a part of a considerably larger system, the United States, which, in turn, is a part of a still larger system, the world. To treat Montana as though it were independent of these systems is to treat the heart as separate from the body.

We've come a long way since travois crossed the land as the only means of transporting goods. Although many of the inventors and inventions discussed in this chapter had their beginnings in other eras, it was only after World War II and its post-war prosperity that they became a major part of the Montana, and American, scene.

By 1950, the automobile had definitely established itself as an important component of American society. These machines were no longer a luxury, but rather a necessity, around which America revolved. Michigan, a part of the *old* Northwest Territory, solidly controls the automotive business. Detroit is its "capital." Because of this, many spinoff industries were created to "keep America on wheels." It wasn't any different in Montana; in fact, all of this mobility gave rise to a tremendous new industry in the state, tourism. By this time Montana had thousands of miles of hard surface roads which enabled people and products to flow into and out of the state.

At the same time, the airlines were beginning to transport greater numbers of passengers in, out, and around the state. Airlines have become extremely important in Montana due to the state's size and the long distances between its cities. The other side of the coin, however, shows that the airlines, because of Montana's small population, lose money. Large federal subsidies, which assure a *fair* profit, have been, and still are, given to airports and airlines to keep air service at an *acceptable* level. Maybe *this* is what people mean when they say taxes are too high?

With the increased popularity of both automobile and airline travel, there has been a corresponding decrease in railroad use. Simple innovations, such as the rent-a-car services, have taken a toll on rail travel. Trucking, too, has bitten into the freight business. Trucks not only have the advantage of door-to-door service, but can carry larger loads than *ever* before.

Some say the fall of the railroads is inevitable. It is a mode of transportation that has merely outlived its *effectiveness*. It will live on only in museums and memories, much the same way the travois, river boat, and covered wagon do now. In today's world, who wants to spend some 32 hours on a train getting from Missoula to Chicago when the same distance can be covered in four hours by jet plane? After all, time *is* money, to most people.

But the other side of the argument might be that Montana *needs* trains. Its products are best suited for rail transportation. Besides, time is relative; as long as the supply remains constant, who cares about the speed? Trucks crowd our highways and use precious oil that might be better used elsewhere. Trains can return to the romantic days of the coal-fired steam engine. Save the oil for jobs not suited to coal. For instance, there hasn't been a person around lately that could shovel coal fast enough to keep a 747 in the air. Trains have played a major role in our "manifest destiny" that to give them up would be to give up an arm and a leg.

These are the real problems with which Montana and the country must deal. How does government regulate (if at all) transportation industries to the benefit of all? The name of the game is competition, and the railroads, trucks, and airlines, and in many places, ships and barges, are all competing for their "piece of the action." What must be kept in mind is that there is a limited amount of things to be moved. With *that* in mind, it isn't hard to figure out that when one industry gains, another must lose business. When one industry loses enough, it drops from competition in that area, unless it can get additional money from the federal government to make up for its losses. In a state that has so many miles and so few people, these losses can mount pretty fast.

Wheels and wings weren't the only things that transported "things" into Montana. Starting in the early 20's, the magic of radio began bringing the "outside world" to people's homes. Montana had only a half-dozen or so stations in those early days, but it was a start. The 30's and 40's were undoubtedly the "golden age" of radio. During these difficult years, radio provided a much-needed escape into the world of make-believe. Names such as Major Bowes, Burns and Allen, Rudy Vallee, Amos 'n Andy, and, of course, the products that sponsored them, became parts of everyday conversation.

The big "wooden box" in the corner of the living room got plenty of use. By the 1950's the radio, due to the invention of the transistor, could be carried about anywhere. The number of radio stations in Montana, both AM and FM, continues to grow, a sign of its continuing popularity.

By the early 1950's, another form of communication came to Montana. It had, and has, awesome influence on people. Of course, this invention is the television. The "T.V." filled in what the radio left out, the picture. What a revolution in communication and entertainment! Now people could see and hear their favorite personalities. They could see the news as it happened. The success of T.V. could be measured by the failure of many local movie houses and theaters. Hollywood now directly came into the home, and so did Presidents.

From their onset, people have been concerned about the affects the new communication systems would have on the country. People in every walk of life and every age group can be reached and influenced concerning everything from what kind of gum they should chew to which presidential candidate to vote for.

At the same time these spectator-type forms of communication were coming of age, a more personal form of communication was crossing Montana. This was the telephone. The telephone not only joined the many little towns which dot the state, it connected Montana with the rest of the country and the world.

Little by little, Montanans were getting "the word."

"The word" was also being spread by the newspapers. We all know that newspapers have been around for quite some time. Published in 1864, the *Virginia City Montana Post* was the first in the Montana Territory. Though they weren't noted for their objectivity, Montana papers sure made for interesting reading. Clark, Daly, and Heinze led the way during the final years of the 19th century. Their use of the news media inspired the Anaconda Copper Mining Company to do "great" things with the press.

Trying to ensure no further problems, such as the ones brought on by Heinze, the A.C.M. controlled more than half of the state's circulation. In other words, they wrote what *most* of the people of the state read. For the first 30 years of this century, the A.C.M. papers "breathed fire" at the Company's opponents. After the mid-30's, however, most of the excitement was provided by the newswire photos that had just come into use. By the late 1950's, the A.C.M. decided to unload its papers.

Some viewed this as a change in the Company's attitude. Others merely saw this as part of a nationwide move by the larger newspaper chains to consolidate and put out a better product. It also reduced competition. A.C.M.'s papers were purchased by the Lee Newspaper chain, which is based in the Midwest. In fact, all of Montana's major newspapers have since been purchased by large newspaper chains. The only remaining "home press" is made up of the many small weekly papers which serve smaller communities.

So what we now have "crossing our land" are means of transportation and communication that can, in a matter of days, hours, minutes, or seconds, depending on the task, connect any part of Montana with any place in the world. Technology has, in many cases, thrust Montana into the mainstream of modern living. But, in some ways, Montana remains, and pleasantly so, a two-lane highway in a four-lane world.

Chapter Two

Few people would deny the statement that Montana's most heated debates in recent years have been generated by problems originating "beneath the land." The open-pit mining of copper in Butte had a drastic impact on that town. The Berkeley Pit is a fully automated operation. Where untold thousands of miners once toiled, in thousands of miles of tunnels, explosives, power shovels, and trucks with enormous capacities now carry the precious ore up from deep within the earth. To get an idea of the size of these trucks, one has to first envision their 12-foot *tires*. Only then can one picture the trucks, which are capable of carrying *150* tons of rock and ore.

With such heavy mechanization, one could only expect heavy payroll cuts. Half the miners were let go immediately, victims of progress. A.C.M. could hardly be faulted for such a move; after all, across the nation industries of all kinds were being mechanized. Besides that, hardrock mining was, and is, dangerous. Lastly, most of the high grade ore had already been extracted, leaving the less profitable, low grade ore behind. To make a profit from this ore a safer, less costly method had to be used. So, in 1955, the A.C.M. began the Berkeley Pit. Bye, bye Meaderville! This once lively suburb has fallen victim to the ever-growing Pit.

Initially, this open-pit mining caused quite a stir. For the most part, it was confined to the area to be affected by the layoffs and destruction. Outside the immediate area, and especially in the eastern part of the state, people didn't seem to care. Perhaps they were tired of hearing about Butte and its problems.

Such was not the case in the 1970's in eastern Montana, however. Little did anyone know that the strip mine operation south of Forsyth, begun over fifty years ago, was going to be the center of controversy throughout the 1970's. This, of course, is the now famous, or infamous, Colstrip.

The Northern Pacific began mining operations and set up the town back in 1924. The coal provided the much needed fuel which kept the trains rolling. In the mid-1950's, the N.P. finally gave in to competition and purchased diesel engines. Because of what had been a relatively inexpensive fuel source, the NP was one of the last railroads to mothball its coal burning steam engines. Once this was done, however, the N.P. saw little use for its coal operation. By 1959 the Western Energy Company, a subsidiary of Montana Power, purchased the surface rights in and around Colstrip. At the same time, they took out long-term leases on the coal deposits. *Someone* was planning ahead.

Montana Power opened a new steam generated power plant at Billings in 1969. Its fuel source was not natural gas, like the nearby Bird plant, but rather it was coal from Colstrip. The success of the plant and a few others in the state obviously led Montana Power and its partners to consider more, and larger, coal-fired steam generating plants.

To spice up the debate, along came the "energy crunch," which *should* have, or *may* have, or *could* have, made people think, or at least consider, conserving oil products. Coal was the answer. But why burn it in Montana? Why *not*? Most of the power is going to be transmitted for use in other states, anyway. Let *them* burn the coal and put up with the smoke. But, big cities already have enough pollution, say the companies. Burn it in rural Montana where it won't hurt anything. The arguments go back and forth. Legal hassles are still going on in the courts.

The problem is a complex web of federal, state, and Native American tribal issues. Mixed together with private enterprise, energy shortages, water rights, average annual runoff, ranching and farming interests, the problem gets more complicated. Add to this the issue of power lines, taxes at all possible levels of government, escalated building costs, and countless other con-

This would be a great time to stop and listen to the song "Paradise." It's on the *Rocky Mountain High* album by John Denver.

This would be a good time to read *The Rape of the Great Plains* by K. Ross Toole.

siderations that *should* and *must* be solved, and you can see that Montana has its hands full.

In many ways, coal mining in eastern Montana sounds all the familiar. Fur boom! Gold boom! Cattle boom! Silver boom! Copper boom! Homesteader boom! Coal boom! What we have to remember is that there was *always* another side of the boom, called BUST. Montana must take into consideration viewpoints of *individuals* as well as corporations, counties as well as tribes, and other pros and cons of any decision to stop or promote an industry which could cause drastic changes in the environment.

Read the 1972 Montana State Constitution and see if the issues of the day colored the document. Unmistakably, they did. Montana, for the largest portion of its existence, has been considered by many to be a "company state." Because of this feeling, if indeed it was not a reality, the people who drew up the new constitution were going to see that the pattern could change. If Montana *has* to give up its coal, it appears it will do so only at a price that will ensure the least possible harm to man, animals, plants, and the physical environment. Finally man is considering the whole problem instead of just the profits to be made. "Progress" may take longer due to the time needed to study alternatives; at least such study might break Montana's past pattern of "two steps forward, one step back."

Besides these much sought-after deposits of underground treasure, there are many other mining and drilling activities across the state. Even western Montana is getting into the oil picture with operations in the Drummond area. Phosphates taken from mines near Garrison provide a good percentage of the U.S. total. (Phosphates are used in fertilizers as well as other products.) Another of Montana's lesser known but equally important products is talc. Found mainly in Madison and Beaverhead counties, it is used in talcum powder and the rubber and paper manufacturing business.

Many of the smaller operations are on an "on again, off again" schedule determined by the price of the material. If the price is high, mining is active, or "on." If the price is low, operations are shut "off." Simply a case of supply and demand.

At this particular point it might be interesting to read a short excerpt from a book by Tom Dole and Vernon Gill Carter, both experienced ecologists. The book from which the excerpt is

238

taken was published in 1955, well before the current ecology "craze."

THE PROPER USE OF LAND

Civilzed man was nearly always able to become master of his environment *temporarily.* His chief troubles came from his delusions that his temporary mastership was permanent. He thought of himself as "master of the world," while *failing to understand* fully the laws of nature.

Man, whether civilized or savage, is a child of nature — he is not the master of nature. He *must* conform his actions to certain natural laws if he is to maintain his dominance over his environment. When he tries to circumvent the laws of nature, he usually destroys the natural environment that sustains him. And when his environment deteriorates rapidly, his civilization declines.

One man has given a brief outline of history by saying that "civilized man has despoiled most of the lands on which he has lived for *long.* This is the main reason why his progressive civilizations have *moved* from place to place. It has been the chief cause for the decline of his civilizations in older settled regions. It has been the dominant factor in determing *all trends* of history."

The writers of history have seldom noted the importance of land use. They seem not to have recognized that the destinies of most of man's empires and civilizations were determined largely by the way the land was used. While recognizing the influence of environment on history, they fail to note that man usually changed or despoiled his environment.

How did civilized man despoil this favourable environment? He did it mainly by depleting or destroying the natural resources. He *cut down* or *burned* most of the usable timber from forested hillsides and valleys. He *overgrazed* and *denuded* the grasslands that fed his livestock. He *killed* most of the wildlife and much of the fish and other water life. He permitted *erosion* to rob his farm land of its productive topsoil. He allowed eroded soil to clog the streams and fill his reservoirs, irrigation canals, and harbours with silt. In many cases, he *used* and *wasted* most of the easily mined metals or other needed minerals. *Then* his civilization *declined* amidst the despoliation of his own creation or *he moved* to new land. There have been from ten to thirty different civilizations that have followed this road to ruin (the number depending on who classifies the civilizations).

Topsoil & Civilization by Tom Dale & Vernon Gill Carter (University of Oklahoma Press, Norman Okla., 1955)

After reading these few paragraphs one gets the idea that man has traditionally entered an area, changed it somehow, grown unhappy with the surroundings, and finally moved to a different location. This, in turn, brings up obvious questions, such as where should we move next? Why should we move? Is there anyplace left to which to move? Maybe, just maybe, where once it was "Custer's Last Stand," is now man and his environment's last stand?!

Chapter Three

GROWING UP IS HARD ON THE LAND

With the end of World War II, millions of men were thrown back into a peacetime setting and a peacetime economy. Learning from the past, the government was somewhat ready to aid these men reenter society more rapidly. Federal programs were set up to encourage further education, start small businesses, and buy homes or land at reasonable interest rates. Because of such programs, plus the fact that the war had held up many marriage plans, many people settled down quickly.

This settling down was the cause of a famous "baby boom" and "housing boom" across the U.S. People who had been apartment-dwellers in large cities were now invading the farm land surrounding the urban areas to form "suburbs." A look at any major city will show the various rings of suburbs surrounding it. A rule of thumb is this: the nearer to the city, the older the suburb. This growth is called "urban sprawl."

So what does all of this have to do with Montana? Besides many of the state's larger cities experiencing urban sprawl, any western Montanan can tell you the names or locations of numerous mills or wood manufacturing plants that supply the studs, joists, and plywood necessary to construct the houses that were needed.

Montana's lumber industry really didn't get into the big time till after World War II. It was then that the terrific demand for lumber caused the lumber industry, as a whole, to look for new areas to harvest. Enter the lumber industry on a big scale in the land of the "Big Sky." No longer was the industry in Montana confined to small mills. Outside money was coming in. Diversification was the name of the game.

By the late 50's, Waldorf Paper Products and Hoerner Box Company had settled in the Missoula-Frenchtown area. Evidently the Montana air was both good and bad for them. Good because the Company grew; bad because they altered the air with their own brand. Yuk!! The Missoula area soon jumped into the top ten of the "most polluted cities" in the U.S. The sleepy University town was right up there with New York, Los Angeles, and Pittsburg. Needless to say, the "honor" wasn't appreciated by the people. Breathing evidently had a higher priority than

working. Anyway, due to pressure and, finally, legislation, and an awakened sense of responsibility, the since-combined Hoerner-Waldorf plant has "cleaned up its act" to a great extent. This "particular" problem, however, exemplifies the problem that faces the entire state.

The Hoerner-Waldorf Company in Missoula has had a great impact on the economy. Many jobs were created. That means groceries on many tables, and taxes for local and state government. For many it was, and is, a job or career. But for many more it was, and sometimes is, a foul smell. The situation is particularly bad during winter inversions. Although *much* has been done to eliminate this "particular" problem, the statewide problem breaks down to jobs versus environment. In a state that certainly needs jobs, the answer has *usually* come at the expense of the environment.

One need only look around the state to see the battlefields on which nature has suffered defeat after defeat. The difference in the lumber industry is that some past mistakes, such as the "cut and get out" policies followed earlier can be dealt with (to an extent) through reforestation. Forest management is an idea that has prospered as a valuable means of making the best of the existing forests. Even the once-controversial National Forests have proven to be a good move on the part of the federal government. These areas, some 70% of Montana's forestlands, are excellent recreation and game preserves.

Throughout this period the lumber industry has progressively grown in the state. However, due to its reliance on the construction industry, any construction slowdown immediately affects logging and other lumber-related industries. This, needless to say, is not the most comforting thought for the over 10,000 people who work in these areas. Already this decade there have been two minor recessions, or periods of tight money. This means people were laid off for a short period of time. Try living for a "short period of time with no money; somehow stomachs need to be filled *all* the time. Try not paying your bills for a "short period of time" — then see how the term "minor recession" takes on new meaning.

239

Missoula Draws National Attention

Although Montana's air pollution problems are relatively minor in comparison to those of industrial states, air pollution in Missoula is bad enough to draw national attention.

The CBS television documentary on air pollution Tuesday night included Missoula in its list of cities with bad pollution conditions. The New York Times carried a story in 1963 about the bad pollution problem in Missoula.

The CBS air pollution program and a similar one by NBC a week earlier focused national attention upon the growing air pollution problem which is estimated to cost the nation $11 billion a year. Both network programs emphasized that something can be done to control pollution — when an aroused and alert public demands action. The nation has the technology to control pollution, the programs pointed out.

The documentaries showed how cities like St. Louis and Pittsburgh with severe pollution conditions put effective control programs into effect.

A wise man learns from the experience of others. Will Montana take a lesson from other states that have been studying pollution for many years? There is some question in the state about the air pollution bill that will be introduced in the 1967 Legislature.

Will the bill, termed a compromise by one by the Air Pollution Legislative Study Committee have sharp enough enforcement teeth and adequate financing to make it effective? Experience of other states shows that both enforcement teeth and good financing are vital to the success of any control program.

As we have contended before, a pollution program lacking strong enforcement teeth and adequate financing is equivalent to expecting a 90-year-old toothless woman to chew a tough slab of bear meat without a knife or a fork.

Great Falls Tribune
Friday, Sept. 23, 1966

Missoula Air Among 25 Dirtiest In Nation, Sampling Survey Notes

By THE ASSOCIATED PRESS

Missoula's population of 27,090 persons has something in common with the 7,781,984 residents of New York City — dirty air.

Montana's third largest urban center ranks with 25 others as among the nation's dirtiest-air communities.

According to the National Air Sampling Network survey of several hundred cities, each of the ones at the top of the list, has more than 150 micrograms of suspended particulate matter per cubic meter of air.

What does that mean?

"It means that if you look at a sunbeam you can see particles floating in it," answers Raymond Smith, chief of NASN's Air Quality Section in Cincinnati.

"It also means that if you live in such a city you will dust your home every day, change your shirts each day, paint your house more often, have less sunlight, use more electricity, and probably experience more frequent respiratory illness."

This also would be true of any community having particulate matter concentrations of 100 micrograms per cubic meter or more — which includes Libby, Garrison and Butte in Montana.

No sophisticated scientific devices are needed for the housweife who goes from a relatively clean air area to the dirty-air area of an urban center. She can tell the difference as soon as she begins sneezing or as soon as she realized she has dust on the table she just cleaned a few hours earlier.

"People can notice by their eyes and nose," Smith said. "For example, they often remark how much cleaner it seems on Sunday than during the rest of the week.

"The reason is very sound. It usually is cleaner. For one thing, there is a reduction in automobile traffic, which reduces the amount of worn tire and engine exhaust mattern thrown into the air, and industrial activity also is reduced. As a rule it might be said that the air is 25 per cent cleaner on Sunday than the rest of the week."

Forester Relates How Pair Escaped Inferno

By K.A. EGGENSPERGER
Publisher
Sanders County Ledger

THOMPSON FALLS — The story of how two Thompson Falls loggers miraculously escaped after being trapped in the roaring inferno of a windswept forest fire Monday was unfolded Wednesday by a Forest Service official.

One of the two loggers, Allen Heuscher, is in the Sanders County General Hospital at Hot Springs with second degree burns on his arms, head and back. The other man, Al Wulfekuhle, escaped without injuries.

According to Jack Vicher of Missoula, investigating officer from the Lolo Forest supervisor's office, the loggers were operating a bulldozer to build a fire line around the Indian Gulch fire in the Little Thompson River drainage when they were trapped.

Vicher said they only had about 100 feet of fireline to build to reach a road when the fire exploded in heavy underbrush. They turned the dozer around and headed away from the flames but were overtaken.

Heuscher shut off the engine and ran through the wall of flames to safety. Wulfekuhle crawled under the dozer and crouched between the radiator and the blade. Vicher said the heat was so intense that it boiled all of the oil out of the engine and transmission, burned all the diesel fuel and engine seals and scorched the paint off the machine. He estimated Wulfekuhl was under the dozer 15 to 20 minutes.

The fire was in the mop up stage Wednesday with about 120 men at work. It was confined to timer on land owned by the Anaconda Co. The two loggers are employed by the Rossignol Ranch and Logging Co., contractors for the Anaconda Co.

Missoulian
September 28, 1967

240

At the *same* time, on the other side of the Rockies, the farms had changed dramatically. Wait a minute! They didn't *all* change dramatically. Some changes were ever so slight. Let's try again. Montana farming has come a long way from the day of the homesteaders. Major patterns can be seen in reference to the eastern two-thirds of the state, but each farm is indeed different, and each family has its own story to tell.

Precipitation. Elevation. Areas of strong wind. Irrigation. Lay of the land. Type of crop. Pastureland. Numbers of acres. These and many other considerations are the variables that make each and every Montana farm its own agribusiness. Neighbors get different yields depending on these variables. Because of this, generalized statements really don't apply to everybody, or maybe even *any*body. Even during the terrible droughts, *some* people did well enough to avoid the problems that plagued the vast majority. About the only things that do apply to *all* Montana farmers are the weather and the market price for their products. Worrying about the weather was given up a long time ago, so worrying about the market price has dominated the anxious, and often angry days of the farmer-rancher.

241

Some people may have noticed a slight change in that last statement. The farmer-rancher? Right! You see a good number of ranchers saw benefit in putting the plow to some of their grazing land. At the same time, many farmers have jumped into the cattle business. These outfits have been commonly referred to as "combination" outfits. Anyway, keep in mind that generalizations have the tendency to "water down" or categorize all farms as being identical operations.

Here goes! After World War II the trend which began with the lesson earned from the drought, that farms should diversify, began to reverse. Farmers began to put their land into one or maybe two cash crops. These primarily were wheat and barley. Why the change from diversification? Primarily the switch was caused by changes in the transportation business. With larger, faster, and refrigerated trucks, fresh produce, mostly from California, became readily available throughout the country. The world had shrunk a bit more. This time it affected the farmer. Because of this competition, Montana farmers went back to raising large-volume crops.

Drylanders went into growing grains such as winter and spring wheat and barley. The land's elevation, precipitation, and general climate determine which crop is planted. The triangle area of north central Montana is big on winter wheat, while in the northeastern corner of the state spring wheat is raised. Both areas have considerable acreage in barley and other types of wheat. Southern and southwestern Montana, more noted for grazing land, tends to produce winter wheat and barley.

Irrigated farms are a different story altogether. For the most part, these farms lie in fertile valleys alongside the rivers that cross the state. Water is usually not a problem since it is provided by melting snow from the mountains. However, mild winters can provide problems. These farms generally fall in the higher-labor category. That is, they require more manhours to tend to them. Products of such farms range from apples, cherries and potatoes in the west to sugar beets, beans, and peas in the east. Both eastern and western farms put up considerable amounts of hay, the general pattern being that the southern half of the state leads in hay production. Truck farms, usually near the larger cities, produce all kinds of vegetables, from radishes, asparagus, lettuce, corn and squash to even a few melons.

Probably the changes in Montana farms and ranches has been due to the obvious increase in the size of each outfit. Realizing there is a limited amount of land, you can see that *bigger* farms mean *fewer* farms. Since the 1920's, the average size of a Montana farm has jumped 400% to over 2,500 acres. And that is an *average*! For each outfit smaller than that, there is one larger!

This increased size was made possible because of the vast changes in farm equipment. Sitting atop an air conditioned $40,000 tractor is a far cry from the days of the horse-drawn plow. Innovations have their price, however. Boy, do they! Paying for the necessary equipment, fertilizers, and weed killer at a couple of dollars per bushel makes worrying about crop prices a lot more easy to understand. A long list of legislation, mostly originating in Washington due to the prompting of U.S. Senators and Representatives from farming states, have continued to give more reasons for farmer's hope, confusion, and frustration.

While there are problems such as weather, price fluctuations and storage facilities, there are a few interesting developments. One has been the relatively new foreign markets which have opened up for high-protein Montana wheat. Much of this business is in the Orient, where high populations mountainous terrain and harsh climates make necessary to import wheat. Sounds like the ideal situation, both humanitarian *and* profitable. So profitable, in fact, that the greater part of our harvests in recent years has gone overseas.

Chapter Four

LIVING OFF the LAND

This would be a good time to read *Where the Grizzly Walks* by Bill Schneider.

As was mentioned in the last chapter, the ranch and cattle industry has changed to a great extent. Why should it have changed? Cattle haven't. Yes they have! Since a set *amount* of cattle for market was established, (just an estimate, of course), the race was on for *quality* control. It was this push for quality that caused some ranchers to specialize in the production of breeding stock. Others went the route of selling their animals before they reached two years of age. Then there are still others who prefer to keep their animals until they mature. Yet another approach is to buy young cattle and graze them, avoiding the breeding end of the business.

Feedlots in Midwest were the last home for Montana beef for a number of years. But since the post-war era, local feedlots have sprung up. Although small by national comparison, the Montana feedlot business boomed throughout the late 1950's into the early 1970's. But a combination of weather and market price of grain and low beef prices all but "did in" the feedlot business in the state. The years 1974 and 1975 may be remembered as good years in the wheat business, but the high price of grain caught many cattlemen in a bind which cost them thousands.

Unlike the farmer, the rancher has a problem in that he or she can't put products into storage. No one has yet come up with a "beef elevator." While the farmer can wait for grain prices to increase, the rancher must wait for increases in the price for beef. The difference is that cattle waiting to be sold must be *fed*. And feed costs money. High-priced feed means high-priced beef. But, once again, remember that cattlemen don't set the price. The demand, or market price does that. Some years are *good* and some years are *long*.

Regardless of the economics, the cattle business is a big one in Montana. If measured only in the amount of land set aside for either grazing or hay, the cattle industry is far and away number one. As with the farmer, the rancher has gone to a highly-mechanized operation. Expensive but necessary equipment and irrigation systems have greatly increased the amounts of hay put up. At the same time these mixed blessings have increased the "overhead" of cattle industry.

Meanwhile, Montana's sheep industry, which for a brief period of time at the turn of the century held the number one spot in the nation, continued in its downward slide. Why? How?

Remember how after the "hard winter" of 1886-87 many cattlemen switched from cattle raising to sheep raising? Or that many added sheep to their cattle operations? At the turn of the century, there were some 6,000,000 of those four-legged sweaters roaming the state. The sheep were looked upon as the product of the future. This idea didn't last too long, however, for as the homesteader moved in, the sheep and cattle were confined to smaller ranges. This was the first major blow to an industry that was to suffer a series of setbacks which have not been reversed.

First of all, the winter of 1906-07 was almost as bad as the more infamous of one twenty years earlier. It was only the changes made by the ranches that saved the herds and flocks. Even so, nearly three-quarters of a million sheep died. The drought years of the 1920's and 30's didn't do the sheepmen any more favors than they did for anyone else. Add this to a depressed economy and the results were similar to the stagnation experienced by the cattle business.

Probably the worst blow to the sheep industry was World War II. The war enlisted labor necessary to maintain any kind of profitable operation. You see, the sheep industry needs more workers than the cattle industry does to keep things running smoothly, from herders to wool processors.

The final blow came to the industry in the form of alternatives to wool. As synthetics proved to have some advantages over wool, the demand for wool dropped. Today, Montana has a mere 10-15% of its turn-of-the century sheep population, or about 750,000 head.

In the meantime, Montana's wildlife was getting more breaks due to the increasingly more sophisticated Department of Fish and Game. Rangelands have been acquired across the state. Data is constantly being compiled to benefit both man and beast. In an effort to keep Montanans informed about wildlife and land usage, the Department issues a magazine entitled *Montana Outdoors*. It's printed six times per year and provides interesting reading for anyone who appreciates the west as a place where the "deer and the antelope play."

Chapter Five

RULERS

It is probably human nature that makes people fail to recognize up and coming powers because they are looking at old heroes or enemies. For instance, for many years people never even noticed Hank Aaron because they felt that no one would *ever* break Babe Ruth's record for home runs. A classic example of people not knowing who controls power is the election of Jimmy Carter as President of the U.S. in 1976. In 1974, hardly anyone outside Georgia even knew his *name*. Then, presto, two years later he is in the White House. One's climb to power is often unnoticed. Existing powers or declining powers receive attention because of their past importance.

Such has been the case in the Montana over the past quarter-century. The once all-powerful Anaconda Copper Min-

ing Company has lost its grip on Montana. With the advent of open-pit mining, A.C.M. not only bit into the Butte hill but also depleted its own traditional source of strength, the miner. As long as "The Company" controlled a sizeable payroll, it exerted power. There was definitely a correlation between paychecks and power. So when the almost totally-mechanized Berkely Pit went into operation, its payroll, and influence, decreased markedly.

Meanwhile, in Great Falls and Columbia Falls, A.C.M. opened aluminum plants, its last big operation in the state. In 1955, the Company also changed its name to just "The Anaconda Company." Montanans, however, still refer to it as "The Company," or "A.C.M."

OF the LAND

Four years later, in 1959, A.C.M. sold its statewide chain of newspapers. Regardless of its reasons for so doing, it voluntarily gave up its public voice. At the same time, A.C.M. increased its efforts to make itself heard in Helena. Heck, the Company was diminishing in grassroots strength, *not brains*. They knew where the action was. In Helena. Big business in the U.S. has known for years that "happy" legislatures pass good laws. Helena was full of lobbyists and occasionally happy legislators. The leaders of A.C.M. and Montana Power, like those of so many other major industries, felt that by keeping the legislators *properly informed*, sensible legislation would and could be passed to the benefit of all. Rumors of lobbying "above and beyond the call of duty" abound, however, because where there is controversy there is suspicion.

The early 1960's provided Montana with some really interesting developments. Besides the fact that Montanans could now read about state developments, they read of the end of Montana's most celebrated "marriage of convenience" since Clark and Heinze. The Montana Power Company and A.C.M. were splitting up. It was inevitable, according to many. A.C.M. was due to be challenged for its role of corporate supremacy sooner or later. M.P.C., on which A.C.M. depended for its electricity, and gas, was in a perfect position to do this.

The A.C.M. had long since grown dependent on M.P.C. and is M.P.C.'s largest customer. But both corporations are in business to make money, not friends. There was a dispute over utility-rate increases. One has to wonder how John D. Ryan would have felt about all of this, especially since he was the "stepfather" of A.C.M. and the "father" of M.P.C. Regardless of what Ryan's feelings might have been, A.C.M. and M.P.C. went their separate ways. Neither company suffered greatly. They still cooperated, and even lobbied together. Old habits are hard to break.

In reality it wasn't as much a "divorce" as it was a case of one corporation becoming powerful enough to go out on its own. M.P.C. was, and had been for a long time, a power to be reckoned with. The hassle of the early 60's was merely the proverbial "last straw."

A look at a few events preceding the split may be helpful. The 50's were good years for M.P.C. They should have been, because the age of electric conveniences had just begun. All of a sudden many people could afford electric washers, dryers, televisions, radios, clocks, blankets, toasters, hair dryers, and so on. The list could go on almost forever. Anything people are too lazy to do, electricity can. Some of these appliances are a little extravagant; electric pencil sharpeners, for instance. But, as a result of people using products like this, M.P.C. experienced a tremendous demand for its electricity.

The Company expanded. By 1960 M.P.C. had nearly $250,000,000 invested in facilities. More than half of that figure was spent between 1950 and 1960. An example of this expansion was the 1959 purchase of surface rights, and long-term leases, on Colstrip coal. They felt the coal could give them an almost unlimited low-cost fuel for future use. If the 50's were that good, why couldn't the 60's be better?

By 1961 M.P.C. decided to move its corporate headquarters from the east coast to Montana. And so M.P.C. became a *Montana* corporation. The following year was its 50th birthday. Both M.P.C. and the state had come a long way in those 50 years. With justifiable pride, Company officials could boast of having upgraded the standard of living of tens of thousands of Montanans. It was at approximately this time that M.P.C. and A.C.M. "parted company."

By the late 1960's M.P.C. had put some of that coal to use in its Billings steam generating plant. It, and others like it, were successful operations. Naturally, they planned more. Wham! The firey 1970's came in, with protests loud enough to qualify as "noise pollution."

Today there are arguments from all sides; private business, environmental groups, government officials at all levels, people from all over the state who are trying to influence the Company's course of action. As was stated in chapter 2, the problems are complex and numerous. Each and every group, no doubt sincere in its particular viewpoint, should be heard. *All* Montanans have a stake in the state's future, and every opinion, from the well-educated to the gut reaction, should be considered.

In the meantime, A.C.M. was taking care of its own business. Because of its past actions, some people had forgotten that its primary concern was copper. Looking back at the 60's, A.C.M.'s position can be compared with that of a person aboard the *Titanic*. The sailing could have been a bit smoother.

Though a strike in 1967 disrupted things a bit, business in those years was fairly good. The 70's however, have been a different story. In 1971 the Chilean government proved to be the "iceberg" that sank the Anaconda Company. In that year, the Chilean government nationalized the huge copper mines owned by A.C.M. In other words, the Chilean government took over the mines and threw out A.C.M., along with all other foreign-based companies which had operations in that country.

The once-mighty A.C.M. began sinking fast. Something had to be done. John Place, A.C.M. president, decided to get rid of all excess "company baggage." Immediately, less profitable operations were halted. Layoffs mounted. By mid-1972 a deci-sion of immense importance was reached, and the Company cast adrift its lumber operations. A single transaction with Chamption International stripped A.C.M. of countless emp-loyees, equipment, and over 670,000 acres of forests.

They weren't going down without a heck of a fight. Mexico in 1974 decided that Chile had had a good idea, and it followed suit, taking over control of mines in that country. The cuts have continued throughout the 70's.

Mining operation in Butte are now in the Pit, using highly automated methods which employ relatively few workers. In January, 1977, Montanans all over the state, regardless of their age or previous feelings for what had been "The Company," felt twinges of nostalgia. In that month, A.C.M., once the allpowerful creation of Marcus Daly, was sold to the Atlantic Richfield Oil Company. Montana's homegrown corporate giant now had an out-of-state address.

Strike Loss Figured At $50 Million Plus

BUTTE (AP)—The Anaconda Co. announced Saturday that total loss to Montana's economy from the copper strike through Jan. 7 is $50,988,922.

That represents losses in wages, services, freight, supplies and taxes, the company said. It does not include loss of savings, credit extensions by banks and finance companies, utility payments or unemployment compensation payments to strikers.

The copper strike will become Montana's longest Jan. 12 when it enters its 182nd day. The previous longest strike was 181 days in 1959-60.

The Anaconda Co. estimated wage loss to all striking employees through Jan. 7 at $23,976,000. The average wage loss to date was estimated at $3,330 per striker.

Loss in federal income tax payments was estimated at $3,060,000 and the decrease in federal Social Security tax payments was estimated at $2,080,000.

County commissioners estimated welfare payments in Silver Bow County (Butte) at $357,000 so far in the strike and more than $150,000 in Deer Lodge County (Anaconda). Estimates in Cascade and Lewis and Clark counties would push the total figure to $650,000.

The strike began last July 15. There is no prospect of settlement or even of negotiations.

The strike, which has been in progress since July 15, has shut down 95 per cent of U.S. copper production and idled more than 50,000 workers.

The issues in dispute are wages and bargaining practices.

Phelps Dodge, the big Arizona producer, and the unions recessed their talks before the year-end holiday to study each other's offers.

American Metal Market, the daily newspaper of the metal-working industry, reported that the fact that Phelps Dodge and the unions are still talking indicates they are engaged in serious bargaining.

However, there remained a considerable gap between their two positions.

There are no talks going in or scheduled between the unions and the other major copper producers — Anaconda Co., and Kennecott Copper Corp. and American Smelting and Refining Co.

Some industry sources believed these companies were waiting for a possible settlement to come out of the Phelps Dodge-union meetings.

Copperweld Steel Co. of Pittsburgh, said last week that it would lay off another 100 workers because of the copper strike.

The company furloughed 100 workers two months ago. The plant employs 800 persons but only those who work on the production of copper-coated steel wire are affected by the layoffs.

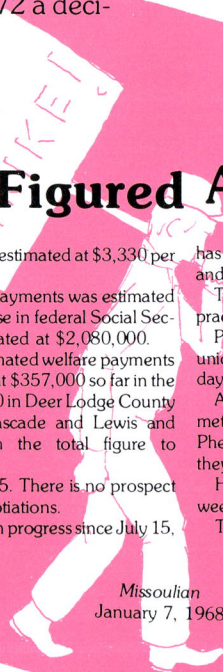

Missoulian
January 7, 1968

This strike ended in late March, 1968, after 260 days. It was the longest in the history of the miners.

246

As for the federal government, depending on your own political leanings, it continues to be meddling, or responsibe, to many aspects of life in Montana.

To get another perspective of the "rulers of the land," following is an excerpt from *Montana: Magazine of the Northern Rockies.* Before you read it, however, read over the first paragraph of this chapter. Also remember that these individuals may change as rapidly as the organizations they represent. Remember, too, that this article is based on a survey, and reflects the point of view of the man who conducted the survey.

In the editor's note preceding the article, replies were encouraged in the form of "responsible and factual comments." The following issue of the magazine carried no replies.

WHO INFLUENCES STATE GOVERNMENT! THE 10 MOST INFLUENTIAL by Thomas Kotynski

EDITOR'S NOTE: This article, and the information listed with it, does not necessarily represent the feelings and opinions of Montana Magazine. They are the opinions of the author as tabulated by a survey he undertook. Mr. Kotynski is well qualified to do an article of this nature. He has been covering the legislature for the Great Falls Tribune for the past three sessions and has been very involved in covering the state political scene in general. Tom Kotynski is currently employed as a reporter for the Great Falls Tribune's Capitol Bureau. Responsible and factual comments to this article are welcome.

It is pretty safe to say that Tom Judge, as Montana's governor, is the most influential individual involved in and with state government. But, have you ever wondered who those people and forces are who can influence Judge's direction? Or, in and of themselves work an influence on the state? Who are these people, businesses, groups and coalitions that make state government work, or even change its course?

As a newspaper reporter it is part of my job to be aware of who and what these forces might be. The following is a list of who I think the "Top Ten" in influences are in and with state government.

My list is drawn from my own experience as a reporter working the Capitol beat and a survey I conducted.

I surveyed 30 people from a broad range of interests in Montana including those involved with business, industry, politics, agriculture, the environment, education, labor, low income interests, the minorities, the public interest, women and journalism. I excluded Judge because I believed him to be such an obvious choice. I asked those answering my survey to do the same. I was hoping that by excluding Judge that those individuals and forces which influence him, but who are generally out of the public eye, might turn up in my survey responses. I think they did. I asked those responding to list their Top Ten in a numerical order of importance and I used that system to come up with my Top Ten as follows: 1. Lt. Gov. Ted Schwinden; 2. The Corporations; 3. The Supreme Court; 4. The Press; 5. AFL-CIO Executive Secretary Jim Murry; 6. House Appropriations Committee Chairman Francis Bardanouve of Harlem; 7. State Budget Director Mike Billings; 8. Judge's executive assistant, Keith Colbo; 9. Helena attorney Ross Cannon; and 10. Public interest advocate Rick Applegate of Bozeman. There were some 54 names nominated for my Top Ten.

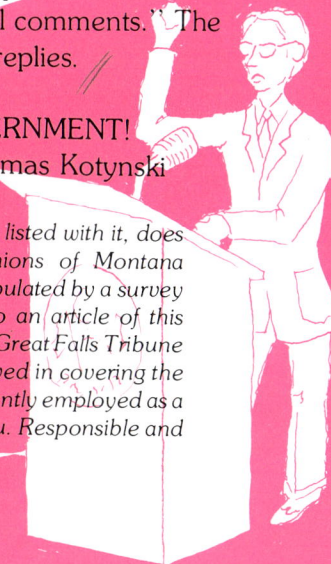

Schwinden

Schwinden was mentioned by nearly everyone I surveyed. Most ranked him "No. 1." Schwinden, who began his term as lieutenant governor in January, was State Lands Commissioner for seven years, and a state legislator before that. He also operates a farm near his native Wolf Point.

"Schwinden commands more respect and authority than the position itself (lieutenant governor)," wrote Phil Tawney, lobbyist for the Helena based Environmental Information Center. "It is a result of Schwinden's personal operating style and long time ties with the Democratic Party," Tawney said of Schwinden's influence.

Helena Lawyer Jim Zion, of the American Civil Liberties Union, said Schwinden's influence is derived as a result of being a spokesman for "middle of the road business and agricultural interest." *Unfortunately, Zion says, Schwinden is responsible for the change in Judge's environmental stance to a "more pro-energy and less conservation policy."*

One Democratic Party official said, "His (Schwinden's) personal integrity, fairness, good political sense and willingness to confront tough problems made him influential even before he was lieutenant governor and have only increased his value since."

A tribute to Schwinden's political abilities is that former Lt. Gov. Bill Christiansen had selected Schwinden as a running mate before deciding not to run for governor in 1976.

The Corporations

Burlington Northern. Montana Power Co. Joe McElwain (Montana Power's president). The Montana International Trade Commission. Jim Hodge (The Trade Commission's executive). Atlantic-Richfield Corp. (which owns Anaconda Co.). TENNECO.

Taken altogether those corporations, and names linked with corporations, were listed as second most influential. If I had listed the corporations individually several would have made the Top Ten by themselves, such as Montana Power. Burlington Northern and the Trade Commission. I chose rather to list them as a group because they often work together for their advantage and influence.

A case in point is the Trade Commission which has in its membership both Montana Power and Burlington Northern.

Montana's history is one marked by corporate domination. While some believe that corporate domination and influence is on the wane, such coalitions as evidenced in the Trade Commission may be a sign of corporate resurgence. By listing so many corporations on my survey, many believe that this is the case.

Surprisingly, no one mentioned the coal companies. Without a doubt, the coal companies exert an influence on the state. *For openers, Decker Coal Co. has now replaced the Anaconda Co. as the state's largest single taxpayer.* The 30 per cent sales tax on coal, as set aside in a constitutional trust fund is going to enrich the state by billions of dollars before all the coal is dug. Every future legislature will argue over how to spend that money.

The politics of coal is being played by the Indian tribal governments now as well as eastern Montana farmers-ranchers, water users and developers. The federal government owns much of Montana's coal and will loom even larger in the future as force to be reckoned with because of that ownership.

The Montana International Trade Commission and its executive director Jim Hodge were mentioned more than any other entities representing the corporations. The Trade Commission has in its membership agri-business as well as the traditional Montana corporate powers.

It has negotiated a trade agreement with Saudi Arabia and is working on others with countries of the Far East and Algeria. Its emphasis is to seek international markets for Montana's products — to broaden the state's economic base. Yet, although the Commission has as many of its members the historic exploiters and exporters of Montana's natural treasures, *its lofty aim is to vitalize the state's small businesses by securing them markets abroad, now beyond their grasp.*

The Commission has caught heat from environmentalists and the Bozeman based Center for the Public Interest, Inc., through its director, Rick Applegate, for its secretive operations. The Commission has also had a hand in some major state deliberations such as the Governor's Coal Gasification Task Force and an Economic Development Task Force. Hodge, a former Port of Butte director, is believed to have the Governor's ear.

With its corporate based membership this writer would have to agree that the Commission is in a position to be a major force in the future of Montana. *Hopefully, it will be the corporations combined in an effort to feed the state's economy rather than to bleed it.*

The Supreme Court

The Supreme Court is the final word in everything in Montana. When the Legislature passes a bill and the Governor signs it, the law means nothing if the Court says it won't pass constitutional muster.

In 1975 and 1976 the Court showed how truly powerful it can be. It overturned a state Public Service Commission utility rate decision; it brought an outspoken former Atty. General Robert Woodahl into line for his statements on pending work-comp scandal cases; it stripped an interim legislative committee of a coveted interim budget power and it strengthened, then changed its mind and weakened Montana's unique environmental policy act.

It was tempting to place the Court ahead of Judge as the single most influential power in the state, but the 1976 general elections have changed the Court's membership and it hasn't gotten its feet on the ground and given the public a feel for the sort of influence it will wield.

The former Court, under the direction of former Chief Justice James T. Harrison and under the influence of former Associate Justice Wesley Castles, had a decidedly conservative, pro-corporate slant. The new Court, under the direction of new Chief Justice Paul Hatfield of Great Falls and with new Associate Justice Dan Shea of Missoula, on its face, will be the old Court's antithesis. Both Hatfield and Shea campaigned against the Castles influence. Their election is a signal to a *"new order."* But, what that order will be remains to be seen.

The Press

While few mentioned "The Press," per se, almost everyone had some member of the Montana press mentioned on their surveys.

Among members of the press mentioned were: Great Falls Tribune Editor, William D. James, The Tribune Capitol Bureau and its columnist Frank Adams; Billings Gazette Editor, William Roesgen; the Lee Newspapers State Bureau; Missoulian editorial writer, Sam Reynolds and the Associated Press.

From my perspective I'd pick Associated Press reporter, J. D. Holmes as the most influential among the Montana Press although he was not mentioned by name on any of the surveys. Holmes has covered the state capitol scene out of Helena for AP since 1949. His stories are picked up by all of the state's daily newspapers and many of the radio and television stations *as their sole source of state news.* To avoid duplication, the Tribune and Lee news bureaus in Helena discourage coverage of stories which Holmes might originate from his beat. *Therefore, Holmes has an almost virtual lock on news from the Capitol "beat." Over the years he has been able to pick and choose the news.*

I estimate that no other man has had his name in print more times in the history of the state. Because Holmes rarely analyzes the news and because his reports are little more than barebones information it has been said that his uncritical coverage of the Supreme Court led to the 20 years of "Castles' Court."

Much credit has been given the Tribune's Frank Adams for exposing that court and causing Castles' unseating in the 1976 election.

Likewise, in other areas Holmes has chosen for 30 years what information about state government Montanans should or should not read. That is real influence. I was quite tempted to choose "J.D." ahead of Schwinden as "No. 1."

Jim Murry

No doubt about it, labor is a powerful force in Montana. *Labor,* for instance, *had the largest single lobby before the 1977 legislature.* And, when one is asked to pick the most influential laborite one would be hard to come up with a name other than Jim Murry, the state AFL-CIO executive secretary.

"Contrary to popular right-wing doctrine," says Mike Pichette, the Democratic Party's state executive secretary, "Murry does not come by his influence through threats involving labor's clout at the polls." Pichette believes Murry is persuasive because of his commitment to "people programs," because he can successfully portray the effects of his proporsals and because he is willing to work twice as hard as anyone else to accomplish his goals.

Significantly, Murry has been able to maintain an environmentalist stance despite labor's historic given image that jobs and a pristine environment aren't always compatible. It is a stance which has brought some tough opposition, particularly from Operating Engineers and the newly formed industry-business-labor lobby — THE Western Environmental Trade Association.

Rep. Francis Bardanouve

One of the favorite tactics of Rep. Francis Bardanouve's opponents is to question his power base. "How does a farmer from little Harlem have so much power over state government?" They ask with a tone of voice implying that others elected from statewide constituencies should have more say than he.

Bardanouve's power is many faceted. The most obvious source is his *chairmanship of the House Appropriations Committee.* The state budget must pass through that committee, as well as many requests for money beyond the budget for the pet projects of the state legislators. He has been in the House *since 1959,* longer than any other House member, making him Dean. His tenure and grasp of complicated budget matters combined with his eloquence, unquestioned integrity and openmindedness have given him almost total say over how much of a budget the state will have and which of the legislative pet projects will be funded.

Besides that, Bardanouve is chairman of the Legislature's *interim Finance Committee* which watches how the state budget is spent during the period between legislative sessions. *His watchfulness has caused the state bureaucracy to be more careful with the state's cash and has resulted in a more conservative attitude towards the state's acceptance of federal money which might some day obligate the state to programs it can't afford on its own.*

Bardanouve is responsible for the creation of the Legislative Fiscal Analyst's office (lesislative counterpart to state budget director) and brought John LaFaver in to fill the job. The result has been a legislature for the first time acting as a coequal partner to the executive branch of government, in fiscal affairs.

Bardanouve's influence is not limited to financial matters.

He has impeccable environmental credentials and is author of the Major Facility Siting Act, the law which set up the criteria for judgment of power plants.

"Rep. Francis Bardanouve is one of the few legislators who can be considered truly influential," House Speaker John Driscoll said on his survey reply. Driscoll credited that influence to his committee chairmanship, his respect from both the legislative and executive branches and the fact that he introduces successful legislation each session of the Legislature.

"His personal relationships are strong and his advice is not sought just because of his powerful position," says Democratic Party executive secretary, Mike Pitchette.

"He would make a superior governor if he only wanted it," said public interest advocate, Rick Applegate of Bozeman.

Mike Billings

The Billings name has a rich place in recent Montana history. Harry and Gretchen Billings ran the liberal-labor-anti-utility "People's Voice"

which pricked the conscience of state government, the status quo and rode herd on the Montana Power-Anaconda Powerbase. Their son, Mike, is Gov. Judge's top budget man, the state's top government management man. There is irony in the fact that his parents are so associated with anti-establishment issues.

In state government, Mike is the establishment. Billings has brought coherency to state government through his management by objective approach which has surfaced in the governor's six year planning process. He was a moving force in helping clean up the mess at Warm Srpings State Hospital in 1974.

"He is a practical 'numbers' man who has given factual basis to innumerable important decisions made by both the legislative and executive branches," says House Speaker John Driscoll, who should know.

Billings has been the governor's key spokesman for the clashes with the legislature over its interim budget powers, opposition to the 1976 budget ceiling initiative and most recently the 1978-79 state budget. And, if something issues forth from the governor's office of financial nature, odds are that Billings has had a hand in it.

Billings' power can be subtle, too. His office writes the "fiscal notes" — the cost of bills to the state. These notes have meant the death of many pieces of legislation, even before public hearings can be held. *Billings is the executive branch's final word on managing the state's $1.9 billion two year budget.*

Keith Colbo

Keith Colbo is Gov. Judge's executive assistant and in that position earns more money than Judge. He runs the governor's staff from day to day. It is Colbo with whom the public confers often when dealing with the "Governor's Office." When a decision is made by Judge, it is Colbo who sees to it that it is executed. But, more than just executing decisions, Colbo is often on the inside helping make them.

Colbo, who was for awhile Judge's Director of Revenue and Budget before Billings, is a money and figures man who softspoken, even handed ways have won him respect and made him easy to get along with in pressure situations. He is not the wheeler-dealer that his predecessor, Ron Richards was. But, he has a good understanding of the political game and plays it well.

House Speaker John Driscoll believes Colbo to be the most influential man in state government. "His influence is based on his intelligence,

experience, political perceptiveness and unusual loyalty to the Governor," says Driscoll.

"Rescind ERA" leader John Driscoll believes Colbo to be the most influential man in state government. "His influence is based on his intelligence, experience, political perceptiveness and unusual loyalty to the Governor," says Driscoll.

"Rescind ERA" leader John Zormeir of Lewistown says, "The secretary to the governor (Colbo) can have much influence about which matters are or are not brought to the attention of the Governor."

State Indian Affairs Coordinator Merle Lucas said of Colbo that he is influential "because he is the Governor's chief adviser."

Ross Cannon

Admittedly, choosing the most influential is risky business. Everyone has his point of reference for choosing who influences whom, Rumors are rampant in the Capitol's halls about who has Judge's ear.

Frequently, the names of Helena attorney, Robert Cummins, Montana International Trade Commission executive director, Jim Hodge, State-Federal Coordinator, Dean Hart, and Broadcaster-Agribusinessman Dale Moore of Missoula are mentioned. But, no name is mentioned as frequently as that of Helena attorney, Ross Cannon.

Cannon, a wealthy and dapper son of former Lt. Gov. Paul Cannon, who was once a perennial candidate for office has an *active law practice which includes some tribal business, state employee collective bargaining and several clients lobbying the 1977 legislature.*

Bozeman Public Interest advocate Rick Applegate calls Cannon "a close confidant of the Governor's."

Civil libertarian Jim Zion, a Helena lawyer too, said, "Ross Cannon is a lawyer who has a good deal of personal influence on the Judge Administration."

One Democratic Party official listed Cannon because "Ross exemplifies the group of Tom Judge's personal friends (such as Tom Hanrahan or George Sherwood) who comprise a set of informal advisers with access to the Governor and advice he respects."

Only the Governor knows whether this is accurate speculation. I sent Judge a survey to fill out and he declined to reply.

Rick Applegate

Rick Applegate's name provokes extreme reactions. He is rapidly becoming the "*Ralph Nader of Montana*" and is the scourge of the state's corporations and state agencies which operate in secret. Although I chose him to round out the Top Ten as a personification of environmental influence in the state, he is much more than that.

It was Applegate who singlehandedly wrote the *"Right to Know"* section of the new state constitution as a Con-Con staffer. He has been a constant reminder of what that section should mean to the state in the way of openness in government. He has doggedly tried to get state government to implement the citizen participation act which became law in 1975.

Through the Bozeman based Center for the Public Interest, which was founded in 1975, he has thrown the glare of public scrutiny on the Montana International Trade Commission. Burlington Northern, women's status in state government, the utility rate structure, public funded regional energy organizations, the Forest Service, Ski Yellowstone and Big Sky.

This list is actually longer than that, but I've made my point, *he's been active in areas which wouldn't have been examined by the public unless he stepped in.*

Further, his research is known for its thoroughness and perceptivity.

Applegate is married to House Majority Whip Dorothy Bradley, Democrat of Bozeman, who in her own right received significant mention as "most influential" on my survey. Bradley has indicated that she may run for Congress in the Western District in 1978.

Others Mentioned

It was difficult to leave out of the Top Ten Atty. Gen. Mike Greely, Billings State Sen. Tom Towe or Sen. Jean Turnage of Polson. Each received significant support for being listed among the Top Ten among those I surveyed.

A major surprise to me was that the only member of Montana's Congressional delegation mentioned was U.S. Sen. Lee Metcalf, and only on one survey.

If I had taken my survey a year earlier I'm sure that former U.S. Sen. Mike Mansfield would have popped up on every one and wound up on the Top Ten.

With the vast amounts of federal lands in Montana there is no question but that our Congressional delegation can do a great deal to make or break Montana.

Much is owed to Mansfield for upgrading Malmstrom Air Force Base in Great Falls, bringing MHD (Magnetohydrodynamics) to Butte, saving Flathead Lake from dams and the fact that *Montana gets back about $130 from the federal government for every $1 in taxes that residents pay.*

Much will hinge on our Congressional delegation's ability to convince a nation and a President that the purity of our state's resources should be considered while the country is attempting to glut itself on Montana's vast energy and natural resource supplies.

There are tremendous decisions to be made on the use of Montana's National Forest lands and Bureau of Land Management properties; will there be intensive development, more wilderness or more of the same?

Legislators were frequently mentioned.

In addition to Bardanouve, Towe, Bradley and Turnage there was Rep. J.D. Lynch of Butte, Sen. Larry Fasbender of Fort Shaw, Sen. Bill Mathers of Miles City, House Speaker John Driscoll of Hamilton, Sen. Dave Manning of Hysham, and Sen Gordon McOmber of Fairfield.

From education, Commissioner of Higher Education Larry Petit received mention on four of my surveys. Board of Regents Chairman Ted James of Great Falls, received one. To my surprise Superintendent of Public Instruction Georgia Rice received no notice.

The superintendency carries with it all the trappings of power, control over vast sums of money and a network of hundreds of small school districts, the most numerous political subdivisions in the state, dependent upon her administration.

One of my respondents listed Gov. Judge's wife, Carol, as the most influential of all.

"Carol's intelligence, concern and energy have won the respect of all who work with her. To my knowledge she uses her influence sparingly, but *effectiveness is enviable,"* he wrote.

Although state Chamber of Commerce executive vice president, Forrest "Buck" Boles declined to name a Top Ten, he said that, "those agencies and individuals who control the development and distribution of energy will ultimately have the most influence on the type and amount of development in Montana."

"The scope of that development will in turn determine the opportunities available to Montanans and will have considerable effect on virtually every resident of the State."

While I'm sure that my exercise in choosing the Top Ten will bring protests from those who disagree with my choices, I believe that the effort has been worth the time, *Hopefully, it will have caused some to ponder who and what influences the state and its future.* Hopefully, many will be more knowledgeable now, because of my effort, who and what those individuals and forces may be.

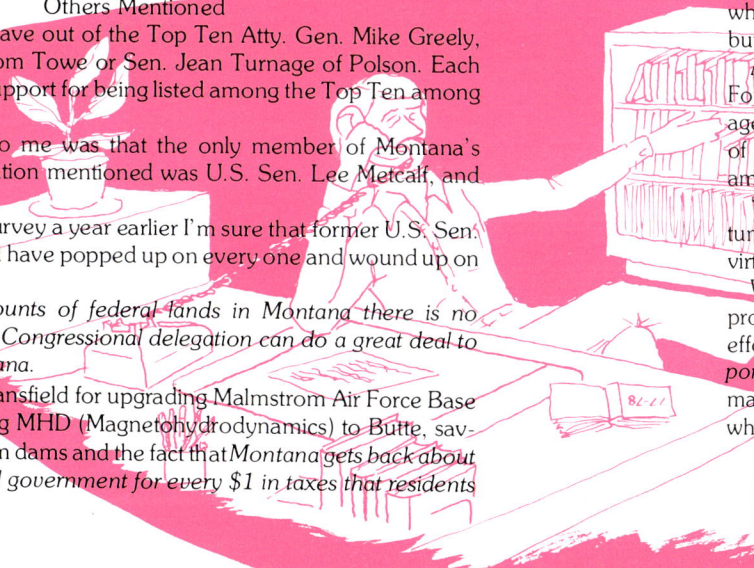

AT HOME ON the LAND

Chapter Six

Discussing recent history and current events is a very risky undertaking. At no other time is the historian so open to criticism. The reasons for this are not always obvious.

First of all, the amount of material out on any given subject is bulky. Because of this, a biased selection process, and they are all biased, must determine which bits of information will or will not be used. Not only that, but "first hand" accounts rarely match. That is, everybody sees things differently and through some complex mental process categorizes and prioritizes items differently than anyone else might. Police understand this when, in investigating an accident involving two cars, they hear ten different stories from ten different witnesses. Similar things happen when teachers and students, parents and children, and rural and urban folks get together to discuss issues.

By now you have the idea that people see things differently. The French writer Voltaire was saying this when he defined history as a "pack of tricks we play on the dead." An anonymous cynic put it like this: "History is merely a collection of agreed-upon lies." Probably the most popular point of view is that history, generally, is a system of recording data to be studied in the future, or a collection of past events studied now. The idea of "tricks" and "lies" surely comes into play, in part, due to omission of information. If, for no other reason than needing to limit the number of pages in a book, omission is a must.

With all of that out of the way, Montanans today at home on the land need to know that no single book, magazine, newspaper, radio, or t.v., or anything else, can possibly present the information needed to make decisions concerning this vast and beautiful state.

To categorize today's Montanans in any way other than as individuals would be an injustice. Attempts are made using such labels as urban or rural, employer or employee, native-born or "out-of-stater." These groupings are necessary to spot trends and understand relationships, but they always ignore someone for some reason or another. Maybe what we should do here is list everyone who lives in the state. On second thought, collect phone books and go from there.

The "average" Montanan of 1977 is considerably different than the Montanan of only 25 years ago. Since 1950 more than 30,000 of the state's residents left the professions of agriculture, railroading, and mining. Picking up the slack have been the state's booming service-oriented professions. These include retail stores, the housing industry, and the food-service industry.

As you might guess, the largest service organization in the state is the State of Montana. Combined state and local government employees number twice what they did in 1950. Another good percentage of Montanans, some 13,000, work for the federal government. By 1970 about *one of every five* working Montanans drew county, state, or federal *government* paychecks. At the same time, more than *one of three* was employed in other *service* industries.

It has to be difficult for the student from Ekalaka, Raymond, Red Rock, Babb, or Zortman to look around near his or her home and see all of the land that has been made to conform to man's needs, either through farming, ranching, mining or lumbering and then visualize the *average Montana worker as the Avon lady.* As the old World War I song asked, "How can you keep them down on the farm after they've seen Paris?" The tremendous decline in the number of needed agricultural workers has changed the character of employment in the state. More dependable engines plus air travel caused a decline in railroad employment. Mechanization of mining and other uncontrollable events put many miners into the ranks of the unemployed.

What does the average Montanan look like? Go look in a mirror and be glad you're here.

your picture goes here!

Chapter Seven

Few people, if any, would deny that Montana's wealth has always been tied to the land. One might notice the pattern of how wealth has been derived from the land in an attempt to provide for the future. One way of looking at it, and there are many, might be to see just why the white man came to the area in the first place. Lewis and Clark first came to observe; they were Montana's first tourists. Next came the men who trapped and hunted. On *his* heels came the miners and loggers, followed by the ranchers. The last major group to arrive was the farmers. Although these groups actually overlapped each other, this was the general pattern.

Now, given that the resources within the boundaries of the state are limited, it may make sense that these groups would *leave* in the same order.

If one were a "prophet of doom," one might say that as wildlife is gunned down, hunters "unload" the area. As the metals and minerals disappear, so do the miners. As the trees are harvested, the loggers "buzz off." As droughts and poor market conditions cause prices to drop, the rancher "hits the trail." As saline seep spreads, farmers "uproot." When this is all done and the economy of the area is destroyed, the tourists stop coming. Who would spend money to see where the "deer and the antelope" *used* to play?

Montana in the late 60's and the 70's has seen a resurgance of an older pattern, a pattern of the "People of the Plains" described in Book II. Repeating a couple of lines from chapter seven of that book, we begin to see their ageless wisdom. "Their idea of conservation was total utilization of the land about them with the least amount of disturbance to its natural state." The Indian exploited the land in such a manner that the land would continue to maintain his lifestyle endlessly.

Conservation in the white man's terms is not a new idea. But it has only been practiced sporadically. In recent years things seem to be going better, on all environmental fronts. The danger with that feeling is that we immediately tend to relax and say that problems have all been solved. Wrong! As long as humans live in an area there is a struggle in the ecosystem, for only humans utilize the concept of "wealth."

For this very reason, we have to use controls. The Fish and Game Department monitors animal populations and sets hunting limits. When trees are harvested, more are planted. As drought causes soil conditions to change, new ways of improving the soil are developed. If these practices continue at a reasonable rate, tourists will continue to pay to see the state.

If Montana is the state of extremes, as it is described by historian K. Ross Toole, it would seem only logical that the answer to the problems of growth is *balance*. Economic and environmental balance.

your class picture goes here

WEALTH...

It's time to "hand over" the past to the present. The present, being only an instant, soon gives it back. This is the never-ending cycle known as history. The future is upon us. In some cases, the future of our ancestors is already behind us. The future is in the hands of the dreamers and planners. Their efforts will affect all of us. With that thought in mind, we've provided a few news clippings that will hopefully place you among their ranks.

Amtrak Threatens End To Service in Montana

WASHINGTON (AP) — Financially troubled Amtrak says it might have to shut down its entire system next summer unless it can cancel train services costing more than $60 million to operate.

Included in its list of possible cancelations are the two routes serving Montana.

An Amtrak spokesman denied the letter was intended as an attempt to squeeze more money out of Congress. He said House and Senate conferees last week had written the bottom line on how much money the corporation will receive in fiscal year 1978.

Amtrak said in its letter that its alternative was to speed up a process already under way of identifying entire routes to be abandoned or restructured.

"Services costing approximately $60 million to $65 million on an annual basis must be selected for discontinuation," the letter stated.

"Services costing approximately $60 million to $65 million on an annual basis must be selected for discontinuation," the letter stated.

"If we were not to take these cost-saving actions — and the process must be initiated immediately — then Amtrak would face a severe funding crisis in July or August next year," it said. "At that time, if the requisite savings have not been programmed, the only remaining option would be to shut down the entire system, including northeast corridor operations in their entirety."

The letter listed financially troubled lines which will be examined for cancellation.

The following routes also were included but were grouped for purposes of further analysis:

• The Empire Builder and North Coast Hiawatha — two routes between Chicago and Seattle via Minneapolis. The Empire Builder stops at Grand Forks, N.D., Havre, East Glacier, Whitefish, Libby, Spokane, and Yakima, Wash. The Hiawatha operates via Bismarck, Billings, Butte, Deer Lodge, Missoula, Spokane and Wenatchee, Wash. Amtrak said the two routes could be consolidated into one of the other, or both could be abandoned.

Missoulian, Nov. 19, 1977

Rural Zoning: It's Coming

"Montanans have got to face the fact zoning is coming." says one official. "We can't step out of time. No amount of legal fees, no amount of 'frontierism' is going to keep the planners from doing it."

Missoulian, Dec. 2, 1977

Anaconda to Pay $73,600 For Alleged Air Violations

HELENA (AP) — The Anaconda Co. will have to pay the state $73,600 for 108 alleged violations of federal sulfur oxide general air quality standards from October 1976 at its copper smelter in Anaconda.

Missoulian, Dec. 3, 1977

Farm Strike Talks Draw Good Crowds

GREAT FALLS (AP) — A planned nationwide strike in which some farmers would hold their produce off the market and stop purchasing farm-related goods appears to be making headway in Montana.

Missoulian, Dec. 2, 1977

Wood Products Industry Regulates
Western Montana Economics — Judge

KALISPELL — Gov. Thomas Judge, addressing the Kalispell Chapter of the American Society of Foresters Thursday night, said the wood products industry serves as the economic barometer of western Montana.

The governor told the more than 200 persons attending the annual convention in Kalispell that when the timber industry is in trouble, western Montana is in economic trouble.

Judge said Montana plans to participate in a federal review of roadless areas and an investigation of how the state and private forest land owners can improve their resources.

Another area that must be watched closely, he said, is a proposed reorganization of the federal land management agencies. The federal government has suggested the Forest Service offices in Missoula be moved to Denver.

"The all-important thing is that the management of the national forests must be kept close to the states and not centralized in Washington," Judge said. "That would be a disaster."

In another part of his speech, the governor trod a delicate path between favoring environmental interests and the forest industry.

He stated his support for the proposed Absaroka-Beartooth wilderness area and for a bill that would put nine areas in Montana into a study to determine whether they should become wilderness areas. President Carter has signed that bill into law.

But Judge also gave some support to the foresters in saying he backed the "fullest sustained yield production of those lands best suited for timber harvest."

He associated his interest in the review of Montana's 6.5 million acres of roadless areas with concern that the Forest Service be able to allow its full quota of timber cuts.

"The Forest Service has informed me that after two years, it will not be able to meet the allowable cut without overcutting existing areas or building roads into new areas," Judge said. "That is why it is important that the inventory of roadless areas not designated as wilderness be returned to commercial logging."

In his closing remarks, Judge said, "Let us manage Montana's forest land as though it must last forever — which it must..."

Missoulian, Nov. 12, 1977

They did it again

CRUEL CUT OF THE YEAR DEPARTMENT (Anaconda Division, Office of Callous Ineptitude) — In the past Anaconda occasionally timed layoff announcements to fall just before Christmas or — on one notable occasion — on election day.

The company's announcement that it is laying off 190 workers in Anaconda and 50 in Butte hit the papers on Thanksgiving day.

It's from such things that bitter memories are born. What a callous, thoughtless, thoroughly rotten bit of work this latest bit of work is.

Sam Reynolds Editorial Missoulian, Dec. 4, 1977

AROUND MISSOULA

Divorce and Finances Workshop Set

A workshop for men and women on the financial aspects of divorce will be Tuesday from 7 to 10p.m. at the University Congregational Church, 401 University Ave.

State Moves Toward New Ambient Air Quality Rules
By GARRY J. MOES
Associated Press Writer

HELENA — The Montana Board of Health and Environmental Sciences agreed Friday to begin preliminary steps toward construction of a new, enforceable state ambient air quality regulation.

The action came in response to reluctant, almost emotional, concessions by the state health department that it has been wrong for the past decade in insisting that the current state ambient standards are mandatory and enforceable.

Missoulian, Dec. 3, 1977

New Power Plant Apt To Burn Montana Coal

SPOKANE (AP) — Montana coal probably would fuel a proposed power plant in Eastern Washington, a Washington Water Power Co. official said Saturday.

Missoulian, Dec. 4, 1977

Two Industrial Power Users Still Withholding Part of Bills

HELENA (AP) — Two of Montana Power Co.'s industrial customers are continuing to withhold full payment of their utility bills until a lawsuit against the power company is resolved.

Since September the Anaconda Co. has withheld $76,148 from its two utility bills totaling $810,416. Ideal Cement of Trident has placed into a trust fund account $22,721, which is the amount it says it has been overcharged by MPC.

Missoulian, Nov. 20, 1977

Panel Puts Off Decision On Oil, Gas Leasing

HELENA (AP) — The Montana Fish and Game Commission Friday put off for a month a decision on a proposed new policy on oil and gas leases on Fish and Game land.

The Missoulian, Saturday, Dec. 3, 1977

Diversion of Kootenai River Proposed

Libby Dam Generation Would Decrease

By The Associated Press

Residents in towns along the Kootenai River in western Montana may awaken one morning in 1984 to find water levels in the river reduced drastically.

British Columbia officials are proposing a power project that would divert some of the river's waters into another Canadian river.

Diversion of part of the Kootenai River flow into the Columbia River at Canal Flats, B.C. would be a profitable power generation project even with construction of facilities to reduce the project's environmental damage, according to a BC Hydro report issued this week.

The report says answers are yet to be found to some environmental effects the project would have on the river.

However, the report recommends BC Hydro apply for a water license for the project in 1979.

An approved water license "would facilitate the planning of BC Hydro knowing that it had an approved project ready to go," but the provincial government-owned power utility should further study the project's economic and environmental impacts before applying for final government approval, the report says.

The possibility of diverting part of the Kootenai River flow to the Columbia River was written into the 1964 Columbia River Treaty with a provision for Canada to take water from the Kootenai before it crosses the international border, about 30 miles west of Fernie, B.C. after September 1984.

Increased flow in the Columbia would permit the generation of more electricity by BC Hydro

power dams, but decreased Kootenai water would reduce generation on the river in the United States, specifically at Libby Dam.

Summing up the international implications of the diversion project, the report — which BC Hydro characterized as a prefeasibility report — says: "The project would result in an average annual energy loss in the order of 400 million kilowatt hours at the Libby Dam. Coupled with the proposed Libby re-regulation project and the remaining undeveloped head on the Kootenai River south of the border, the potential losses to the U.S. could be about 660 feet — virtually equivalent to the potential gain in British Columbia.

"From a broad viewpoint, it's apparent that the $60 million to $80 million expenditure for the

Kootenai diversion project is being spent merely to transfer the generation location across the border between the U.S. and Canada."

Unanswered is the effect the reduction of flow in the Kootenai downstream from the diversion would have on the river's pollution. "For long periods of time the diversion would reduce the flow in the Kootenai River to about its minimum record level and this effect on the pollution...has not yet been answered," the report said.

North of the international border, a lead-zinc mine, two municipalities and a pulp mill currently are discharging wastes into the river between the diversion point and the border.

In effect, even if effluents did not increase actual pollution might because of cutback flow.

The Missoulian, Wednesday, November 2, 1977

Soon after this my father sent for me. I saw he was dying. I took his hand in mine. He said: "My son, my body is returning to my mother earth, and my spirit is going very soon to see the Great Spirit Chief. When I am gone, think of your country. You are the chief of these people. They look to you to guide them. Always remember that your father never sold this country. You must stop your ears whenever you are asked to sign a treaty selling your home. A few years more, and white men will be all around you. They have their eyes on this land. My son, never forget my dying words. This country holds your father's body. Never sell the bones of your father and your mother." I pressed my father's hand and told him I would protect his grave with my life. My father smiled and passed away to the spirit land.

I buried him in that beautiful valley of winding waters. I love that land more than all the rest of the world. A man who would not love his father's grave is worse than a wild animal.

I believe that the old treaty has never been correctly reported. If we ever owned the land we own it still, for we never sold it. In the treaty councils the commissioners have claimed that our country had been sold to the Government. Suppose a white man should come to me and say, "Joseph, I like your horses, and I want to buy them." I say to him, "No, my horses suit me, I will not sell them." Then he goes to my neighbor, and says to him: "Joseph has some good horses. I want to buy them, but he refuses to sell." My neighbor answers, "Pay me the money, and I will sell you Joseph's horses." The white man returns to me, and says, "Joseph, I have bought your horses, and you must let me have them." If we sold our lands to the Government, this is the way they were bought.

I can not understand why so many chiefs are allowed to talk so many different ways, and promise so many different things. I have seen the Great Father Chief (General Butler), and many other law chiefs (Congressmen), and they all say they are my friends, and that I shall have justice, but while their mouths all talk right I do not understand why nothing is done for my people. I have heard talk and talk, but nothing is done. Good words do not last long unless they amount to something. Words do not pay for my dead people. They do not pay for my country, now overrun by white men. They do not protect my father's grave. They do not pay for all my horses and cattle. Good words will not give me back my children. Good words will not make good the promise of your War Chief General Miles. Good words will not give my people good health and stop them from dying. Good words will not get my people a home where they can live in peace and take care of themselves. I am tired of talk that comes to nothing. It makes my heart sick when I remember all the good words and all the broken promises. There has been too much talking by men who had no right to talk. If the white man wants to live in peace with the Indian he can live in peace. There need be no trouble. Treat all men alike. Give them the same law. Give them all an even chance to live and grow. All men were made by the same Great Spirit Chief. They are all brothers. The earth is the mother of all people, and all people should have equal rights upon it. You might as well expect the rivers to run backward as that any man who was born a free man should be contented when penned up and denied liberty to go where he pleases. If you tie a horse to a stake, do you expect he will grow fat? If you pen an Indian up on a small spot of earth, and compel him to stay there, he will not be contented, nor will he grow and prosper. I have asked some of the great white chiefs where they get their authority to say to the Indian that he shall stay in one place, while he sees white men going where they please. They can not tell me.

I only ask of the Government to be treated as all other men are treated. If I can not go to my own home, let me have a home in some country where my people will not die so fast. I would like to go to Bitter Root Valley. There my people would be healthy; where they are now they are dying. Three have died since I left my camp to come to Washington.

When I think of our condition my heart is heavy. I see men of my race treated as outlaws and driven from country to country, or shot down like animals.

I know that my race must change. We can not hold our own with the white men as we are. We only ask an even chance to live as other men live. We ask to be recognized as men. We ask that the same law shall work alike on all men. If the Indian breaks the law, punish him by the law. If the white man breaks the law, punish him also.

Whenever the white man treats an Indian as they treat each other, then we will have no more wars. We shall all be alike — brothers of one father and one mother, with one sky above us and one country around us, and one government for all. Then the Great Spirit Chief who rules above will smile upon this land, and send rain to wash out the bloody spots made by brothers' hands from the face of the earth. For this time the Indian race are waiting and praying. I hope that no more groans of wounded men and women will ever go to the ear of the Great Spirit Chief above, and that all people may be one people.

In-mut-too-yah-lat-lat has spoken for his people.

Joseph, Nez Perce, 1899

BIBLIOGRAPHY

There are several general texts dealing with Montana history. Any research into Montana history may begin by consulting one of these: Merrill G. Burlingame, *The Montana Frontier,* (Helena, State Publishing Co., 1942); James M. Hamilton, *History of Montana: From Wilderness to Statehood* (Portland, Binfords and Mort, 1957, 1970); Joseph Kinsey Howard, *Montana: High, Wide, and Handsome,* (New Haven, Yale University Press, 1943); Michael P. Malone and Richard Roeder, *Montana: A History of Two Centuries,* (Seattle, University of Washington Press, 1976); and K. Ross Toole, *Montana: An Uncommon Land* and *Twentieth Century Montana: A State of Extremes,* both published by the University of Oklahoma Press, in 1959 and 1972, respectively. The Roeder and Malone book contains the most comprehensive bibliography, although the reading level of the book is aimed at advanced high school and college level readers. Written especially for younger readers are Ralph Henry's *Treasure State: The Story of Montana for Junior Historians* and *Our Land Montana: The Story of Our Treasure State,* both published in Helena by the State Publishing Company.

Also useful are edited collections of essays dealing with all aspects of Montana history. Two of the best are Merrill Burlingame and K. Ross Toole, eds., *A History of Montana,* (3 vols; New York, Lewis Historical Publishing Co., 1957) and Malone and Roeder, eds., *The Montana Past: An Anthology,* (Missoula, University of Montana Press, 1969). An invaluable tool for research into Montana's past was compiled recently by the Montana Library Association in cooperation with the University of Montana Library. Entitled *The Bibliography of Montana Local Histories,* (Missoula, University of Montana, 1977) it lists over 500 books, articles, and unpublished manuscripts dealing with the history of Montana's towns, counties, and regions. The *Bibliography* also indexes each item according to location, which enables one to locate instantly the sources pertaining to a specific place. For those especially interested in knowing what sources are available, the Montana State Library regularly issues a "Montana Newsletter" which lists all new Montana items recently added to the State Library. Write the Montana State Library, 930 East Lyndale Avenue, Helena, Montana, 59601.

A periodical which contains many good articles dealing with Montana history is *Montana: The Magazine of Western History,* which is published quarterly by the Montana State Historical Society in Helena. Of special interest to the younger reader is *The Montana Historian,* which is published by the University of Montana Publications in History, in Missoula. It contains essays written by high school students from around the state, as well as short articles by noted Montana historians. Teachers might also wish to acquaint their students with Margery H. Brown's *Montana: A Student's Guide to Localized History.*

Book I

Books dealing with pre-historical Montana are sadly lacking. One useful book is David Alt and Donald Hyndman, *Roadside Geology of the Northern Rockies.* A project recently completed by Robert Taylor, Milton Edie, and Charles Gritaner, *Montana in Maps: 1974* (Bozeman, Big Sky Books, 1974) could be used to acquaint students with Montana's geography. J.P. Rowe's *Geography and Natural Resources of Montana* (Missoula, University of Montana, 1935, 194) is useful, as are Eugene Perry's *Montana in the Geologic Past,* Montana Bureau of Mines and Geology, Bulletin 26 (Butte, 1902), and essay, "Montana before Man," in the book of essays by Burlingame and Toole mentioned above.

Book II

There are many books dealing with Indians of the Great Plains. Some are anthropoligical, some are historical, many are outdated. Carling Malouf, University of Montana anthropology professor, wrote a very useful pamphlet which can easily be used in conjunction with this unit. Entitled *A Brief History of the Indians of Montana for the Elementary School Student,* it was published in 1969 through the University of Montana Foundation. Also good is Professor Malouf's essay, "Indians of Montana," which originally appeared in the *Montana Almanac, 1959-60,* and was reprinted in the collection called *Montana's Past,* edited by Michael Malone and Richard Roeder. Good introductory material of a more general nature is found in Alice Mariott and Carol Rachlin's *American Epic: The Story of the American Indian* (New York, Putnam, 1969).

Specific tribes are covered by a number of books. One of the most prolific writers on Plains Indians was naturalist George Bird Grinnell. His best known (and while old, still outstanding) accounts are *Blackfoot Lodge Tales, The Fighting Cheyenne,* and *Pawnee, Blackfoot and Cheyenne.* Other accounts are R.H. Lowie's *The Crow Indian* (New York, Farrar and Reinehart, 1934), O.W. Johnson's *Flathead and Kootenay* (Glendale, California, A.H. Clark, 1967), H.H. Turney-High's *Flathead Indians* (New York, American Anthropological Association, 1937).

Book III

Students generally enjoy biographies and there are several pertaining to this period, along with some first-person accounts. There are many versions and editions of the journals of the Lewis and Clark expedition; those kept by the leaders themselves are too detailed and statistical to interest intermediate-level students. One member of the expedition, however, wrote a journal which is easily read, though not too excitingly written. Sargeant Patrick Gass, who survived the rest of the members of the expedition by many years, made public his own journal, and it was reissued in 1958 by Ross and Haines in Minneapolis. He makes good reference to wildlife, changes in landscape, and the diet followed during the course of the journey. Its reaching level is well within reach of most junior-high level students. John Colter, who was on the Lewis and Clark expedition, later became one of Montana's best-known fur trappers. Stallo Vinton's biography of him, while old, (1926), is also easily read. Burton Harris wrote the more standard biography of Colter (New York, Seribner's, 1952).

Some of the best literature written about this period is just that. Fictionalized accounts and short stories treating these early years abound, and many were written by Montana authors. Especially good in describing everyday life, these books succeed in recreating the mood of early-day Montana. A.B. Guthrie's *The Big Sky* originally published in 1947 remains one of the best accounts ever written of the fur trade. It is available in several paperbound editions, and while perhaps a bit difficult for the average intermediate reader, is well worth the efforts of the more advanced. Dorothy Johnson's *Indian Country* is really a collection of stories, including the ever-popular, and highly readable, "A Man Called Horse." James Schultz's *Bird Woman, The Guide of Lewis and Clark,* (originally published by Houghton-Miflin in 1918), is an excellent biography of Sacajawea. Frank Linderman's account of the life of a fur trapper *Liege Mounts: Free Trapper* (also published as *Morning Light*) is also excellent for this age group. Vardis Fisher's *Mountain Man* (New York, Morrow, 1965) is a fictionalized account of the life of Jeremiah Johnson.

Book IV

Richard Roeder and Michael Malone wrote an excellent series of articles dealing with Montana as it was in 1876; originally appearing in *Montana, the Magazine of Western History,* they have since been published together under the title *Montana As It Was: 1876.* The articles deal with mining, agriculture, Indians, and politics, and are well-illustrated.

There are many published volumes of memoirs dealing with this period of Montana history. Most are easily read, but some of the older ones were written in flowery prose which today seems quaint. Granville Stuart, an Iowan who later became one of Montana's first *Forty Years on the Frontier* (Cleveland, Arthur Clark Co., 1925). Stuart mentions the Vigilantes; this infamous group is treated in greater detail in Ed Bartholomew's *Henry Plummer-Montana Outlaw Boss* (Ruidaso, New Mexico, Frontier Book Co., 1960), which is a compilation of newspaper articles appearing at the time of the Virginia City gold rush. The "standard" work, *The Vigilantes of Montana, or Popular Justice in the Rocky Mountains* was written in the 1860's by Thomas Dimsdale, the Virginia City schoolmaster. It was republished in 1915 by the State Publishing Company in Helena. A similarly contemporary account is N.P. Langford's *Vigilante Days and*

Ways, which was published in 1912 by a New York publisher. An excellent, but unfortunately unpublished source, especially for intermediate-level students, is J.M. Miller's diary of Virginia City life in the 1860's. This is part of the manuscript collection of the Montana State Historical Society, Helena. W.C. Vanderwerth's *Indian Oratory: Famous Speeches by Noted Indian Chieftains* is a good source for use when dealing with the Indian wars. Finally, along these same lines, the Montana Historical Society just published *Not in Precious Metals Alone,* a manuscript history of Montana. Included are excerpts from letters and state documents which illustrate different topics and issues, and while many would be tedious for junior-high students to read, it would be a good sourcebook for every school library.

Book V

There are many books on the topic of the copper industry in Montana. James A. MacKnight in 1892 wrote a book on the current status of the mining industry. While it is definitely pro-industry in its outlook, its statistics are useful. Entitled *The Mines of Montana: Their History and Development to Date,* it was published in Helena by the C.K. Wells Company. The standard work on the Copper Kings is C.B. Glasscock's *War of the Copper Kings,* which was published in New York by Bobbs Merill in 1935. Other accounts of the copper kings include C.P. Connolly, *The Devil Learns to Vote* (New York: Crown Publisher, 1938), and Marian Place, *The Copper Kings of Montana.* Most interesting for the intermediate-level reader is Dan Cushman's *The Old Copper Coller,* a fictionalized account of the Clark-Daly feud.

Best biographical information concerning W.A. Clark is the volume, *The Clarks: An American Phenomenon* (New York: Silver Bow Press, 1946). Sarah McNelis, *Copper King at War* (Missoula, U. of M. Press, 1968) is a good biography of F.A.

Heinze. Unfortunatly, only a few volumes of this book were printed, and are now almost impossible to find. A shortened version of Heinze's early life is in an article by the same author in *Montana the Magazine of Western History*, Volume II, #4, October, 1952. No good biography of Daly exists; check Joseph Kinsey Howard for the information he has compiled in *Montana High Wide and Handsome*. Numerous articles concerning mining days in Butte have been published. Check both the *Montana Historian* and *Montana the Magazine of Western History*. An excellent source of interesting anecdotes and photographs is the recently published *Butte's Memory Book*, (Don James, Caxton Printer, Caldwell, Idaho, 1975.)

There aren't too many books which describe in detail the ordeals faced by the early twentieth century homesteaders who moved to eastern Montana in such great numbers. Both of K. Ross Toole's books mentioned above contain excellent chapters on the "Honyokers," and would be worth checking. Another excellent account is contained in E.J. Bell Jr.'s *Homesteading in Montana: Life in the Blue Mountain Country*, which was published in Bozeman by the Montana State University's Big Sky Books in 1975. The topic of homesteading would be a great way to introduce students to local oral history; many of their grandparents and great grandparents probably came to Montana at about that time, and would have countless stories and recollections to relate.

Book VI

Accounts of famous Montana politicians are scarce. Burton K. Wheeler wrote his autobiography, *Yankee from the West*, in collaboration with Paul Healy. Published by Doubleday in 1962, it would be a good choice for the advanced reader. Jules Karlin, University of Montana history professor, recently published a massive study of Joseph M. Dixon (Missoula: University of Montana Publications in History, 1974). The era of Montana politics in which both Wheeler and Dixon were notable was a turbulent era which involved rather complex economic and social issues, and until a biographical history is written with intermediate-level students in mind, the sources available are out of reach to them.

Students should, however, be able to utilize local sources in conjunction with this chapter. Relatives and neighbors can be consulted, especially concerning the depression and war years. Local papers, though many were Company-owned, contain accounts of political battles, statistics, and human interest stories. In addition, *Montana, the Magazine of Western History* and the *Montana Historian* contain numerous articles on Montana communities during these years. Finally, a good library project would be to use the *Reader's Guide to Periodical Literature* in order to track down articles about Montana which appeared in national magazines. A good example is a lengthy article in *Life* (Nov. 23, 1936) about the Fort Peck Dam.

Book VII

Unfortunately, there are few published sources on this era. Richard Roeder and Michael Malone's *Montana: A History of Two Centuries* is one of the few books available that goes beyond World War II in its treatment of the state. Also available is former Governor J. Hugo Aronson's autobiography, *The Galloping Swede* (Missoula: Mountain Press, 1970). Newspapers would probably be the best source of information. Noted events of this era, copper strikes, forest fires, floods, the environmental movement, and politics all received extensive coverage in even the smallest of the local papers, National publications also took note of Montana during these years; the December, 1970 *National Geographic* summarized Missoula's anti-air pollution drive, and the 1972 Constitutional Convention received good coverage in an April 10 issue of *Time*. In covering this period, students should be encouraged to investigate local sources, both written and oral.

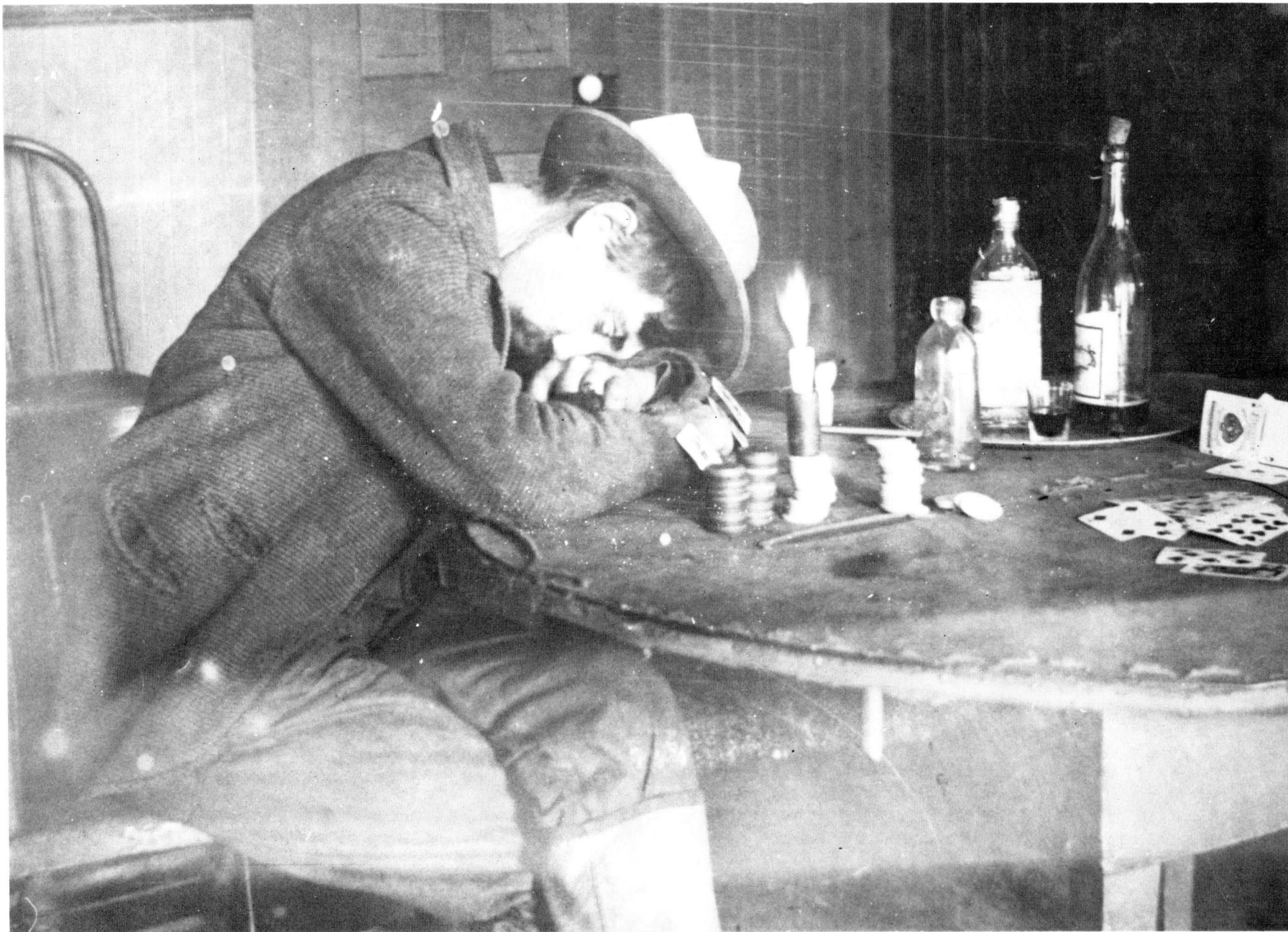

DONE!...For Now...